LIVING ON CYBERMIND

Colin Lankshear, Michele Knobel,
Chris Bigum, and Michael Peters
General Editors

Vol. 24

PETER LANG
New York • Washington, D.C./Baltimore • Bern
Frankfurt am Main • Berlin • Brussels • Vienna • Oxford

Jonathan Paul Marshall

LIVING ON CYBERMIND

Categories, Communication, and Control

PETER LANG
New York • Washington, D.C./Baltimore • Bern
Frankfurt am Main • Berlin • Brussels • Vienna • Oxford

Library of Congress Cataloging-in-Publication Data

Marshall, Jonathan Paul.
Living on Cybermind: categories, communication, and control /
Jonathan Paul Marshall.
p. cm. — (New literacies and digital epistemologies; v. 24)
Includes bibliographical references and index.
1. Internet—Social aspects. 2. Electronic discussion groups—Social aspects.
3. Cybermind. 4. Social interaction. 5. Online identities. I. Title.
HM851.M373 303.48′33—dc22 2007000753
ISBN 978-0-8204-9514-9 (hardcover)
ISBN 978-0-8204-9513-2 (paperback)
ISSN 1523-9543

Bibliographic information published by **Die Deutsche Bibliothek**.
Die Deutsche Bibliothek lists this publication in the "Deutsche
Nationalbibliografie"; detailed bibliographic data is available
on the Internet at http://dnb.ddb.de/.

Cover design by Joni Holst

© 2007 Peter Lang Publishing, Inc., New York
29 Broadway, 18th floor, New York, NY 10006
www.peterlang.com

All rights reserved.
Reprint or reproduction, even partially, in all forms such as microfilm,
xerography, microfiche, microcard, and offset strictly prohibited.

To Alan Sondheim, in particular, and to everyone else who has ever been on Cybermind and helped with the project. I hope I live up to all of you and convey something of what the List has meant to me, and something more of the thought you have engaged in.

Contents

Acknowledgments	xi
Transcription Conventions	xiii
Introduction	**1**
Preamble	1
Patterns of Disunity?	2
Outlines of Interests	5
Fieldwork on Cybermind	7
Outline of the Book	10
Chapter 1 Toward an Analysis of Communication	**13**
Introduction	13
Categories	14
Boundaries	16
Problems of Communication	17
Framing	18
Groups, Identities, Norms and Categories	23
Values	28
Summary	29
Chapter 2 Cybermind — A History	**31**
Preamble	31
Growth of the Internet and Email	31
The Origins of a Social Group	32
Early Days on List	40
Further Happenings	43
Chapter 3 The Internet and the World	**47**
Introduction	47
Temporary Association and Western Society	49
List Discussion of the World	51
Recapitulation	70

Chapter 4 Structures of Communication and Internet Groups — 73
Structures of Communication — 73
Mailing List Organisation — 73
Internal Structures: Hierarchy and Subgroups — 79
Groups and Other Groups (Us and Them) — 82
Conclusion — 87

Chapter 5 The Virtual Life: Asence and Experience — 89
Introduction — 89
'Asence' — 89
Lurking — 92
Flames — 96
Burnout and Reading — 101
Histories — 102

Chapter 6 The Reign of Authenticity — 105
Introduction — 105
Authenticity in General: Offline, Public and Private — 106
Authenticity Online — 111
Bodies and Authentic Expression — 118
Gender, Authenticity and Intimacy — 120
Conclusion — 122

Chapter 7 Bounding the Body: Moods, Intensities and the Haunting — 125
Introduction — 125
Boundaries and Offline Bodies — 125
Sustaining Mood (Death and Netsex) — 129
Cybermind Discusses Netsex — 134
The Haunted Computer — 141
Virile Bodies, Asence and Politics — 145
Conclusions — 147

Chapter 8 Existence and Exchange — 151
Introduction — 151
"The Gift" — 153
Exchange, Melanesia and Mailing Lists — 155
Time and Exchange — 164
Place and Exchange — 165
Gender, Gift and Intimacy — 165
Property — 170

Chapter 9 Control and Crisis — 175
Introduction — 175
Exchange and Hierarchy — 177
Authenticity — 178
Political Categories — 179
The 'Holocaust Debate' — 180
Conclusion — 185

Chapter 10 Invasions, Fragmentation and the Mobilization of Gender and Politics — 189
Introduction — 189
Invasion Freaks? — 189
Fission — 197
Iraq — 204
Gender — 208
Clustering — 210

Chapter 11 Constructions of Online 'Community' — 213
Introduction — 213
'Community' — 213
Origin of the Cybermind 'Community' — 221
Cybermind and Community — 225
Problems and Pleasures of Online Life — 234

Chapter 12 Intersection of the List with the Offlist and the Offline — 241
Introduction — 241
Organizing as a Group — 241
Offlist Meetings — 242
The Aura of the Offlist — 248
Offline Benefits — 254
Comparisons — 256
Conclusion — 258

Conclusions — 265
'Culture' — 265
Categorisation — 265
Control and Communication — 267
Community — 275
Paradox — 277

Appendix: Demographics and Statistics — 281
Introduction — 281
General Population — 281
Surveys — 282
Active Population — 291
Activity by Gender — 295
Summary — 298

Glossary — 301

Notes — 307

Bibliography — 335

Index — 353

Acknowledgments

Clearly this book could only emerge with the help and co-operation of far too many members of Cybermind to acknowledge all of them. However, I would specifically like to thank the following people:

Alan Sondheim for his support, openness, provision of information, and intellectual stimulation. Without his aid this book could not have been written; Bernadette Garner for encouragement, ideas, interviews, information about MOOs, and comments on several chapters; David Hoberman for a copy of his thesis; Elizabeth Barrette whose influence is wider than might appear; Fanny Jacobson for interviews, films and comments; Gauti Sigthorsson for his perspectives; Glen Ropella for debate and permissions; Jerry Everard for discussion, clarity, rescuing the archives, and for early drafts of his book; Jim Reith for keeping everything going; Karen Melzack for interviews and the huge work of organizing the Cybermind Conference; Kerry Miller for constant debate on problems; Laurie Cubbison for insights and information; Lexie Don for ideas, discussion and pre-publication versions of papers; Lynne Harding for support, interviews, comments and articles; Martin Wheatley for correcting me in such a genial way; Mitchell Pravatiner for copies of his archives, email-interviews and comments; Michael Gurstein for email interviews; 'Morning Glory' for email interviews and ideas; Nan Williams for email interviews; Richard MacKinnon for writing the first 'internet sociology' article I ever reacted to, his good humour at my response to it, and his helpful comments; Robert Kezalis for debate, comments and much information about the United States; Rose Mulvale for kindness, insight, commentary and reading some of the original thesis; Salwa Ghaly for information, insights and support; and, finally, Tom Ellis for email interviews, comments and much political debate.

Thanks also go to Malgosia Askanas and Kent Palmer for historical interviews and commentary.
On the Alchemy list, special thanks to Adam McLean and Tom McRae.

Financial assistance was provided by a Sydney University Postgraduate Research Award, the Carlyle-Greenwell Bequest, and a Githa Connolly Award.

Without the kind support of Professor Michael Allen, I could never have begun the return to Anthropology or started this book. My thesis supervisor, Dr. Vivienne Kondos deserves much thanks for putting up with the chaos of working with me, and providing the flexible intellectual environment in which the thesis could be written. Particular and grateful thanks go to Colin Lankshear for his support in getting the book published and to Angela Thomas who provided the pathway.

My parents have given me support and encouragement beyond any calls of duty, especially during the long illness.

Luke Kendall introduced me to the Shadowrn mailing list, and thus started this whole project. He also has given much insight from his non-Cybermind experience of mailing lists, and made many valuable suggestions.

Finally, there is my wife Sally Gillespie, who is the pivot of my life, and nothing I have written or done could exist without her.

Transcription Conventions

Quotations of material taken from the Internet and Cybermind are generally as written—unless a particular spelling introduced an ambiguity which was clearly resolved by the whole (unquoted) document.

Sometimes spelling has been modified to disguise a source.

Ellipses have been reproduced as written. Ellipses added in the book are enclosed in square brackets, i.e. [...] single dashes (-) have been replaced by long dashes (—)

I have kept Australian spelling and punctuation for the body of the text, but have not altered the texts which are quoted.

Introduction

Preamble

Over the last fifteen years interest in, and use of, the Internet has grown enormously in Western societies. However, compared with the plethora of general articles about pornography and pain, or business books telling us how to exploit the Internet for profit, or commentary on how Internet society *should* work, there are relatively few detailed studies of how people actually do use the Internet socially[1].

This book investigates the social life of a group of people who interacted, via an Internet mailing list called Cybermind, between mid 1994 and 2007[2]. Topics considered include the social make up of the group; perceptions of the political and social forces surrounding them; the role of categories in the process of construction of identity (both of the participants and of the group as a whole); the organization of communication and its effects; and the vagaries of power and conflict in the maintenance of the group. Given Cybermind was five months old at the start of the study, it is of interest to observe the changes and development within this social form, and the way people's strategies have changed during this history.

Clearly one society's way of using the Internet may not be the same as another's, and premature universalism should be avoided. Only with studies of, say, Aranda, Nepalese or Bantu net culture will we have any idea of what is driven by the Internet itself and what by the user's embedding culture (see Miller & Slater 2000 for an excellent beginning). This book only considers Internet usage within what will be called WES (Western English Speaking) cultures.

The introduction argues that 'culture' is a form of interpretive knowledge about how one should act with other people and the world and how they are likely to react in turn. There will be many cultures operating in a society and we cannot assume that there is a pure ideal type of culture which everyone possesses in part. Disagreement is as important as agreement. In this book we are also interested in: the wider processes that social action is embedded within; the organisation of communication; the ways boundaries are conceived, broken and maintained; the way systems control or disrupt themselves; the way that power ratios operate within these systems; the ways that exchange is conducted; and the advantages provided by the group to its members. Finally, I suggest that ethnography is similar to the kinds of processes that people engage in to function in online societies; that is, in finding out the culture of others.

Online Society

Online society differs from offline society in many obvious ways, such as:

a) There is no necessity for face-to-face contact (so communication is often considered to be comparatively denuded of richness);
b) It is difficult to use physical force to settle disputes;
c) It supposedly removes cues indicating gender, race or age, allowing people to express themselves 'as they are' or 'as they choose to be'; and
d) Interactions can be much more governed by fantasy, or by freedom and anarchy.

These kinds of statements are often presented as analytical insights (as some of them will be here), but they are also part of the standard discourse of online life. There is nothing foreign about them, and they are frequently used to separate online and offline life, and denigrate one in comparison with the other. In order to discuss online life in more detail we need to have at least an outline of a theory of culture or social processes, and a theory of communication. The theory of communication will be described in the next chapter; the rest of this chapter deals with issues of ethnography, culture and power.

Patterns of Disunity?

Ethnographic research is what anthropologists do when they interact with others to gather information so as to analyse or interpret a society[3]. Making ethnography may differ somewhat from the normal interpretive and analytic activities of humans, but much is similar. The anthropologist lives in a society, at a fairly local level, trying to build a model of people's behaviour in that society, just as everyone in that society attempts to build a model (including those who try to understand, act with, or use the anthropologist). Writing for an audience elsewhere, an anthropologist's interests and problems may be different[4], but their attempt to model, to interpret, to render coherent is similar—an 'interactive' learning process, which makes use of what others tell them and of what they experience themselves. The model produces what we may call 'culture' as a form of knowledge. People are not exemplars of an abstracted 'cultural essence', but develop "insights into life" (Barth 1995: 66), and their culture can change and develop. Knowledge may vary with available techniques, social position, life experience, degree of involvement and so on, but in general it involves categorization, manipulation and linkage (see Chapter 1). As with interpretive processes in general, our attention is drawn to those aspects of life which we don't understand, or which seem different. Events which apparently make sense are ignored, until we find our understanding or ability to act is inadequate. As Michael Agar writes, culture is "what happens to you when you encounter differences" (1994: 20).

We build culture for ourselves and others in order to understand what people do, and to act with them. Culture is, therefore, not just an abstract series of 'rules' located nowhere, but is present within the efforts of humans to coact with[5], and interpret, the activities of others. Difference and error is as important as accuracy—any ethnography never succeeds entirely. A 'ritual symbol' may 'mean' one thing to one group and another thing to another group. Some groups may be aware they do not know its meanings, but they can undoubtedly invent one. We cannot say who is right—although one group or another may make that claim[6]. The effects of the 'ritual symbol' occur *through* these variations. There is not One Culture but a whole series of idio-cultures produced by people in coaction. We can never write or talk of society directly, only as a model and resistances to that model. We may also assign 'a society' boundaries, for heuristic or political purposes, but that does not mean that it is actually bounded. Analyses are descriptions which selectively delete; often, the more elegant the analysis the more is deleted. As anthropologists, we may assume our models are more sophisticated than local models (even if only because we assume they are not accurate), but they are still models, still 'cultures'[7].

Therefore, we cannot assume that what we explain is a falling away from an ideal type model, of the Weberian kind, which is somehow *never* manifested, because mess and complexity are essential to sociality. As Barth argues, variation or misperformance within a society cannot simply be considered an epiphenomenon, or 'noise' produced by an underlying order, and thus irrelevant. Variation "should emerge as a necessity from our analysis" (Barth 1993a: 4). We tend to perceive 'order' as imposed upon 'chaos', when particular kinds of social order might depend upon, or create, particular types of 'chaos'. "Societies are not simply problem solving mechanisms: they are also problem creating mechanisms" (M. Strathern 1988a: 33). WES online societies seem to create problems of power, presence and authenticity.

Cultural artefacts or institutions may not have the same meaning or function for different people, or groups of people, and these differences may have important social consequences. Again to quote Barth:

> Culture is distributed and major aspects of its structure inhere precisely in its patterns of distribution... Actors are... positioned, and the interpretations they make will reflect this positioning and the knowledge that they command (1993a: 176).

In WES social life people disagree in many ways over issues they regard as fundamental and present many recognised differences or counterpositions. People act while aware of the disagreements between them concerning the meanings and functions of symbols and institutions, and of the insufficiency of acts, although they may not accept these divergences.

People act not just because they believe in a 'custom', but because they believe others will act as if they do[8]. They also try to make others act in ways which fit in with their own categories and expectations. People, who self-categorize as members of particular groups, will tend to try to impose category agreement on each other as a condition of group membership. This gives members a set of 'cultural aspects', shared in *varying* degrees, which enables them and others to abstract a cultural model.

Analysis is further complicated as, in societies like Cybermind, people are creating and learning as they go, rather than learning from experienced others, and social processes could change with this learning. Analogically people are inventing a game and, as they play, the rules are modified. Cybermind has functioned differently at different times. However, learning always occurs in the context of conventions existing in the embedding society. These have an effect and so, contrary to popular stories, online life is not, as Argyle implies, an anarchy or 'Carnival' in which "all codes of conduct, all rules of behaviour are abandoned" (1996: 137). Furthermore, as Gluckman (1955) points out, such 'rituals of rebellion' can be temporary, can be ordered, may take their value in relation to 'normal life', and don't have to institute permanent change.

Despite these proclamations of multiplicity, spurts of spurious unity are generated in this book by tales of conflict. Perhaps when a group is apparently 'functioning well' for a WES person, there is little to comment upon; a lack of dramatic markers with which to make a narrative or analysis, when observed from without[9]. Or perhaps cooperation and conflict are not unrelated opposites, but mutually creating, or always present together in different patterns in differing situations, giving each other whatever meaning they have.

It may be that production of uniformity in ethnography occurs by the same processes by which members of our own group or category appear to us as individuals while we make 'others' the same in some ways. If so, then ethnography can manufacture culture through a process like stereotyping. If culture resembles ethnography, then it may be useful to ask about the methods by which people learn culture, or attribute it to others, and the circumstances within which they do it.

Outlines of Interests

The key terms of this analysis are undoubtedly 'Category', 'Social Control', and 'Framing'.

If these represent my interests, then these interests are brought to bear via perspectives, as the interpretation of a process depends largely on the perspective taken, the theories brought to it, and the data selected to make these theories and perspectives valid or refutable. The following kinds of perspectives have been chosen— although the order of presentation should not be thought of as significant.

1) The *Embedding*. All human lived experiences, interactions and representations occur within different levels of framing: for example, they occur within a macro *and* micro sociological framework. The division between these framings is a matter of analytic perspective. Processes are always embedded in other processes, although not necessarily in a hierarchical fashion. To use an analogy, processes may embed each other as if overlapping or intersecting circles, as well as if concentric circles. These macro and micro sociological factors are themselves coalescing and passing patterns of human activity. They restrict *and* enable possible kinds of behaviour. 'Importation' of effects can occur, because it is difficult for people to deal with 'microsociological' events without using categories and framings developed for dealing with 'macrosociological' events and vice versa. The embedding also includes linguistic factors as discussed in Chapter One.

2) *Infrastructure*, or the organization of fundamentals. What is 'fundamental' can change from group to group, and from perspective to perspective. In this case, it is proposed that the 'organization of communication' is important to the kind of sociality which can develop and to its (dis)organization. The organization of communication influences the way people and groups can interact, and provides the online 'ecology'. Although, offline, it may be dangerous to abstract a structure from the behaviour of people which then determines that behaviour, in the case of online groupings this organization of communication is indeed independent of the actions of the people who use it. People may shift from one kind of group to another to gain different potentialities, but nowadays they are rarely able to change the group's organization of communication themselves.

3) *Boundary*. Concern with boundaries manifests in conflict, integration and separation; as well as in more personal concerns, such as with the use of the body and intimacy. Particular problems arise because WES people often conceive boundaries as sharp, firm lines rather than as multiple, permeable or graded[10].

4) The *Control System*. All processes are 'regulated' in some way. They have potential modes of (dis)organization and (in)coherence which arise out of themselves and out of their embedding processes. Social control is a primary mode of group coaction which limits divergence of categorization, and provides, or manifests, further opportunities for the temporary development of meshing identities.

5) *Power*. Power is *sometimes* important in control systems. As Norbert Elias argues, power is not a thing collected by some and exerted by them on others, but an aspect of the patterning of human relationships. Power manifests in various kinds of balance, or ratio, with varying degrees of stability, between people or groups. Power ratios "are bi-polar at least, and usually multi-polar" (1978: 74-5, 131). Even dictators and absolute monarchs are not completely free to act, but are constrained by the activities of others (1983: 277ff.). However, the options open to some 'players' may be significantly more limited than others (Van Krieken 1998: 64). Power can operate in different ways. Some people may be able to command others, while other people may only be able to modify the course of the dispute (Elias 1978: 82). Some people may only be able to prevent[11]. Previous events may influence the current power balance, making certain acts more or less likely to succeed. Power ratios are an expression of the dynamic patterning of human coaction[12]. Those patterns which are easily

activated express the established modes of power. However, power is risked and resisted each time it is displayed. Newly manifesting patterns may disrupt the smooth expression of established power ratios and enable easier expression of new kinds, and ratios, of power. Discussing the 'control system' is also meant to imply that power may not reside, with individual people or groups of people.

6) *Exchange*. Most social processes involve forms of exchange. The 'items' exchanged and the methods of exchange are often connected to the control system and the infrastructure, although they are not reducible to epiphenomena of these perspectives. It is posited that the fundamental unit of exchange for mailing lists is the item of mail, and that this has specific consequences.

7) *Returns*. The question of the 'functional' benefits of a process is always a matter of its benefits for whom or for what and for how a process maintains or fragments other events or processes. I ask what functions the List (Cybermind) has in terms of the wider society and for list members. Returns can be direct or compensatory or both. Systemic returns can be opposed to personal returns. Not all returns will be conscious, although it is probable people will aim for some kind of return, even if it is impossible to achieve.

Fieldwork on Cybermind

Cybermind was founded by Alan Sondheim and Michael Current in July 1994 to discuss "the philosophical and psychological implications of subjectivity in cyberspace". The official topic of the list is often overwhelmed by discussions of the participants' personal lives and interests. This has made it ideal for the study of "subjectivities in cyberspace", not only because of the ideas presented by list members, but because of the subjectivities displayed. Autobiographical and social data are available to a degree which seems unusual in this kind of environment.

People using Cybermind openly discuss their relationship to the list, and many participants appear to consider the group as a 'community' which they feel strongly about. There are many long-time members, some of whom have been present from inception. Active membership requires dedication as the volume of communication can be high. During fieldwork the average volume of mail has been between 30 to 60 messages per day and has occasionally reached well over 100. This volume has tapered off after conflicts over the Iraq War and the Bush Administration, but can still reach relatively high levels.

Initially I joined the list because of its subject matter but it soon became clear the group was of interest in itself, and I decided to do fieldwork there if possible. I discussed this possibility with Alan Sondheim in late February of 1995. He was cautious, as he feared that questioning and observation might alter the nature of the list. I thought this unlikely as the group already seemed extremely introspective and self-questioning. However, I made it clear that nothing would be done without his permission. This proved acceptable, and I participated without informing the list of the project until Alan suggested I do so, about six months later.

Onlist I was always open about being an anthropologist, and my interest in particular events "as an anthropologist". Private email of any extent always included a mention of the research.

Initial restrictions caused few problems, and it was possible to ask questions and run surveys with good response rates. Other people also conducted surveys of varying types, and the results have been incorporated into this work.

Although my experience online is not a universal experience, it was one way of socialising. I cannot claim to be more of an 'outsider' than most other members of the group, and thus privilege my cultural models over theirs. At the same time I was hardly central to the group. The analyses made here did not arise in abstraction or detachment, but in passion, joy, bewilderment, anguish and occasional boredom.

Cybermind was also a group in which WES concepts of study were not foreign. People shared my concerns and questioned my assertions. Anthropology or sociology is part of the discourses WES people use to describe themselves (however informally), and as such it is both social and partisan. There can be no pretence such disciplines are isolated from the society being discussed[13]. I cannot claim to be fearlessly stripping away people's delusions to reveal the actual authentic workings of a society, or even presenting a privileged view of that working[14]. The interpretations in this book are not 'pure' and abstracted from the group; they are always part of some narrative or theory about groups, politics or existence. They are, at best, counterpositional to another interpretation, and to another way of life. They emerge from the same set of possibilities.

Contacts and Informants

At one time, going out to the field meant searching out good informants who could tell the enquirer about whatever aspects of life, from politics to salmon recipes, they were interested in. Complications could ensue if the people's social categories differed from the anthropologist's[15] but, in general, people could be persuaded to give data showing they had religions and economies and so on. Ethnographies often become the account of the society by the informant (their personal culture) as translated by the anthropologist, with the apparent unity produced by that source.

Informants are as liable to give biased or fantastic accounts of their own society as anyone, perhaps more, as they enjoy talking about these kinds of problems. Informants might be those with a compulsion to appear central to somebody, and this itself could be a social position. Informants are as prone to use anthropologists for their own purposes as anthropologists are to use them. Many anthropologists have found their understanding of a society has radically shifted with a change of informants (e.g. Berreman 1972: prologue)[16].

I failed to find any dedicated informants, and did not have to live with a particular subgroup, although it is true that most of my closest associates were also Australians. However, I frequently might ask someone for an account of something after they had mentioned it themselves, and receive no reply, or be told they would reply later and receive nothing. Even when information was made available, it was hard to check against other sources[17]. People may have "information managed" my observations, although hopefully they did this in the kinds of ways they information managed others in general. Consequently parts of this book may be largely fantasy, and yet these kinds of fantasy may be important for the workings of the group.

Unlike many ethnographers, I am in the position of being able to present the actual words used by people. However, the mere selection and framing of statements in a book distorts and gives foreign meanings to those statements. Any implication of uniform statements, meanings, or functions is unintended. It is not possible to write "Cyberminders say": it is always "this person wrote, now".

Usually the names of the group and the people being described would be disguised, but I have generally not done so as it deletes my indebtedness. Other list members, writing texts for publication, have posed the question of attribution of texts to the group, and the majority response has always been that the texts were public and if correct attribution were given to the original author, or anonymity granted where requested, then there should be no problem[18]. People who specifically did not want remarks attributed to them, have either been quote anonymously or not quoted. There has, at time of writing, been no objections to the use of people's words as they appear in this book.

Population of Cybermind

Though it is hard to generalise about the members of Cybermind, and such generalisations should not be taken as indicative of other such groups, certain things can be said[19]. The group is overwhelmingly well educated, yet job security or wealth is not marked: survival fear is justified. A variety of occupations *is* noticeable, with a tendency towards student or part-time academic. Business people are largely absent. Members often seem caught in the divergence between the mytheme of the 'knowledge worker' as vanguard of the future, and the actual difficulties of living by their knowledge. Members of Cybermind usually participate in many other kinds of Internet forum.

Outline of the Book

In the next chapter, I will argue that members of a category are rarely linked by uniform definition, and have degrees of membership within that category. Some members will be considered to be 'better' members than others, or 'prototypes'. 'Category-norms' are defined as the properties which express prototypicality. Communication is not seen as a transfer of contents between people but as a continual process of mutual adjustment which depends upon the framing and interpretation of communicative events. Important framings include mood, the public and private divide, exchange, excess or redundancy, and etiquette. A *mytheme* is defined as an explicit theory or story which explains an aspect of the world, justifies action and aids framing. Sometimes a 'true' story functions as 'myth' giving a charter for behaviour, and scientific theories can attempt to maintain 'scientific practice', group memberships and relative statuses, as well as explain the world.

Chapter 2 outlines the development of Cybermind, referring to the major events touched upon in the course of the book. Mythemes of 'freedom' prove important shared references for list establishment and mutual control of members.

Chapter 3 discusses the current WES social situation, and the role of the Internet and electronic communication within that world. I suggest that the power ratios within contemporary corporate capitalism have shifted in favour of the corporate world. As a result, the life of 'middle-class intellectuals' is becoming far more uncertain. Information technology, while exaggerating 'traditional' features of capitalism, allows the construction of possibly fragile survival networks and presents new possibilities of exchange and action.

Chapter 4 outlines two different types of Internet-based sociation and identifies the effects of the organization of communication upon the patterns of interaction, the kind of hierarchies which develop, and the types of relationships which exist between Internet groups.

Chapter 5 describes particular online experiences arising from these organizations, such as '*asence*' (a neologism which refers to a suspension of presence needing confirmation in exchange), 'flaming', 'lurking', 'burnout', and lack of history.

Chapter 6 considers the widely shared WES mytheme of authenticity and the etiquettes surrounding it. It is shown that expectations of authenticity lead to problems when linked to aggression, concerns with gender, and WES divisions between 'public' and 'private'.

Chapter 7 discusses the use of mood as a maintainer, or framing, of communication; the bodily anchoring of experience, through netsex and mourning; and problems with boundaries, which lead to constructions of 'cyberbodies' as ghosts, and the problems this can engender.

Chapter 8 compares mailing lists and Trobriand exchange. List processes are elucidated by comparing emails to prestations (formal and competitive gift exchanges), and exchange is considered as a framing for communication. The feedback which establishes the 'prestation hierarchy' is found to be of particular importance. Connections between gender, intimacy and exchange are also explored.

Chapter 9 describes the group's attempts to deal with a disruptive member and the construction of values. It shows how etiquette is fundamental to the interpretation of discourse, explores problems arising from etiquettes of authenticity, and investigates how social behaviour develops in encounters.

Chapter 10 focuses on conflictual relations between and within groups: dealing with attacks from outside; fragmentation and subgroup formation; and the relevance of gender and political category clusters to the interpretation of conflict.

Chapters 11 and 12 consider cooperative relations within groups and the use of the term 'community'. I am not interested in forming a new definition of 'community', or in determining whether online groups are 'real communities' or not. Community is not a term with a specifically sociological meaning. It enters into politics and expectations, and is entirely part of 'popular' discourse about groups and their validity. People on the List appear to recognise List community in two main ways: firstly in particular forms of excess or redundancy which elaborate otherwise relatively 'simplex' bonds between people, reducing uncertainties, giving reassurance during argument, and indirectly informing people of approved behaviour; and secondly though offlist activity between members. Organising or acting as a group is difficult, while individual or small group contacts seem relatively easy. Online societies allow the, now insecure, 'intellectual middle class' to extend their range of contacts and survival networks when faced with newly uncertain living conditions.

Appendix I includes a statistical analysis of aspects of the population and use of Cybermind.

Appendix II contains a glossary of terms and neologisms used both in the book and by members of Cybermind. If readers, perhaps rightly, forget what 'WES' means, this is the place to look.

Chapter 1: Toward an Analysis of Communication

Introduction
This chapter introduces and explains some of the theoretical terms used in the rest of the book. If the reader has no particular interest in the justification for these ideas, then the book can be followed by perusing the summary at the end of this chapter. The theory takes seriously the unfixed nature of human communication, and discusses how, given the expected variation in culture and the shifting nature of signs, there can be any consistency in meaning, or collaboration, at all. To deal with this question it is necessary to discuss the ways that linguistic and social categories are formed, and the consequence of these modes of formation. Recent work on category formation suggests that rather than linking things or events which are all the same in some way, categories can link things which are similar in different ways. Thus, category formation depends upon possible modes of manipulation and presentation of the things or events being classified, and the context of use. The chapter explores the ideas of prototypes, terminators, category boundaries, and framing, to provide a series of tools to allow us to analyse the ways that people go about trying to stabilise communication, persuade others of something, evaluate their place within a group, or make a category identity for a group.

If we dispense with the idea of culture as an overriding or uniform 'thing' which dominates people, and replace it with the idea of diverging forms of knowledge which are created, distorted and received by people in interaction with each other and the world, then we have the problem of accounting for the degree of uniformity which we observe. If categories are not simply reflections of things 'in nature', but result from social interaction with the world and if, as a result, communication cannot be a simple transmission of data from one place to another, then this problem is emphasized. Collaboration, feedback and the resistance of the world to our conceptions and actions may normally reduce these variations[1], however, this becomes problematic online, in a 'discourse based group', as there is little resistance offered by text (or fantasy), and there is rarely any collaboration which is non-textual. Furthermore, with such a view of culture and communication, it is particularly useful to consider the problems of how language relates to knowledge and persuasion, and to be as explicit as possible in our formulations. This chapter attempts to provide some tools for dealing with these problems and directing our attention toward significant factors which might otherwise be ignored. These tools include:

1) Awareness of the non identity of linkages between members of a category, so that people are not automatically members of a category in the same way;
2) The distinction between 'concept' and 'congerie' categories;
3) The notion of category 'prototypes';
4) Awareness of problems of divergence in communication and the related issue of 'framing';
5) The conception of groups as categories, with 'norms' being defined as category properties; and
6) Taking self-identity as a form of self-categorization taking place in concert with the categorisation of other people.

Categories

John Taylor suggests that the traditional Western view of categories is: that all members of a category are similar in the same way, so that membership can always be defined by necessary and sufficient conditions; that boundaries are clear so that things are either in or outside the category; and that there are no degrees of membership (1989: 23-4). Since the 1920s all of these positions have been challenged, largely through examination of how people come to learn and to use categories[2].

People do not receive all categories instinctively, but learn category usage in exploration of the world, as part of a way of life and as guided by people who have socially recognised knowledge or greater power. In his study of category formation in children, Vygotsky discovered two common kinds of category: the chain category and the radial category. Chain categories link things or events by similarities, which vary from link to link. Thus, a red square could be linked to a blue square, which could be linked to a blue triangle and so on. With radial categories, members are linked to a 'central item', possibly by different 'features'. Thus a red square is linked to a blue square, and then the red square is linked to a red triangle and so on (Vygotsky 1986: 96ff; cf Lakoff 1987: 91-5). These 'central' members of a category have become known as 'prototypes'.

At roughly the same time Wittgenstein suggested that, in many categories, members are not linked by a common similarity but, like members of a human family, resemble each other in different ways: with "a complicated network of similarities overlapping and criscrossing: sometimes overall similarities, sometimes similarities of detail" (1968: #66ff.). This we might consider a combination of chain and radial category. Linkages occur because of *perceived* properties which are not necessarily properties of the category members, but arise because of their social mode of presentation, or even because of a person's apparently similar emotional response to them[3].

Not following Vygotsky's terminology exactly, I will call categories whose members can be linked by uniform similarity 'concepts', and every other type of category 'congeries'[4]. In the case of congeries membership cannot be given by *definition*, as members can be linked by the varying attribution of a set of properties.

The 'congerie' form of the category is most obvious when humans are trying to conceive the inconceivable, the new, or the hard to manipulate. Concepts arise when the process being conceived is manipulable, and there is some pressure towards system. We might think of scientific or philosophical progress as, ideally, a process of people beginning with congeries that are then developed into concepts which promote new research which, in turn, may shatter the concepts leaving us to work with congeries again[5].

Prototypes

Eleanor Rosch (1973, 1975) was perhaps the first to point out that some category members are 'better' than others. For example, people in the US generally hold that a 'robin' is a better example of a 'bird' than a 'duck' or an 'ostrich'. Likewise they hold a 'chair' is a better example of furniture than a 'vase' or a 'refrigerator' (Taylor 1989: 43-4). As already implied, these good members are termed 'prototypic'.

Prototypes are more easily activated than non-prototypes. The more prototypic an example, the easier it is to identify it as a member of the relevant category. Mention of a category, in turn, serves to make prototypes more recognizable. Anything which can be labelled as belonging to a category can then appear to take on characteristics of the prototype (Taylor 1989: 45). Prototypes are easy to remember, and memory tends to make situations more prototypic (ibid: 53).

When there are multiple ways of determining whether or not something is a member of a category, then its apparent membership can be influenced by the comparisons with other categories which are being made at the same time. Similarly, what constitutes a good prototype can also vary, depending on the comparison being made, and the situation it is being made in.

Terminators

Some congeries appear to gain their power through the role they take in discourse. It is impossible to ever justify the 'axioms' of a discourse without going outside that discourse into another discourse, which also cannot be self-justifying. Neither is it possible to bring everything under signage. Therefore, some terms fill in these inevitable gaps in the language, and act to terminate arguments or infinite regression in the search for axioms. These terminator categories are wide enough to allow an illusion of mutual understanding to occur. Levi-Strauss implies that the term 'mana' in both Polynesian cosmological discourse and in Marcel Mauss's discourse, takes its force from being a congerie and terminator[6].

Such congeries as 'truth', 'good', 'beauty', 'community', 'information' and so on, tend to be taken, in Western discourse, as abstract, existent and as fully worked out concepts which, however, are difficult (Ellis 1993: 20ff.). They often become taken as an actual existent and people may come to ponder the complexities of the 'similarity' between a 'good work of art' and a 'good person'[7].

Sometimes these congeries are linked to institutions which act to help them function as terminators. Such institutional categories can be used to support or justify a particular class, or power pattern, or way of life. Thus Plato finds it easy to show 'the good' are 'the best', are the 'aristocrats'[8]. Capitalist States can use the congerie 'freedom' to justify the lack of control 'ordinary' people have over corporations. Other times it seems that congeries like 'beauty' may generate, or become the subject of, particular fields of discourse, like aesthetics.

Boundaries

Category boundaries are not always distinct: they can blend into one another or overlap; they can fade out; they can be arranged in a mutually dependent system or be treated as isolated (Taylor 1989). Boundaries can allow one-way or two-way flow, they can have different thresholds of permeability, they can be abrupt or gradual, or be extending or excluding. Different styles might be used in particular categories of situation and these styles could vary throughout a society. Kosko (1994) also points out that categories may be vague, blend into each other, or be *fuzzy* with degrees of membership, rather than having 'all or nothing' memberships. Given these boundary variations, and the notion of degrees of membership; then liminality cannot be a given (as implied by Mary Douglas or Victor Turner). For a group, or process, to be liminal it has to be made so, and this needs to be investigated. The nature of boundaries, and how people will deal with them, cannot be assumed in advance.

Problems of Communication

Without interactions between people using the same language, categories tend to diverge and eventually become different languages. Different groups using the same language can have different schema for interpreting people and terms, in effect making the same language different[9]. If this occurs then communication cannot be a *transfer* of internal states or representations from one person to another (what Lakoff (1995) calls the 'conduit metaphor' of communication), and thus category matching and 'comprehension', become problems to be explored[10].

If communication is not 'transfer', then it can be regarded as a process in which people interpret the responses of those with whom they are communicating, and check whether those interpretations match with their expectations. If the interpretations and expectations do not match, then people may use this feedback to change their response and so on. Meaning cannot usually be abstracted apart from socially known tasks. Basically a person emits a statement and behaviour, which to them has a particular content: the 'receiver' then interprets this as another content, which may well be different. Having expectations and making interpretations is a necessary part of communication, but having congruence of either mental states or 'meanings' is not.

People can apparently agree on things, even though they may have divergent maps. This does not matter as long as expectations are met well enough to allow coaction. These different mappings may be discovered through failure of mutual action, but they may not, and this may influence the coaction in other ways. If people are collaborating, then feedback and shared experiences may help the mappings mesh so that categories become more and more shared. People will remark on it if they don't understand something, or they will give back an interpretation of the other's communication so it can be checked and corrected. Cooperation may slow category variation better than conflict due to the shared resistances of the worked with the Real.

When adults talk to children, these kinds of disjunctions are clear and the adult usually corrects the child, trying to get the child to respond according to the adult's expectations. Each responds to the other, but it is unlikely the adult's language will be permanently modified to match the child's. Power ratios are directly involved in communication.

Difference in power or status ratios can affect the feedback process in other cases as well. People may hide mistakes, incomprehension, or ignorance, through fear of loss of status, fear of revealing the secrets of power, through fear of punishment, or through their relatively limited correctional options. Consequently, considering the power opportunities and patterns the discourse is embedded in will help any investigation of communication.

As Cybermind is a voluntary discourse-based group with little coherence given by interaction with a shared real, it is intimately associated with problems of making language and systems of interpretation stable, and thus ensuring the relative continuity (or regular fluctuation) of discourse and response behaviour. Significations need either a) a pre-existent and shared set of terminators, or other modes of 'clusteration', to hold them steady enough for functioning; or b) for these terminators to be created in coaction. Different types of groups may demand different types of functioning and steadiness of signification. There is no necessity to assume the clusters will remain stable in all circumstances. They are subject to argument, to the effect of 'external' forces (such as politics, economics, gendering and so on), to the various changes of power ratio, and alterations in personnel and foci of the group, so such factors cannot be ignored.

Framing

Some of the ambiguity in communication is reduced by language being embedded within, and partially consisting of, a 'framing' of ritual, etiquette, gestures, artefacts, tasks, forms of speech, tones of speech, types of font, modes of deference and so on, which comment upon the situation, telling people about the message and reducing ambiguity[11]. Framings tell people how things are likely to proceed; give a person expectations of other people involved and the likely results; and inform them of the likely expectations of others and thus how to function within the situation. Framings may indicate who can speak or write and who cannot, and who may listen or read and who may not. They indicate the relative degrees of power, or influence, of those who speak or write, and may determine the distribution of instructions or performances. They may indicate subjects which can or cannot be mentioned, and the ways they must be mentioned or not mentioned. Framings may indicate preferred styles of language use (in contrast to other uses), such as repetition, rhythm, 'plainness', obscurity and so on. Framing displays, or reinforces, the situation of coaction and can make an utterance performative[12].

Framings are not distinguishable from the situation as the participant's framings make the situation what it is. Different framings can intersect. Framings are not necessarily stable, they may be challenged. Different groups in the society may use the framing differently, and interpret the framed communication differently; framings may remove ambiguities for the interpreter, but may add meanings unintended by the emitter. Being able to 'define' the framings allows a person or group to define the debate.

Framings, when compared with the messages which occur within them, are cruder, more widely taught (often in early childhood), more habitual and repetitive, and often enforced.

Framings are influenced by the social uses of technology. A book distributes and allows access in a different way to a megaphone or telephone. On a mailing list the range of types of collaboration is much smaller than in face-to-face interaction and possibly different, so the probability of fragmentation into monologue is perhaps higher—there is a tendency for topics to wander. This implies that social control, and assertion of framing, becomes extremely important, as it is one of the few ways in which people can collaborate. Social control might even be more fundamental to online society than to face-to-face society, because there is no 'survival necessity' cooperation such as gathering food together, bringing up children together, building houses together, etc. However people can join together in trying to make stability, to keep the 'feel' of the list present, and to drive away the 'deviate'.

Types of Framing

It is useful to indicate the kinds of framings, or features of framings, which have arisen in this research as the most important for online life. Several of the features overlap. They are: locale, mood, exchange, redundancy, etiquette, conflict, public/private, and what I will call 'mytheme'.

Locale

In WES society, locales (such as banks, living rooms, classrooms and so forth), provide framings for the activities going on within them. They indicate appropriate behaviour and interpretations of behaviour, and often imply social roles[13]. Particular groups may control conventions for particular locales. This control may be reinforced or contested in other locales. The convention of locale helps give 'cyberspace' its sense of place (Marshall 2001). The Internet makes a collection of locales rather than a single locale, although people frequently write as if the Internet was a single locale with a single set of conventions. This may result from the developmental period in which the Internet was largely controlled by people of the same profession, something no longer the case.

Mood

Mood provides one mode of category linkage. It also guides expectations and the likelihood of statements being interpreted in particular ways. King writes that "emotion provides the fundamental way in which memory is organized. Information that is affectively congruent to the contents of a memory node are more accessible to it". Evaluations of ambiguous material will be interpreted according to the most easily activated, or current, mood (1995: np).

Continuity of mood is relatively rare online, particularly onlist with the disjointed topics and attitudes in different mails, and when it occurs (as with mourning of death, flaming or netsex), it is frequently remarked and often almost overpowering. A common experiential mood is the suspension of presence and absence, which I have called *asence* (discussed in Chapter 5). People engage in fairly routine efforts to resolve asence, which will be shown to affect patterns of list behaviour and communication.

Exchange

Exchange provides a framing, in that every communication is, in a sense, an exchange, enmeshed within other patterns of exchange. Such exchanges may be of gifts or commodities, equal or unequal, generous or stingy, relatively free or forced. Styles of exchange tell people something about the communications which occur within these exchanges, and can be used to influence the behaviour of others. People may be evaluated (as to status, worth, importance, etc.), in terms of their place and performance in a pattern of exchange.

Redundancy

In communication theory, redundancy is a way of avoiding errors, by giving more information than is actually needed. To give a simple example: if we repeat a message twice, then any difference between the two messages as received will indicate the occurrence of an error. Public framings tend to be redundant, or excessive, so that audiences have more chance of deciding which frame is in use; ritual gestures, vocal tones, the invocation or execration of Names tend to be common. The use of multiple, but specific, symbols can add redundancy by marking out a situation as of a particular type (Sperber 1975). Thus the combination of church-like architecture, silence and a crucifix each reinforces patterns of expected behaviour and authority. In this case, symbols are not necessarily 'standing for' something, but indicating and evoking a specific situation, and perhaps a 'mindset' to go with it.

Etiquette

It seems probable that there are nearly always constraints upon acceptable behaviour and meanings. Breaking constraints implies a breakdown of predictable response and category-matching. The handling of such a breakdown will depend upon the ease of assigning particular prototypes to the emitter of what has been interpreted as breakdown, the relevant power ratios, and the correctional styles of the groups involved. Many misunderstandings can be driven by 'small' things like the etiquette about who initiates conversation, how turns are exchanged, what duration turns should be (in themselves and relative to each other), how a change of turn is indicated, how many turns a person should take relative to others, and how closure comes about (Agar 1994: 164ff.).

One usual function of etiquette is to express what kind of person you are, your status, and how you are likely to behave. ("I'm normal, I'm not hostile, I'm keeping these small rules therefore I am likely to keep more important conventions"). Simultaneously, perceptions of etiquette are used to interpret the behaviour of other people involved, to discover how they are likely to behave, and so are involved in the creation of trust. In some societies it might take longer than others to establish this kind of trust, and the intensity of the trust required may also vary. Acting in a way which breaks these conventions, effectively gives out messages implying the emitter is uncontrolled at best, and renders it probable they will be fitted into prejudicial categories. The emitter can become perceived in terms of a hostile prototype, and people will not hear the intended content. This may be even more so if, like many WES people, the participants do not believe in etiquette. In this case there is less chance of an emitter, perceived as breaching the etiquette, being perceived as incompetent, or as using a different etiquette—they will be perceived as deliberately provocative, or as a particular type of outsider. As shall be shown later, WES modes of framing often involve an etiquette of authenticity, and this has marked effects on online sociality.

Conflict

Conflict, as well as resulting from different framings (which lead different groups to interpret events differently), can also be a framing in that it indicates what people should be doing, and how they should interpret the activities and communications of others. Although in WES societies it seems easy to explain conflict as deriving from aggression, the relationship may be more complex. As Elias suggests aggression may not trigger conflict, but conflict triggers aggression (1996: 461), just as the justifications for conflict can arise out of the conflict rather than cause it (Harris 1975: 62). We should be wary of explaining behaviour by commonly used explanatory terminators, even if we cannot avoid terminators of some sort or another.

Public/Private

I do not assume that public and private distinctions are universal, and they appear to vary with situation, and the comparisons being made, but they do act as framings in WES society. As shall be shown later in this book, communication in private settings is associated with greater intimacy and truth than public communication; and a great deal of effort is expended in distinguishing one from the other in order to determine the kinds of behaviours and truths expected.

Mytheme

I use the term 'mytheme' to include theories, myths and stories about the world irrespective of their claims to truth. These mythemes draw attention to aspects of the world (social and otherwise) and usually act as a template for interpretation, usually in a dramatic way. The user of a mytheme is already situated within a story that categorizes them *with* some others, and *against* some others; thus giving them expectations about the communications which are made. Mythemes guide and express experience, linking survival to identity, as they imply categories of people have particular motivations and actions and survival needs. At least some of their description is equivalent to prescription. Events contrary to the mytheme *tend* to be unperceivable to users in comparison with those that confirm it.

Even common mythemes are often challenged. Other people will propose *counterpositions*—different mythemes which disagree with, or object to these common mythemes. Any reduction of a complex of mythemes to the 'one underlying' mytheme, the one complete myth etc., must carefully demonstrated.

Mythemes link categories in clusters, so that the presence of one category tends to activate the others, and the clustering of categories supports their mytheme.

Mythemes often assign causal explanations to events, causality being, as Hume observed, merely temporal contiguity given a human linkage (1888: 72-78). The kind of explanations which attribute ingroup failures to the activities of outgroup others, are a traditional feature of 'sorcery' mythemes and apply in most groups.

Groups, Identities, Norms and Categories

This study makes use of a variant of the identity theory developed by John Turner, who proposes that self-identity arises in relationship with others, as an act of categorization, and as a mode of framing which helps people interpret others. People categorize themselves, and are categorized by others, as belonging to particular groups, which are categorized in relationship to other groups. These categorizations are related and dynamic, as people attempt to determine the attributes which allocate themselves and others to various groupings and demonstrate closeness to group prototypes. People may have differing self-categorizations as members of different groups, some of which will change during their lifetime, and others of which (as appears with gender), are always relevant[14]. Identity categories are not just chosen but imposed.

A category of people often need only be named to have an effect; it need not have any other 'real' properties. In experiments people who were randomly allocated group membership, without knowing the other members of the group, were biased in favour of their group (Turner et al 1988: 27-8). Further experiments showed that people listening to arguments on tape were more likely to be persuaded by argument if the arguments came from a group they were told they would be joining, than if the arguments came from a group they were told they would be opposing. Persuasiveness increased if people were told the arguments came from a group to whom they were similar, and diminished if they were told the arguments came from a dissimilar group (ibid: 160; Haslam et al. 1996). Similarly in experiments involving 'prisoner's dilemma' type games, cooperation increased if people were told they belonged to the same group (Turner et al 1988: 36)[15].

The implication of this naming effect is that 'real' distinctions between groups are not always required to promote perception of difference. Desired and ascribed group membership can drive the perception of differences from other groups, and of similarities within groups. Discovering, inventing, implementing and persuading others of these differences then becomes a prime social dynamic. Behaviour which approximates that attributed to a prototype is both noticed and confirms the prototype, while behaviour which does not approximate a prototype is less noticeable and is rarely taken as falsifying the prototype. Perceiving a person as belonging to a category not only defines them as similar or different, but it selects the similarity or difference as normative (Turner et al. 1988: 131). I propose that those properties (conscious or unconscious) which 'determine', or are announced by, category membership, be called 'category-norms'[16]. Category-norms often derive from categories over which the actor has no control such as gender, race or age (Cancian 1971: 142-3)[17].

As category-assumptions, category-norms both guide 'audience' expectations of a category member's behaviour, and the member's expectation of how others will behave towards them. Category-norms not only constitute identity but express identity, and thus are subject to reformulation depending on situation and adequacy. As category-norms gather around, or create, reciprocal identities they may induce mutually rejecting, exaggerating, complementary or cooperative behaviour. Categories linked by opposition gain salience and existence from comparison with their 'opposite', and hence people may try to enforce the existence of an opposition. Thus, in many societies, males and females may try and prevent the other from engaging in behaviour which 'belongs' to their own category and which sets it off from the other.

It might be possible to observe in the history of a group a kind of hierarchy of norms, shown through the stability of some behaviours and interpretations, and the fluctuation of others. However, if category-norms only arise in, or are mobilised to deal with, particular types of situations, then the appearance of hierarchy may be given by the recurrence of certain happenings and the rarity of others. This appearance may change completely with the introduction of new events or challenges to authority. Again, care needs to be taken in deciding what 'norms', if any, are 'fundamental'.

Category Bias

Category assignment seems to affect evaluation. People tend to evaluate the categories to which they belong positively, although it is possible for people to identify with groups with which they would prefer not to be associated (Turner et al 1988: 107)[18]. People tend to be evaluated positively (or found attractive) by fellow category members to the degree they are perceived as prototypic of the category to which they all belong (ibid: 57). Outgroup members are less attractive the more they can be perceived as prototypic of a negative outgroup (ibid: 60). Elias writes:

> an established group tends to attribute to its outsider group as a whole, the 'bad' characteristics of that group's 'worst' section... In contrast, the self image of the established group tends to be modelled upon its most exemplary, most 'nomic', or norm setting section (Elias & Scotson 1994: xix).

Elias goes on to suggest that weaker outsider groups can only begin to positively self-evaluate, and engage in 'counter-stigmatisation' when the power differentials diminish (ibid: xxi).

The internal influence of a person or a statement is connected with perceptions of what a group or category shares, or of what distinguishes it from other groups. The degree of persuasiveness of a statement is "exactly equivalent" to the degree it is perceived to exemplify some ingroup norm/property (Turner et al 1988: 154). The most prototypic ingroup member is the most persuasive (ibid: 155; Van Knippenberg et al 1994). Persuasion from a current opinion is also easier if the opinion is not relevant to self-identity as a member of other groups (Festinger 1960: 294). Hopkins & Reicher (1997) show how effective persuaders:

a) define category boundaries so as to include as much of the audience as possible;
b) try to make the audience and speaker part of a common category;
c) construct the recommended actions or beliefs as congruent, or prototypic, with this category; and
d) try to make opposing arguments represent an outgroup category.

Such strategies constantly appear in online disputes.

Prototypic Variability

Prototypes can vary. There is no need for the group prototype to be the same for members of a group, and for members of other groups who are interpreting their behaviour. Struggle can arise over what constitutes a prototype, both internally and externally.

Conflict framing can strengthen categories, thus causing 'ambiguous' individuals to be expelled or become 'taboo' or dangerous. As prototypicality "depends upon increasing differences from outgroup members and decreasing differences from members of the same category" (Turner et al 1988: 155), groups in moving away from the perceived prototypes of rival or negatively valued others, can move to an 'extreme' position rather than towards an existent 'median' position, which might be closer to the other group (ibid: 151). The prototypic response of a group does not necessarily correspond to the ingroup mean of responses (ibid: 80-1).

Category-norms are not only validated by group acceptance. Cybermind may have created and validated some of its identity norms by rejecting Glen (Chapter 9), but it is equally possible that his norms and self-identity were also validated by the rejection.

Category Imposition

That category-groups exist in relation to other groups, leads to the situation in which people are forced to belong to a category by the actions and reactions of others. If they possess some salient properties of a category, a person may be treated as if they possessed all the properties of the category. Certain property-clusters exclude others. Cancian gives the example that in the old American South "it would not have been possible for a male Negro member of a predominantly white group to be [perceived as] both (1) responsible and trustworthy and (2) angry and aggressive" (1975: 145). Enforcement is particularly likely if the category is cast as an 'opposite' to the enforcing category by the enforcing category. Normative statements and behaviours are expressions of a particular view of reality.

People may go along with such impositions not only to avoid enforcement but because communication and coaction is otherwise constantly disrupted by 'incorrect' interpretations by others. With prolonged exposure and use of these conventions, people may internalize at least some of them as expressing their own identity and may use other aspects to present this identity in a beneficial way. It may also be exceedingly difficult to select those parts (properties) of their assigned category which they prefer, or which appear more accurate, from the other parts as these are reinforced by the clustering of other categories, and the 'systemic-reference' of terminators.

Simplex and Multiplex Relations

A slight modification of Gluckman's distinction between simplex and multiplex ties is useful in considering the way that self-identity categories can be linked. Gluckman proposed that in small-scale societies many relationships are 'multiplex'; the relationship serves many purposes, and a person has a number of separate roles, or self-categories, with respect to the same audience, some of which may be in conflict. Ritual may be used to mark the category relationships in current use and to regulate this conflict (1962a: 26-7). In the city, relationships tend to be 'simplex' in that the audiences for different self-categories are more likely to be separate, and conflicts are more likely to arise without mutual ties to other people, and without mutually recognised rituals to frame the events (ibid: 35, 38-9). Gluckman suggested that multiplex ties lead to people negotiating and compromising[19], while simplex ties lead to win or lose situations. This distinction can prove useful in elucidating some aspects of online life, and its worthwhile wondering how simplex relationships might become multiplex over time, or not.

Categories Online

In online groups, ease of leaving the group selects those who abide by, or do not noticeably violate, at least some group category-norms. However some, perhaps prototypic, people are more important for maintaining group identity than others. In the disputes considered later, a relatively small proportion of the group make public comment, though the majority of the most visible people make at least one comment. However, even major participants like Alan can leave the group (as has happened occasionally) without a change of norms appearing immediately. Previous selection processes maintain coherence for, at least, a short time. People will also be influenced by the category-norms affecting their offlist lives—hence these offline norms cannot be ignored.

Because, online categories are largely conceptual, and as we shall demonstrate, not particularly influenced by interactions between online groups, these offlist categories might tend to become exaggerated to achieve shared reference, and to easily assign people into categories which govern recurrent behaviours and to frame events. This, as shall be shown, is the case, in particular with gender and with political divisions. Gender tends to be an important ingroup demarcator, and politics an important outgroup marker.

Values

Category-norms, as category properties, always exist, but in the case of Cybermind explicit statements about category-norms (or *'values'*) need to be created and the formulations agreed upon. They have to be presented, negotiated and mobilised. Though some kind of informal normative discourse exists on Cybermind, this is not a formulated discourse of rules. Values formulated in times of lesser stress may have little impact on behaviour or values formulated in times of greater stress. People who make the dominant formulations for the group may differ depending upon the situation. Thus, Alan was of little importance in 'normal control' and of great importance to 'control under pressure' while, another list member, Rose, was the opposite. When explicit values emerge to control, or remove somebody, or keep them quiet, they tend to cluster in patterns which are themselves created within the values of offlist life. These clusters may further be associated with what we call 'institutions' or 'rituals', though these may not appear in *all* types of Internet society.

Values are used to justify, or delegitimate, behaviour. However they need not cause behaviour. Cancian writes of:

> the vast number of previous studies on attitudes and behaviour. Most of these studies had found little relationship between what people do and what people say is right and proper (1975: viii).

Moore states:

> For every occasion that a person thinks or says 'that cannot be done, it is against the rules, or violates the categories', there is another occasions when the same individual says 'those rules or categories do not (or should not) apply to this situation. This is a special case' (1975: 219-20)[20].

However, although values may not terminate explanation of behaviour, they may have some effect as: firstly some statements are 'truer' than others; secondly some values are defensive of identity and abandoning them might cause one to be linked with a devalued category; thirdly because different framings may keep the contradictions separate; and fourthly because of the clustering of norms which determine the probability of arguments being acceptable. An argument which activates the most stable, largest and 'emotional' value clusters will be more persuasive than one which activates small clusters. Such clusters may be associated with the patternings which are usually called institutions.

We can however, ask with Barth "what produces value convergences?" and investigate the processes at work in orienting people's choices (1993b: 34, 36), which is part of the complexities of communication and category matching. As Barth further points out positive values may be less important in directing behaviour than people's awareness of potential states which they wish to avoid like sorcery, anger, or system failure (ibid: 37-8). It shall be shown that there are feedback processes built into the control processes of online societies, which depend on people avoiding 'dysfunctional' states.

Summary

Categories link unlike things together. This is not simply dependent upon the properties of the processes under categorization, but also upon the social mode of presentation, the psychophysical state (or mood) of the people involved and so on. Thus things can be linked in categories by the feelings which people have towards them, or the uses people make of them. Thus the linked category members may have little in common themselves. When there is pressure towards coherence, and the aspects of the real under categorization are manipulable, it is possible to generate systematic *concepts*. However, many categories remain at the non-systematic *congerie* stage. Some of these categories act as *terminators* to discussion, summarising many disparate processes into the one term which is taken as 'conceptual' or as 'real'. Many categories have *prototypes* which are 'good' examples of the category, which serve to illustrate it, and which are easily recalled.

Identity is a process of categorization which involves the allocation of membership of people into groups. I am an academic, a footballer, a soldier, a wife, etc. The properties of the group are emphasised in relation to other groups and to the situation. Those people who are (or become) prototypic of an ingroup are high status and persuasive: those who are (or become) prototypic of an outgroup also take on the assumed properties of that group and become less persuasive. The 'properties' of a category do not have to remain stable but depend on perspective and the social dynamics involved. The persuasive force of a statement is influenced by the degree to which it is made by a member of a group the hearer identifies with, and by how prototypic the stater is, and by how much it conforms to the *category norms* which help define the group prototype and, simultaneously, render outgroups more clearly defined.

Communication is not a transfer of content, as categorization tends to divergence and difference of interpretation. Communication involves a complex set of processes whereby people attempt to prevent this divergence. *Framing* gives added information, redundancies, or an excess to the message which helps its interpretation. However, it is possible for interpretations to vary wildly from intentions, and modes of framing can be contested, or simply different. This difference of framings can influence the course of discussion. I allege that important framings online include: etiquette, conflict, values, locale, mood, exchange, redundancy, and mytheme.

Framings and associations of a category can *cluster* so the use of one part of the cluster tends to evoke other parts of the cluster.

Finally, relationships can be crudely defined as *simplex* if the audiences for different self-categorisations of a person tend to be different, and *multiplex* if those audiences overlap.

Chapter 2: Cybermind — A History

Preamble

This chapter outlines the history of the Cybermind from the period before its inception, when the co-founders met on the FutureCulture and deleuze mailing lists, to the current day. It discusses the politics of the group's instigation and birth in the Spoon Collective—briefly outlining the statistics and demographics of its first month. Events leading to the move away from Spoon are described and the context is provided for all the events which are discussed in the rest of the book, up to the partial breakdown of the List in the period leading up to the second Iraq War and after.

Growth of the Internet and Email

By 1995, when this ethnography begins, Computer Mediated Communication (CMC) had moved from a limited number of universities, the military, internal corporate nets and commercial email suppliers into the public or commercial arena. The successor to the ARPANET; the government funded NSFNet, had been transferred to a consortium run by Merit, MCI and IBM who used the government subsidy to provide a network which would link commercial information suppliers with the users of NSFNet (Salus 1995: 199-200; Mackie-Mason & Varien 1994: 2; Cerf & Aboba 1993). By mid 1997 the five leading Internet backbone suppliers, responsible for 80% of US Internet traffic, were owned by major telecommunications carriers (D. Schiller 1999: 33).

Although in-house use of email was quite common in large corporations by the 1980s, the majority of interactions through the Internet, specifically, were confined to scientists and the military. Commercial provision of email and 'chat rooms' began in the 1980s with the founding of such companies as America Online (AOL) and CompuServe. In the 1990s the growth of such companies was phenomenal. Between 1991 and 1999 AOL, which eventually provided Cybermind's infrastructure, increased its subscriber base from 130,000 to more than 17 million. This coincided with AOL providing a gradually increasing full Internet connection to subscribers (figures from AOL Annual Reports)[1]. Although this changed the demographics of Internet usage, the majority of users were significantly better educated than the majority of WES populations, and largely came from the 'middle class', which has been so affected by the changes discussed elsewhere in this book. This does not imply uniformity in the views embraced by this group, as discourse is relatively diverse; however, the groups formed by these people tend to be locally uniform, and may act to provide support and contact.

The Origins of a Social Group

I was not onlist for the first five to six months and so missed much of the experience of this time including the density of messages and offlist correspondence, which shapes what happens onlist. This problem is compounded by the apparent reluctance of people online to reminisce, or tell each other stories of the past, or of what they have shared, which is normally a way of maintaining group values and identities (see Chapter 5). When people do reminisce, chronology is often inaccurate. A consequence of this reluctance is that events are selected for their drama or potential as origins or causes. Yet life is not always dramatic or an originary point. The most important processes of existence may be entirely routine and not easy to perceive, or they may (as is perhaps particularly the case with a mailing list) actually occur out of sight. This is especially so of the administrative work that Alan (and subsequently pip, Laurie, Jim and Drew) put into keeping the list moving and which is only visible when it fails.

A consequence of this chronological vagueness is that the exact date of Cybermind's first appearance on the net is unclear. The earliest records I have suggest it began about the 1st July 1994[2].

Alan Sondheim, one of the founders of Cybermind, and the current listowner and moderator, describes the origin as arising from an issue of the *Art Papers* magazine he was editing on "Future Culture"[3]. At this time he discovered an Internet mailing list with the name FutureCulture which he joined. While on that list he met Michael Current, the future co-founder of Cybermind. Michael was also running the Deleuze and Guattari list under the ownership of Kent Palmer at Thinknet[4], which Alan also joined. Soon Alan and Michael began to talk about starting a new mailing list[5]. Later Alan was to write to me (pc 24 Feb.95) that:

> [At this time I] wanted to get into this badly; all my work [...] deals with issues of body, sexuality, language and I wanted to have an email list devotedto this. So Michael and I began talking; he wanted something dealing with Cyberspace, and we agreed to co-moderate

A letter from Michael to Alan "probably from May, 1994" and posted to Cybermind by Alan on 21 June.96 reads:

> As for the proposed list itself, it can pretty much be whatever the moderators decide to frame it as. The moderators would be allowed to draft the description that goes in the "info" file on the list. My thought was that this would be a place a.) to discuss work devoted to, or relevant to, the philosophical, etc, issues related to the impact of cyberspace on subjectivization (or, as I prefer human becoming); b.) discuss these same issues in more general terms; and b.{sic}) provide a palace to share work-in-progress (this would especially involve student work, a great deal of which is now focusing on cyber-issues. Thesis-net and a couple of other lists have tried to perform this function, but don't seem to have succeeded, despite what looked to be a fair amount of interest.) So I guess that would mean general conversation, conversation focused around specific theorists/texts (perhaps some group readings from time to time), and discussion/critique of works-in-progress... I know this is vague, but I just made it up :)[6] and it is late at night.

Alan continues (pc 24 Feb.95):

> I had opted for 'Cyberpsych', but 'Cybermind' was his invention; he was part of a psychological support group on the Net[7] and wanted no 'psych' involved in the title. We argued for a while, then I backed down and Cybermind stuck. We wrote the info sheet together. I think the ideas were both of ours, the final wording his. But it was really a collaboration

Michael may have briefly considered setting up Cybermind with Kent Palmer and the Thinknet group which was running his Deleuze list, but Kent had apparently "interfered" with Michael's running of that list on some occasions and according to Alan "there was a huge storm"[8] (21 June.96 & pc 22 June.96).

Malgosia Askanas, who was involved in the events around the founding of Cybermind, wrote to the Spoon list-proposals list on 16 June.95 that "Kent... had certain ideas of propriety of list-conversation and occasionally Kent would intervene in discussions on his lists when he thought they overstepped the limits of good taste". fido wrote in reply (16 Jun.95) to this letter, that:

> Kent, not really knowing a thing about Deleuze, started a Deleuze list in the hopes of learning. (I believe he's working on a tome about how the world works.) Kent has many advanced degrees. But Kent was unaware of the import of the action he'd just completed: that is, starting a list for people into Deleuze or people into what they thought Deleuze might be into: people whose writing slams in the megalopolis, people into becoming-genera, people-against-oedipus, people into rubber clothes, people who weren't

offended by edgy language, people who didn't give a fuck about advanced degrees, you get the pitcher...[9]

in the first weeks of Michael's tenure as moderator Michael had a number of bizarre embodied syntax errors--he changed his medication, and was having a lot of trouble adjusting. Rather than duck out and come back all fresh Michael made his body part of the text of his list, and from the start Deleuze had an emotional quality, a PHYSICAL quality, that I don't think Kent was ever able to understand.

Kent Palmer wrote to me (pc 5 May.99) that he:

> thought that absolute freedom of speech would soon degenerate into inane chatter and nihilism... However [I] only attempted to stop the use of profanity and posts that had nothing to do with the stated purpose of the list. The major concern was with possible legal issues revolving around the viewing of inappropriate material by minors. Eventually things came to a head when profanity began to be used on the Deleuze list... When it became clear that most of those on the Deleuze list wanted 'absolute freedom of speech' whether it was philosophically relevant or not then [I] suggested that those who were active on those lists take over the administration of the lists themselves and set up their own policies as they saw fit.

Malgosia writes that she was not on the deleuze list, but:

> was having this infinitely long and painful and lonely-seeming fight with Kent [about the nature of rules of behaviour on lists], and suddenly in the middle Michael joined the fight on my side. This is how I first met him, and how we came to join forces" (pc 12 Jul.96).

As a result of this, and their mutual reaction to Kent's intervention in the deleuze list, Michael and Malgosia decided to form their own organisation ("Spoon Collective") running from the same machine[10]. Over a few days the deleuze-guattari, film theory, avant-garde and technology lists which they were running were transferred from Thinknet to Spoon—"the opening of the account was an emergency measure to prevent the danger of Kent closing these lists down"[11]. According to Malgosia, both she and Michael wanted to avoid the problems which had arisen with one person doing all the administrative work. They therefore decided to establish the "specific collective-work solutions that... are characteristic of Spoon" and gather new list owners. Hence Cybermind opened under the Spoon banner.

It is important to note that Spoon, and hence Cybermind, were partly established as a proclamation of a particular kind of 'freedom'; as forums for authentic and open expression which might otherwise be impossible. Self-identity and distribution of the products of that self-identity were important in the founding of these lists.

The social positions of the founders of Cybermind and Spoon should be emphasised. All three were well-educated, intellectual people of 'middle class' upbringing (for want of a better term), interested in art and philosophy, but without a recognised place for the expression of their interests and activities which offered steady remuneration[12]. Alan, aged in his 50s, according to his resume has held a truly phenomenal number of exhibitions, grants[13] and committee positions, and a similarly large number of temporary teaching positions at colleges and universities. His financial and survival insecurity bother him, and with good reason. Michael, during this period, was unemployed and seriously ill with diabetes and a heart condition[14]. Malgosia, though financially more secure as a computer programmer, was also obviously not able to live by following her main interests. It is perhaps not surprising that Alan and Michael should wish for Cybermind to be not only a forum for their interests and a way of propagating their work and thought, but for it to be welcoming in a way in which the formal intellectual and artistic worlds of their society did not seem to be for them.

This original 'manifesto' gives some ideas of the ambitions with which the group was established.

ANNOUNCING
CYBERMIND

AN ELECTRONIC FORUM FOR THE DISCUSSION OF THE PHILOSOPHICAL AND PSYCHOLOGICAL IMPLICATIONS OF SUBJECTIVITY IN CYBERSPACE

We are all dwelling in cyberspace, coursing through the wires, becoming cyborg and becoming human[15]. We are subjects of a realm which is totally charted, and completely unknown. CYBER-MIND is devoted to an examination of the new subjectivities that have emerged and might yet emerge in this arena. We are interested in particular in the philosophical, psychological/psychoanalytic and social issues engendered, particularly as they concern the user and the social.

Some issues that might be relevant: the psychology of intimacy, the role of gender, the phenomenology of the terminal screen, neurosis and paranoia on the Net, the relationship of lag to community and communication, sex/gender/sexual orientation theory and electronic subjectivity, the role of the symbolic or imaginary in computer communication, the implications of symbolic extensions of the human ("external memory", and so forth), fantasy and the hallucinatory aspects of email/USENET groups/MUDs, and the psychoanalysis of lurking.

This will be an "open list"—posts on all aspects of the above issues and more will be welcomed. It will be open to general discussion, group readings of published works, and the sharing and critique of participants' works -in-progress. We would stress, however, that our intent is to explore these issues in the broadest sense. Discussions focused on IRC, MUD's/MOO's, Virtual Reality, etc. are already readily available on the Internet. While it is perfectly acceptable to discuss these issues when relevant, we do wish to discourage threads that are too narrowly limited to any particular medium or "sub-realm" of cyberspace

Similarly, while critical examination of cyberpunk literature can yield important insights, and we will welcome discussion of work in that genre, "fan"-type discussion of cyberpunk, of the type available on alt.cyberpunk, etc., is not appropriate on this list[16].

One concern we hope to address is the way in which much theoretical work on cyberspace to date reflects an exclusive, hegemonic[17] bias, thus foreclosing some of the most interesting and radical of possibilities for the development of Net culture. We plan to challenge ourselves and the list members to integrate issues of race, sex, class and multiculturalism in our efforts to think cyberspace together.

We believe this list will be an important forum for opening up new perspectives on cyberspace and cyberculture, and are anxious and excited to begin a dialogue with all interested parties on the types of issues we have described here. Our list is open to all interested parties, be they academics, Net "technicians," or ordinary citizens of cyberspace who wish to join us in thinking and discussing the present and future of this fascinating, exciting, and sometimes frustrating realm—and, ultimately, of ourselves.

To subscribe, send the message:
subscribe cybermind
to
majordomo@world.std.com.
You should recieve a message confirming your subscription.
If you have any difficulties, or more general questions, contact the list-owners:
mcurrent@picard.infonet.net—or—sondheim@panix.com
Michael Current and Alan Sondheim

When I joined the list in December 1994, the message was more or less unchanged with the exception of the addition of the following[18]:

CYBERMIND is brought to you by the Spoon collective, a group of Net citizens devoted to free and open discussion of philosophical issues on the

Internet. Based on the Collectives philosophy, PLEASE BE AWARE THAT POSTS CONTAINING LANGUAGE OR DEALING WITH MATTER THAT SOME MIGHT FIND OFFENSIVE MAY APPEAR ON THE LIST FROM TIME TO TIME, AND SUCH POSTS WILL NOT BE CENSORED. However we would like you to know that racial or other bias slurs will not be tolerated; there are other sites on the internet for them.

Absolute freedom could not be maintained, as it prevented discourse and rendered the presence of some people less likely. More sadly it also contained the following remark:

Please note: Michael Current, co founder of this list, died in July 1994. Those of us who have known him miss him terribly. We dedicate this list to him.

Initially the Spoon Collective ran from World.std.com, a commercial supplier in Boston. According to an early Spoon document, "A short guide to Spooning", the account was requested by Malgosia, and the costs were supposed to be shared among the collective although she was officially responsible for them. Members of the collective were also responsible, in alternating weeks, for cleaning up the error messages from the server and carrying out any acts arising from these messages.

Members of the Collective could communicate amongst themselves via a public list ('spoon-administration'), but the instructions made it clear that this "should NOT be used for any communications with even the slightest internal flavor". This disjunction between onlist 'public' and offlist 'private' communication is an important part of mailing list life—although it may be useful to distinguish between offlist 'social' communication between list members, and communication relating to the 'administration' of the list, which is usually hidden and occurs among a much more demarcated collection of people.

At about the time of Cybermind's inception Spoon was running the following lists, which also show the interests of the collective:

avant-garde	run by Malgosia Askanas
blanchot	run by Dan Kern
deleuze	run by Michael Current
film-theory	run by Malgosia Askanas
foucault	run by Steven Meinking
frankfurt-school	[no info]

marx	run by Flannon Jackson and Jon Beasly Murray
spoon-administration	
spoon-announcements	
technology	run by Malgosia Askanas

This list would expand considerably in a fairly short time, as would the size of the collective. At this time the collective consisted of eight persons; at least four of whom (Sondheim, Current, Askanas, and Meinking) were initially active on Cybermind, and three of whom (Sondheim, Current and Askanas) were among the first month's most prolific posters.

Alan also founded 'Fiction of Philosophy' or FOP, within the Collective, posting the original FOP announcement to Cybermind on 9 Jul.94, so it was founded between one and two weeks after Cybermind. Several years later Alan retired from moderating FOP and the position was taken over by Laurie.

Fiction of Philosophy was, in some sense, Cybermind's 'sister list'. Posts on one frequently appeared on the other, and personnel were frequently on both. Technical problems prevented me from subscribing to FOP at the beginning of my fieldwork, but most of the posts to FOP seemed to come to Cybermind. Later some members claimed the "life" of Cybermind migrated to FOP for a short period of time. One member, who left Cybermind for FOP, commented to me that it was where people from Cybermind went after reaching maturity. I was concerned that this migration might link with my presence as an observer on Cybermind, and decided not to participate on FOP despite occasional suggestions that tensions between members of Cybermind were often more explicit on FOP. I was, however, frequently told about events on FOP. Later still, the lists diverged as more people entered Cybermind not knowing of FOP and vice versa. Later still, in May 2000, the name of FOP changed to 'Wryting' and since then the lists seem to be largely separate.

Shortly after I joined Cybermind in December 1994 the Spoon Collective transferred its lists to a computer (jefferson.village) operating from IATH (Institute of Advanced Technology in the Humanities) at Virginia University on the invitation of John Unsworth of the Department of English. Both Alan and Malgosia agreed this change occurred because World.std.com was about to charge for email lists. The use of the new machine was free, though the collective had to become "IATH fellows, etc" (Alan pc 15 Mar.96).

In response to the question "Did this lead to any kinds of administrative changes?" Malgosia replied:

> On World, we were basically dependent for everything on the sysadmins. On jefferson, we have been given a free run of the system as far as list-matters are concerned. We can create lists as we please, set up complicated schemes, make our own updates to majordomo, install whatever software we want, etc. We are also considered an asset, and an important part of the IATH, rather than an indifferent commercial customer.

These changes in patterns of access to programming power, perhaps inevitably, meant decisions would be taken either by those who had the time to be continually involved, or by those who were programmers, and would tend to sideline the others. Or as Malgosia wrote, there was:

> more of a tendency for internal stratification in Spoon: the people who understand the system and the people whose commitment is to 'spoon as a project' tend to acquire greater indispensability and de-facto power than the others [...] in this environment, people who really, in the long run, don't want to become more involved, are in danger of feeling marginalized and pushed out. So in spite of the fact that we have a collective horror of coercion, there _is_ a certain degree of coercion towards a certain style of being-in-spoon. This would not have arisen if we had stayed at world, where we were all basically equally powerless.

Granted the circumstances of the group's founding in a rebellion against intervention and control without consensus, tensions probably became inevitable.

About twelve months later, differences between Alan and some other members of Spoon led to Alan's resignation from the Collective, and Cybermind moved to a commercial provider, America Online (AOL), for a listserv account[19]. Initial contact was made by Alan. The account was free, and was to last for a year, with a guarantee of free speech (pc 15 Mar.96). The latter part of the arrangement aroused skepticism on Cybermind, due to AOL's reputation for 'policing' areas within its provenance, its forbidding of various words, and the progress of what became known as the "Communications Decency Act" through the US legislature, which was expected to make AOL even more sensitive to external pressures. The vocal hostility of longer-term (non-Cybermind located) nethands to the "invasion" of the Usenet by "newbies" from AOL in 1993-95, which, to some extent, gave an AOL address a bad reputation, probably increased some people's reluctance to accept this as Cybermind's home base. However, AOL has been completely cooperative, never interfering with Cybermind's operation and Cybermind has stayed with AOL ever since. The only commonly remarked problem with AOL has been the way they only keep archives for the past two to three years.

The politics of life, between the List owners, seems to have been largely influenced by: a) the structures of communication with which they had to deal and which gave potential for uneven or conflicting responsibilities and powers; b) the difficulties of interpreting other's behaviour; c) the opening up of a new 'space' for their own interests or activities and; d) reference to existing offline values and conflicts.

Early Days on List

It is worthwhile looking at the opening month of Cybermind's existence to see the kind of expectations and experiences brought to the list by its potential users, the problems and unities that emerged, the forms of control used and subjects evoked and to see if these concerns continued.

Records for the start of the list are relatively good. Alan and Jerry Everard both kept edited selections of the initial posts, and Mitchell Pravatiner kept an almost complete record. Marius Watz also kept some archival material. All of this has been kindly made available to me. These selections are all 'expurgated' either in accordance with the selector's interests or by accident, but the volume of mail and references within the mail make it clear that Cybermind had a relatively heavy traffic from the beginning.

Between the first recorded post of the 1st of July and the last post dated the 6th of July, there were at least 330 posts. Even at this stage the group posted an average of over 55 messages a day. At least 2 of these posts would have to count as substantial essays—one taking over 15 pages of single-spaced type when printed, the other being just slightly over half that length. In this first week, at least 60 people seem to have posted. About half of these people (33) came from university addresses and a fair number of these seem to have been academic staff. Eighteen people came from commercial suppliers and the rest from other, or unknown, sources. Actual numbers were much greater. Malgosia wrote (6 Jul.94): "this list alone has close to 300 members". Even this estimate of the first week's population may be low as is shown by a post from Marius of the same date: "the 'WHO cybermind' command yields quite a different list than it did two days ago [...] some names I know have disappeared from it".

This number of members suggests some fairly effective promotion of the list occurred before its establishment. When asked if most people came from other spoon lists, Alan replied: "No, we did extensive advertising all over other lists including Future Culture—I forget which. Michael had a huge list of places to try" (pc 15 Mar.96). Jerry learnt about Cybermind from the "Announcing Cybermind" manifesto quoted above which had been posted to the Spoon's foucault list[20], so it can be assumed Cybermind was advertised on the other extant Spoon lists.

Presumably most of the people who joined Cybermind did so because the Manifesto suggested it would be interesting, but at least two posters (Malgosia and Marius) explicitly stated they joined because they knew Alan and Michael. The number of people from the FutureCulture list also implies there was an attempt to follow the 'community' of that list into another 'space'. Alan later wrote (26 Jun.96) "both [Cybermind and FOP] drew from Future Culture [...] Cybermind more so"[21].

Over 300 people subscribed to the list during the first month, and at least 80 people posted. However, well over half of the total known posts were made by the 12 most prolific posters, or by less than one sixth of the total active group. Alan was easily the most prolific poster. As is shown in Appendix I, this pattern of posting has continued.

Six of these twelve most prolific posters were women. Women have always been in the minority on Cybermind, and yet have had a significant visible presence. This was clear at the time to some members—fido, one of the more prolific posters, wrote (3 Jul.94):

> One of the things I've found really refreshing about this list—and this will be the first and probably the last time I hitch my post to a fe/male observation where I equate such distinctions with something positive—is the number of female names attached to messages. I don't think I have ever been on a list with so many (presumed) female voices.

In the first month 25% of the active population was female and made 32% of the posts. Almost 60% of these women had a .edu address implying they came from an academic base.

Life in the First Month

Conditions for reading Cybermind were not at their best on the opening weekend. Mitchell Pravatiner subscribed to Cybermind on Friday 1st of July 1994 and remembers (1 Jul.96):

> When I next connected on the following Tuesday morning, the Fourth having been on Monday, I was greeted by an email reader filled with new messages numbering somewhere in the 400s or 500s--much more than normal after a long weekend. Many of them, as it turned out, were duplicates, the product of an infinite loop caused by a rogue address. Many others, though, were the product of spam and flame wars.

By my reading, the most talked about subjects within the first week were: a) spelling and style—this was the cause of the first 'flame war'; b) the nature of community, and whether virtual communities were similar to other forms of community; c) the nature of identity and the problems of congruence between 'virtual' and 'real' identities; d) virtual reality and its uses and consequences.

This is in fairly good agreement with Alan's summary of the first week as posted on (6 Jul.94):

> We've had our first flamewar and a heavy overturn of subscriptions, in part related to it. We've had enormous quantities of posts [...]
>
> I myself have gone through days of exhileration to days of depression and back. I worry about the discussion turning into flurries of brief postings, an atmosphere of cameraderie but very little substance to some of the topics [...]
>
> An example—the discussion about beauty on the net, beyond poetic descriptions, opens up whole areas in terms of aesthetics, the sublime, disembodiment and beauty, and so forth. Another example, which did go into some depth, community—simply put, can there be disembodied communities? Are telephone party-lines capable of communality? What does teleconferencing say about our potentially alienated state? [...]
>
> Some of the other topics that have been covered or come to mind — desire/seduction in cyberspace, the voice of the ASCII correspondent, the role of etiquette (typos _beyond_ the flamewar)—perhaps in relation to other forms of language/languages, nationalism and CMC, the use of MUDS in technical communities, the syntax of flamewars, trans-gender and general issues of identity/identification.
>
> There are also troubling issues about the ontology and alterity of cyber-space; Malgosia raised the question of the _translation_ from this space to actual physical _care_ of someone. What are the interrelationships then between virtual space and real life—what sorts of fuzzy boundaries?

As implied above, within its first three days, the list was troubled by a dispute over spelling which centred on the kind of norms governing what was an acceptable message to the list. The dispute orbited around the questions of the list's 'alternate' nature, problems of inclusivity and freedom, and were largely governed by the focus of 'authenticity' (see Chapter 6). Offlist and privately Alan and Michael discussed implementing full moderation, in which all mails would be read by the moderators before reaching the list, but this did not occur.

At the end of this first month Michael Current died, and the group collectively mourned his loss. People found it necessary to wonder about their grief, how they and the group should organise the expression of this grief, and to establish that, although in some ways they did not know Michael, nevertheless their grief was real and legitimate. After the first two days most of the reaction to Michael's death went offlist, perhaps in accordance with the usual extensions of privacy in the WES world around the dead and the mourners of that death.

Further Happenings

In November 1994, the US Republicans won what was commonly called a 'landslide' victory in the US House of Representatives with promises of radical cutbacks in government services and outputs. This was widely construed by US list members as marking a period of increased survival difficulty for those involved in artistic, intellectual or educational pursuits. Shortly afterwards attempts to regulate freedom of speech on the Internet were linked to an Act to deregulate commercial ownership of all media. Hostility towards the so-called *Communications Decency Act* and other attempts to regulate online behaviour was marked on Cybermind.

I joined the list on the 5th of December 1994. Shortly after my joining, the first meetings of members, not already known to each other from offline life, occurred in New York and Canberra. The list also transferred from 'World' to Virginia University.

The first formal group meeting on PMC (Post Modern Condition) MOO occurred in late April 1995. Shortly afterwards Jim Reith built the Cybermind Lounge on the MOO. I conducted the first "Great Cybermind Survey" in May 1995. Soon after this survey 'Gordon' wrote in stating he was interested in the psychology of flaming and began flaming. Eventually this correspondence took so much space that Alan decided to remove him from the list. A large debate about issues of free speech and the nature of the group resulted. The volume of mail also threatened group identity, as people unable to cope with this volume left (see Chapter 10)

In late July 1995, another dispute arose which focused on a returning list member (Glen), largely because of incompatible styles of communication. Glen found himself accused of anti-Semitism. During the dispute Alan began to question, onlist, the continued functioning of Cybermind and his involvement with it. This could be seen as a threat to end the list. Glen eventually curtailed his writing after the second threat to unsub him. Alan claimed, both onlist and offlist, that he had received many requests to unsub Glen from other list members, and wrote to me that though he thought it would be extremely disruptive to do so, he couldn't see an alternative. Glen left of his own accord shortly thereafter (see Chapter 9).

During August and September of 1995 PMC MOO was 'reformed' by its Wizards—and made more relevant to discussions of Postmodernism. This caused discussion on Cybermind, again focusing on issues of 'free speech' and 'community', and effectively ended PMC as an offlist centre for communication between Cybermind members.

Shortly after this, Gordon returned to the list with several friends, most of whom belonged to another list, which we shall call 'Freaks'. The attack was not particularly competent and this time the 'defence' was largely conducted offlist, calming down recognised members, and identifying 'attackers' and unsubbing them if necessary. Not only was this attack dealt with more efficiently because of learning and recognising some of the people involved, but it was also relatively easy to discover the boundaries between recent and longer-standing members (so as to group the attackers as a category), and set up a temporary hierarchy.

During this attack, Cybermind was 'closed' so that people had to be registered on it to post to it, and, for a while, new applicants had their addresses looked at more closely than usual. There may have been an increased level of suspicion towards newcomers who behaved unusually, and it is probable quite a few innocent people were jumped upon.

The list was less able to cope with a series of internal disputes, mainly based in politics which occurred in the five months after these external disruptions. Partly this problem occurred because messages tend to be monotonic or simplex. Offline it is easier to create other relationships simultaneously with the person you are disputing with, and to give messages that reassure at the same time as they dispute. As a result, dispute was easily channelled into polarities, with categories perceived as opposites. The only sanction for either side was either enforced exile or splitting off, neither of which maintains group integrity. Only the moderator can enforce exile, and it is exceedingly unlikely they would be able to interfere in a dispute between long-standing members, unless they were personally involved, without further disrupting the list. So the tendency, in the event of such an internal dispute, is for longer-standing members or groups to split off, or leave the list. Sometime after September, some female members of Cybermind, FOP and FutureCulture formed a secret list called 'emma' to avoid what they considered excessive male hostilities.

In December 1995, there was an attempt to run meetings in London and New York, and connect together via PMC MOO. Inspired by the attempts to organise this, Karen Melzak proposed holding a Cybermind Conference. Organising this conference took most of the following year. It eventuated in November 1996 in Perth, Western Australia, deliberately preceded by my "Second Great Cybermind Survey".

In February 1996 intragroup hostilities were high. It was alleged to me that a particular subgroup were isolating themselves from the list, making ingroup postings with no list relevance, and not respecting the differing views of other list members. Most of this subgroup departed from the list over a two-week period and one member subscribed some of these people, and others, to a list of their own called 'Offlist' (see Chapter 10).

Another sublist formed in September 1996 to discuss the communicative and educational ideas of Antonio Rossin, after it appeared to list members Kerry Miller and Antonio that the discussion was not strictly relevant to Cybermind and was taking too much space on the list. In contrast to the two other lists, the formation of this list was public, and seems to have continued for some considerable time.

The election of George Bush II as president of the USA in 2000 and the controversy about vote counting in that election sparked much conflict on the group, even though the majority of the members seemed to agree that he would probably turn out to be a disastrous incompetent President, increase the problems and precariousness of their lives, and be a significant threat to world peace. More right wing oriented members vocally disagreed with this diagnosis. The attack on the two towers in New York in September 2001, produced temporary political unity on the list in general commiseration with, and between, the American members, some of whom lived in New York. This soon disintegrated before the actions of the Bush Administration, encapsulated by his 'you are with us or against us' and 'Axis of Evil' speeches. Despite ongoing conflict, the List still functioned well until the year leading to the invasion of Iraq when many non-American members thought that the Bush administration clearly wanted to go to war and would not allow UN weapons inspection to proceed. Many of these members were accused of being 'anti-American', even by US members who did not support the President. Arguments grew increasingly heated, broken largely by various series of one-liner sex jokes initiated by those not involved in the arguments who were increasingly depressed at the state of the world and the List. Membership slowly dropped off and since the invasion the List has been relatively quiet with a much smaller active population than previously, and with conversation tending to be much less on the subjects advanced in the Manifesto, and much more oriented towards personal chat and contemplation, perhaps making it harder for newer people to understand what is going on.

In late 2002, Cybermind weathered the long illness and death of another central member, Rose, who was frequently described as the 'heart' of the list. This time there was little expression of people's surprise at their grief, although many people expressed their fear that the list would not be able to continue without her, as she had on many occasions acted to cool the tempers of members of the list, and had prompted people to explain themselves in more detail when the limitations of short texts became too apparent. It is possible with the loss of Rose, the disputes which led to the fall of the List population, were more disruptive than they would otherwise have been.

The List has always had a varied set of topics though, and is full of self-reflection. Cybermind member Skip tried to describe the list and its wanderings as follows (14 Feb.03):

> "Philosophy and psychology of cyberspace," says the description. One might expect a serious, academically-minded list, long on footnotes and polysyllabic terminology.
>
> But what do we see here instead -- discussion of mundane concerns, long threads of puns, humor, experimental texts, cris de couer, obituaries and mournings, propositions, political diatribes, conspiracy theories, clearly psychotic or at least highly neurotic rants, and on and on... WTF is going on here?
>
> Here's the way I take it: this list explores by actual usage the possibilities and limitations inherent in computer-mediated communication. In this way, the list exemplifies and typifies various aspects of the topic... in other words, we talk about it by doing it.

Jim wrote in response: "Yes, we're the case study".

Chapter 3: The Internet and the World

Introduction

It is impossible to give an accurate description of the social processes which are affecting the world, affecting internet use and surrounding Cybermind in the space of a chapter. There are many other analyses (for example: Castells 2000, Hardt & Negri 2000, 2004), most of which disagree, and these analyses are not separate from, or above, their embedding social processes any more than the people on Cybermind. Consequently, this chapter mainly outlines the kinds of views about the world which are presented on Cybermind itself; although my formal analysis would be similar.

Since the late 1970s, it can be argued that power ratios within the State appear to have become less balanced and increased in favour of corporate interests[1]. Computers and computer networks have allowed the intensification of features of capitalism, which were previously restrained by struggles with other factions in the State. These features include: concentration of wealth; decrease in dependence of corporations on the middle and working classes; competition between labour in different countries; free movement of capital to areas of greatest predicted profit; increasing vulnerability of non-capitalist ways of survival, and the reduction of most values to economic ones[2]. The biggest section of the economy is now involved with speculation; with such things as forex and capital markets, which not only deal in huge amounts of money, when compared with conventional trade, but which require extremely small numbers of workers. These markets are difficult to predict, tend to be chaotic and, as a result, hinder long-term planning.

Such changes have disturbed the survival expectations of many people, in particular those of the 'intellectual middle class' who form the basis of Cybermind's population[3]. The jobs, careers and security they may have expected are no longer as available. However, as well as currently reinforcing capitalist hegemony, information technology also provides a tool whereby people can attempt to overcome, or survive, these changes. It can be used to make contacts; to build support networks; to engage in new work; and to protest at, accommodate to, or explore these new circumstances. Information technology may change capitalism 'from within' by causing uncontrollable instability in markets, changing modes of ownership and property, and rendering control systems vulnerable to sabotage. It can even advance terrorist activity and communication. Even those we might consider to be powerful often express their sense of lack of control, and locate power elsewhere.

Simultaneously in WES societies with the 'triumph' of corporatism, there has been a widely reported decline in the sense of participation in the political process. This sense of diminishing involvement is not confined to one class, or to one or another of the two mainstream political party-based views. There is little specific support for left or right. As will be seen below, although government support for the corporate sector at the expense of the populace appears unpopular, neither is there any trust in the possibilities of a more even representation. It has been suggested that 'refusal', or category separation, has become more important than positive choice (Taylor & Saarinen 1994: 'Superficiality 8'). People vote against what they like *least* rather than for what they want *most*, or they define themselves in terms of rejection by others (Greenberg 1996; Castells 1996: 23; 1997: 343). With capital being nomadic, it is hard to identify, never mind protest against, or exert force upon, those who might be dominant. However, this does not capture the passion with which politics was argued by people. They seem to care passionately, but also seem to think they will not be listened to.

The politics of Cybermind list is overwhelmingly 'left-liberal' and the kinds of analysis reported below reflect this. There have been only two *long-term* members whose politics can be consistently categorized as 'right wing' in the List's history and one of these became more leftist in orientation with experience of the Bush Administration's failures in Iraq. Although more pointed left political posts may generate little support, posts from the right tend to generate criticism. This is a left politics which expresses the need for self reliance, and lacks vision of alternatives to the 'free market'. Its primary fears centre on the death of diversity before capitalism, the diminishing possibility of personal survival and fulfilment, and the displacement of current internet users before commercialisation. The spread of corporate values may make finding work without sacrificing one's own self-identity harder still, and this is not just recognised by Cybermind members. A study of a mailing list for General Practitioners by Fox and Roberts shows that similar status and value issues arise among other 'middle class intellectuals'. One of their list members writes:

> We are in a position analogous to a subject people which has been taken over by a colonial power which not only wishes us to change our behaviour, but believes its attitudes and culture are superior (1999: np).

As a result of these difficulties these Lists supplement what remains of civil society and are related to other temporary group, or 'third place', manifestations. It is a 'built community' or 'club', which does not need to pay for rooms, or require much effort, by many, to run. It can be fitted in when time is available from other things in life and provides a way of meeting people, making friends and contacts, searching for prospective lovers, pursuing career moves, writing and thinking. Cybermind allows people to explore the dilemmas of their lives and the forces around them with others in similar positions. As such, it becomes important for list members to protect what appears to be an only fragilely safe 'space' in a hostile environment. These factors allow the List to continue long after its official topics are greeted with exhaustion.

Temporary Association and Western Society

A 'decline' in 'The Family' or in 'The Community' has been a remarked feature of WES life for a considerable period of time (see also Chapter 12). Separation between kin groups through distance, work (or lack of work), divorce, the lack of integrating roles or lack of mutual trust is a standard mytheme. Census data support the position that more people are living alone or with non-kin and that marriages are occurring later and breaking up more frequently (see below). As Giddens writes: "Kinship relations often used to be taken for granted on the basis of trust; now trust has to be negotiated and bargained for, and commitment is as much an issue as in sexual relationships" (1992: 96). Declines in State support renders people's situation more insecure, as there are few kin or local ties to 'fall back on'. According to a survey conducted by Wuthow in 1989, about 37% of people felt they could not rely on relatives to help in sickness (1994: 424n14). Castells writes "at the moment when the traditional family becomes indispensable as an instrument of both financial and psychological security, it has been falling apart" (1997: 97). Whatever the causes, people enter into a large variety of household arrangements, and may seek to replace uncertain kin ties by negotiating temporary ties with non-related people. Building temporary or permanent ties of friendship is one way of dealing with this situation, and such negotiated ties are often not with neighbours, but with others who are defined as similar, or who are met in groups. Wuthnow claims that 40% of American adults are members of small groups which meet regularly to provide support for members. Of these people, almost half had been involved in such a group for five or more years, while only one in seven had been with a group for less than a year. Of those currently uninvolved, 40% had previously belonged to such groups and a further 25% would like to be involved (1994: 45-50). Over 90% of group members wanted to make friends, receive support, and discuss things of interest to them (ibid: 52-3). Wuthnow argues that these small groups fit in with present trends: allowing people to adapt, to separate from other people or positions, and to cope with the stress of life or work. They do not necessarily require people to adjust or change their lifestyles, or to publicly protest at their alienation from society (ibid: 12, 21-5). According to Census data posted to Cybermind on 11 Feb.03, 44% of US based adults did volunteer work, contributing an average of 15 hours per month, which also suggests participation in groups outside family and work. A small survey by Katz and Aspden (1997) suggests that Internet users tend to belong to voluntary organizations, and do so more frequently the more they use the Internet. Therefore the same kind of forces and benefits found in offline groups may operate online. Online groupings in the WES world could therefore arise for the same reasons as these other forms of 'temporary voluntary association', not tied to kin, workplace, locality, or political action, which are prevalent in these societies, yet subject to little ethnographic research outside of leisure studies[4]. Much of this latter work seems to be concerned with whether participating in voluntary associations furthers 'democratic values', although this is not always defined. Investigations do show that people in voluntary community groups participate in their 'community', and that participation gives members more resources and human connections (Glover et al 2005a, 2005b), both of which points seem almost tautological.

More usefully, in a brief consideration of US student groups in the 1960s, Moore and Meyerhoff point out that these groups continually need to recruit new members to replace those that leave, and so reiterate expressions of collective identity. People involved in these groups are often embarrassed when they expel someone. In several such groups with an 'anarchistic' ideology, expulsion was declared to be a private matter, and group decisions were postponed to avoid conflict or 'organization'. If conflict became inevitable, it would frequently be distracted by the introduction of activities which were enjoyed by most of the group. Sometimes group conflict was declared to result from the actions of the external hostile world (1975: 15-19, 30). As we shall see, these points suggest similarity between these student groups and Cybermind, perhaps as they contain populations similar in some ways. Elias suggested that European student society had certain characteristics such as: suspension as well as anticipation of achievement; people being less restricted than others by jobs; largely self-regulating; and they experience blockage of promotion, and ambiguous relationships with immediate authority (1996: 275-6). This certainly seems to be the case with Cybermind's population.

There is a large body of work on psychoanalytic therapy groups, which have structural similarities with mailing lists (see Cano 1997; the essays in Kreeger 1975 are also suggestive). However, most of the writers do not specify whether the groups they are studying are voluntary or compulsory, and the accounts are primarily illustrative and scattered in their presentation of data. Nevertheless, occasional reference will be made to this literature.

Given the prevalence of these temporary groups, it seems that this project, as well as describing a relatively new social form, will elucidate WES social processes more generally.

List Discussion of the World

As suggested, List members are aware of the kinds of problems discussed above, and are concerned about them and discuss them amongst themselves. In mentioning some of these discussions there is no suggestion of an absolutely uniform Cybermind viewpoint; any post faced the possibility of being disputed. However, there is a direction to the kind of analysis which was put forward. Many political posts were 'Forwards' from other lists, which makes the posts appear more authoritative, with the argument less likely to be seen as personal or disruptive.

The discussions have been arranged under several headings, but they bleed from one to another. Although the views presented here are generally what would be known as leftist, similar types of complaints and analysis with different labels, also expressing alienation and a sense of power being elsewhere, could be found in other groups. I participated in these debates, generally in favour of a left position, and so am likely to select mails which harmonise with my political and analytic position. However this bias in selection is no greater than it would have been were I to present a more formal argument. Carrying the argument out in this way emphasises that the mythemes and categories of sociology and economics are not completely above the world and that 'ordinary' people are well informed and able to argue with these analyses.

Social Transformation

First let me quote a heavily abridged version of list owner, Alan Sondheim's description of the transformation of society from "modernity to postmodernity" (1 Oct.96). Such a transformation involves:

> Transformation of society from industrial to service to information economy.[...]
>
> Increased ad hoc attitudes towards labor, coupled with vocational disinvestment (i.e. flexiwork).
>
> Transformation from late capitalism to ad hoc transnational managerial capitalism [...].
>
> Weakening of the nation state and growth of bricolage governance (local mafias).[...]
>
> Increased gaps between richer and poorer, in terms of both economic and cultural/informational capital.
>
> Emergence of subcultural-noise cultural phenomena, simultaneously using micro-technologies (pirate radio) and abjuring technology altogether.
>
> Ecological destabilizations and managerial or fundamentalist responses.
>
> Intensification of apocalyptic and survivalist subcultures.[...]
>
> Destabilization of world economies coupled with exponential population growth. [...]
>
> Proliferation of shack cities (favellas, colonias) without sewage, water, electric, and the growth of world-wide shack cultures.[...]
>
> World-wide growth of the Internet, including dark-net domains.[...]
>
> Confluence of genders, transgressive sexualities operating within an _engendered field._ [...]
>
> Commercialization of the university, alliance of business and education—i.e. _the business of education,_ _education of business._[...]
>
> A split among _postmodernisms_ themselves into _apartment postmodernism_ characterized by wealth, personal telecom terminals, and a mobile urbanism; and a _postmodern poor_ characterized by nomadicisms, urban intensifications, information economies [...]

> Postmodernism occurs within a critical space, a space of the catastrophic, emptied of symbolic legitimation and stability. Because of capital flow, emigration, and struggles for individual survival and autonomy, the space begins to "fill up," creating a cacophony of (informal) regimes competing for cultural and economic power, gaslines, water, labor, prostitutions, and so forth. The resulting struggle produces competing domains in which the symbolic itself is at stake; nothing, not even communication, can be taken for granted. The zone is a chaotic accumulation of intensities, condensed matter and languages, a dead or deligimiized zone. The planet itself is becoming an accumulation of such zones.

This is clearly a presentation of the 'information society' as a mode of fragmentation, separation, chaos, and the growth of inequalities and new strategies; and many of these perspectives are reflected in the mails quoted below. For example, another discussion in September 2006 touched on the dystopian idea of 'Feral Cities' (as proposed by Richard J. Norton in the *Naval War College Review*). In such cities buildings are decaying, disease and ecological devastation is both rampant and life threatening, criminal and terrorist organisations provided whatever order there was, while the city is still globally connected through the internet and commercial linkages. Norton proposed this as happening in the future and elsewhere, but List members wondered if the condition was already present. Elizabeth Barrette wondered (26 Sept.06) whether Detroit was already such a half-wild city and Alan responded with his experiences in Ciudad Juarez where:

> the city seemed unmapped, unmappable, with large parts beyond the Pale, unbearable amounts of pollution of all sorts, and violence rising exponentially... I wrote about it all the time as a post modern city characterized by 'radiations and dusts'; I knew I was seeing the future—there can be no other with population increase.

An earlier discussion (Jul.04) of a similar topic referred to a report by the United Nations Human Settlements Programme called "The Challenge of Slums", which had suggested that the truly massive increase in urban slums had occurred simultaneously with a more or less complete global 'liberalisation' of trade and capital flow.

In this chaotic world, even the basis of the so called 'information society', knowledge and information itself, were seen as precarious. Alan wrote (25 Nov.06):

> Future knowledge will no longer be at the beck and call of its past; if anything, it will be vastly reduced as power grids collapse, desertifications and extinctions set in. What I am writing now, what you are writing, has no chance for survival. Records, archives, require potential wells which become more and more difficult to maintain in environments which are increasingly adverse.

Others disagreed, but everyone realised the vulnerability of electronically stored information, and hence the fragility of any society based upon this alone.

The author of this book suggested on another occasion (30 Aug.03) that in an 'information age' there were tendencies which reinforced the distribution and use of inaccurate, rather than accurate, information and that similar forces also reinforced the distribution of certainty or dogma, rather than the kinds of suspensions required to generate creative solutions to problems or, "to paraphrase Gresham, bad information drives good out of Circulation". This indicates a suspicion of the easy equivalence of information with knowledge and productive endeavour.

At the best it was feared that the potential openness of the information society could be undermined by intellectual property rules, the extension of which can prevent discussion. Phlo (1 Mar.06) wrote that there:

> is a battle of different concepts of intellectual-property. On the one hand you have the content-industry doing everything to maintain their "old" concept of intellectual-property, on the other you have global file-sharing networks which couldn't care less.

Intellectual property was an ambiguous area, as without it, most members could not survive or gain status, yet it was generally seen as unenforceable and restrictive, especially as applied by the corporate sector. This was reinforced by the vagueness of the information congerie.

The 'information society' was recognised as global, and increased contact and cross cultural connection was usually seen as good, yet the processes known as globalisation were approached with caution, largely because of competition between this openness and corporate or military dominance. Dian remarked (27 July.03) "We're done in. By corporate greed and globalization". People forwarded in reports (11 Sept.03) of a group of artists protesting against culture being reduced to its economic value. The letter stated that "Many governments are under pressure to bargain away their cultural identity in the race to liberalize all sectors of the economy". A forwarded essay (3 June.04) from the Bay Area Situationists claimed that globalisation was also a form of internal colonisation creating weak citizenship and failed States. Skip posted (11 Sept.06) the URL of an interview with Niall Ferguson of Harvard arguing that as the first age of globalisation was ended by the First World War so the current age could end through a similar process involving overstretched power, escalation of rivalry and the growth of terrorism. Tom, who self-defined as a conservative libertarian, responded: "You just want to get me started on why Globalization is a Bad Thing(tm)", Skip added "what I don't like is the globalization of exploitation, of the mobility of capital". Maurizio (13 Mar.03) saw globalisation as a day in and day out group psychodrama of agonising over world events extended through media.

List analysis also tended to relate globalisation to US power. Ian described (2 June.03) comments by Thomas Friedman as "one of the more accurate US opinions" about globalisation. These comments argued that a central feature of globalisation was the extension of US power and culture which touched people's lives in an intimate way, and them wanting some kind of input into this—especially when that nation turned into "Godzilla, a wounded, angry, raging beast touching people militarily". Ian (30 Mar.03) also commented that British Prime Minister Tony Blair:

> wants to save the power/violence based system advanced by the American Empire from being lost sooner than necessary by the incompetetent Bush. He is on a mission to save US/UK power based in military strength and avoid a new globalization where the many nations of the world each have a say.

However, Ian also thought that the internet had the tendency to destroy centres, or portals of control, and that the war in Iraq was "the last gasp of the portals". Salwa (30 Mar.03) agreed that Blair differed little from his colonialist forebears. Alan referred to (21 May 03) an article by Jean Baudrillard, which argued that terrorism was "the contemporary partner of globalism" and that while technology, the market and tourism were being extended, human rights and democracy were on the way out. Baudrillard claimed this has led to homogenisation and fragmentation; to dislocation, discrimination and exclusion; and to a clash between uniformity and "whatever domain, retains a quality of irreducible alterity". On the whole, people on Cybermind liked the idea of globalisation as promoting cross-cultural contact, and as expanding their experience, but worried about the power aspects of it.

This was so even given perceptions of possible power shift in the world, independent of the attacks on America of September 11 2001. In particular China, and potential Chinese hegemony, seemed to be a source of concern. Around the turn of the millennium, the more right wing members of the group seemed to be expecting a war with China even though they did not want one, while at least some other members of the List thought that President Bush was more of a danger to the United States than China was at that moment.

Almost everyone, of every political persuasion, seemed worried about their rights and survival being compromised in the contemporary world or in the near future, through political, economic or social movements, although the sources of such attack might be seen as different and what constituted freedom might be framed differently.

Economic Factors

Concerns about this 'new society', and the resultant transformations of power and wealth, arising from a shift towards the corporate elite, remained fairly stable over the period. Mike forwarded (20 Jan.96) an analysis of "Agile Production" by Bruce Allen of the Auto-Workers Union with the significant comment:

> this analysis which concerns the automobile industry also directly applies to the emerging structure of the university, IMO...

Allen suggests that Agile Manufacturing is necessary to survive in an "environment of constant and unpredictable change". While this agility generates more cooperation and sharing of resources by corporations, labour "becomes completely subordinated to Capital". There are a few secure workers, but "a large and fluid body of temporary workers", marking the end of collective agreements, increasing the pressure to turn skills into software, and forcing workers "into a race to the bottom, where they will eventually find themselves earning 19th century wages and enduring 19th century working conditions while using 21st century technology".

A further forward of 24 Jan.96 consisted of an interview with US Secretary of Labor, Robert Reich, originally published in MEME 2.02, and prompted by AT&T sacking over 10% of its workforce. Reich argued that capital is more mobile than it has ever been, while the middle class, with their wealth in property, are becoming less mobile. When an area declines in employment, house prices decrease and so it becomes harder to move to an area of high employment where house prices are increasing. New jobs often require new skills, whereas in industrial society skills were transferable. The manoeuvrability of capital also means that Nation States have less power, and communities conflict with each other in bidding for corporations to set up in their area. Unemployed people are no longer laid off in accordance with business cycles and reemployed when times improve: most people who lose jobs lose those jobs permanently. However Reich states that the "top 20 percent of income-earners in this country are doing exceedingly well. The top 5 percent are doing superbly well". In his opinion "connections" have become extremely important in getting new jobs. This increases the division between the top strata and the rest: "we are, as a nation, segregating by income to a much larger extent than ever before", and this segregation affects the kinds, and distribution of, public services to people.

Forwarded excerpts from an article by Jeremy Rifkin (22 Feb.96) pointed to the decline in jobs in the industrial sector and argued that the service sector was automating, with the result that millions of people would become unemployed. Another set of excerpts from Rifkin forwarded in 2004 referred to a report by Alliance Capital Management which claimed that manufacturing jobs were being lost over the world, even in China, despite global industrial production rising by 30%, and that the same automation process was being applied in white collar occupations "through software, computer and telecom revolutions, and the proliferation of smart technologies". With more and more people being replaced or becoming unnecessary, Rifkin was not sure where the consumer demand would come from to buy all these extra products and services. Another forwarded article by Lester Thurow discussed the decline in wages for 80% of the US workforce and the cutting back of social security. An OECD report, described in another forward (16 July.96) pointed to the US and the UK as places with a "persistent and large rise in earnings inequality". Dobie (24 Mar.96) forwarded a humorous article by Michael Jay Tucker in which it was proposed that the best way for a company to increase its stock value was by sacking people; irrespective of whether this helped the company perform better.

Mike forwarded an interview with Ian Angell of the London School of Economics (21 Dec.96), in which Angell argued economic growth no longer required employment, and this applied to computer literate people as much as to others. The only relevant skill was "knowing how to take information and broker it and make money out of it" and, at the most, a relatively small percentage of the population had the expertise to do this. Angell would later write a book arguing that there would be opulence for the talented and wonderful few and poverty for the many (Angell 2000).

Kerry (17 Sept.96) sent in an article analysing how American companies were shifting to cheaper overseas based labour. The article states:

> In the 1890s, most Americans were struggling to reach a middle-class lifestyle. By the 1990s, an overwhelming majority, having achieved it, were either losing it or struggling to hold on. The losers? Working Americans who have been forced to live in fear—fear of losing their jobs, fear of being unable to pay for their children's education, fear of what will happen to their aging parents, fear of losing everything they've struggled to achieve.

Other emails discussed Wal-Mart's attacks on unions, on workers conditions and pay, and the way that it destroyed local retailers by undercutting their prices until they collapsed and then charging whatever the market would bear. One forward (21 Dec.04) stated that Wal-Mart encouraged its workers to apply for State assistance so that taxpayers ended up supporting the decline in wages and that it conducted massive campaigns to prevent stronger labour laws. This was despite claims in another forward (3 Dec.04) that even in States which voted for President Bush, voters overwhelmingly favoured an increase in the minimum wage; however the political establishment was not interested in such projects.

An article forwarded on 27.Jan.06 described a report by the Center on Budget and Policy Priorities and the Economic Policy Institute, which claimed that over the past twenty years incomes had increased far more for people in the top quintile (by 59%) than for those at the bottom (by 19%). This was blamed upon globalisation, decline in manufacturing, expansion of service jobs, and the decline of unions. Broadcaster Bill Moyer was quoted (1 Jul.04) as saying:

> Nothing seems to embarrass the political class in Washington today. Not the fact that more children are growing up in poverty in America than in any other industrial nation; not the fact that millions of workers are actually making less money today in real dollars than they did twenty years ago; not the fact that working people are putting in longer and longer hours and still falling behind; not the fact that while we have the most advanced medical

care in the world, nearly 44 million Americans—eight out of ten of them in working families—are uninsured and cannot get the basic care they need.

Astonishing as it seems, no one in official Washington seems embarrassed by the fact that the gap between rich and poor is greater than it's been in 50 years—the worst inequality among all western nations...

In 1960, the gap in terms of wealth between the top 20% and the bottom 20% was 30 fold. Four decades later it is more than 75 fold.

Another article, by Paul Krugman, forwarded (7 Oct.06) claimed that:

The Dow is doing well largely because American employers are waging a successful war against wages. After-tax corporate profits have more than doubled, because workers' productivity is up, but their wages aren't.

Krugman goes on to describe some attacks on the rights of US workers to join unions, and concludes that corporations are trying to treat workers as if they were disposable commodities and that the government supports their efforts. A humorous compilation by Maurizio (2 Sept.06) concludes that:

The median hourly wage for American workers has declined 2 percent since 2003, after factoring in inflation. The drop has been especially notable, economists say, because productivity —the amount that an average worker produces in an hour and the basic wellspring of a nation's living standards— has risen steadily over the same period.

As a result, wages and salaries now make up the lowest share of the nation's gross domestic product since the government began recording the data in 1947, while corporate profits have climbed to their highest share since the 1960's.

Another mail (19 Aug.06) reported that the US Treasury Secretary had also announced that economic inequality was rising in America and that Krugman was arguing that "between 1980 and 2004, real wages in manufacturing fell 1 percent, while the real income of the richest 1 percent—people with incomes of more than $277,000 in 2004 —rose 135 percent" and that this was due to the dominance of pro-corporate forces in government. Other emails mentioned that Delphi proposed cutting its standard worker's wages from $27.00 per hour to $10.00 per hour while increasing executive bonuses, that Continental Airlines proposed to cut wages and benefits by $500 million a year and that US Airways got court permission to scrap its employees' pension plan.

A central concern of the people making these forwards and references was to detail the fall in wages, working conditions and job security, which affected all levels of society except for the already well off; the creep of these declines into 'information worker' areas, and to declare that these economic concerns resulted from the excessive power of the corporate sector.

Thus, it was widely expected by members of the List that the tax cuts awarded by the Bush administration to high level earners would leave the burdens of supporting the State and the Iraq War on the poor and middle-income earners. One forward (1 Jul.04) claimed that the Bush tax cuts amounted to two trillion dollars, with half the benefits going to the wealthiest one percent of the population. It seemed generally thought that the wealthy would not spend their extra money so as to stimulate the general economy, and that the tax cuts would be used to bankrupt Social Security.

Consequently, there was general skepticism about the Bush Administration's attempts to privatise Social Security. Elizabeth Barrette wondered (4 Jan.05) why:

> we charge the poorest people a portion of their meager wages to support them and others in old age, but [we charge less] for the richest people? That's bloody stupid, or more to the point, bloody plutocratic. I'll bet the entire "Social Security is insolvent" problem could be solved by taking the SS percentage from ALL wages ... with enough left over to give the elders a bit of a *raise* in benefits so that fewer of them would be living in poverty.
>
> Instead, some people are proposing that we privatize the SS system. Why? So they can keep more of their already unfairly large wad of cash for themselves, while others suffer. Oink, oink.

Jim thought (6 Jan.05) that moving to "personal investing puts money headed into the system at risk". Skip responded that it seemed "like a mechanism for increasing corporate dominance in all areas of American life; and corporate thinking tends to be shortsighted and limited in scope". Later on he wrote (7 Mar.05):

> The Republicans have received huge campaign support from the brokerage industry and other financial professionals, who stand to make a substantial amount of money from Bush's proposed changes.

He also reminded people of recent scandals involving high-finance companies which did not inspire trust in their ability to look after the funds for the benefits of pensioners. He also suggested that the investment of people's funds would be used to make arguments against lowering profits by installing controls on pollution or paying decent wages.

There were many arguments about the benefits of 'free markets', as might be expected. On the whole, with one or two notable exceptions most people seemed to believe that there was too much dependence upon them for the solution of social problems. Some argued that the idea of free markets were contradictory, as with Rowena (17 May.01):

> a really free market is a totally unworkable, at the very minimum one needs a regulation (agreement) about the worth of things and (and for a more sophisticated market where one uses some intermediary instead of direct bartering goods for goods some kind gold (or other) standard) and a measurement standard. These regulations (=things that regulate) don't impose themselves spontaneously/organically/ freely there is some kind of state/power needed for that.

GordR added:

> If one were to take apart the phrases that describe the market, like the "Invisible Hand" the theology of it, the superstition of it, becomes manifest.
>
> There is even the apocalyptic element that posits a heaven on earth if the market is allowed its full sway. "If the market were free then paradise would come soon after!!!!"

This harmonises with Salwa's description of an article by Pierre Bourdieu (23 April.03) in which Bourdieu argued that the neoliberal corporate economic order was a desocialised and dehistoricised utopian ideal, backed by structural violence, which protects corporations and atomises workers while destroying forums for collective action. This set of actions severs the system from its social base, making the theory appear real in the fear of spreading poverty. Bourdieu suggests that we need to rescue collective action, but is vague on how this is to be done.

A discussion, based on a *New York Times* article of 19 May.01, found general acceptance of the proposition that although the US had grown wealthier people had not become happier. Indeed surveys suggested that the satisfaction levels of Americans had declined. If this was true then an economics based on the idea of wealth bringing happiness could be seen as pathological. Other forwards protested issues such as the increase in child abuse and child poverty, resulting from harsh economic conditions; closing of help for the homeless; interference with the provision of free food; corporate attempts to prevent accurate food labelling; increasing levels of youth suicide and so on.

Even with this general suspicion of corporate free markets, fear of decreasing wages, lowered working conditions, and insecure social security there was, as was suggested by Daniel Bell (1976: 374-7) and Alvin Toffler (1984: 38), no evidence that members of Cybermind, as primarily information workers, saw themselves as a self-identified group with 'class interests'. There was little sense that members could, or would be able to act together to change the world or to intervene in it, even though they might, and frequently did, act as individuals.

General Demographics of the United States of America

Alan regularly sent in press releases from the Census Bureau, such as that which made the point, yet again, that over the last three decades income inequality among the nation's households had risen (20 June.96). Another release (13 Mar.96), reflected concerns about 'the family', showing the increasing age of first marriage, the increasing numbers of unmarried people, the increasing numbers of people living alone, and the increasing numbers of children living with one parent. These kinds of figures were supported in later releases posted to the list in 2001. One such demographic forward lead Elizabeth Barrette to write about this abandonment:

> We have no health care to speak of, we throw our mentally ill patients on the streets, we have a sky-high personal handgun rate, we've got shockingly poor school systems, in big cities like NY, the poor are getting poorer while the rich are getting exponentially richer—it's amazing we've managed to survive as well as we have. It's probably due to our enormous garbage output and bloated bellies that we've made it this far...

> Leave us not forget the appallingly high rate of teen suicides, especially among homosexual, Pagan, artistic or other young folks who for some reason are made to feel like they don't belong. Like they literally have no right to live. Well, when you make someone's life unlivable, a lot of them... decide not to keep living it.

Survival for Non-Corporate People and List Members

These kinds of demographics and problems were manifested on the List. I have already mentioned the career difficulties faced by Alan, Michael and Kent, but just to quote one further example posted to Cybermind from an artist:

> In our culture, your "profession" tends to be that for which you are paid. For most artists I know, myself included, that for which I am paid is not my "profession." I keep slamming up against this dichotomy w/people who insist on referring to my work as a "hobby" which shows, primarily, that they have not a fucking clue.

Other List members discussed their issues with unemployment or relative poverty, or with living alone, or in couples, with no kin or other support. People faced self-proclaimed financial ruin, homelessness, lack of health care, and prolonged ill health affecting their abilities to earn a living. Even those who were programmers with a long history of work faced unemployment. Members did not seem to particularly crave wealth but claimed that they did not have much leeway for the inevitable occurrence of misfortune or ill health. They were living on the margin. People also discussed collapses of sponsorship, precarious teaching or academic careers, and the difficulties of living as artists.

Ecological Crisis

There was general agreement that the world faced ecological peril, whether this arose from human nature, stupidity, or capitalism. Only a few people suggested that corporate capitalism would solve the problems, and they rarely if ever gave any evidence for these assertions. Maurizio (8 Sept.06) pointed to the problems of a burgeoning Chinese economy "1.2 billion cars using, say, 3 gallons a day is 3.6 billion gallons a day, or roughly 120 million barrels _a day_." Many forwards discussed global warming, or potential animal extinctions, and the reluctance of corporations and right wing governments to do anything to prevent this. The presence of such arguments seemed to intensify with the arrival of the Bush Administration with its close ties to the oil industry and its refusal to ratify the Kyoto Treaty. There were forwards and general allegations that Dick Cheney, the Vice President, had allowed power and resource companies with connections to him to draw up US energy policies. The claims of the administration to be dealing with the issues were regarded with cynicism. Thus one member wrote:

> with Bush at the wheel I'll believe it when I see it. He's already doing his damnedest to gut what regulations *have* been put into effect. I don't see him pissing off his sponsors by telling them to clean up their act.

Another writer quoted the Vice President as saying "Conservation is not a sufficient basis for a sound, comprehensive energy policy" despite the continuing decline in global and US oil production. Other forwards by people included descriptors such as "ethnic and religious diversity bad for crops, says Bush agriculture appointee" or "crudely written propaganda defending polluters turned environmental regulators".

Using other forwards, List members claimed that since the industrial revolution levels of CO_2 in the atmosphere have increased from 280 parts per million to 365 parts per million which is an increase of about 30% in the gasses which produce global warming. Similarly at least half of the forests on the planet have been destroyed, and other forests such as the Amazon, the lungs of the earth, were being cut down. Ice shelves are breaking up, glaciers on mountains are melting, and fish are moving from the tropics to what used to be temperate climes. Fish are also being fished out leading to the possible crash of food stocks, and water is to become the new resource over which wars were fought, and was already important in some Middle Eastern struggles. In 2001 there was a discussion of the ideas of Partha Dasgupta, a Professor of Economics at Cambridge University, who claimed that the world was largely getting poorer, despite increases in Gross Domestic Product in developing countries because of the depletion of natural assets, which meant people were more and more hard pressed to survive.

On the whole the implication was that those in power would prefer to risk general destruction rather than a temporary loss of profit for their friends or a class, and that their seemed to be little people can do to change this or to oppose it in general.

Right Wing Censorship and Attack

The US Right worried List members, not only because of its dominance in Congress, its proclaimed release of corporate power from government 'interference' and cutbacks for everyone else, its removal of support from the arts and some academic or scientific positions, but because, in the US, the Right is associated with a Christian Fundamentalism which advocates strict control over the lives of sinners. Thus Gary forwarded (9 Feb.95) a long mail which claimed the Religious Right was taking over the Republican party, planning to eliminate public broadcasting, to seize control of education, and to channel the funds from government welfare into church-controlled charity. This projected programme eventually happened. Caitlin forwarded (6 Nov.95) an article which claimed the Religious Right had a "campaign to shut down cyberspace" and "destroy online speech as we know it" by prohibiting "indecency", thus "dumbing down every conversation, web page, newsgroup, and mailing list on the Internet to the level of what is not offensive to children". This was something that did not occur. Stephan wrote (21 Jan.95) "Republicans are planning to cut government spending for everything except killing people". The success of Pat Buchanan in the Republican Primary Elections in early 1996 produced a spate of analysis of why people were turning to him. To quote just one example, pip wrote:

> The reality is that l/c and m/c americans _are_seeing their wages declining, possibilities for advancement narrowing, etc. But, since there is no effective Left in this country, there is no convincing voice out there to place the blame for this where it belongs—on increasing concentration of wealth in the upper percent of the population, facilitated by the natural evolution of capitalism plus particular policy decisions. So, populists wind up on the right instead of the left, blaming immigrants, minorities, etc, instead of corporate/government interests.

Later forwards covered the proposed cutbacks of art, education and scientific funding by Congress, and political censorship of biology, stem cell and climate change science by Republican administrators. These posts imply that holding views critical of this establishment was not safe, and people could suffer for it, especially given the precarious nature of employment.

The Media was also perceived as affected by the Right. There was considerable wonderment over right wing attempts to prevent children reading or seeing the movie of Harry Potter. At a more conspiratorial level, it was often perceived that there were coordinated right-wing media campaigns in favour of George Bush which were largely distortions of truth. An example of this centred on widespread media allegations that members of the Clinton Administration had looted and vandalised the White House and the Presidential plane, despite later (and much quieter) retractions. Another series of discussions centred on why American newspapers largely did not discuss issues around irregularity of voting, the disenfranchisement of voters, or vulnerabilities in electronic voting machines; particularly those associated with Diebold, which were reported as being relatively easy to hack and whose software could not be checked independently because of commercial confidence.

Later on some people wondered why the American media, especially that owned by Rupert Murdoch, was generally so supportive of the push to go war in Iraq. People seemed to learn much about the doings of the Bush Administration through what were perceived as more independent overseas newspapers and through group comments, and this was widely perceived as a benefit of the internet. As Ian wrote (10 Dec.06):

> I pay much more attention to Skip and Salwa and trust them more than Lou Dobbs or the New York Times.
>
> Can anyone really deny they were consistantly more accurate on Iraq than any major news source in the U.S., or any senate committee?

However, even here this freedom of information was often perceived as being under threat by attempts to regulate the internet either corporately (by charging for content) or by government—examples were given of the government removing or altering documents on the web.

In all cases people worried about Information Technology being used to further government and corporate surveillance of the populace or workforce, although the more right wing members tended to regard corporate surveillance as less of a problem. However, rumours of surveillance programs being built into Microsoft products was greeted with hostility by everyone.

The Bush Administration

The Bush Administration was generally not welcomed as this intensified the possibility of total right wing Christian or corporate dominance. This was especially the case given that in 2000 the President had earned less votes than his competitor, and that the election hung on the refusal of the courts to allow a recount in Florida, and (again according to forwards) that even if there had been a successful recount the President's brother, who was governor of that state, would still direct his representatives to the Electoral College to vote for Bush. Even those who supported the Bush Administration beforehand tended to become more cautious over time. The member of the List with the most consistently right wing opinions and who always tried to balance his disgust with the Bush Administration with his disgust for the previous Clinton Administration, even talked about armed insurrection as a way of solving problems with Bush. This was not, I think, a serious proposition and not particularly welcomed by other members of the List, although some members seemed to think that the US Army would not put down a popular revolt. The other consistently long-term member with more right wing views became completely opposed to Bush; before the 2000 Election he had argued that even if Bush was an idiot we could trust Dick Cheney and other members of the administration to control him. He later wrote when discussing what he perceived as the Bush threat to use nuclear weapons:

> When a former sot truly believes that a higher being is talking to him person-to-person, without the aid of any artificial sweeteners, distilled liquids, funky pills or little scraps of specially treated paper, then the best position we can take was best described in a manual I saved from a drawer from my deceased Grandma; You sit, grab your ankles and place your head between your knees. Breathe deeply, keep your eyes closed. If you still have time, get away from any window to avoid flash burns and flying glass.

After Bush came to power forwards tended to focus on Haliburton, the Vice President's old company, and its apparent frauds at taxpayer expense; the legitimacy of the President's conversations with God and his affiliation with millenarian right wing Christians; fears of the administration's inability to deal with ecological crisis; fears that it would not govern equitably; fears that its economic policies were dangerous and destructive; fears of its reliance on force and suppression; and, in particular, fears about the intentions of its foreign policies. Before the invasion of Iraq, List members discussed the *Project for the New American Century*, and other neo-conservative documents which seemed to propose that the US should establish an empire and impose its will upon the world. It was generally thought that the new administration was deliberately bellicose and, even before the attacks, some suggested that it was deliberately searching for a war. Judging by the number of forwards many members were upset that the Bush Administration was repudiating international treaties the US had signed, and was hostile to the UN. This included not working against landmines, chemical weapons, nuclear proliferation, child soldiers, women's rights, global warming, international tax laundering, and working against an international criminal court and bio-weapons inspections.

People also wondered why, in its early days, the administration was focusing on 'Star Wars' defence systems against nuclear attack when it was clear that this would increase the spread of nuclear weapons, unless the US also reduced its nuclear weaponry, and that the main threat to the US probably came from internal terrorism rather than 'conventional' warfare.

Posts also tended to be satirical. Thus there was discussion of 'faith based' missile defence, air traffic control, and global warming prevention. There was considerable amusement and dismay at the President's well documented errors such as: "Rarely is the question asked Is our children learning?" "Will the highways of the internet become more few?" (both from his primary campaign in Jan.2000); or the remarks at the signing of the Defense Appropriations Act for 2005: "Our enemies are innovative and resourceful, and so are we. They never stop thinking about new ways to harm our country and our people, and neither do we".

The administration did win uneasy loyalty and support after the attacks of 2001, but this started to dissipate after the overt failure of the invasion of Iraq, and the Bush Administration's apparent favouring of the corporate sector at the expense of everyone else. Forwards from non-US newspapers consistently contradicted the Bush line on weapons of mass destruction, the alliance of Iraq with terrorists, and other pieces of supposed intelligence. People asked why the Bush administration should be so keen for weapons inspectors not to carry out their work. However, disputes about the administration, at this time, did initially generate fragility on the list, as national identity categories seemed to become more prominent.

Some members took more personal approaches, thus WA wrote (10 May.01):

> We are, I believe, on our last legs, set to drown in our own corruption. Bush is part of the whimper with which we will exit. I weep for that nation I was taught to love.

Rose added:

> The multinationals are on their way to owning governments all over the place, and they like Bush and Cheney just fine the way they are, thank you.

Other claims included posting headlines to the effect that Bush used the War on Terrorism to fight a war against America's Social Security (as implied above), that Attorney General John Ashcroft could suspend the law if it was convenient for the administration, that the country could not support tax cuts and a war at the same time, that medical costs were increasing for the elderly, that benefits were being cut back to war veterans, and so on. There was a long vituperative debate over whether the anti-terrorism laws, especially the suspension of habeas corpus for those defined as enemy combatants, could be used to attack people's freedoms.

On the whole, it is fair to argue that although people felt strongly about politics, they tended to regard politics as beyond their influence, and as involving people with largely different, or even hostile, interests. Although it is easy to find statements which attack politicians it is relatively hard to find statements which support them. As Alan explains (13 Mar.03):

> I protest and write and forward constantly now, so I'm definitely engaged. But I honestly feel it will do no good, that war is a foregone conclusion. I don't think there are options, and I feel that email list discussions of such are as dead as negative posts. So why do either? Because:
>
> 1. it shows the rest of the world that there _is_ an opposition in the US, that this country is being held hostage as well at this point;
>
> 2. it lets off steam and anger that otherwise might boil up in our personal lives […];
>
> 3. at least with my texts I hope to create a very specific sense of the apocalyptic nature of the actions of our government—and the world crisis in general—for example the MOAB pieces deal with annihilation and the blanket cauterization of communication;
>
> 4. it creates a sense of commonality and even communality that is critical at this point—it's an issue of identity as much as anything else;
>
> 5. the forwarded news articles keep us informed of other oppositions of course;
>
> 6. this situation is such a crisis that _any_ response, even pro-war ones, has value—elucidating discussion and thought; and
>
> 7. I frankly think the current actions of the US government can only create negative responses—who is listening to future-culture or cybermind for that matter—but at the same time, the situation is so utterly bleak. I don't want to read of 'options' I don't believe in (I know I'm being contradictory here) when Bush and thugs will never act on them. I want to go the utmost, the limit, of the darkness, in order to deal with the situation in whatever way I can.

Cynicism about the political system was rife. Tom, the libertarian, wrote (12 June.01):

> Most Americans don't believe our politicians, which is part of why voter turnout is so low. That, and the general malaise that comes over a fat, overfed,

lazy bunch of people who think that they can't change anything, and don't want to rock the boat of their own prosperity.

Elizabeth Barrette, who was one of the most consistently optimistic writers, wrote (20 Dec.2006):

> I am sadly in agreement with the bumper sticker, "We don't have a democracy. We have an auction." [and that we have a] Culture in which money takes the place of virtue.

On reading this section of the book, Ian wondered if this was also a matter of US based culture. The List did tend to discuss US issues, rather than issues in Canada, the UK or Australia. He wrote:

> Certainly I feel that I have no impact on US politicians, but do correspond with Canadian politicians and am active in local, provincial and international issues—all of my political activities are outside of the realm of most discussions on Cybermind....
>
> We are all guilty of playing into the American ambit

Although this may be true, it also makes the point, people felt helpless before the main kinds of politics discussed on the List.

Recapitulation

The point here is not so much the accuracy of the general observations people on the List make about the world, but that they seem as coherent and documented as most others, and that people make use of the Internet to spread ideas from recognised writers that support the sender's worldview, which seem interesting, or which express a shared experience of life. Although the analysis of WES society described here may be simply a development of the mytheme of 'corporate rule', it has effects in the way many people on Cybermind conceive the world, and affects the expectations they have and the way they behave. In my experience more right wing groups have a similar sense of alienation: believing that the media does not reflect their interests and that immoral people who do not understand the true nature of the world, namely 'liberals', are in power and subverting attempts to make things right and destroying virtue in the populace and politics. People seem to miss a sense of participation, power is elsewhere and all they can do is shout and worry.

While there are no data to allow us to decide whether the survival security is actually lessening for members of the List, there is certainly a suggestion that it is because of relatively constant discussion of changes in patterns of work, diminishing wages, the winding down of Social Security and government support, cutbacks in the extent and role of civil society, lessening of kinship or community support, and feelings of alienation or disenfranchisement from wider political or social processes.

Continuing post World War II mythemes of impending nuclear, population or ecological doom, probably compound this apparent experiential insecurity. List concerns arise amidst an apparent growth in, and concentration of, corporate power and wealth, leading to a widening division between the very wealthy and everyone else; and a change in the power ratios within the State in favour of the corporate world. It could easily appear that the middle level organisations, which might have employed middle class intellectuals, are either being absorbed by the corporate sector or being fragmented.

In this system, the survival chances of those without access to 'contacts', or without skills which are in demand, such as programming (but even here a person's skills always risk being superseded), do not seem as good as they might have been 20 to 30 years ago when Alvin Gouldner (1979) could speak of the rise of the 'new class' . For 'middle class intellectuals', career paths in universities, education, or in the institutions of State and civil society (the locales of postwar 'new class' power), are either no longer present or subject to increasing pressures and insecurities. Unemployment and competition between workers has led to the expectation that workers will become 'flexible' to fit the demands of the company. Hours of work become more random, or increase, with no growth in income. Jobs become temporary, rather than long-term. It should not be assumed that people are happy with these demands for *their* constant flexibility, even though they may adapt. The 'inflexible' demands of the system appear to overwhelm personal preferences. Ideologies of individualism (backed up by weak kin and local ties, and disparate work), diminution of the importance of middle-level organisations, and the alienation of people from positivity into refusal means that organising to resist these movements is difficult. Those organisations of refusal, which seem effective, arise within identity categories not formed in the workplace and outside the corporate power structure: religion, race, intellectual interests or cultural localisms.

As argued earlier, many people within the WES world attempt to deal with these situations by joining voluntary organisations, or support groups. People are not compelled by the demands of these groups, as they can leave, but they can obtain levels of verbal or temporary support from them, and some help in problem solving and the shaping of concerns. They can also make contacts which may prove useful elsewhere. Such formations are in a sense experimental; if they work they are continued with, and abandoned later when they no longer work. Such formations have appeared on the internet, further freeing people from locality, kin and group demands, while offering benefits and aid in pursuing their lives and survival. Because of the need for access to a computer, understanding of how to use it, and access to the Internet, at this point people who go online for these purposes tend to be relatively well educated, although this has become less important over the period of study.

There is no necessity that those 'dispossessed' by capitalism have much common experience, or are able to unite in opposition. Commonality may be further diminished by the partitioning of groups allowed by the Internet. However, there is no simple opposition between global and local. Some locals will use the technology which furthers global capitalism to oppose the global, to join the global, or to entice the global into their region. Others will attempt to select parts of the global and reject others; some will attempt to construct new locals and new globals. Political movements can conceivably be given new publicity and possibly new influence and so on.

Although it is often argued that we are heading towards a radically different society, largely because of 'information technology', at the moment it appears more accurate to claim that information technology magnifies functionings of capitalism, which had previously been impeded by other interests within the State. These magnifications may well give rise to an unstable system which could radically change its state. However, although fears or celebrations of this change are important mythemes, which may feed into such changes, it is not necessary to assume that radical change is already here.

Chapter 4: Structures of Communication and Internet Groups

Structures of Communication

Theories proposing that social organisation is determined, enabled or limited by an underlying economic, technological, or ecological basis are well known (e.g. Marx, Marvin Harris). The difficulties in abstracting out such 'economic' or 'ecological' bases from other social activities are equally well known (Bateson 1972: 62-4, 84ff.; Elias 1978: 64). However, most Internet societies are based around standard types of organisation of communication which may not *determine* sociality, as imported social factors make certain types of enablement more probable, but they do affect the kinds of behaviour that are easy to manifest. This includes the ease, or difficulty, of establishing internal hierarchy and internal differentiation (such as the formation of subgroups); and the ways that groups can interact with each other and maintain their boundaries. I will briefly compare two types of online groupings; the Mailing List and the MOO, MUD or MUSH[1], to demonstrate that not all Internet groups are the same, and need to be considered in specific, rather than in general, and that people may use different groups for different purposes[2].

Mailing List Organisation[3]

On a mailing list, each member 'subscribes' by registering with a particular computer which runs the list. They then receive all the mail mailed to that computer for that list (including their own, unless they choose otherwise). For most of the course of the fieldwork there were two main forms of list-operating software: 'majordomo' and 'listserv'. Cybermind has used both, and although making some difference for the list owner or moderator, effects on the list seem minimal.

Having to subscribe implies that people who stay subscribed are fairly committed to a list, even though it is possible to stay for years with the setting on 'nomail'. Despite this commitment, on every list I know of, only a relatively small proportion of the list population is 'visible', or contributing regularly (see Chapter 5).

The 'listowner' is the person or group responsible for that list (in the case of Cybermind, this is Alan Sondheim). Lists may be moderated, in which case someone (usually the list owner), exerts control over the list. This control may range from almost nonexistent, through largely public discussion and refereeing (Alan's style) to 'fully moderated', where the moderator reads every piece of mail before sending it to the list. The moderator can remove or 'unsubscribe' people from the list, is able to check the addresses of those who subscribe, and sometimes demands conditions of those who subscribe. Thus joining the 'scholarly alchemy' list requires an applicant to demonstrate a 'bona fide interest' to the moderator[4]. As the moderator is the only person on the list with these powers they are frequently focused upon as the solver of list problems and the subject of considerable offlist mail. Social control depends upon the moderator for ultimate sanctions. In theory the power of the moderator could be total; however, given the embedding values of WES life, the moderator is often unable to direct the list, and disputes about their decisions can bring the list to near halt[5]. The tendency towards autocracy increases the more being on a List has value in defining membership of a group offline. Professional Lists tend to maintain boundaries and often have more extreme sanctions.

Lists usually have a topic which is supposed to be the central focus of the group, but the amount of leeway to post off topic varies from list to list. As shall be shown later, on Cybermind there is a tendency for people to define the 'community' of the list in terms of the presence of off-topic posts (see Chapter 12). One person told me they were initially unhappy on Cybermind as they found the irrelevant postings hard to endure, but changed their mind as they became more involved with the people. In this group, long-term users may be happier to delete mails than to become aggravated.

Within lists, postings generally have a subject heading. Replies to that subject are distinguished from the original by the insertion of 'Re>' or 'Re:' into the subject heading as with normal replies to email. Thus if I post on 'cyberalchemy', any replies, or replies to replies, will have headings like 'RE>cyberalchemy'. Posts connected to each other in this way are called a 'thread'. Threads, however, tend to fray almost immediately. Contents of postings headed 'RE>cyberalchemy' may diverge from the original topic when someone replies to a side point and effectively starts a new topic. Several unrelated discussions may be carried on simultaneously under the same heading, until someone decides to formally mark the change of subject with a new subject header; for example, 'Hamburgers (was Re>cyberalchemy)'. However a letter with a heading of Re>cyberalchemy may still contain writings more properly associated with the subject of hamburgers[6].

On Cybermind the average thread is usually over within a week. Threads with no postings made to them for more than three days can usually be assumed to have terminated. It could be argued that discussion tends to be fairly 'shallow' or inconclusive, due to the reluctance of people to post on a subject to which no one else has responded after such a period. Lists, therefore, tend to have a short attention span: a letter a person did not have time to respond to can be buried by new mail calling for new replies. Unusually, in the early days of the Alchemy list, replies to a post could commonly be made weeks later and stimulate fresh discussion. This behaviour lessened with an increase in the number of postings per day, which increased the 'burial' factor. Volume and immediacy demote elaboration.

Threads do not seem particularly important in organising list topics or the contents of mail. People frequently write about topics external to the current thread, and as often react to the totality of 'conversations' on the list as they do to specific threads.

Due to the time lapse between posts and replies, short-term memory and the usual ways of organising a conversation fail. Yet this lag is not long enough for the monologic conventions of correspondence to prevail (this is also lessened by the possibilities of multiple response). Quotation from the letter being answered is a common solution to this problem[7]. This tends to render communication an exchange of commentary which may encourage people to be more tart in response, and to 'throw the other person's words back in their face', as it were. It can also lead to people focusing on an aspect of a mail, particularly if replying to a reply, and apparently dismissing other parts of it. Certainly it can disrupt the smooth flow of the respondent's prose. As people exchange commentary, rather than focus on a subject, the probability of topic divergence again increases.

On a mailing list people can generally be certain as to whether their message has got through, as they should receive it themselves (unless they elect not to), while private correspondence, particularly between list members, can 'get lost' within the volume of the list. This seems particularly dependent upon mailer software; with some programs it is possible to separate personal mailings from mailings to a list, in others not. When I used one Mail program, mail from Cybermind appeared as 'from Cybermind'; with another it appeared under the name of the original sender.

Correspondence, unlike conversation, is often not closed. Conversation usually finishes with all participants knowing that messages have been received or acknowledged even if by 'grunts, or goodbyes'. Email communication tends to close in silence, when one participant feels they have no more to say, or when mail gets lost. This produces a potential suspension, and lack of closure in discourse, which contributes to the effect I have called *asence*, which is discussed in the next chapter. This effect contrasts with the finished form of a person's own mails—i.e. 'utterances' are not incomplete, or interrupted whilst being made, as they often are in conversation, but only sent when ready and probably after rereading.

MOO, MUD, MUSH[8]

MOOs are artificial, usually text-based, partitioned 'worlds' in which members take on character roles, and interact according to the rules of the world—both social and embedded in the program. Nowadays, graphic MOOs are popular, but this seems to make little difference to the kinds of behaviours described below, with the exception that graphic MOOs are conventionally three-dimensional in their maps. In this form of sociality people can be in different parts of the MOO and not interact at all. It is customary to think of the partitions as 'rooms' (even though they may be described as 'deserts' or the 'inside of an old shoe'), which connect in multiple ways. This renders the sociality far less 'universal' in its reach between members, and there is far more potential for casually hidden behaviour.

The described size of a location has no effect upon the numbers of characters which may be packed into that location. It is also generally impossible to interact with most of the description of a location or room; however, the description may set the *locale*. As then Cybermind member Caitlin Martin wrote:

> I build rooms and complexes of spaces which become stagesets upon which we interact... And this building does impact our interaction. You talk differently to me on my Roof Garden than you do in a sex room (C. Martin 1999: 11).

People with characters on the MOO will frequently 'build' their own rooms via the *@dig* command[9]. Building involves being assigned an abstract numbered location (which usually requires some recognition of a person's status by the MOO administrators, or Wizards) and then describing it[10]. People entering the location are then presented with the room description. Thus, on entering the original 'Cybermind Lounge' you would read:

Cybermind Lounge

A comfortable space for Cyberminders to meet and talk

You may make this your home or mail [A] if you'd like to connect your personal space to here.

There is an exit to the south. You see a blue sofa, a rocking chair, and a beanbag chair here. Above you see a balcony with seating and a porch with chairs and a porch swing through some glass sliders. Or you can sit on the floor.

[A list follows telling who is in the room]

If the room builder is sufficiently privileged, the room may contain 'objects' which are manipulable in limited ways. MOO rooms are thus extensions of the MOO persona. The room may connect to the main architecture (although a Wizard may have to do this for the person), but is more likely to connect to the rooms of friends (if both people agree to the connection), and even this is rare as it is unnecessary for transfer from room to room. When the 'Cybermind Lounge' was built, various members of the list did connect their rooms to this room, and the room description became more complex as it described these connections. People may 'occupy' a room together by using the *@sethome* command to have their characters appear in this room when they enter the MOO, rather than at the MOO entrance. This is often a mark of close friendship, romance, or loyalty to a group. 'Moving into' another person's room is a statement. The pattern of architecture in the MOO becomes more a map of friendships and associations than of geography, and is subject to the variations of these relationships[11].

Jim Reith set up the 'Cybermind Lounge' on PMC MOO, at a time when people from Cybermind attempted to interact on the MOO regularly and formally en masse. The group venture failed after about three attempts, largely because of the time lag[12]. Suggestions to go elsewhere (Media MOO, and Chiba MOO) did not draw any unanimity. However, it was common for individuals, pairs or small groups, to meet on MOO, and occasionally for people to 'recruit' new members there.

At one of the meetings at the Cybermind Lounge, some people appeared with pseudonymous characters and refused to give their list based names. Some felt this claim to anonymity to be a blatant contradiction of the 'community' nature of the list[13]. However this difference of opinion occurs because MOOs are structures which enable the anchoring of 'roleplay', so MOO characters can be considered more expressions of a persona than marks of authenticity. MOO activities can be framed differently and people can engage in behaviour which might be considered inappropriate on a list, as it is a blatant persona that is acting[14]. However this public roleplaying is still not expected to continue as much in pair relationships, which become dominated by demands for authenticity again. The upset produced by the refusal of some Cybermind member's MOO characters to be transparent, marks off a conflict in framing, and emphasises the importance of authenticity and intimacy to List life (see Chapter 6).

Even though MOOs can use similar software[15], an initial set of programmers has to set up the 'MOO world', its 'theme', and its possibilities. This indicates the kind of interaction expected from users. Some are primarily sites for adventure gaming, similar to roleplaying games such as *Dungeons & Dragons* with marauding monsters, or fights between giant combat robots (cf. Ito 1997; Reid 1999: 120ff.). Others mix adventure and sociability. Some are primarily places of sociability such as Lambda MOO, or they can, supposedly, be reserved for particular types of discussion such as Media MOO or Postmodern Condition MOO (PMC-MOO). The 'Wizards' can control what it is possible to do and what is acceptable behaviour as they have the ability to stop entry from various addresses or sites.

Unlike mailing lists, interaction time is fairly rapid, and the ability to enter text with no necessity to quote previous comments means dialogue proceeds more like normal conversation. However, lag can mean that nothing appears on the screen for quite lengthy periods of time, followed by a rushed catchup, as previous dialogue scrolls past the viewer at speed. As well conversation in the same room appears in order of typing, and frequently overlaps with other remarks, so that it can be quite difficult to follow the intercrossing dialogues. As a result, MOOs can be confusing and hard to anchor. Often people become frustrated with this confusion and log off, or attempt to lower the number of people whose dialogue they are reading by moving into a 'private' room.

The immediacy of interaction between people on MOOs is a noticed factor. Rodion writes to Cybermind (17 Apr.95):

> It is a similar community to our lists but the interaction is immediate [...] The friendships have a delicacy and relevance that seems more direct then the communities on lists.

Caitlin adds (18 Apr.95):

> It is more immediate, more intense for me. There are people I know from MOOing who I see everyday. Whose lives are intertwined with mine in a kind of connectedness I've never experienced before (primarily because so much of it *is* disembodied, even though we wear assorted bodies— borrowed or otherwise)

Bernadette claimed (pc 19 Apr.99) that this kind of intertwining, together with the ease of discovering when a character was last on MOO, meant a person's absence was far more noticeable than their absence from a list, and people would try harder to keep in touch.

Internal Structures: Hierarchy and Subgroups[16]

The next section of the chapter investigates the differences in the degree of internal structure (hierarchy and subgroups) between types of group, and the kinds of relations possible between groups (focusing on boundaries and cross-membership).

Internal Group Structure and Hierarchy

Hierarchy on the various kinds of Internet group, particularly on MOOs and Lists, tends to differ.

Wizards on MOOs can often appear distant. When there are several thousand characters on a MOO it is unlikely most people will be aware of, or interact with, the Wizards much, and the Wizards form a mutually recognising category-group set off from the rest of the people on MOO by their access to programming powers. This means a hierarchy develops which, ideally, corresponds to the Wizard's programming skills, experience, or access to tools. Social control tends to become more codified and more committee based[17]; there is a recognisable group that has to be consulted on many decisions.

As people on MOOs generally have considerable time and effort invested in the construction of their character, its room and props, the tendency for people to protest against what they consider to be an arbitrary or unfair decision by leaving the MOO altogether and abandoning this investment, diminishes. This gives the Wizards considerably less tenuous or uncertain power than a listowner, who is faced with continual placation of those objecting to their decisions[18]. Spreading power around makes it more absolute. As well, individual solutions on MOOs are not particularly workable. Caitlin wrote, in response to the advocacy of *@gag* commands which make the gagged person's comments invisible to the gagger (16 Nov.96):

> @gag prevents you from seeing whatever nastyperson may be saying/emoting to you, but does not prevent everyone else in the room from seeing [it...] All of this sort of harrassment is frequently conducted on a couple of levels— there's the personal spam attack, for example, but there can also be the endless discussion of who you are irl ['in real life'], your faults, etc. [...] One could say that none of this should bother you, but it's very difficult to counteract and defend against things you can't see. [...] Another issue [with respect to] these defense mechanisms is that the use of them penalizes the 'victim' by adding to eir personal lag.

Unlike listowners, Wizards can grant resources such as programming rights or extra characters; they give others 'secret information' about identity or private conversations; and support people in disputes, as application of MOO 'law' is often a matter of patronage. Therefore, they are often courted by other members, and can build small empires within the MOO.

On PMC-MOO, during August/September 1995, the Wizards decided there was not enough discussion of postmodernism and tried to ban 'recreational mooing'. This caused passionate debate, on Cybermind as on PMC-MOO itself, largely over who 'owned' the MOO, the users or the Wizards. Ultimately, the Wizards had the power to shut the MOO down, and did so, to re-open on their terms. However, even in this case I am not sure how long the prohibition remained enforced, although the MOO seemed to decline and periodically someone would tell me that PMC-MOO was no longer as good as it had been.

In contrast, on mailing lists there is little formal hierarchy, or category structure. On Cybermind the only hierarchy is the position of Alan as List-owner and moderator and possibly someone else as co-moderator. Co-moderators tended not to last for long before Jim took up the position. The shallowness of this hierarchy made it difficult for Alan to construct a lasting intermediary class dependent upon him for their rank. Unlike MOO Wizards he has no formal rewards to offer and so no intermediary group can manipulate access to his largess, or distribute that largess themselves. His main power is the threat of unsubscribing individuals or of closing the list down, rather than any power of positive direction[19]. His power is unstable and depends upon his ability to persuade others. Conflict could, and did, arise over authority. As there was no ritual or symbolic differentiation of Alan as moderator from other list members (other than the volume of his mail), it was possible for others (particularly newcomers with whom he had not built recognition) to categorise his power as arbitrary or illegitimate[20]. Given the 'left liberal' orientation of the list such categorisations were to be avoided, although it was always much easier to remove people who were new or did not post very often, as they were not recognised and had built no alliances. However, if the online group was related to an offline group, then it again becomes easier to organise such committees and the power base becomes more complex.

Informal hierarchy exists in Lists and depends upon volume of posts. There are those who post more and those who are responded to more, and these tend to be the same people (see Appendix I and Chapter 8). Those most likely to be reprimanded are new or unfamiliar, so there is an informal hierarchy between familiar and unfamiliar list members. This was rarely explicit, and those who stayed and posted frequently would move out of the lower category (just as those who ceased posting might 'move down'), so the hierarchy is constantly changing. Perceptions of hierarchy can also vary throughout the group, as those not currently active have no presence. However, previously active people can be recognized by currently recognized members and retain a degree of influence even though unknown to most users.

It is useful to replace a static notion of hierarchy with a modification of Elias's phrase 'established-outsider relations' (Elias & Scotson 1994: passim; Elias & Dunning 1993: 55ff.), namely 'recognized-outsider relations', with the provision of negative as well as positive recognition: that is when the person is recognised as strongly outgroup. These terms remind the analyst there are only degrees between unknown (and possibly hostile) people and people who are rarely visible, and that fame and infamy both have rewards.

Recognition is achieved rather than ascribed. There is no system of formal roles other than moderating. Even on MOOs with their hierarchies and committees, power will tend to be achieved rather than simply ascribed, but afterward these hierarchy roles are marked.

Cybermind did have informal subgroups, which were usually fairly invisible; for example, the people who knew each other from FutureCulture, or the people Alan might contact to discuss List 'strategy'. On the occasions when a subgroup became visible fissioning was probable (see Chapter 10). This probability seems to increase with numbers of visible subgroups, and can leave the group with either the one visible subgroup or no subgroups at all. Given the constant change of personnel, any such inner structures are unlikely to be firm or lasting. Again, this is not the case with MOOs, where the partitioning of communication into 'rooms', makes subgroups common.

This inability to easily form subgroups on Lists, because of the organisation of communication, has the further result that it is difficult for people, as a group, to continue discussions which are not interesting to the rest of the group, without threatening group disruption. The more mailbox space these 'uninteresting' discussions take up, the greater the potential for disruption.

Groups and Other Groups (Us and Them)
Almost all people who use Cybermind, use other online groups as well, some of which are shared with other Cybermind members — in particular FutureCulture, FOP (later Wryting) and Cyberculture. Some of this arises because of shared interests. People may ask close associates what other online groups they use. People also use these groups for different purposes, and may move from one to another to 'achieve' these purposes. Thus intimacy first broached on Cybermind may be developed on MOO with more synchronous communication and greater 'privacy'. People used FOP to better express, or develop, the tensions which arose on Cybermind, not restrained by questions of 'topic relevance'. People may start private lists to discuss issues away from other list members, and so on. People will tend to know the people who share many groups with them better, and this may have consequences for how they act on these groups. The effects may not always be those intended. For example, a MOO was set up to help organise the Cybermind conference. An unintentional result was that disputes arose in the conference MOO because the established authority, control and privacy patterns did not match those of the new environment. Offlist relationships became visible and intrusive and were resented.

Heterogeneity/Homogeneity
No group can be entirely homogeneous as humans differ and are unlikely to only have contact with the same people, and no group can be entirely heterogeneous as its members could not understand each other or cooperate. Perceptions of homogeneity or heterogeneity change by comparison with other groups, with the framing, or with the site of the perceiving.

Cybermind perceives itself as heterogeneous, although outsiders have perceived it as homogeneous. It has included visible list members from Canada, the US, Britain, Australia and, less numerously, from Germany, Norway, Finland and India. All visible list members have been proficient in English. By far the majority of recognized list members have some university education, are familiar with the humanities and generally supportive of the congerie of theories categorized as 'postmodern'. Uniformity of political views is marked, the group being primarily, to use the US term, 'left liberal' in orientation, and this seems to be the case for new, as much as for long term, members (see Appendix I). The polarity distinction between 'left-liberal' and 'right-conservative' seems important in constructing this group's identity and its difference from other groups. However, the group had vocally right-conservative members, although they tended more to the libertarian aspects of the pro-capitalist right than the moralism of the 'Christian' right, and the list's view of its heterogeneity is arrived at by not excluding others in advance, and by not specifying what is likely to lead to exclusion, with the exception of "racial or other bias slurs" as stated in the Manifesto.

During my first six months onlist, there was a relatively low interest in politics or religion or in converting people to a particular religious or political viewpoint. There was no explicit attempt to get the group to subscribe to particular sets of propositions. It is possible the group avoided politics or religion due to the status these have in WES societies as disruptive subjects[21]. Homogeneity was obtained by not discovering difference. Later on, when politics did come to the fore it often proved intensely disruptive, and the difficulties of resolving communication were obvious. People could strongly feel that they were being misread or their words were being distorted and leave in disgust.

Homogeneity or heterogeneity of *all* list members is never visible. Prototypicality has to be constructed out of the activities of the most visible members. As prototypicality might be expected to include the property of 'posting a lot', most list members may exclude themselves from being prototypic and thus risk feeling they are marginal to the group. At the same time, however, exclusion is not thrust upon them. The phenomena of 'degrees of membership' is marked despite the apparent all-or-nothing nature of being on list.

As is argued in Chapter 12, the list's homogeneity is primarily maintained by strenuous requirements for participation rather than by exclusion. It is easy to imagine mailing lists far more homogeneous, and formally so, than Cybermind. Kinds of homogeneity can vary; the alchemy lists, although restricted to those interested in alchemy, seem more heterogeneous in class, nationality, politics and education than Cybermind. A specific, rather than a general, topic might allow more diversity, as these differences are less likely to surface. Similarly the stronger the demand for 'community' the more open heterogeneity may decline. On MOOs people can easily form isolated groups, so heterogeneity on non-topic MOOs is probably encouraged, though subgroups may be more homogeneous.

A further kind of homogeneity may arise from the populations from which an Internet group gains its members. For example online 'professional groups' may be restricted to people within the same company, department or profession either deliberately or by default. Behaviour on such groups may have consequences in offlist professional or personal lives. At the beginning of the fieldwork period, most academic Mailing Lists were of this type and, from my experience and that reported to me, tended to be quiet. Few people risked comments, other than to announce papers and conferences. Activity might increase if a 'non-professional' joined up and wrote something which was not academically acceptable. As time passed these kinds of lists seemed to become more active, but they always seemed to be in danger of appearing exclusive to those not culturally proficient, and moderators often seem to shut down factious conversations without much protest on the List itself.

Relations Between Groups

The relationship of a group to external or inclusive groups is important to its member's self-categorization. Other groups can be categorized as similar or different. The way this similarity or difference is constructed may also have an effect. The group could act as isolated, or as actively differentiating itself from other groups, or as part of a hierarchy or collection of groups. Its relationship to other groups could be cooperative, competitive or antagonistic; or symmetric or complementary. This coaction may relate to internal regulation, or to the regulation of others.

Few Internet groups have formal relationships with other Internet groups. When such interactions exist, they are often based on interactions and category divisions in the embedding societies; as with the newsgroups about Indian and Pakistan described by Mitra (1997: 67-8), or the left-liberal, right-conservative division in the US. Connections between online groups appear, in general, to be at an individual level as people belong to many other such groups. Even though there is likely to be an overlap of personnel there is rarely prior commitment, *as a group*, to another group. Although people on Cybermind belonged to FOP and FutureCulture and used PMC-MOO, they rarely acted together in those groups (especially towards other groups) as 'members of Cybermind'. No one 'spoke for' Cybermind to any other Internet group or was expected to organise coaction with another group. Voluntary intergroup coaction is rare to non-existent. People rarely discussed (as opposed to expressed) problems with one list on another[22]. Social control focuses on the ingroup rather than on other groups. The only attempt to motivate Cybermind to act as a group elsewhere on the internet occurred during the reorganisation of PMC-MOO, and was not particularly effective. Neither does Cybermind attempt to differentiate itself from specific other groups; even ingroup praise rarely implied contrast with other groups. The list can be said to exist, as a group, in isolation from other groups. There is no hierarchy of groups or categories, which includes Cybermind. The next most inclusive category would be that of all Internet users, which might be referred to as the 'Internet community'. For example, although Cybermind was initially a member of the Spoon Collective, this was primarily at a moderator level and rarely impinged upon group life. When tensions between the moderators of the collective became a problem, Cybermind could end the connection with little disruption to the groups on either side.

Conflict and exchange between groups is rare. Forwards might sometimes count as intergroup exchange but, in general, few people respond back to the group of origin. Similarly, conflict is more common within rather than between groups. People on a list would have to be persuaded, rather than ordered, into combat with external groups, whereas internal combat is spontaneous, and unlikely to be directed. In internal combat people are likely to have ties with those they might conflict with, and there are likely to be people with ties to both sides who will try to calm things down whether publicly or offlist. Prolonged conflict tends to interfere with normal forms of exchange, and the weapons available are likely to be non-lethal or involve danger to the user. With a small population, the loss of one or two recognized people can be significant enough to diminish the conflict. Finally, the results of overwhelming victory are usually not that beneficial, and there are no power structures that will maintain the victory.

Because of the downplay of intergroup interaction there is little in the way of categories of generalisable 'others', despite a degree of suspicion towards unrecognised people or towards those categorised in terms of embedding society conflicts. There are some 'others' with which the group interacts conceptually, such monolithic and vague, if powerful, groups as 'the Government', 'the Corporate World',' the Media' and those not online, although people from these groups are rarely seen as persuasive. People using Cybermind are not necessarily hostile to these groupings, but seem to expect these groups may be hostile towards them[23]. Most net-based groups are categorized as fellows in comparison with these vague others. However, there is little evidence of intergroup cooperation in opposition to these 'non-Internet groups', even when people were protesting against the Communications Decency Act or the Iraq War[24].

The general lack of relationship between groups may mean that self-categorisation is unlikely to come from membership of Internet groups alone (people are not members in relation to members of other groups), but has to come from external categories. The more marked these external categories are in the embedding society, the more, when invoked, they will be exaggerated in Internet groups, and the more these categories may overpower group membership categories which have no other reinforcement than the online group. Hence the importance of male/female, 'right'/ 'left', and so on.

Boundaries

Internet group boundaries are generally permeable, although they can be controlled as in some academic lists. 'Comms-MOO' had a registration procedure which filtered out people[25]. However, such marked boundaries are rare. I do not know of any group which demands an initiation ritual from would-be members which is observed by the group. Likewise I have not encountered any sanctions against contact with 'outsiders', although suspicion can be raised if such contact is discovered when the outsiders are perceived as hostile. However, for all Mailing Lists it is never clear to most members precisely who is also participating. Active group membership is continually vague.

As the difficulty of entering a group, or the severity of initiation into the group, increases its attractiveness to WES people (Aronson & Mills 1960; Festinger & Aronson 1960: 220-1), we might hypothesise that the attractiveness of Internet groups, in general, is not great, and they are easy to leave, 'emotionally' as well as practically, unless a person fought for, and achieved, recognition.

Intragroup contact between the members of lists or newsgroups is sporadic. However, contact between certain members may be frequent, may go offlist, and be more intimate than contact with people in their offline lives. This contact may affect the group adversely (see Chapter 11). On MOOs, contact between subgroup members is fairly constant, but between the general membership is probably rare.

Internet groups generally do not have strong and *perceivable* boundaries, although it could be possible for the boundaries of mailing lists to be strong if fully moderated. Mailing Lists tend to have a lower internal set of boundaries than MOOs where people can be locked out of rooms.

Conclusion

Although it is not possible to be certain, because of the lack of cross-cultural research into social forms arising via the Internet, it seems probable that the organisation of communication has an effect on the enabled social form in the kinds of opportunities open to members, the kinds of internal differentiation that is easily possible, and the kinds of relationships possible between groups. Members of Cybermind most frequently interact via Lists, MOOs and private mail, using each modality for different purposes.

The online group exists as a named category with vague boundaries. To some extent the name and the organisation of communication make the group. Only in MOOs does the category involve interior distinction, or markers of status, which affect many members, and this arises because the organisation of communication allows partition; gives more control over the group environment to some than to others; and allows distribution of resources and favours. Borders can be most clearly demarcated on mailing lists (although internal borders are still not perceptible to members), and the capacity to form complex subgroupings is most marked on MOOs. Styles of authority vary between the types of grouping from none, or earned (based on cultural competence and exchange), to committees and personal rule. Authority in MOOs is more 'feared' as people have time and effort invested in characters, rooms and programmed items, whereas on Lists all the person has is personal history, which is always in danger of evaporating anyway. Mailing Lists can be autocratic but this autocracy tends to only allow prevention, especially where membership is not connected to offline livelihood or an offline group. Otherwise, partly because of WES social conventions and the dangers of losing recognised members, authority in mailing lists is contested and unsure. There is little the moderator can do to gain sustained support or construct a hierarchy dependent upon them, without an offline power base. However, as the list moderator is the only person who can enforce 'exile', moderators are often lobbied by people involved in disputes, and held responsible for what happens.

The simultaneity of MOOs implies a greater sense of involvement between members and makes recognized members more noticeable when absent. It also means that it is easier to check ongoing reactions to what a person is writing, and harder for 'alienating' exchange of commentary to develop.

It is easier to split public and private, and to do this as groups, within a MOO, because of 'rooms' (which can keep others out) and *@page* commands (which allow private communication), whereas on Lists 'private' contacts tend to be dyadic, and it is harder for subgroups to discuss matters offlist. In effect subgroup discussion rather than being hidden, tends to be thrust into everyone's view.

Despite frequent overlap of participants, Internet groups do not generally have connections to other Internet groups. Cooperation or conflict between groups tends to derive from the relationship between groups in the embedding society, and it is difficult to organise intergroup activities. Each group tends to function as if it was a group alone, surrounded by others who are potentially hostile.

Chapter 5: The Virtual Life: Asence and Experience

Introduction
This chapter describes some experiential aspects of life online (particularly list life), which result from the structures which have just been discussed. These features include the mode of being, which I have called 'asence' (or the suspension of presence), lurking, flames, burnout, secrecy and the absence of history.

'Asence'
One of the most obvious features of list life is a blurring between presence and absence. In offline societies, it is generally possible to tell whether a person is present or not. Presence and status are acknowledged by others making, at the least, eye contact or grunts in a person's direction, or by their pointedly ignoring that person. Identity is reinforced by reaction. People are generally aware of who is listening to the conversation and of their reactions to each other so that these listeners and the reactions become part of the conversation itself. Online this is usually not the case. It is possible for a person to be present without others being aware of them; there is often no marker of existence beyond the act of communication itself.

Even in email 'conversation' between people who are aware of each other, this blurring is present in the closure of email. In offline conversation, reception of a message and the ending of communication is marked by a negotiation of grunts and/or formal phrases; however, email conversation is usually ended abruptly with suspension of closure and no response. There is no certainty whether you have been received, or read, or of the nature of your reader's reaction. As Skip asks (27 Oct.06):

> was the person responding with silence, or did their message simply get lost in the Net somewhere or otherwise fail to transmit properly?
>
> (Or, for that matter, was it erroneously detected as spam and deleted?)

As a result, your presence is always drifting away.

This drift to invisibility is reinforced by lists having a shallow history. Generally mail, or a subject which is not commented upon for several days, will vanish beneath the influx of new mail or new subjects. Little continues to remind people of your presence. A person who is not posting now, to some extent, does not exist.

'Asence' is a term coined to indicate this relationship between presence and absence. It represents the state of being present without the people you are present with being aware of you—to them you are absent—and without you being aware of reception, or able to fine-tune communication as it proceeds. It is a suspension of recognition. Ruesch and Bateson draw attention to this kind of factor in complex communication networks generally, discussing particularly how people can feel helpless or insecure if they do not receive acknowledgment of their messages. Further, "the individual feels paralysed if correction of erroneous interpretations is impossible" (1987: 39-40). This is in continual effect online.

Because some people post regularly and are read by almost everybody, they have a real presence to the reader. The reader comes to know their personas and to become emotionally involved with them, to feel friendly or hostile etc. towards them. This process is increased by the apparent emptiness of the text, which has few social or physical markers upon it. Processes of categorization can operate without resistance. This can lead to a feeling of deep intimacy with people. Others essentially live out their lives before you. They may even interact with you, without particularly noticing you. Thus, people can assume the existence of an intimacy, which is in no way recognized by the recipient. If the person tries to take this felt intimacy to its object, they can meet with quite radical and unexpected rejection. In some ways this resembles WES ways of relating to 'celebrities' who can be present and apparently known to us, while we remain unknown to them and unacknowledged by them.

Asence is not just a problem for the infrequent poster. The only way a person can know they exist online is through reading their own mail on list, or the response of others, and yet only a relatively few mails to lists receive acknowledgment, even if people like the post. Although a few writers may receive many replies, both on and offlist, there is little reinforcement, or feedback, to most communication-presences. The problem can be exaggerated by heavy volume of mail, as it diminishes the number of mails from any particular person which elicit a response, while at the same time increasing the apparent presence of other people. This may lead to a sense of discouragement or dislocation. This may be one reason for previously silent list members ('lurkers') appearing, only to disappear again.

Asence is also emphasized by uncertainty about 'audience'. List members have little idea who is actually present. People you think might be present may not be receiving mail. They may have left the list for a few days without notification, or be skipping mail if they are busy. Messages to which you anticipate a response, can go unnoticed. As a result, you may be engaged in conflict with someone, or 'risk' personal revelation, and those you expect to notice or give support do not; so your presence seems snubbed or absent and 'community' seems fragile (see Chapter 11). The opposite can also happen—on one occasion a list member announced they had discovered someone from their offlist past was reading the list, and left.

There can be mild dislocation for a person who has been absent, as the group will not necessarily engage in any welcome-back rituals or greetings when they do return. When people leave there may be no farewells. In one case, when a person who seemed reasonably recognizable and popular on Cybermind wrote to the list that he had to leave, he received little in acknowledgment. He replied to my offlist farewell by writing that it had been a chastening experience, as he had only received two goodbyes in total.

Asence, together with the short memory span, affects status or social identity as a person is only present in their acts; thus reputation must be continually re-earned. New people, perhaps whole new 'generations', may appear on a list in a period of a few months[1]. None of this new generation may be aware of long-time list members who are currently not active, even if these 'long-time members' are reading the list, are engaged in correspondence outside the list, and feel themselves to be active members of the list. The new members do not know the old, and have not received the previous prestations of text. Therefore, the new generation may construct a completely different view of the 'community' of a list and its accepted practices (as such practices only exist in the postings currently made), and longer-time members may feel continually displaced. As a result, a list member's persona and social identity are continually on the verge of drifting away and must be continually recreated. Alan writes (4 Sept.06)

> Years ago, when I was first writing about the Net, I talked about "rewrite"—that one must constantly write oneself into the net—into existence for others—otherwise one disappears. So that the self becomes a kind of continuous rewrite—this relates to the "uncanny" feeling one has… when you realize you haven't heard from someone for a long long time…

To use a metaphor, status in cyberspace is like a continual potlatch, new gifts of text must be repeatedly given, and in that giving are consumed (see Chapter 8). Nothing is returned but short-lived respect, of which the receiver may be completely uncertain or unaware. Not surprisingly some find this tiring.

Lurking

Of the 100 to 350 people on the list, only about a maximum of 20 to 40 people are *regular* contributors at any one time. Some people will post at a high volume for their entire time on the list, other people's postings come in cycles or bursts. Most people on the list never contribute to discussion, or contribute to such a small extent their names and personas are largely forgotten, or never noticed, by the vast majority of readers. This apparent absence may be emphasised by the marked presence of particular people and by the general list volume.

Although this silent audience has little effect upon the main participants, who post largely to their known audience of regular posters, there are occasional discussions of 'lurkers' (people who read but do not post). These discussions often arise during disputes, when people might expect the dispute to drive lurkers away, as when Steven writes (26 Feb.96):

> I feel much more reticent (not that it stops me)...
>
> if I feel reticent...how about the lurkers and tender new ones?

Most commonly discussions about lurkers focus on how to encourage them to 'de-lurk'. These discussions have little effect, despite occasional expressions of delight such as Bazza (6 Apr.03):

> Love it! Lurkers coming into the open are like finding an extra layer in the choccy box that you didn't know was there.

At other times, people can express worry about lurkers and the unseen audience, as one member wrote: "after all on the Internet anyone can be John Ashcroft! [the attorney general of the US]".

McLaughlin et al. suggest, that lurkers do not think of lists as communities but as more like magazines, or epistolary novels[2] (1995: 103). This is not necessarily so, lurkers may feel membership. Thus Mari wrote, describing some features of asence and lurking (2 Apr.03):

> i lurked for the longest time at first, and loved every minute of it. i read everything avidly. i can't remember my first post, but everyone just ignored it, and i felt humbled and then i sank back into lurking for another while. then i posted something that was controversial and suddenly, everyone answered me and that was almost more horrible than the being ignored was. but i lived. but it is a wonderful thing to just lurk sometimes, even now. i can sink into myself, but you're all still there around me.

In November 2001, Rose and Renata reported receiving mail from lurkers. Renata wrote:

> I'm always kinda flattered when I get mail from lurkers; also I like the idea of having an unknown audience. When I write a post to CM and nobody replies, I think of all the non-posters reading it—I feel kinda heard then. ;-)

Later Jim stated (27 May.03) that some lurkers "have blossomed into good net friends without ever delurking". Perhaps they feel incapable in some way as did the following writer (23 Mar.96):

> I mainly lurk and find most contributions stimulating and thought-provoking. Some of it is way over my head but if I keep reading perhaps one day I will understand what you are all saying. [...] There are probably many other lurkers like myself who appreciate CM but are happy to let the more knowledgeable and articulate do the talking.

Another lurker wrote similarly (1 Apr.03):

> It is certainly educational reading.
>
> I've honestly not read much in the past 4-5 months until a week or so ago.
>
> I don't have the time needed to put my thoughts together in order to respond to many of the issues presented here in a timely manner. Thus, I don't make my presence known often.

Or perhaps they think of themselves as outsiders; they have posted and were ignored. Often, however, a lurker will 'break cover' to announce they really enjoy the list, and perhaps tell a little about themselves, or contribute to an ongoing discussion. For example, one person (23 Feb.03) described the list as:

> An all-round enjoyable experience. I have to applaud you all for providing constant entertainment for...... oooh...... lots of lurkers, no doubt, the world over. Speaking as a confirmed lurker myself, which, of course, I am.
>
> What's a performance without the audience?

In general, lurkers return to silence, rarely to be seen again[3]. Not announcing, but describing, such a transition is this post from Richard (9 July.96):

> I lurked for almost a year in the bushes on the edge of the village. I witnessed Michael's funeral. I observed attacks from roving brigands. I saw the departure and apparent suicide of respected opinion leaders. And I was there when they returned to us—either from a long journey or beyond cyberdeath. And all the while, the village tried to govern itself through all of these crises.
>
> But I had been tricked. I had come to learn about cybercommunity, to research it, to analyze it. It took me a long time to actually find it because not everything that I described above was self-apparent in Cybermind. It was obscured by flames, tedious off-topic threads, seemingly irrelevant and poorly written poetry, audaciously graphic sexual texts, and such. The community exists at the meta-level. It's not like an online shopping mall with clearly marked signposts pointing "Cybercommunity this way---->"
>
> Community here, like everywhere, doesn't come easily. You just can't look for it. You have to work for it. And for me, it meant that I had to de-lurk out of the bushes and start typing. If you are coming to Cybermind to find community, I have a secret for you: you have to bring it with you.

Richard makes the important point that abstract observation of mailing list behaviour is completely different from participation. Participation separates out the 'voices', makes allies, debating partners, and sometimes difficult relationships, etc.

Lurkers may also break cover to tell the list they hate it, and threaten to unsubscribe as for example (2 Nov.95):

> I ran across this list while surfing and thought it would be invigorating. Instead I seem to have found a large group of people (apologies to the few intelligent posts I've read) who can do nothing but whine, whimper and stab each other in the back. I hope it doesn't stay this way long or I'm gone. I get enough childish angst from my 3 year old and at least with her it's all new.

Sometimes people's first mail is to announce they are leaving. This frequently brings forth mail from regular posters trying to find out about the problem, or suggesting the person starts up a topic they *are* interested in. However, as such suggestions are necessarily usually made after the person has had time to unsub, they serve more a function of re-establishing group solidarity than placating the lurker.

The relation between asence and lurking is shown when dobie wrote (15 Mar.95) about lurkers on Cybermind occasionally harassing recognised posters by asking for netsex, presumably because of an expected intimacy, and people's fear of opening up because of this[4]. On another occasion a person taking an unpopular position onlist was flamed offlist by several lurkers. In response to a query about this he wrote to me:

> yesterday, I believe it was, I got 4 nastygrams, only one of which was from anyone that had posted before to the list...some of the terminology used was 'dittohead', 'fascist' and 'shithead' (the only one of the three that has *ever* been applicable to me :>). [...] I did find it curious that the nastiest epithets were from 'lurkers'.

Perhaps this occurred precisely because these lurkers had no other ties, or interactions, with him — their relationships were extremely simplex and easy to risk. He was easily made prototypic of an outgroup category.

Long-time, and recognised list members, may move into lurking after extensive participation. This may result from 'burnout', too much offline work, feelings of depression, or from a greater personal involvement with other list members thus developing an offlist correspondence which replaces onlist correspondence.

Jim kindly gave some information on the possible numbers of lurkers onlist, writing (20 Aug.04): "There are 264 subscribers at the moment [with] 123 set to receive mail". During that, relatively quiet month only 23 people posted leaving 100 lurking, if merely temporarily.

If all lurkers participated onlist, the volume of the list would increase massively and people would either leave, or skim or ignore a greater percentage of mail. If, for example, a list has 300 members and they all post 4 times a week, that is 1,200 messages per week, or over 170 messages per day. If we assume that those members who don't post less than 4 times a week continue to post at the same rate as previously, then the total number of posts per day could easily approach 200. With this volume not only would the list become unreadable other than by truly dedicated people, it might also become harder to recognise individuals, so weakening the sense of 'community'. Therefore, there is a feedback limit to the maximum number of active participants who can use a list (which number undoubtedly varies with the list). Often this number is given by List members as being 'about 20' which undoubtedly refers to the most active and recognisable participants.

Flames

Mailing lists and, more particularly, newsgroups have a reputation for what are called 'flame wars': basically increasingly vituperative mailings, in which the purpose becomes demolition. These disputes can monopolise much of the mailbox space of list members, and possibly destroy the list for its original purpose. This is so much a part of Internet folklore that newsgroups for flaming were started, to try and confine it to parts of the net[5]. However in counterposition to this walling off of flame, some people espouse the view that only 'intense' debate is worthwhile or authentic, and demand it everywhere.

Some comments made about flames during Cybermind's first couple of days (largely within the 'Spelling Wars'), give some ideas of conventions developed elsewhere on the internet and brought to the list.

That flames were a source of dread to some is shown in Ann's letter which, by pointing out some careless spelling, started the dispute (2 July.94):

> On this list, words are everything. I fear a glut of words that lack thought or conviction or style. Please—no flames. I offer this observation with the best of intentions and the hope that this list will indeed prove valuable.

This suggests the author knew the capacity of her letter to provoke such responses. An early reply concluded: "This is not a flame. It is a discussion", and Ann responded: "Thanks. I appreciate that. I have found flames to be so psychically intrusive that I will leave lists where they are too easily triggered". Marius illustrated his concerns about what happens to lists in flame war mode, by describing some happenings on FutureCulture (4 July.94):

> The flame war situation on FutureCulture [...] that has been referred to was important because it was causing people to leave. These were not participants, mind you, but passive on-lookers, frowning at what they saw. And some of them got fed up and left. Unsubscribed. Disappeared. That scared me. Some idiot foaming at the mouth about guns had driven away interesting people. The distance created by that flamewar was a threat to the community.

Another list member also wrote emphasising the trauma of flame (12 July.94):

> I would still argue that exposure on the net [...] is more fearful than presenting one's own self if one values one's thinking. What if the assertions

are responded to with a flame? Or if one's spelling errors/typos are criticised? It can be demoralizing...

Other members considered fear of flame to be foolish. Fran responded to the letter above (13 July.94):

> Are not these risks we have to take in our daily lives even more so than in what we say on the net? With risk taking comes a sense of assurance. So what if you're flamed? Flame back. Correct your typos before you send things out. Why let it demoralise you? Some guy with a lead pipe isn't going to _do_ anything to you on the net.

Dan called another member a "clueless newbie", for worrying about flame, as flaming was standard on the Internet (3 July.94):

> The phenomenon described above has happened on all lists at one time or another, at least unless they are VERY tightly edited
>
> One flame...call for banning the flamer...switching into a discussion on intellectual freedom, freedom of speech, whether the moderator (if any) is doing his/her job well, and so on and on...until it burns out until the next time.
>
> Stick around...you'll see it on EVERY list at times, even the lame over on netiquette...

As these posts suggest 'flame war' is a paradigm for net dispute, and even for net existence, despite the difference in responses and expectations. The reputed consequences of flame war (its causing people to leave, destruction of community or driving away 'hopeless newbies'), by repetition becomes a method of maintaining unity. Either it gets rid of incompetents or, more commonly, the predicted consequences are non-specifically disastrous and to be avoided at all costs. Contradictory framing about what makes a flame, and what its effects are, is common.

One of the first letters posted to Cybermind before the dispute began, bears this latter anxiety about disintegration and disaster. Marius wrote (1 July.94) about the newsgroup alt.syntax.tactical, which had gained some fame for deliberate disruption, and occasional destruction of other newsgroups[6]: "The method: Prolonged flame wars and trickery drawing people into a whirlpool of confusion and ange, exploiting the weaknesses of the net to make communication all but impossible". He goes on to write of "sociopaths... psychopaths, the violently paranoid and the clinically schizophrenic. Has it struck you they are all out there, and they may thrive on the net?" Alan added (2 July.94) that:

> In general there seems to be an underlying tension and paranoia evident on the Net... On the one hand there is the very real threat of control from above... and on the other the equally violent threat of disruption from below[7].

Motivations of 'others' are hidden and thus potentially conspiratorial. The 'projection' which allows asent intimacy also allows asent hostility and paranoia. Every communication is launched with no guide to its reception until it is out; it cannot be changed while response is being interpreted by the emitter. Response becomes a kind of fantasy. Ann, who has little power to change anything, has her image magnified and stereotyped into a 'dragonlike' teacher. She herself thought people were not seeing her 'as she was'.

Different standards for what constitutes "flaming" existed in the group. Ann gave her definition (4 July.94) as "personal attacking as distinguished from a spirited interchange on the issues", but this distinction was not clear. When she announced she was deleting the mails of Livia unread after Livia used an obscenity in response to her, Liz thought this an over-reaction[8] and wrote (4 July.94): "I did not find that Livia was 'flaming', I only found a strong reaction". In the same letter Liz took the view that a "flame" could be easily defined: "If it were flaming, there would have been personal insults". This justifies the accusation of over-reaction: what was happening was not "flame war", but discussion. Some members appear to have seen both Livia's replies to Ann and Ann's reply to Livia as attacks, while others saw Livia's remarks as justifiable expression and Ann's public deletion of Livia as over-reaction, while fewer others saw Livia's comments as 'personal attacks' and Ann's remarks as an avoidance of conflict.

As indicated, flaming and list insecurity were already on people's minds. Though many knew each other from other lists, there were strangers on this new list, and there had been no time to develop a list style, or sense of continuity, to buttress its existence. It only takes a few people to create a flame war. Although many people commented indirectly on the dispute (and it certainly influenced the mails on community, uncertainty of identity and presentation which occupied people in this first month), the number of people directly involved was small, most mail came from five people, and not more than twelve commented directly, yet the perception was the dispute was overwhelming the list. This arises as mail creates the locale-framing of the group, and so mail of one mood (in this case hostile) dominates over the more fragmented moods of other mails. In offline social life people can walk away from, or otherwise avoid, arguments. Online argument is more or less impossible to avoid, and the normal gestures of presence and reassurance of offline conversation do not occur[9]. Offline relationships have more facets and connections than online relationships, particularly when the online relationships are new. Offline relationships are more multiplex than simplex. Online arguments tend to be before an audience, rather than offlist and private. In offline WES social life, arguments before an audience are usually regarded as more serious than arguments in private.

In such an environment, where physical force is difficult to bring to bear, and it is next to impossible to exclude people (particularly in newsgroups), public condemnation and humiliation are the only obvious ways to exert social control. Thus flames are often used to establish membership boundaries and to point out those not familiar with the conventions of the group and, presumably, get them to learn or leave. The list may become almost unreadable in a flame war, which also tends to drive away those without commitment to it.

There have been frequent claims that the removal of identity markers releases inhibitions, or that it is easier to express hatred in email as there are no 'real life' consequences[10]. Thus Amy asks (4 Aug.97):

> What is it about e-mail that provokes these types of 'flame wars?' I think it's partly a result of 'instant' communication. We write something and zap it off without putting enough thought into it sometimes. (And we're more likely to say something nasty because we're not face to face.) I think there's potential for this to be a negative impact of e-mail.

Andy replies:

> Virtual anonymity. Some people do not filter what they say because they are not worried about a punch to the nose or a knee in the groin.

TS adds:

> Lack of inhibition is the key here.

Alan writes:

> [email] mediation creates the simulacrum of an emptied_chora,_ locus of drives, inchoate affect. It's here that action is taken, because the action

> appears free-form, without culture, without consequence, with only the primal rupture of eliminating the token of the other. There's no gaze, no voice; it carries the ethological notion of deferment/deterrence one step farther.
>
> Like cyber-relationships, flaming is thereby involved with projection and narcissism; it's a textual void one attempts to annihilate.
>
> The wonder is, not that flaming is present, but that it's not more pervasive than it is[11].

Such an argument assumes an underlying tendency to aggression or 'uncontrollable emotions', held in check by society. However flame war might arise from the structure of lists and newsgroups.

If I suggest something offensive to my reader in 'one to one' email, then they can either ignore it, or respond and discuss it. If we are close, the correspondence continues because a decision is made (involving only two people) that the 'relationship' is too important (or multiplex), to engage in abuse which might threaten it. If, however, I write something offensive or irritating to a proportion of a group of 300 people (which is possibly hard to avoid), most of whom don't know me or vice-versa (that is, our ties are exaggeratedly simplex), then by force of numbers someone is likely to respond strongly on some occasions. This may stimulate others, who may in turn stimulate others, until the volume becomes large enough for people to flame people for flaming—even if I have decided to make peace, or even if there are only a few people involved. The resultant struggle has nothing to do with whether it is easier to express hatred or not in email, simply that it is harder to get all 300 or so people, with little other interconnection, to stop responding[12].

Explanations, which focus on emotions, aggression and authenticity alone, are socially constructed outside the net, and brought into it. Thus, there seems to be a social knowledge or expectation that low flaming groups will be predominantly female (cf Baym 1995: 158), and hence that flaming is an act of masculinisation, perhaps tied to the construction and preservation of a defined men's space as a mode of identity. This association with masculinity may be a factor in one attack made on Cybermind, and is an often remarked gender difference (see Chapter 9). Just after the 'spelling war' in which *all* the most vocal participants had been women, a list member asked "Are women netters less likely to be flamethrowers? Are we marginalized on the net?".

As well as stemming from communicative organization, flaming may also stem from asence, as the easiest way to get acknowledgment is to irritate or attack people, particularly people with whom the flamer has no connection. The responses received demonstrate the flamer's existence, and so reduce their asence. In this vein, Shirky points out that if people agree with a post then discussion and presence stops. The main way that online discussion and presence can continue is with disagreement, so "the liveliest and longest running discussions tend to be the ones in which the most people disagree with each other" (1995: 44)[13].

Burnout and Reading

Burnout, weariness or exhaustion, are frequently mentioned phenomena of Internet social life. Initial enthusiasm can give way to a haze of boredom and frustration. Some people back away from the net, and some keep aimlessly hanging around looking for the same excitement. Sometimes the burnout declines and the person can reinvolve themselves with their online groups. Two people have reported to me that the experience is unlike that generated by any other social activity — most of which continue to get better as one becomes more proficient.

Exhaustion arising from the continual need to re-present one's existence to others has briefly been mentioned. Another possible cause of 'exhaustion' arises from the circumstances of the act of reading. As this writer remarked (9 June.95):

> I frequently get overwhelmed by the sheer quantity of mail, and the correspondence i want to maintain.

As well as lack of acknowledgment, feeding into any lack of self worth a person might already have, online life may tend to induce melancholia as, at the limits, not everything can be done. It is difficult to be both on top of things and completely involved. If list activity is high, then not everything can be read and reflected upon. Mail can be saved like a burdensome memory, perhaps revealed in the size of the mailbox. Not only did I end up with mail which I found interesting saved into folders, but the active box would often contain over 700 mails requiring attention or reply, and as mailboxes got bigger this number increased. Periodic purges of my mailbox removed the solidity of memory and I could begin again in a more manic mode.

Another explanation for burnout might stem from the lack of formal roles and obscurity (asence) of personal boundaries. A society with formal roles, can provide restrictions upon demands made by others, and give strength and direction to actions one takes. Trying to deal with a society in which the absence of roles is marked, and where there are few limits to possible demands or responses, could intensify burnout. As suggested earlier, as a person only exists in their current actions; status and recognition onlist must be continually maintained, or the person becomes unknown, unnoticed and subject to the stringencies of being unrecognised. There can be little rest in such an occupation.

Histories

In offline societies the use of reminiscence to say how things were done or should be done, and to tell stories of mutual triumph, or to relate present events to some distant past, is clearly common even in gaming groups that only meet once a week (see Fine 1983: 139ff.). Tradition is reinterpreted to prove the current and continual existence of the group[14]. This occasionally, though rarely, occurs on Cybermind. However, as onlist communication is text based, it is possible to keep records of the group's activities and to render human memory less essential.

On Cybermind it seems to have been decided, within two weeks of the list starting, to collect the postings in 'archives'. Such archives are vulnerable to their keeper's lack of interest, or lack of time available for maintenance. The original archives held by Marius Watz, which ran from just after Michael's death, were lost after he left the list. Archives were kept at the University of Virginia from the time of Spoon's arrival until Cybermind left for AOL, when they were deleted. Richard McKinnon tended another set of archives on his personal web site between March 1995 and October 1996 when he ran out of computer space. These archives were transferred to a site in Hong Kong were they lapsed, taking no new items, until Jerry Everard rescued them, installing them at the Australian National University from May 1997, where they ran until 2000 when they stopped taking new items. AOL also collects archives but deletes so as to only keep three years worth of posts. Some list members also kept private offline archives at various times. Archives are not stable.

Although I have no idea to what extent these archives were consulted by 'the average list member', some people collected selected posts to Cybermind[15] and very occasionally past posts resurfaced. Alan, in particular, occasionally reposted some of Michael Current's writings to keep the sense of his presence alive, and Michael's death is the only historical event recorded in the manifesto.

There is very little in overt reminiscence about the group, despite plenty of reminiscencing about the personal (or the public; as when George Burns, the comedian, died), which makes this absence all the more marked. The general feeling is of a place with little or no history, in the sense of shared story, and no time—just a collection of events. There is no formal reiteration of 'group learning'. If Cybermind continues, then the events described in the history chapter will be largely forgotten. As Alan writes (pc 2 Apr.98):

> The list has a long and complicated history, as every list does, but there seems to be little reference to it, which I also find interesting; instead, it seems to look forward.

This may have to do with the general futurity of net discourse, but it may be a generational effect. If, for example, the majority of people posting to the list were not there five months ago, then what can a long-term member reminisce about which will have any common understanding or support? The 'new generation' will only have a fairly shallow history to share. By asking for clarification they may risk revealing their newness (to those even newer) and risk status.

The lack of public reminiscence, and perhaps uncertainty about the presence of others, may mean that people are only able to publicly remember or discuss things they think everyone remembers, or which are traumas with 'no blame' to anyone on list—such as the 'freaks' escapades discussed in Chapter 10. Absence of common story may reinforce a sensation of fragility. The infallible memories of the machine seem to weaken the memories of participants, and history is only vague. In the period in which the archives became non-current, there may have been more group reminiscence. Pickard reports the suggestion of a 'MR_D' that online groups have no history because events can be checked in the archives, and this leaves no room for people to exaggerate, improve or otherwise change stories to fit the current situation adequately (1998: ch.4). However, people did not seem to check the reminiscences of others in this way; challenges to the narrative tended to be made in terms of the other person's memory of events.

Douglas argues, "Public memory is the storage system for the social order", and that "Certain things always need to be forgotten for any cognitive system to work" (1987: 70, 76). So we need to ask if this lack of tradition serves, or arises from, a social function. Difficulty of cooperation in performing group-recognized tasks might mean there is little to anchor the passage of time, and little sense of group development. Historical time might, to WES people, be a record of change, so if change is not obvious, then time may not be noticeable. Attempts to petrify change through telling of the past may serve more of a negative than a positive function. Though the recognised might have an interest in history to justify their status, their status really depends upon current action, and the more recent members have little to gain from learning the history of the group. Ease of leaving suggests that if it is too difficult to gain 'cultural competence' within a group, and there is not that much recompense for learning it, then people will go elsewhere. Similarly the common recent response of established List members to queries about what has happened in a person's time away is that the List is not as good as it used to be, which perhaps situates status in a largely uncheckable past. A direct question about what people remembered in January 2007 primarily elicited the recall of member's deaths (cf Chapter 7) followed by the trolling episode described in Chapter 10, the conference and the writing of the novel; all of which suggest that memorable moments are those in which the List was almost completely focused on one topic, and which did not involve combat amongst established members. This implies history could be integrative, making it still more interesting that it is indulged in so infrequently.

Douglas also suggests that groups with hierarchy and ascriptions have far more need to use history to justify and naturalize the current ascriptions, than groups without them (1987: 80). Although Cybermind has no need to justify ascriptions and hierarchy, it also implies behaviour might be justified not by historical tradition but by some situational, or possibly, eternal or 'natural' tradition. I shall suggest in the next chapter the importance of a factor which is considered non-historic, namely, authenticity.

Chapter 6: The Reign of Authenticity

Introduction

This chapter investigates some of the problems arising from a demand for, and an expectation of, authenticity. Although it has frequently been suggested that people use the Internet to explore a 'postmodern' multiple or decentered self, this does not appear to be the case in practice. On Cybermind and the other lists and MOOs I have experienced, the main aim, or expectation, seems to be to uncover, or display, the authentic self. This causes problems because authenticity has to be indicated by conventions, whilst at the same time defining itself in opposition to conventions, etiquettes or rules. It will be argued that ways of indicating authenticity on Cybermind make use of references to the body, to gender, to breaking rules, and to the public/private division.

Authenticity behaviour is often portrayed as therapeutic as it reveals hidden, truthful, and therefore genuine, parts of the self. Thus a list member writes (27 Sep.95):

> For me, […], it is a place of freedom from all the masks I must wear in my daily life. This is a little hard to explain briefly. Also, it is a space which provides at least an illusion of freedom for a while from some of the 'thrown' aspects of our lives. I can speak to you as I perceive myself to be, free of the accidents of age, sex, race[1], physical status, economic situation… those things which I am but which I did not choose to be.

Another woman writes to me (25 Nov.01):

> How much of the supposed real has a hefty dose of the "unreal" already built-into it… Why do we call cspace virtual if we find ourselves in it more truthful sounding to ourselves than we usually are at work or at home?

Authenticity is a congerie and it is not unchanging. Here I use this term in the manner of Trilling (1974) and C. Taylor (1991) to specify a more rigorous moral demand than 'sincerity'; a demand to truly and *consistently* express a person's real self. Contemporary WES models of authenticity are intertwined with ideas of individualistic, self-determining freedom and self-expression. Other pre-existing and overt social rules are usually considered to restrict authenticity. However, authenticity needs to be recognized, and itself has to be indicated by conventions which, in this case, include references to 'the body', to 'underlying emotions', to breaking rules, and to gender. Authenticity is also influenced by distinctions between public and private; particularly as the private constitutes the intimate which is particularly under the sway of the authentic.

In Chapter 1 it was proposed that all communication requires framing to allow interpretation, and that etiquette was important in demonstrating this framing. It is not possible for us to perceive inner states or intentions—we can only infer them, make predictions and explanations of actions, or hope our inner states 'resonate' with those of others—all of which we do by interpretation. Similarly, it is not possible to express ourselves without 'tools', which both enable and channel the expression and what we are able to express. Effective expression is further influenced, with varying degrees of mutuality, by the interpretations made by others, and the situation as defined by others.

Etiquette, or ritualized communication, functions to establish the nature of a situation, its predictability and whether the people involved can be trusted. Etiquette may serve to establish status and power differentials but, as Whigham points out for Elizabethan England, concern with etiquette can also function as a tool of social fluidity (1984: 5), and it may even protect the 'oppressed' by rendering certain overt behaviours difficult. Etiquette may distinguish members of an ingroup from each other through proficiency, and it may distinguish the ingroup from those who cannot perform adequately—this is as much the case with etiquettes of flame as of 'politeness'. All human societies will have some behaviour functioning in this manner[2]. People in WES society generally call for authenticity. The 'outer' (public face) should not hide or disguise the 'inner' (private face). Trust is established when a person is convinced that another's 'inner' is on display, and that this inner is acceptable.

Authenticity in General: Offline, Public and Private
'Authenticity' has a history. Norbert Elias has argued that a successful 'Parliamentary regime' requires the suppression of physical violence between participants, and an increase in their restraint levels, allowing peaceful dispute and change of power. The more the regime is inclusive the more this is the case (Elias & Dunning 1993: 27-40, 171-4). It also requires that people have some sense of their interdependence. This change in explicit hierarchy correlates with a feeling that formal deference behaviour is not as relevant as

previously, and (given mobility) it is harder to enforce by those who previously received deference. He summarises by writing, "The tendency [nowadays]... is towards the same behaviour in all situations" (1996: 29).

This sameness of behaviour attempts to represent a truth, an authenticity, or openness which is itself compulsory, yet requires great control over certain behaviours and feelings (Brinkgreve 1982: 52-3). These restraints are supposed to be mutual, irrespective of status difference (Wouters 1990: 69). Wouters argues that:

> many people may not even experience or recognize any constraint, as it is a constraint to be unconstrained. As status competition intensified and the art of obliging and being obliged became more important as a power resource, demonstrations of being intimately trustworthy while perfectly at ease also gained in importance... Thus, the rise in public or anonymous intimacy—part of increasing emotional and behavioural alternatives—ran in tandem with rising demands on emotion management (Wouters 1995a: np).

This kind of balance required (or selected for) a relatively controlled personality style, able to negotiate, compromise, and to avoid giving offence to an extended range of ingroup members. Towards the end of the 20th century, this kind of style began to coexist uneasily with a more brash style (valuing being able to live on credit and impulse buy), which also indicates its truth through aggressive authenticity. It might also be suggested that the more corporatism becomes dominant, or the less people feel mutually interdependent, the less people will regard the feelings of their opposition.

Thus, although bound up with counterpositions, the tendency of the WES world has been towards the removal of *formal* ritual and etiquette from social life and their replacement by demands for transparency and 'authenticity'[3]. This is not entirely possible as ritual and etiquette frame, or comment upon, events making it possible to interpret them. Denial of formal etiquette and ritual, interacts with the need for it, in specific ways which have particular and important effects online, both in the application of social control and the symbolism of human 'bodies'.

In the embedding WES world we can see removals of formal ritual and etiquette occurring in such things as the disparagement of judges for wearing wigs and gowns or being seated at a higher level than the rest of the court. Occasional 'pageants' are acceptable, but these are not seen as 'meaningful' and are usually explained in terms of tourist dollars or marketing[4]. Many WES people seem to think ceremony distracts from the authenticity, truth and efficiency of the situation, and that its only function is to establish status differences which are perceived as 'wrong'. It is possible that dislike of formal rituals could be a way of denying the contradiction between obvious inequalities of power and supposed democratic equality in WES society. This is not to deny there are not regular events which help define List mood and which could be described as ritual, as when Drew observes (22 April.02)

> ceremony enters in the form of Maurizio's daily musings [witticisms...] and Alan's posts, which are ceremonial, almost to the spiritual degree of daily community prayers.

Such events are not formal and could be seen as accidental (only Drew ever made this kind of remark outside of mourning), even though they do select for a particular kind of audience.

WES people often seem to consider that what they define as unpleasant or aggressive is the real, and the pleasant is a front, particularly if the unpleasant was private. Secret corruption will seem more real than hidden virtue[5]. If a WES person discovered someone was thinking murderous thoughts and they did not previously know this, they would probably think this revealed *the truth*. In other places this might be regarded as a natural condition of no particular consequence, or simply a further thing to know, or only a problem if it manifested as murderous behaviour. A prime strategy of truth or significance is to claim to have uncovered, or unmasked, the underlying, and if it is 'violent' or 'unpleasant' that proves its truth (Trilling 1974: 141; Latour 1993: 44).

Surprisingly, there seems to be almost no counterpositionary mytheme to the virtue of authenticity, of expressing one's inner truth[6]. The 'multiple self' position usually substitutes truly expressing multiple selves for truly expressing one self[7] — and it doesn't actually seem relevant in Internet practice. Even those who claimed to fake selves did so in order to reveal or berate the inauthenticity of those they attacked (see Chapter 10). This lack of counterposition occurs despite the mytheme that modern capitalism requires the continual reinvention, or 'flexibility', of the self to accord with flexibility of employment (E. Martin 1994; Sennett 1999). On the whole, the mytheme implies continual reinvention is not good, and it is furthermore class based as talented executives will still be held to save the company through the talents/self which is uniquely theirs, and which requires special remuneration. More ordinary 'workers' have to be flexible, while management either expresses its inherent talent, or attends 'self-development' seminars to learn to express its inherent talent, status and success (Boxall 2003). Authenticity can thus be related to status and aspiration.

'Authenticity' becomes a hidden prescriptor, a denied etiquette which is, supposedly, not separate from the person as they 'really are'. As such the personal world of the person does not belong to the person alone but to everyone, while at the same time we distinguish public and private and value one over the other. Despite the mythemes of postmodernism, authenticity removes multiplicity from the self, by making only one self or self-presentation acceptable.

Public and Private

The mytheme of authenticity is intersected by another distinction, that between 'public' and 'private'. Although being conceived as exclusive polarities, public and private are relative, they are fuzzy framing categories that shade into each other and are rife with ambiguities which affect arguments relying upon their differences. The private generally takes the realm of the 'authentic' and the public that of display. There is pressure for the public to match the private — yet their difference gives each its value, and each private group is another form of public.

Elias argues that the formal division between 'public' and 'private' originated in the Eighteenth Century with the bourgeoisie. Previously, European Court and Peasant societies did not have the same division (1983: 114; Riley 1992: 184, 213; Mennell 1992: 134). The growth of the contemporary division is linked to divisions between: capital (private property) and State (public property); 'Public life' as the official behaviour of the State and 'Private life' as that of the individual unconcerned with government; between 'home' and 'work'; and to the development of modern male and female roles.

In WES societies the distinction between 'public' and 'private' is a focus of political and social, concern and dispute. Lawyer James Boyle argues that people in WES societies are theoretically equal within the 'public' sphere (when facing the State), but unequal in the private sphere (of culture and commerce). Capitalist political theory must exalt equality while confining this to a particular sphere (Boyle 1996: 26). It might be suggested that much of this particular political theory is devoted to diminishing that which is considered 'public', and extending the sphere of 'private' corporate possession and procedures. WES corporations, in general, act to disengage from 'civil' obligations into private benefits alone (Breslow 1997: 251). As the application of Justice differs depending upon whether it is a matter of public or private law, controversial legal issues are often about the placement of the case in the 'correct' sphere (Boyle 1996: 27).

The distinction between public and private also seems connected with the formal elision of etiquette and ritual. The private is ideally the intimate sphere, devoid of etiquette and transparent to fellow members while opaque to outsiders. As, for most people in the WES world, communication is about transparency and revealing inner truths, so intimacy is measured in lack of privacy, or even a hostility to the public[8]. We feel *all* of ourselves should be acceptable to the 'intimate other' (Bauman 1992: 84-8), and that the private is 'true', rather than 'a truth'. However, formal ritual and etiquette may provide a greater range of tools for 'self elaboration' than a less visible or denied etiquette.

We are morally supposed to have a perfect match between public display and the private 'reality', which leads either to personal suppression or overvaluation of the uncontrolled. At the same time the difference between the public and private indicates intimacy. Hence the people on the List fear State or Religious censorship (see Chapter 3), as that would turn the private and intimate into the public and barren.

If most people manifest different selves in different locales then management of these selves and situations, and control of spillage from one area to another, is part of the demand of living in those situations[9]. Different publics are kept private or separate. So, despite a demand for a single authenticity, the multiplicities of publics requires multiple self-presentations, and the intimate requires a marking of difference from the public. This is a 'contradiction' in WES groups, which is usually elided by focusing on one side or another.

Public/private distinctions are often said to be transformed by information technology. Meyrowitz argued, before Internet usage was widespread, that electronic media (particularly television) restructures the ways people separate public and private, or on and offstage, behaviours, thus transforming society (1985: vii). Different role audiences can be brought together, or prove harder to keep separate (ibid: 5, 23-4). New connections can sidestep the hierarchies' previous ways of linking people, or presenting them to each other (ibid: 63-9, 161-2). New forms of public and private are created, though the distinction is not destroyed.

Jones suggests that the Internet is worrying because it brings 'immoral' strangers into the 'moral' home; it blurs impersonal (public) and personal (private) relations (1997a: 21). In Meyrowitz's terms it shows children how adults can behave in ways which are usually hidden from them.

A similar change is often held to transform the political realm. Thus Harrison writes to Cybermind (6 Dec.94), "Is not the net perhaps the only kind of public space to appear since the 18th and 19th Century forms have ceased to function?" Frederick (1993) argues that the Internet allows the birth of a global civil society, particularly instancing the case of agitation to free Tibet from Chinese rule. Likewise Derrida gives the conventional opinion:

> electronic mail today, even more than the fax, is on the way to transforming the entire public and private space of humanity, and first of all the limit between the private, the secret (private or public), and the public or the phenomenal... [This] must inevitably be accompanied by juridical and thus political transformations (1996: 17).

Much of the concern about Internet regulation focuses around the argument of whether the Internet should be defined as a 'private' exchange of messages like phone-lines or the mail, or 'public' like television[10].

In the course of this book we shall have cause to see how the ambiguities of the expectations of public and private play out online. Online, people appear to grade the levels of privacy and occasionally contest the classification. In general, people consider privacy to be greater offlist than onlist, and greater onlist than in a newsgroup. Posting offlist mail to Cybermind was almost universally considered an offence. Surprisingly Witmer found that people would engage in "risky" communications on newsgroups, even though they could be identified, and concluded that privacy was not an issue (1998: 140). However, this may well have changed with the storage of newsgroup archives which renders 'speech' more permanent; and posting from anonymous addresses has always been common.

Authenticity Online

Authenticity is sometimes seen as inevitable online[11]. Thus Karen, praising the warmth and openness of Cybermind, writes (4 Feb.96): "we are all *essence* here... there is absolutely no way you can hide here". DLR writes (14 Aug.96): "Here I am more truly myself than I have ever been in PL". Another member writes (22 Jan.96): "I think the attraction of this dwelling is that to a certain extent one can be the persona one chooses"[12]. In response to this, some people were quick to point out that inauthentic expression is, likewise, easier for the same reason.

Counterpositionally the Internet can be seen as encouraging inauthenticity. Mark writes (22 Feb.95):

> the fragility of the net is a blessing because it reaffirms the fixity of FTF [face to face] comm... The net is powerful; as powerful an illusion our culture has produced to date. But it is ultimately a diversion; its not being in the world... what makes the net possible and sustains it is precisely the knowledge that there is so much more when you jack out...
>
> And isn't that just the worry? That people who thrive on the net help erode humanity in *all* its ramifications?

Assumptions about 'underlying truth' also contribute to flaming, as people assume that by goading a strong response they are getting a genuine response. Strong 'emotional' responses are supposed to be uncontrollable and 'underlie' the person. However, a strong response can be generated as easily as a bland one. As we shall see, an apparently careless or quick response with spelling errors may be construed as 'genuine', as it has (presumably) not been tailored. Lack of etiquette locks into a formality only slightly less rigid than the etiquette disparaged.

This insistence upon authenticity as a focus governing net discourse might be challenged by frequent reports of the use of multiple identities on the net, or the free play of idenity, particularly when joined with theories of a 'postmodern' decentering of the self. For example Turkle writes:

> in the daily practice of many computer users, [computer interface] windows have become a powerful metaphor for thinking about the self as a multiple distributed system... Thus more than twenty years after meeting the ideas of Lacan, Foucault, Deleuze and Guattari, I am meeting them again in my new life on the screen. But this time, the Gallic abstractions are more concrete (1995: 14-15).

Reid describes people on Internet Relay Chat (IRC) as engaged in "deconstruction" and enabled:

> to escape the assumed boundaries of gender, race and age [and] create a game of interaction in which there are few rules but those the users create

themselves. IRC offers a chance to escape the language of culture and body and return to an idealised 'source code' of mind (1991: np)[13].

However multiplicity is not particularly 'postmodern' (Zizek 1997: 140ff.). The multiple self is a standard part of late 19th century psychology[14], and in practice authenticity is taken to be the truth behind appearances. Potential multiplicity may make this more complex, but it does not delete people's quest for the single, private, inner truth of others[15].

This is brought out in the responses to a question of Alan's (18 May.97): "Are you certain of your own identity when you are on-line? If not, does it seem to matter to you?". Despite knowing of the postmodern multiple self, and some respondents' admission of confusion about their selves (which might come from expectations of one true self), most respondents claimed the net expanded their sense of self rather than liberated new selves or allowed new selves to form. At the same time others made statements like "my identity is constant. it doesn't shift...", or "I am always certain of my identity". Enok writes: "That's why I am on the Net—to ge searching for my identity, which I feel is greater then I am told it is". Paula writes:

> online I can explore different aspects of myself that aren't possible offline. Being online doesn't make me feel I am becoming someone else, I have never feared that. Rather I feel this is a place I can learn more about myself, both through the contact I have with other people and through my characters at moos.

This kind of discourse of therapy or self-enhancement is common, as the authenticity gained online is carried into offline life. KNS writes: "Being online has helped me to integrate parts of myself that I could not express otherwise. I can now express them more in everyday life". and G writes:

> I feel there is a trend towards greater disclosure of feelings, more naked self, in any form of written communication Vs spoken communication. However, I have noticed that after indulging in 3 years of e-mail I tend to express my feelings more IRL and am unafraid of making myself vunerable in this way. So I would say that the two states are converging[16].

Virtuous WES discourse implies a single authenticity for each being, which can be revealed or uncovered. Even masks are held to reveal what is truly there and otherwise not expressed. Thus, even though many knew that Gordon, who attacked the list, was 'wearing masks' and his self-presentation could not be taken at face value, it is doubtful members would have guessed he might have been, among other things, a children's book illustrator. Transparency is the ideal, but as a mode of organising it creates problems.

Authenticity in Action

Concern with authenticity, and the need to resolve asence, explains features of the opening weeks 'Spelling Wars'. The problem proposed by the initial complainant, was lack of clarity of expression, and the lack of proofreading. However, almost the whole debate shifted to issues of correct spelling. The typo was used by the complainant as an organising focus for questions of "unclarity", "ill written verbiage" or "unthought out arguments", but, in being appropriated by others, became the axis of a debate about authenticity, equity and personal truth, abandoning the complainant's stated problems.

An etiquette of transparency means that adherence to certain kinds of forms, which might be criticised by 'polite' norms, can be seen as indicators of authenticity. For example Liz (2 Jul.94) takes 'irregular form' as a pattern of genuineness: "The typos denote a certain haste, a certain 'must-speak-now'... a certain emotional charge...". She claims this implied "that in fact we are communicating, mind to mind./Or learning to do so". So despite denial of the importance of "style", certain styles denote "Thought and conviction", and in this case the removal of (bodily) barriers to communication ("mind to mind"). Likewise Cynthia (3 Jul.94) claimed typos were not "indicative of quality of thought or capacity for thoughtfulness" and that they could be a virtue ("typos or fast-speech-in-e-space or whatever it is, can produce positive effects"), citing the original error "realativity" as "actually pretty provocative", although never developing this "provocation".

Discussion began to break down, with Ann's response to Liz's statement that Liz did not want to have to avoid words which "may offend shall we say, more delicate sensibilities". Ann wrote (3 Jul.94):

> As for resorting to obscenities, I find it offputting. I tend to judge people who use obscenities quite negatively. I assume that they lack cogent language, they've run out of real arguments.
>
> Plus, I feel they show a lack of respect for the reader, especially for the many very young readers on the net, and, frequently, for women (whose minimal presence is often noted).

As might be expected, some list members considered that 'obscenities' lay on the valued side of the assumed-to-be-transparent/authentic, line of communication, along with 'non-standard grammars'. Cynthia responded (3 Jul.94):

> and on obscenities: don't assume. i'm a girl and i use them all the time, and not because i am at a loss for words or can't manage an argument. they have other uses, that is, aside from indicating a lack of breeding or specific acculturation (they can be a sign of specific acculturation).

Yet another, apparently female, reader was even more direct. Livia wrote a one-line reply[17]: "Cogent language, yet? Gimme a fucking break".

Ann then publicly stated her rejection of Livia, rather than taking a private decision: "Sorry, you get no break. My negative judgment is upon you. I will delete all further messages from you unread". Livia responded (3 Jul.94):

> What do you other cybers think? I happen to be 'off put' by the Freshman Comp teacher mentality. Yeah... of course I was a Freshman comp teacher. Never had the mentality, though... kids learned to write just fine... without idiotic attitudes about 'writing cogently'

Here Livia uses authenticity by implying Ann is teaching a subject which is taught easily, which people learn automatically (as expression results from authenticity), and which she has taught successfully herself[18]. Ann, it is implied, is setting up elitist barriers, or promoting 'falsity', and Livia makes an appeal to an unspecified creativity of not acknowledging 'rules'—which, as seen earlier, marked the spelling mistake as "provocative".

With authenticity as a virtue, freedom to be one's true self is a prime requirement, and thus must not be excluded or silenced. Alan's first reply makes appeal to net discourses of freedom and anarchy and to Cybermind as an alternate outside normal academia which accepts more and different people (which again can be perceived as variant on authenticity, as people are to speak online without worrying about offline power and status issues)[19]. He writes:

> No one has authority here beyond the words he or she speaks. I for one would regret anyone unsubscribing because of someone else's faulty spelling, but I would rather tolerate the unsubs than set down protocol—
>
> there are no grades in cyberspace (sounds like a Clash song[20])!

This phrase "beyond the words he or she speaks" illustrates that email tends (unless the person is being specifically careful), to be characterised as speech rather than text[21]. Thus, comments on proofreading have the potential to be read as comments on speech rather than comments on text. Email has a perceived closer relationship to 'identity' than does the essay. Informality maps to intimacy. Tendencies for email to become "essays" can appear to remove intimacy from speech, not only through their formality, but the length also suggests a lack of spontaneity. Livia writes towards the end of this discussion (7 Jul.94):

> I worry about screensful upon screensful of postings which may have 'lots' of substance of without an 'atmosphere of comraderie' in which to chew on them become just somebody's disembodied essays. I find myself hitting the SAVE key [...] when things get too lon, too crafted offline, too print, ... just another one of those essays you saved without reading [...][22]

To comment on writing style, is a form of exclusion, as tactless to this audience as commenting negatively on someone's appearance or accent in front of others would be in their offline lives. Text is their being, or only evidence of being, which again explains why typos (marks) rather than unclarity (absence) became the focus.

Tension may arise, in the wider middle-class US culture, between: a) standards of avoiding conflict in intimate (private) relationships; and b) the demand for transparency or authenticity which translate into a "strong emotional statements are the only true or genuine statements" position. However, even within the same framing, strong emotional statements can be flagged as either truthful, or as aggressive or antagonistic. As a result, and to solve the dispute while avoiding conflict, a number of writers suggested that Ann should "use the delete key" to solve her problem, that is, to delete mail unread without complaining or protest. The implication she should delete mail by particular writers is NOT mentioned. Openly mentioning particular people, as opposed to privately doing it without comment, would be perceived as a hostile act. Ann initially responded to the suggestion by writing that she has too much mail for this to be workable[23]. No one suggested that those who found Ann's comments annoying or irrelevant should simply delete *her* posts. The problems were not seen as equal and it seems people perceived the disruption as originating with her, rather than with those who responded to her. By her comments she had marked herself as an outsider, which implies the norms broken were norms existent outside of this particular group.

Another method of trying to avoid personal conflict, yet remark on the problem, is to "forward" posts from other lists which comment on the situation or act as evidence in the dispute. Presumably the person forwarding such items agrees with them but, if the posts are criticised, then it is not the forwarder being criticised as it is not *their* words. Such a prestation is a form of distancing, of using the 'impersonality' of the public. One person forwarded a review of a *Time Magazine* article "Bards of the Internet" from the newsgroup *alt.culture.internet* to support their position. The original article asked why there was so much bad writing on the Internet and the forwarded reviewer, David Sewell, states (3 Jul.94):

> Fact is, people write better here than they do in class. In class, you're writing up, to an artificial audience, an authority figure who enforces rules that you had no part in drafting, on the Net, you're writing to a vast audience of peers who are collaborating with you in creating an entirely new set of rules [...].
>
> I think the Net is the place where writing is being reinvented more vibrantly and creatively than anyplace else right now. And I don't mean the subdomain of the online world populated by the traditionally articulate [...] I mean good old filthy, flame ridden [...] Usenet [...].
>
> I've lived in a place where writing is genuinely 'awful' and dying because of it, the academic English department [...],
>
> Hacker culture has led to a fruitful marriage of language and technology, the likes of which English (at least) hasn't seen since Shakespeare and Ben Jonson were mixing botany and alchemy up with their Latin-based rhetorics.

This review uses similar strategies to those used by the list: firstly an appeal to democracy, lack of authority, and the irrelevance of rules; secondly, a more intimate connection than usual between writer and audience is postulated; thirdly the reviewer declares their academic competence while deriding the sterility and turgidity of academic writing; and finally, the flat assertion that writing on the Internet is creative, and is particularly creative at its most "impolite" and hence authentic. 'Creativity' here functions as an empty sign, a magical congerie like 'mana', guaranteeing potency. The assumption is that formality constrains an inherently good creativity, and that creativity is detected when formality is broken. Hence creativity's connection with the rules of authenticity. Ann may assume that creativity must involve a concern which is indicated by the removal of 'noise'.

Bodies and Authentic Expression

WES people often use metaphors implying the experience of body, sensation and emotions as being 'underlying', 'separate', 'force-like' and inchoate. We remark upon 'letting off steam', the 'animal within' (not referring to any 'real animals' but to a vision of vicious nature threatening society), or have notions of the pressure-cooker-like emotional id. Westerners often talk as if their body was struggling against them, as if they were divided. This view of the underlying becomes indicative of the authentic or real truth.

The question arises of whether this 'natural other' should be controlled or expressed. As Douglas might lead us to expect in groups supposedly devoid of ascribed roles or elaborated ritual codes and with a valuation of authenticity and transparency, people have usually valued expression. However, this causes problems as this expression is also defined as expression of the uncontrollable (e.g. aggression, emotion, desire) and there is no regular means to channel it or otherwise deal with it. People tend to fear 'outgroup' members expressing themselves as that expression may be particularly uncontrollable and disruptive, as seen in some explanations of flaming and some of the alarm about lurkers and what they might do.

As online discourse involves asence, signs of the body are brought in as an anchor to make what people are writing valid, or real, to them[24]. Gaps of contact are filled by importations of bodily constructions ('kiss', 'hug', 'smile' etc). This is perhaps more so when intimately private[25]. The more emotional involvement increases and becomes private intimacy, the more authenticity becomes important and direct typing is taken as transparency. In this society, as the relationship becomes important, ritual (particularly public ritual) is discarded. Deuel suggests that preprogrammed MOO actions are used less the more that netsex becomes 'real' (1996: 140). Messages given offlist, or offline (in private), are more likely to be considered authentic than messages received onlist or online. As Kendall writes:

> [People] privilege offline identity information over information received online... This allows them to continue to understand identity in the essentialized terms of a persistent and consistent self, grounded in a particular physical body (1998: 130).

Offline, one way we recognise intimacy is with the ease with which the other person's gestures and physical states evoke apparently similar or complementary states in ourselves. To recover this lost gesture, people use emoticons to try and express voice tone, and yet we have written for centuries without feeling the need for them. However, out of the vast range of emoticons depicted in dictionaries of such things, we commonly only use three:

;) [smile, or I'm not being serious],
:) [wink] and
:([sad expression/frown]

The glyphs ;-) :-) and :-(are equivalents.

We can easily imagine possible cultures which might not use these particular signs, or would use others[26]. Therefore, we need to ask 'why are these particular signs needed in this particular culture?'

Using these particular emoticons arises from the WES conventions that authenticity involves saying exactly what you mean and directly revealing your 'interior' or perhaps 'natural' state, yet, usually doing this without causing offence. 'The body', or 'body language', is taken as an underlying truth beneath discourse and hence is referred to in expression. This demand for transparency might lead to a reading that looks for only one value (although it may privilege certain recognised texts as multi-valued). In such a culture, irony and joking is fraught with the dangers of appearing to be either deceit or an expression of hostility. Hence the need to resolve these problems by indicating 'transparently' a person's supposed interior state if it apparently conflicts with the words. A society more pre-occupied with formalities and maintaining boundaries, and less concerned with transparent representation might generate different problems.

The concern with emoticons can be contrasted with the lack of explicit interest in other matters of layout, such as paragraphing and line length, which are of considerable force in providing indications of expression. This suggests emoticons are noticed because they are used in situations of unease or ambiguity[27].

Another way of using references to underlying offline emotions and body as authenticity framings, which is perhaps not unique to Cybermind, but which I have not noticed to the same degree elsewhere, is to comment on the emotional state of the sender as after they sign their name. For example:

[Name] *gnashing her teeth in despair* then clearly thinking better of it and smiling ruefully...

> [Name] (now wishing for chocolate covered strawberries in Memphis... its that time of year.
>
> [Name]wearyofthisworldspainlookingforitsjoyagain

These sentences are clearly separate from the letter, by being set after the signature, but they comment on the way the mail should be read, and usually refer to emotional physical states (i.e. teeth gnashing, smiling, eating, exhaustion), which imply an offlist life. Thus indicating a complex offline authenticity to the mailing[28].

Gender, Authenticity and Intimacy

Writing about online life constantly focuses on the question of whether someone is the sex they claim to be. Voluntarism is supposed to be supreme. McRae writes:

> mind and body, female and male, gay and straight, don't seem to be such natural oppositions anymore... The reason for this is simple: in virtual reality, you are whoever you say you are (1996: 245)[29].

However, it seems more accurate to say that although the occupiers may be fluid, the categories remain as rigid as ever. McRae herself points out that if someone plays a woman and wants to "attract partners as 'female' [they] must craft a description within the realm of what is considered attractive" (ibid: 250)[30]. As Kendall writes: "choosing one gender or another does nothing to change the expectations attached to particular gender identifications", and no one "encountering someone using the pronoun e[31] is likely to believe that this expresses their 'true' gender... Some may respect this desire to 'hide' gender, but others probably will not" (1996: 217)[32].

This supposed flexibility of gender is also a source of worry. Kolko and Reid write:

> The stories of online cross-dressing that abound, for example, often culminate in narratives of betrayal. In this accumulated body of scholarship, participants talk of how their notions of the world and their selves and others has been destabilized, rocked beyond recognition, until they are left feeling adrift, at sea, that they 'cannot trust anyone,' that 'everything online can be a lie,' that 'no one tells who they really are.' (1998: np).

Which leads to the question of why people are so continually nervous about the sex of people they meet on the net? It suggests that the 'true' gender of the other person is important for framing the interpretation of communication—it adds background, which enables text to be read, and suggests the possible styles of communication which can be engaged in.

In WES society, status and role differential is either dismissed, or said to be based entirely on magical congeries such as personal talent, despite vast differentials in access to wealth, power or recognition. The only role divisions recognised as (partly) legitimate are those of gender, and these roles are constructed in relation to sex and intimate bonding, gaining their legitimacy in those contexts. Thus they become tied to authenticity, not only through intimacy, but via the 'underlying' nature of 'the body'.

Online, it is rare for people not to take *a* gendered identity, or let their gender slip. However, all the side communications establishing gender do not exist; men[33] don't take out the garbage or mow the lawn, or women feed the kids and wash the clothes. Women may receive more attention from males in online society than in the embedding society. One correspondent stated that when she is on a MOO men are much less likely to "rave on forever". They listen to her and ask questions, probably because they need to involve her in conversation to make sure she is there and resolve asence.

If gender is the prime way we establish intimacy and make intimate exchange, and if in the embedding society intimacy almost always involves women (Cheal 1988: 180), then a relationship which is directed at the 'private' or offlist dyadic sphere will be influenced by, or even depend upon, gender. In general at least one of the participants might be expected to be female[34]. Intimacy and gender get conflated. Establishing that at least one of the party is a woman, allows closeness to manifest more easily. As already mentioned 'maleness' is commonly identified with aggression and flaming (even when the participants are women), and women are identified with more harmonious interaction, so are more appropriate for intimacy. Such identifications probably increase expectations in offlist exchange.

On Cybermind, most people are identified by their name, and naming conventions, as male or female. Of those few who use ungendered pseudonymous names, the majority are identified as male or female by use of a gendered name within the posts some time within their life on list. When Alan asked people on the list about 'changing' gender (18 May.97), of fourteen replies two implied it might be interesting to do but they hadn't. One had done it to "explore theoretical issues", two chose to make themselves spivak on MOOs (see note 31), and the rest couldn't be bothered. It was only on

MOOs that anyone thought it worthwhile to change gender, no one *admitted* doing it on a mailing list—perhaps because a list is more easily classified as totally private.

Only one prominent poster on Cybermind with a bi-gendered name did not explicitly reveal their claims to gender, and this person's gender was never the subject of overt concern to other list members. In the replies to some questions about gender and exchange discussed in Chapter 8, only one person, who themselves cultivated a degree of gender ambiguity (and did not answer any of the questions), mentioned uncertainty with respect to gender as relevant. The male gender of the person using the name 'dobie' did cause some members surprise, probably because of his 'gentleness' and his habit of writing emotions (e.g. *smile*[35]), but he never 'masqueraded' as female or as genderless. No one ever expressed surprise at discovering someone they thought was male was female. No one expressed any surprise about any particular person's gender after mid-1995. Clearly *among list members* gender was pretty much taken for granted as true.

This common usage of gender to indicate authenticity contrasts with formal declarations that gender does not matter. When DaveS (one of the few Cybermind members ever to openly express membership of the military) expressed surprise that Amethist was male, and stated that gender was fundamental to authenticity writing (23 Mar.95):

> Sex cannot be removed from the persona, it IS who we are! (changers and crossers be damned!)

Response was almost uniformly hostile. Criticisms were frequently made in terms of authenticity and limitation. Amethist explains the strength of the reaction as stemming from "those who resist being limited and defined by gender based ideologies". The mytheme is that gender constructions should not detract from expressions of the authentic self, but in practice gender is a prime symbol allowing the interpretation of authenticity and so can rarely be discarded, particularly when discourse shifts into the private or intimate realm, giving another 'contradiction' in group life.

Conclusion

Formal etiquette, or ritual elaboration as a mode of framing, is denied, and replaced by demands for authenticity. Authenticity itself has to be indicated and this involves a 'denied' etiquette which depends upon displays of strong (underlying) feeling, mistakes, evidences of speed, unpremeditated or unpolished communications, 'unpleasantness', 'unconventionality', references to the body, to underlying emotions, gender, and so on. Creativity is indicated by breaking rules and shows authenticity through this breaking. Private and public divisions, though shading into one another, require privacy and intimacy to be authentic, and expect the public to be inauthentic, which is, however, held to be immoral. These divisions not only frame messages but indicate the types of exchange which are expected. Email is ambiguous because it is perceived as speech (and hence identity) but it is also public and overtly mediated or, counterpositionally, transparent and almost telepathic. Despite suggestions that the postmodern self is deliberately multiple in response to rapidly and uncontrollably changing situations, indications are that people regard themselves and others as having one true self which is to be expressed in intimacy. 'Flexibility' may be 'good', but it is often thought to risk dispersion if it requires multiplicity. Irony and humour may cause problems of ambiguity in a regime of authenticity and thus indications of the body are used, as the body is held to constitute an underlying truth, to resolve these ambiguities. Gender, as particularly involved in intimacy and tied to the underlying body, is a primary tool used in interpreting authenticity and thus concern about the gender of others is particularly marked when it is not 'visible'—even when moral mythemes insist it should not be relevant.

There is also a potential conflict between flags of authenticity and flags of aggression (often revealed in interpretations of flaming), and this shall be considered in more detail in Chapter 9.

Chapter 7: Bounding the Body: Moods, Intensities and the Haunting

Introduction
This chapter explores problems deriving from using body references in an environment subject to asence[1]. The online body is often described as 'ghostly' when contrasted with a virile and active offline body. Online, personal boundaries appear fluid, which contrasts with offline moves to make boundaries impermeable and which reinforces the appearance of immateriality. On other occasions the body may be described as cyborg, which also expresses difficulties with boundaries and borders. Due to the use of the body as an interpretive mechanism, mood becomes a potent mode of framing online, and shapes people's responses when mail repeats a constant subject or style, as with flame, mourning, or netsex. In netsex, problems arise for people as gender exaggeration is frequently used to give charge to the experience, and thus appears to delete authenticity at the same time as supposedly allowing the most authentic contact.

Boundaries and Offline Bodies
Before discussing online boundaries in more detail, it is useful to return to offline body boundaries and some of the mythemes which circle around these ways of categorising and ordering people and selves.

Offline boundary anxiety is shown by the mytheme which holds that our bodies are dangerously porous to attack from ever-present outsider 'germs'. These germs are classically associated with matter out of place and come from other people or the natural world and overpower us when our personal or social boundaries are not maintained (Douglas 1969)[2]. This model nowadays includes other destructive boundary violators, such as carcinogens, radiation, chemical additives to food and genetic modification.

Similarly in the WES world, it appears that boundaries between groups, the methods of maintaining boundaries, and even the legitimacy of boundaries are insecure. People feel unable to control either their own or their group's destiny or security. Forces around people, whether we call them political, economic, criminal or ecological, seem impersonal, beyond control, and likely to overwhelm at any moment[3]. In the workplace the boundaries between work and home seem constantly threatened. In politics the global is said to threaten the local, and so on. People dispute which boundaries are threatened and what causes these threats, but they seem to agree that important boundaries are vulnerable. In response, some people try to construct boundaries which are impermeable to the outside, relatively hard and isolate, perhaps inevitably failing, as no such living boundaries exist. The wealthier middle-class seems keen to move into 'fortress enclaves' to keep out the outside world[4]. Politicians campaign to keep out refugees and illegal immigrants, and blame crime on religious, cultural or ethnic minorities who are defined as different and amongst us.

Boundaries and Online Bodies

As we have seen, online groups rarely have formal boundaries, and almost never have boundaries which are observable by all members. People wander in and out, and the majority of members either don't participate, or participate so infrequently they are invisible. A shifting core of people, who are bonded or joined by presence and seeking permanence, may be surrounded by an unformed sea of others. People might be able to express 'outwardly' without inhibition, thus giving a feel of intimacy, but there may be no response, thus giving the feel of absence and isolation. Asence is a product of unclear or vacillating personal boundaries and presence. Similar vacillation and uncertainty is clear in people's reports about their sense of body and its boundaries online.

On the 18th of May 1997 Alan asked questions of both Cybermind and FOP, relevant to this topic[5]. The first question was: "When you are on-line, do you feel that your body has a specific beginning and ending? Are you aware of your body?"

Several people implied they felt their bodies *extended* online. For example, Alan writes (19 May.97): "it's as if I'm extended into another space, boundariless". Paula, that it "frees me of many boundries. I'm free of my physical limitations and constantly encouraged to expand". G writes "there is no beginning and ending". Jerry (20 May.97): "my fingers reach out into the wires..." These statements, imply that online life reduces restriction, or the 'resistance of the Real', and hence 'materiality'. Nicholas is ambiguous:

> Yes and No. Muscles and cells remain jammed and packed as usual but simultaneously I feel there is a certain flow of intensity that squeezes through,

in and out the connection line. Initially I thought it was purely intelectual pleasure, then I became aware there was a certain involvement of the body

Other people implied that they lost awareness of their body while online. Kerry writes (19 May.97):

> [After logging in], body awareness subsides against the intense linguisticity, the concentration on/of what is being _said_ even as the digits and the pixels conceal and obscure

FOP2 wrote (21 May.97): "If there is ever a time when my body is simply carrying my eyes, this is it". KNS suggested that body awareness varies with activity, but also points to etherealisation (19 May.97):

> Different activities involve different physical sensations: reading on the web, my body is relaxed and I sprawl in the chair; posting I am more attentive, all my awareness focused on my fingers and I 'feel' my mind more;

Extension, and loss of body awareness was not my experience. Discomfort from hand pain while typing always made me aware of limits, and the possibility that if I did become immersed then I would be crippled, maybe for days. Orlando, G and Laurie, all of whom did *not* find that their bodies extended, or that there was a lack of boundaries, also mentioned ongoing pain. Others can suggest that the lack of clear boundaries is problematic:

> Initially I found the lack of resistance to be invigorating, perhaps an imagining of cold Air like Nietzsche's mountain tops, but cold air leads to frostbite— a withdrawal and numbness.

This lack of boundaries is not always conceived to be good, but it seems present if the body 'drops away' and little resistance is encountered.

Another question Alan phrased in terms of boundaries was: "Do you have immersion-feelings when on-line, lack of boundaries? If so, to what do you ascribe these?" Nicholas answered: "Immersion feelings yes, mostly dominated by the visual fascination of the screen". Alan himself suggests 'immersion feelings' are modality and interest dependent:

> I ascribe them to an identification with the site or domain I'm reading/writing. It happens more often when working on, say, javascript or

exploring sendmail, than when reading/writing email. It happens totally with Netsex, the strongest often in cuseeme.

Immersion was frequently linked with lack of awareness of time passing. For example zoogirl writes:

On-line (or whilst at the pc reading and writing) I feel immersed in what I'm doing to the extent that time telescopes and dissappears. I forget to eat (useful when dieting) and can usually carry on regardless of how tired I feel.

In a less extreme sense perhaps, Kerry writes: "Immersed Yes. For evidence, it's enough to look at the clock and see that 2 or 3 hours have evaporated". Rose also mentions time passing in this context: "I'll grant you this: the awareness of 'time elapsed' is suspended in this medium. Remarkably so". FOP1 agrees but is ambivalent about the result: "i have no sense of time passing. i can't gage if being online is the most useful expenditure of my time. should i be doing something else?"

Lack of time-awareness, as well as removing other boundaries, suggests that online time is in some ways removed from offline, or 'normal', time and thus reinforces the vagueness about history and the order, or succession, of events, mentioned in Chapter 5.

Again, this sense of immersion can be interrupted by 'real world factors' and the assertion of unexpected boundaries and categories:

there are boundries here. People still want to know too much. They still want me to reveal my gender and age at many places. Then, ironically, they are often disappointed when I tell them.

All of these responses imply that online, participant's sense of the boundaries to their bodies and selves are much less fixed than they are offline. They appear relatively fluid, although this fluidity can be disrupted by the unexpected importation of offline boundary factors such as pain, imposition of categories, and so on. For the person to become present or immersed online, their body becomes asent and this may be reinforced by the vagueness of group boundaries, or even the lack of boundaries on the web. There is little resistance to movement. It can set up an expectation of freedom, which then is unsatisfiable because of asent or hidden, but still active, offline factors.

One way of trying to overcome these ambiguous boundaries is to attempt to impose a rigid separation between online and offline, or between the net persona and the offline person. This forms another common and explicit online discourse, which rigorously separates the mind from the body, or words from actions. The argument usually alleges that no online social behaviour can affect a person offline, everything is public and people should not be hurt by words. Both Fractal and Richard took this position at the Cybermind Conference. Nearly all list members who commented seemed to disagree, which might be expected given the positive valuation of empathy as a marker of the group.

Given the existence and commonness of performative statements, which make something so by pronouncing it so (in the right framing), such a distinction between words and actions cannot be sustained; at best the difference is a continuum. To be obvious, the phrase "you are a Jew" had an effect in Nazi Germany, just like the phrase "you are an unlawful enemy combatant" can now. The law itself is 'just' words, and naming has consequences. We are defined by words, and particularly so online, where words are our weapons and putting people into social categories defines what should be done with them; possibly even more so than offline because its almost all we have to mark their presence.

Sustaining Mood (Death and Netsex)

As argued in Chapter 5, on an email List there is usually a great variety of messages, and a fairly fragmented discourse and mood. On one occasion Alan summed this up by writing (21 Aug.02):

> Every so often I walk away from my computer and come back, say, fifteen minutes later, and I realize I haven't got the vaguest idea what anyone is talking about.

Sustained mood, as a marked contrast, which can then act as a framing for messages, is rare, and when it occurs is often marked. Flame was discussed in Chapter 6. It can also occur with death and netsex, which will be discussed now.

Death

Sustained mood may explain people's surprise at their intense emotional responses to Michael Current's death. For example, Debra writes some considerable time later (31 Oct.96):

> The most powerful event of my online life (so far) was the death of Michael Current [...] I still don't understand why, as right now when I think of him I find tears in my eyes.

Argyle, lurking at the time, reports in her article that she wondered:

> What was going on with me? Why was I so upset? Why did I have to read all these messages. Why do I still think about it now? (1996: 136).

Even at the time of the death, many list members wrote as if they were surprised at the extent of their grief, and had therefore to justify their ties to Michael, usually by describing offlist contact, which was then taken as showing the existence of authentic and real private ties that could legitimate their grief.

The almost constant reiteration of grief, involving a relatively large number of people, produced a radically different experience from the normal disconnected modes of reading, and for some people this crossed over into other Lists. Fido wrote (24 July.94):

> For me the ritual has already begun in the cycling of messages repeated and repeated from list to list and I leaf through five, six seven copies of the same awkward anguish, one copy for each place we haunted together.

Not only was the mood sustained by these messages of grief, but the mood was a common one with a momentum of its own. We all have experienced grief, and most have ongoing griefs, and these can all resonate with each other. Argyle writes:

> The pain of the other's touched the pain held within myself. Personal experiences of loss, memories of funerals and the sorrow of those left behind all flooded me.... I grieved with them, for myself and my losses, and for theirs" (1996: 140).

Michael's family did not need to be protected from the grief of those distant from the deceased, and so the grief was not hidden. As Michael was both the moderator of the group and deeply articulate, he had symbolic resonances and was easily made prototypic for list identity. His death was defined by his relative youth and its unexpectedness as a 'bad death'; there could be no illusion of control or a gradual sequestration of the dying to prepare others for the events.

Despite people's suggestions or requests, group rituals were not used to maintain mood and there were no markers to remind people of the appropriate mood. Silence and quiet, which are common at WES funerals, for example, would simply imply that List members were not present or interested—an effect of asence again. Thus, even with the intensity of feeling around Michael's death, the list could only maintain the mood for several days, and returned to 'normal'. More pronounced grieving went on offlist and thus could not be observed by the List as a whole.

The death of perhaps the most loved and high-status member of Cybermind, Rose Mulvale, was different in that it was drawn out and slow. The illness and close-to-death period lasted from February 2001 until October 2002. This allowed irregular bulletins from her family to reach the List via List members, and sometimes family members wrote directly to the List using her email address. Occasionally the family would send letters which Rose had dictated herself. People would often ring the hospital and her home and report the news back to the List. People sent her presents and received them in return. At times Rose was well enough to participate on the List to much joy from everyone else.

Two days before she died Ian wrote:

> I have some sad but not unexpected news about Rose. As many of you may know I went to Nova Scotia for three weeks last month to help take care of her. She was failing but strong of spirit and maintaining regular correspondence with many of you when I arrived but each day she became weaker. Her friend Julie came from Ohio to take over her homecare from me and has been constantly by her side for the last two weeks. For the last week she has been confined to bed and having Cybermind and your messages printed out and read to her. She was playing the same friendly, wise, inspiring and generous role on some cancer lists. Early yesterday morning she was taken to hospital and is unlikely to return home. Her daughter and son-in-law arrived this morning to be with her. If you want to take one last chance to write to her, send a card to: [her address]. I know she would appreciate it as many of you meant so much to her.

This letter drew many responses to the List praising Rose and celebrating people's memories of her. The day she died Alan wrote:

> Rose for years and years was and still is the heart and soul of this list.
>
> Her writing was always, always, generous; she called cyberspace "This beautiful place," and made it feel that way. When I met her in Nova Scotia, she was the same; there has always been a great beauty about her.
>
> I haven't seen such warmth for a long time, elsewhere on the Net; the Net has become harsher, more corporate, and now filled with anger and despair over world politics, as much as anything else.
>
> But Rose's voice was a stillness, a calming, for all of us, in the midst of the world, at times an almost unutterable beauty.

Again the continuing presentation of mood overwhelmed everything else onlist, but in this case, perhaps because of the length of time involved and contact with her family, even though people did wonder about their grief when compared with that of those who knew her offline, it seemed more possible to act and write to her family and this was suggested onlist. One person later remarked that Rose's illness had called him back to the List. The group seemed able to deal with its grief without surprise. People still remark on the loss of Rose as I write, and we remember her.

Netsex and Framing

In the last chapter I argued that demands for authenticity and the conflation of gender relations with intimacy made gender and body referents exceedingly important in offlist or personal communication. As we 'choose' aspects of the body to emphasise, it is significant WES people online often emphasise aspects categorized as sexual[6].

Foucault (1979: 6-7) suggests that discourse about sex in Western society is treated as a discourse which is both about freedom and a revelation of 'truth', and hence acts as a declaration of authenticity. Thus, it reinforces online conventions of references to 'the body' acting as signs of authenticity, and suggests the importance of sex in establishing the 'truth' needed to make intimacy. Sex and bonding become more marked, especially on MOOs, to reduce asence and give a sense of physical presence, anchored in a sustained, mutually referenced and common, body response. On mailing lists, the volume of the list itself gives presence, and when members have read and/or responded they move on; sex is not so necessary to maintain presence.

Taking MOOs first, as on MOO boundary problems and issues around asence are emphatic, and List members often met in MOOs. On a MOO the person behind the 'avatar' you are interacting with, can be temporarily absent, having gone for a smoke, or to the toilet, or to eat, or even to talk with another person or persons (even on another MOO), or perhaps the delay is so great they have not received your message (less of a problem nowadays if you have broadband, but in the 1990s 'lag' was a significant part of the MOO experience). As a result of this lack of confirmations of presence, communication can drift, the other person can feel as if they are insubstantial, forever drifting away unless they are held in place by some ritual, or recurrence, which gives them a more 'substantial' body. This is particularly marked as the relationship moves towards intimacy, and yet the conventions of authenticity forbid the use of much ritual to maintain, or mark, states or claims. The only acceptable rituals are those of relationship; the love affair, sex, living together (sharing a MOO room), or even marriage. Therefore people can MOO marry very quickly. Falling in Love seems natural, and people use sex to sustain a mood which is commonly understood, tends to be partially self-sustaining, and is anchored in 'the reality' of 'the body'. With love, which is the prime way WES people justify closeness and intimacy (especially between the sexes), and with netsex, a person can maintain the presence of the other before them via narration. Netsex can fill in for those social rituals of 'being together' in which little is said as 'being together silently' is fraught online. Netsex can also restore commonality when conversation peters out or when dialogue moves away from areas of mutual interest.

Although the gender of the person online may not match their gender offline, the gender they choose usually exaggerates the conventions of gender construction. Particularly on MOOs, where sex is important in reducing asence, most women and men are adorned with an excess of the symbolisms of the gender and sexual discourse they participate within (Chapter 6). As Springer writes, when discussing cyberpunk novels and films "cyberbodies, in fact, tend to appear masculine or feminine to an exaggerated degree" (1996: 64), or as Dom writes to Cybermind (6 June.2000):

> All too often, the elements which make up the chimeric sexual identity invoked in on-line performance are taken from the Central Bank of gender stereotypes, an establishment that I think I'd rather blow up than keep in business.

This comment brings out the ambiguity of gender presentation and issues about gender and authenticity. In a society which values authenticity, the use of recognisably overt gender symbols to enable, and intensify, the performance, may appear to simultaneously delete the presence of 'real gender', or a real self, which might be expressed in uncertainties and hesitations. As Kendall writes, "In the limited bandwidth of text, typed conversation is the only means of communicating gender identity, and communicating it in a complex or nuanced way can be very difficult" (1996: 220). It could even appear particularly disastrous. Most people I have discussed 'online romance' with, seem to fear they could be falling for fantasy (inauthentic) images, and hence need to bring the relationship into the 'real' to check it or render it 'true'[7]. Although online romance may be perceived as intense, it may also be perceived as 'unreal'. The person can become caught in a contradiction between an intimacy, which is supposedly only confirmed offline, and an equally supposed ability to only be 'who they are' online.

Cybermind Discusses Netsex

I will now elaborate in more detail what is involved in netsex by extracting some remarks from discussions on Cybermind[8]. Discussion of its role in the life of the List occurs in Chapter 12. Netsex is often a cause for alarm in the offline world; people repeatedly discuss Julian Dibble's article on virtual rape (1998), and netsex is further associated with addiction, pornography, prostitution and child molestation[9]. However, this is not what is being discussed here. Mitchell (22 Jun.99) attempts to define netsex for a newspaper, in response to yet another online sexual abuse story, as follows:

> netsex (typically spelled as one word) refers to simulated sexual encounters, in which participants type out textual descriptions of their actions. In the overwhelming majority of cases, it is a fully consensual and benign activity.

It occurs between participants sitting at terminals in different locations, voluntarily describing sexual activity to each other, in text, together with their responses to those descriptions. Netsex may also involve net video cameras transmitting pictures of the person in front of their computers, but this has not seemed to be as popular with members of Cybermind.

Netsex is part of the offlist or private life of Cybermind and, as will be discussed in Chapters 11 and 12, it has paradoxical effects on the functioning of the list, acting both to strengthen and weaken 'community'. It occurs between members, as well as between members and non-members, in other online environments. The privacy of netsex was emphasised when two list members mutually posted some 'art' netsex to the List. Many people found it hard to read neutrally. Thus, one member wrote:

> last week [A and B] gave me a real scare when it appeared that she was sending private email to the list. [...] it's a difference between public and private space. bringing something out of private space into public space for the purpose of embarrassing someone is damaging in my opinion.

The man involved wrote that he was amazed at the amount of worried and solicitous queries he and the woman received, although the woman also received queries "from males coming on to her", showing that even in a place which is defined as relatively gender equitable like Cybermind, women who define themselves as sexual can be subject to expectation of sexual availability.

List members seem to have usually conducted netsex on MOOs, although people also used Unixtalk, IRC and instant messaging. Rodion (17 April.95) claimed that there were two important differences between being on MOO and using Unixtalk. Firstly in Unixtalk you could see the person's keystrokes, whereas on a MOO you only got to see the persons fully formed statements, and secondly that as Unixtalk is not self-supporting, you have to form the relationship elsewhere, whereas a MOO can be self contained. Not surprisingly, other people implied that seeing the keystrokes meant Unixtalk sex was more authentic and thus superior.

Despite the acceptance of netsex, it is still recognised by List members as a problem. The first thing that causes perturbation is it intensity and effects. Thus Alan writes (29 Apr.99):

> There are real-life breakups, divorces, and marriages; there are people traveling across the world to meet their partners; there are orgasms of incredible ferocity; there are exhibitionisms and voyeurisms and explorations of sexual behaviors previously considered perverse; there are games with worlds at stake—and everywhere, there are misrecognitions—"I didn't realize how serious this was"—"I didn't realize how much I care for you"—"I can't believe this"—"it just seemed to happen"—"I can't stop now"—"I won't stop now"—"I'm with you"—"I want to meet you"—"I dream of you constantly"—"my marriage is falling apart"—"I don't know what to say"—"this can't be happening".

Knowledge of the surprise of its effects is duplicated by other members. Thus: "people get caught, and suddenly they are hanging on the line waiting for someone to appear and neglecting people in RL", "It is overwhelming, beyond belief what I feel", "she thought it was just a game, but now she is trying desperately to meet him". People often comment on the intensity of their online orgasms, and how much stronger they are than masturbation. One woman tells of her adventures, with the sex moving to the telephone. The move from netsex to phone sex seems relatively common when people have got to know each other, and want a more authentic presence still.

> A few years ago i got into cyber sex. Merely for the purpose of study, but having said that, there were other benefits. Given as i am a writer, it didn't take long to master and within a very short time, guys began asking if they

could telephone me and every night i would get calls from all over the world, some calls as long as 4 hours. It wasn't all about sex. Over the telephone we would make wild passionate love and then kick back, smoke cigarettes and talk about philosophy, art, literature, politics etc all on the telephone. Now the amazing thing was that most guys actually confessed that having sex with me on the telephone was far more exciting and physically satisfying than the actual physical experience with their girlfriend or wife.

Although the strength of orgasm and feelings in online sex is clearly a problem for people, they do not have much in the way of explanation. Thus Alan (23 Jul.00):

I've written about [netsex] in terms of projection/introjection and control—that one simultaneously gives his/her body up to the other in an almost complete fashion (as complete as it can be in fantasy/fiction)—and at the same time, retains a sense of ultimate self.

However, as it stands, this explanation is little more than a restatement of what is observed: that is, that people often find it easy to have online sex and it is intense; it is not explained why projection should so easily take a sexual form. To be useful we need to be able to state why certain projections are more prevalent than others, and if possible to say something about their structure. Ideas of 'fantasy' are usually invoked, in explanation for why online sexual relationships, which may sustain people for years, often fail on meeting (Hammannd; Adamse & Motta 1996: 154).

Projection involves fantasy and the accusation that netsex leads people to retreat from real life—which is usually situated, by people making this argument, offline. It is also possible to argue that fantasy can intensify the sharpness of existent categories. As remarked previously, people on MOOs are often marked by exaggerated gender conventions, even when gender is not explicit. It certainly allows others to appear more prototypic of the kind of person they might be, and hence more appealing or aggravating. With certain categories of people this will make potential markers of closeness seem more real. In that way, potential anonymity, and the limited amount of information transmitted, may allow quicker appearance of intimacy, and it might be that the change from simplex to multiplex communication is enabled to occur more rapidly, thus giving a sense of contact and hence intimacy.

As well as being portrayed as more intense than offline sex, netsex can also be found to be unsatisfactory a diminished copy. One woman writes that netsex is a "pale copy of the Real thing though, don't you agree [...], why not go for the real thing? Why the Ersatz?" A male writes "at its best netsex is like the plastic tomatoes one gets in supermarkets in the winter". Another male writes, "it is too distant, afterwards I am left cold and alone". People can also express how much they used to like it but how burnt out they have become. Thus one woman writes "It can also be horribly empty and lonely and cold. I've found it becomes moreso the longer I'm in this space which is probably why I don't do that much anymore".

Netsex can be seen as parallel to, or as adding to, offline sex. A woman writes (7 Jul.99):

> Cybersex isn't a substitute for the real thing, and yet this is as far as I see it also a wrong why to phrase it. For indeed it would be sad if one only had cybersex or only private sexual fantasies. Cybersex as well as private sexual fantasies can be different sexual _dimensions_ , all of which can add to a rich and varied sexual life.

Others argue for difference. KNS writes (19 May.97): "with my online lover, I am aware of intense erotic sensations very different from RL sex", and Alan (23 Jul.00): "net sex isn't parallel to offline sex —it's different—and for some people—precisely because of the simultaneous control and freedom—considerably more powerful".

All of these statements above imply that netsex is somehow different from offline sex, but usually that it is either more intense or unsatisfactory. So there is the potential for oscillation between involvement and uninvolvement.

Netsex although perhaps solving some problems of asence by helping to maintain presence is caught in several contradictions. The most obvious begins when people often (but not always) express a desire for the netsex to move into offline life, and for the person they are having sex with to become an offline partner. The online relationship, by the canons of authenticity, has to be confirmed in the offline world. One woman explicitly states it is the "possibility of realization" or the prospect of meeting which renders netsex worthwhile: "If that possibility (however remote) were not there, I wouldn't bother—it would be a waste of time". Another writes "Sometimes I fantasize, most times not.... it's been highly probable that cyber-become-physical will become *physical*. Another person writes that he "Can't imagine it being a source of sexual pleasure, unless it is intended as a prelude to a physical encounter".

This also adds to the worries about authenticity of experience. Although openness is held to occur much easier than offline, the 'real' motives of others are held to be harder to discern. Feelings of openness oscillates with awareness of deceit, thus a woman writes (4 Mar.01):

> I wonder whether many of us are not more honest and open on-line than we are in RL. Here I express my opinions more freely and allow my feelings to show with less disguise than anywhere in RL. Even with my sexual partner, who is also my best-beloved and closest friend, I am more guarded than I am on-line. (Example: I fake orgasms when necessary in RL...I never deliberately fake anything on line!)

Jerry (6 Mar.01)

> I would say that I am more open online, although I am just as honest offline ;-). I think the issue for me is one of being more willing to be vulnerable online. There is also a sense of presencing online—the narrow bandwidth is such as to make me want to assert my human-ness more than offline, where my human-ness is all too visible...

But as Rowena writes (20 Nov.02):

> You can be untruthfull in so many ways, you can claim to be a big busted woman while actuallu be a srawnly male, you can claim to wair nothing but back boots while actually still in your workingclothes, you can claim you have your hand between your legs while actually you are filling in taxreturn forms with it etc.) I guess that this uncertainty might for some people be part of the attraction (both for the deceiver (obviously?) but also for the deceived.

Of course, one partner may not expect authenticity at that moment. Developing the idea that 'deceit' may add to the experience Jim writes 21 Nov.02):

> Does the recipient need truth, or just good wordcraft for it to be good netsex? I'm not looking at the person, they are projecting an image into my mind. That big sex organ we all share...

Salwa goes into this further (21 Nov.02):

> I would think that truthfulness has little to do with it; most welcome being lied to and invite cliched statements and untruths. And if you face them with "the truth" they say you're not playing along. From what I know of chatrooms, the discourse that develops between two is one in which they collaborate. One says what he/she expects the other to want to hear; one party

helps actualize the other's fantasy, and does not necessarily come up with its own. The suspension of disbelief is the basis for such interactions.

This ambiguity can lead to different responses to netsex when a person has an offline partner and to moral dilemmas of interpretation and framing:

> I think that falling in love over the web is adultery due to the intent involved and definitely infidelity to a real life partner with whom you are having a steady, monogamous relationship.
>
> I feel nauseous even writing this because what I did was very real.

Counterpositions abound and another woman writes:

> I am an ordinary woman. I work, I have a husband, children and friends. I lead a normal life. I connect to the net. With this person I met online I can be myself, and we had the most extraordinary sex over the net. Which enhanced my own real relationship. My husband knows that I chat, and even maybe that I do have sex over the internet. He is now recommending my friends do the same because he says that chatting has made me change in bed, where I previously always had taboos. He is a formal guy, with ethics, but he is giving me freedom. For him infidelity means physical contact.

Expanding from this last remark, another way of interacting with these uncertainties involves issues of safety. Thus one woman writes:

> It's a safe place to try out new games, games that I wouldn't necessarily want to act out in RL. Just like my private sexual fantasies; an substantial amount of those would kill me (hey—not literally—I'm not into death-type sexual fantasies) if they happened in RL.

A person of unknown gender wrote: "Some people do actually explain their attraction to c-sex with the fact that they are too shy or too inhibited in real life to get engaged in sexual relationship". However, as already implied, the counterpositionary fears of betrayal and trauma arising through netsex are the subject of many stories, and are well known to List members. Tales of failure of relationship on meeting, tales of misrecognised gender, tales of people impersonating each other, even tales of serial killers stalking the internet for victims are not rare. The intensity and the possibility of openness comes *with* a background of fears.

Issues of online sexual attractiveness arouse interest because of the intensity and rapidity of relationships. zoogirl writes that falling in love is "Easy as falling off a log. MUCH easier on line than off". Enok points to ambiguity: "Yes. But also feeling unsecure. May be I have become sceptical". Attractiveness is usually related to writing style or to openness. A woman writes:

> I didn't care if [A] were bi, a total queen, or an Amish preacher breaking into a tiny library in Iowa to type all night to strange women (or men) as long as what he wrote was entertaining.

One male writes (2 Mar.01)

> To me, a person's personality has a lot to do with their level of sexual attractiveness to me. There is of course a physical/chemistry aspect too, but the personality is very important. Does that not shine through in this space?

And a woman responds:

> I think it does ... there's two men on CM I find sexually very attractive, and I'm only judging from their posts. ,-)

On the other hand, a woman writes to me that she:

> used to visit a site just to observe male/female interaction, and the crassness of their language, poor spelling, wrong syntax used to turn me off big time.

She continues:

> there's always a chance that a sustained email correspondence might turn into overt flirtatiousness then romance and possibly more.
>
> Words are made flesh in cspace in a way that I experience viscerally; words shrink distance between people or, converesly, amplify it multifold.
>
> For a while I was very skeptical of the notion of "cyberrape"; I couldn't understand how a woman might feel violated by sheer words alone, but then little by little as I became more in tuned to the subtlety and overwhelming intensity of words and the concomitant bodily/physical reactions, sensations and feelings, this notion became all the more plausible. One can't underestimate the presence of the body in all of this cyber traffic of information and people.

Despite claims to the contrary (i.e. Ferree 2003, another review that assumes people online are both naïve and damaged), there was no observable difference on Cybermind between women and men's expression of their experience of netsex. There was also surprisingly little discussion of possible gender differences in approach to netsex, although most people acknowledged that women were generally more prone to sexual harassment online than men were. It is hard to say whether female members of the List, in general, felt harassed by male members sexually, as this would be likely to happen offlist, and would thus be sequestered in 'private' space. If it did occur, it seems improbable that it would be reported due to the difficulties of gathering together a support group, and the risk of speaking in public. However, in almost none of the offlist gossip that was reported to me, was sexual harassment an issue.

The Haunted Computer

How are online bodies categorised? WES cultures already have a set of 'virtual body' constructions, which are complementary to our constructions of the 'physical body'; those of the 'soul', the 'mind', and the 'ghost', all of which blend together due to their status of being 'not-physical' bodies. This polarity is usually characterised as 'the mind/body split'. A strange thing about this division is that it should not be entirely expected. Plato describes the appetite (*epithymetikon*), the spirit/will (*thymoeides*), and the rational soul (*logistikon*), while Aristotle talks of the 'plant' (*threptike*), 'animal' (*aisthetike*) and the 'intellectual' (*noetike*) souls responsible for nutrition or growth, motion or sensation, and reason respectively. St Paul distinguishes 'psyche' and 'pneuma' from the 'flesh' (which also has its own volition), St Augustine works with a triadic or trinitarian 'psychology' in his book on the trinity—as humans are the image of God the one soul is three. Descartes suggests there might be an intermediary spirit between mind and body. Ghosts vary in their materiality over history and so on[10]. However, despite such traditions, we tend to polarise mind and body as opposites, even while criticising other people for doing so.

A fairly common mytheme is that this mind/body opposition developed in the 17th century as part of a successful strategy deployed by some of the 'intellectual' administrative class to distinguish the realms which were open to its own investigation, theorisation and control (the 'New Philosophy') from the realms which were under the control of the Church. This became institutionalised in the governors, or managers, who undertook mind work and the governed who performed body work and who, ideally, do not question. The association of reason and mind with males has been much commented upon (cf Merchant 1990, Ross-Smith & Kornberger 2004).

One of the problems for this 'New Philosophy' of Descartes, Boyle and Newton was to retain the necessity of God, while removing the possibility of unmediated communication with God, as the latter theory ('religious enthusiasm') was widely blamed for the social upheavals of the 17th century. The 'mechanical philosophy', by stripping matter of life, removed the immanence of divine process, while needing God to design, start and maintain the machine. Eventually the machine became conceptually sufficient alone[11]. The ghost becomes more ethereal as this process becomes more pronounced. It seems that the upheavals of the 20th century loosened this boundary for a while and the ghost became more 'solid'[12].

Nowadays, the polarity between mind/body, seems to easily cluster with the parallel of 'virtual' for 'spiritual', and offline for physical. There are hoards of science fiction novels or movies in which computers become intelligent (*2001*), or in which human minds get projected into computers after the person's body dies (*Synners*). In others artificial intelligences assume an independent and powerful net life of their own (in Gibson, they become voodoo gods, or loas). In *Buffy the Vampire Slayer* demons and ghosts penetrate computers. A theology of 'cyberspace' seems easy (Cobb 1998; Hefner 2003). Scientists, such as Hans Moravec, talk of downloading human minds into machines, as if 'the mind' could easily be separated from the body. Most of the techniques Moravec (1988) proposes involve destroying the original, presumably on the principle that the copy is identical to the original. In a similar vein Ray Kurzweil writes of "when we become software" (1999: 150). Other research shows that many people approach computers as if the computers were 'conscious' social actors[13].

In a historical parallel, this movement might be linked in mutual feedback with the constant attempts to characterise the new elites supposedly dealing with 'immaterial' information, as 'knowledge workers' opposed to 'physical' service workers or the valueless unemployed, which might weaken gender attributions (Marshall 2004a).

Thus it is not surprising that people can treat online bodies as if they where ghosts or spirits. Elizabeth Barrette writing to Cybermind describes haunted cyberspace completely (26 Dec.06):

> Cyberspace is an ephemeral reality accessed chiefly through material means, but it remains ephemeral in nature. One doesn't really need a body in cyberspace. I suspect that the reason it's not overrun with discorporeal entities

is that most of them don't know how to *find* it. As time passes, more souls who are aware of cyberspace will take leave of their bodies ... and I think we will gradually accrue more cyber-angels and cyber-ghosts and sundry other whatsits.

Online Bodies as Ghosts

This view is of course not uncontested, but it is common. It was a readily evoked theme in the Cybermind novel. People on the List mention "virtual bodies' or "disembodied sex". Some write more positively (19 Apr.96) "cybersex does not need a body", Kara claimed (6 Dec.94) that in "virtual relationships [...] there is no physical reality and no desire for it", and Bernadette wrote (pc19 July.96) of her and her netlover that "We desire to merge but our body gets in the way". Perhaps the 'lack' of a body feeds into Western visions of the perfect love as loss of self, where "united *souls* represent the purest form of romance" (Springer 1996: 61 emphasis added).

Sometimes the experiences behind this idea could be complex. A woman writes (30 Oct.02):

> I know that when I have contacted certain people and made certain kinds of connections with them over the internet, I thought that I have "felt" their "energy", their "emotions", or their "presence" in a very palpable way.

Another woman writes (30 Oct.02):

> I had a very interesting cyber experience with a guy in the US for eight months. We would go into split screen private chat. He would be typing while i was typing. I would feel him touch me in a certain place, but i hadn't read it because when i type i have to look at the keys lol. After i felt him touch me ie running his fingertips thru my hair, i would look up at the screen and read and that was exactly as he had typed. It actually got to the point that we didn't need to read the text, we knew ahead of reading what was being said.

Bazza tries to explain this by positing that:

> we are basically electromagnetic machines. It makes sense then, that whilst two of us are manipulating an artificial machine in direct communication with each other, that we may feel vague impulses of the other, or get a glimmer of character and personality traits, as our electomagnetic "energy" mingles with that of the machine.

Other types of explanations were proposed for these effects, from subliminal perception to active fantasy. Here the suggestion is that it has something to do with perception of boundaries. Judith Butler proposes that matter, is not "a site or surface but... a process of materialization that stabilizes over time to produce the effect of boundary fixity and surface we call matter" (1993: 9). This suggests that materiality is linked with rigid boundaries and that, as a result, non-rigid boundaries help constitute a sense of immateriality. Through this proposition, materiality becomes related to categorization, and particularly to the process of making categories firm and exclusive. The lack of boundary fixity in people's experience online, particularly when not interrupted by pain, may create a sense of personal immateriality, which is perhaps furthered by the loss of time sense as an organiser of experience, and the apparent diminishment of restraint or resistance—especially when contrasted with the offline world.

Bodies as Cyborg

The ghost is not the only model of the cyberbody to be found online. The cyborg, a melding of human and machine, is also quite common, although cyborg references seemed rarer on Cybermind, more self-conscious and more fantasies of the future than statements of present experience. Only DavidS and Sasha seemed unambiguously keen on the idea of becoming machines. Most mentions of cyborgs occur via forwards, or through worry about implanted surveillance devices.

When Tom asked (11 Jun.01):

> Would [you] yourself.. have a computer implant that directly linked to your central nervous system? If Yes, would you do so if that implant also had a wireless network link?

Responses were ambiguous and demonstrated further boundary anxieties, mentioning disadvantages such as the risk of being hacked, being controlled elsewhere, bug-ridden software, needing to upgrade, being drowned in spam, being switched off, or at risk of power failures. The only favoured pluses, which tended to be mentioned by males, seemed to be the possibility of increasing assimilation of information, or the possibilities of downloading the mind before death, and perhaps being able to travel through the universe. Another indication of cyborg boundary worries was illustrated when Rajesh asked (21 Feb.02) "Has the machine infected the soul? Or does its noise merely make the soul's gentle whispers inaudible?"

The idea of downloading links the idea of cyborgs to ideas about etherealisation. Downloading can only work if there is a separable mind, and thus its appeal to males may not be unexpected. Many theorists also involve gender explicitly in cyborgization, as sheltering disruptions to the male ego behind armour and identification with the machine. This is usually seen as avoidance of the 'tender', or fleshly feminine, although Harraway famously argues that cyborgs are post-gendered (Bukatman 1993: 303-4; Robins & Levidow 1995; Harraway 1989b). As gender seems vital to WES self regulation and framing online, assertions that cyborgs are post-gendered seem improbable (see Marshall 2004a).

Virile Bodies, Asence and Politics
The cyborg also points to another anxiety, which centres on the ability to work and to survive, to interact with the outside world via technology. As computer programs constantly update, no one can ever develop expertise they always have to be mastering new programs, or worried that they will be left behind, and similarly there is the possibility that their body may not be able to cope with the stress of working with a computer. Hayes claims the rate of Repetitive Strain Injury among the workforce increased by 1,246% between 1982 and 1992. The estimated cost of dealing with this problem in 1992, was US$25 billion per year (1995: 176). In the UK the Trade Union Council estimates that 1 in 50 (presumably unionised) workers has reported an RSI condition (BBC 2002). Another report suggests that 3 out of 5 Swedish office workers have RSI (RSI.org). Responsibility for this is increasingly thrown on the worker. Kome remarks that "the employer tends to dispute claims almost automatically and force the worker to prove that the disorder is work related" (2002: 95).

As well as facing incapacity, the role of the information worker is never clear; they are supposed to be freed from body work, to create, or to work with symbols or intangibles, yet they have to use machines which might injure them. They might be called the 'creative class' (Florida 2003) but their contributions to productions are appropriated as easily as a factory worker's. 'Information' is a congerie often used to terminate mythemes which are held to explain changes in the economy, or the organization of life, as in the expressions 'information economy', 'information companies' and so on. As such a congerie, it has tenuous boundaries, and becomes ghostly itself. Information can even be claimed to be a directly productive force, as if it was self-animated, which adds to this effect. Research, policy, or product can be based upon interaction with simulations rather than interaction with 'realities'. Writers commonly note that this theory promotes the deletion of reference to the social and technological bases which allows the information to exist, and which controls its distribution, leaving 'the market' as an abstract determiner of 'success' (Castells 1996: 371ff; Grusin 1996: 46; Henwod 1995). This deletion is emphasized, because despite claims that 'information' or 'knowledge' is the driving force of the 'new economy' (e.g. Drucker 1993: 181ff.), humans cannot live by abstract information alone. Information needs to be legitimated, or converted into something else, usually through some organization. The mytheme implies that information creates wealth in a never-ending alchemy of self-productive signs. However, only certain kinds of information can be sold; information in demand, or which is not readily aviable. Information must be restricted to be saleable, and in general information workers do not own the information they produce. As a result of these confusions, the nature of the work of 'knowledge workers', and of their place in the world, becomes problematic. Furthermore, all those with superseded skills, or injury, can become unable to 'keep up', joining those without computers and vanishing from the computerised world. Information workers too can become ghosts with no impact.

If 'physical' body is the ultimate locus of power, then the frustration involved in social control renders that body 'immaterial' and/or 'unvirile' if online. We cannot act directly upon the bodies of others. The offline can often be contrasted with the online, as Real, through the common use of RL (real life), for offline life. Online events were frequently described as 'pale imitations' of offline events. Robert muses on the pallid interaction between the embedding world and the net (13 April.95):

> Does a major in the Jonas Savimbi army shudder at the thought that Cybermind disapproves of their attack on a major import/export center [...] Double Bah, tripple humbug and a loud Hah!

Others wrote that the discussion of politics on Cybermind solved nothing and might even distract from solutions. Glen, although hardly mainstream (cf Chapter 9), encapsulates these issues of lack of virility, warning of (6 Mar.95):

> 'analysis paralysis'... this condition arises when a problem which may or may not be intractable causes a temporary or permanent inability to act

He later writes (5 July.95):

> There's nothing I hate more than a bunch of fat or emaciated intellectuals talking about what lies behind our sensory input [...] We're trying to become big, mushy, brains suspended in amniotic fluid with electrodes stuck to our surfaces.

The implication is that online we are weaker, and this is reinforced by political alienation, in the sense that people cannot act on the world politically, so they may tend to experience themselves as 'immaterial'[14]. Further, the web of power appears nomadic, elusive, and always elsewhere; in some ways more alive than ourselves, it too has no obvious boundaries and thus becomes represented as spirit-like, a magic life haunting the net. We cannot act upon it, and the traditional modes of protest, available to all, such as occupying the streets or a building are no longer effective (Critical Art Ensemble 1994).

Yet at the same time people's action in online society is often an attempt not only to act in the world, but to create a new world, or at least to create a safe place in the world. So here again, in the heart of the absence is presence.

What is clear is that information workers have to use computerised technology. While using the computer, the more speedily and well the body functions, the more it can be ignored. As we have seen, pain interrupts the transfer and sense of presence online. While the person is engaged, sexually involved, or intellectually interested, then sensual discomfort is overpowered by the direction of attention elsewhere. When topics recycle, attention is no longer distracted and discomfort, boredom and burnout become more noticeable. Efforts to increase the engagement could explain some of the attractions of flaming or netsex, as these sensations, or involving emotions, diminish the background sensory distress, and demonstrate one is surviving and competent. In which case, people do not approach the net erotically, but *become* erotic to maintain an approach.

Conclusions

Ways of categorising the body seem affected by the ongoing experience of weak or shifting boundaries, and by the tendency to exaggerate categories to resolve and frame communication. The low sense of boundaries seems to flow into category making. Existing mythemic contrasts between mind and body make it easy to contrast offline life, with its supposedly real, 'material' and virile body, with an online authentic but potentially deceitful mind, thus leading to the common idea of the online self as like a spirit or ghost. These ideas are perhaps reinforced by uncertain but semi-alive seeming congeries as 'information', which govern much work life.

Similarly the body can appear both present and absent when online, so it becomes an asent, oscillatory body like a ghost. Sometimes the virtuality is taken as real, as in the mytheme of the virtual world which allows true expression of authentic being, and sometimes it is the offline world which is taken as real, as in the mytheme of computer use as an escape from, or abandonment of, real life.

A low ability to use ritual, some of which seems determined by offline conventions, and some of which is determined by the difficulties of engaging in mutual but silent presence, can increase the impact of events which involve a more coherent stream of message moods than is usually found, as in flame or mourning.

When relationships move into a more dyadic sphere, netsex can act to maintain and sustain a sense of contact and authenticity and sustain a set of exchanges which give people presence to each other, through reference to the body. Although the displacement of being or asence that occurs with lack of acknowledgment, can be temporarily reduced by netsex, it can also increase it by contrast with the embedding. However, people return to netsex because of its mood-stabilizing functions which appear to guarantee communication. On the whole, it seems many people put more time and effort into netsex partnerships than they do into their non living-together sexual partnerships. Online, more effort is needed to overcome asence and prove an existence.

The motif and framing of authenticity becomes a problem related to bodies. A person may have the ability to be who 'they really are' online, but this is coupled with an equal ability to engage in deceit. In netsex this deceit can occur at the same time as the people involved are trying to show their connectedness, through exaggerating sexual symbols, bodily parts and so on, in order to generate the tension that helps make netsex so intense. Therefore, people are caught in a potential clash between being who you are online, while potentially undermining it, and having to have the existence of the relationship confirmed offline.

Similarly the difficulties in using power online also tend to ghost the body and reinforce ideas of the offline body being the virile body, despite the difficulties people may face in engaging in productive offline politics. The online body is in some ways oscillatory, as it is this body that generates information and contacts which can encourage survival, but at the same time it can be perceived as ineffective. It might be that this provides both anxiety and energy.

The body becomes liminal because it is caught in conflicting demands between online and offline authenticity, and online power and offline power. Although it provides framings through gender and through anchoring emotions and realities offline, these framings can be incompatible. A method of solving the apparent problems in online life generates further problems.

Chapter 8: Existence and Exchange

Introduction

This chapter uses a model to describe mailing list social activity and control, which is based on anthropological models of the 'gift economy', with mail items as the 'gifts'[1]. In Chapter 5 it was suggested that identity and status are gained through the constant prestation of messages in a status war similar to that of potlatch or Melanesian exchange. Further, in an email list, the prestation of text gives the space of prestation, and the existence of the prestator and the group. The hierarchy of prestation both gives, and expresses, the accepted status of people among the group, in a feedback process, such that if people without status make more mails than they should, the list protests, ignores them or people leave. Gender is also tied to exchange and studies of offline WES exchange suggest that female List members will tend to be active in offlist mailings between List members.

Therefore, I suggest, contra Richard MacKinnon (1995, 1997, 1998), that the models used by anthropologists to describe stateless societies (particularly traditional Melanesian societies), are more effective than the models developed to describe the activities of Western States such as: 'Social Contract', citizenship rights, rule of law, the sanctity of private property, and so on. Online behaviours may actually clash with the models of private property and exchange established under capitalism, as well as with the theory of social contract.

The term 'social contract', suggests that society is a voluntary and deliberate compact, that there is one social interest, and that society members agree to the power structures, to their 'place' and so forth. However, there might be as much evasion and subversion as agreement. Even in an online society, where this 'contractuality' might apply, there is precisely no contracting, no explicit or formal agreements, no laws enforcing the contract, etc. Some members of Internet groups may proclaim that their group has rules, but there is little uniformity in agreeing what these 'contractual' obligations might actually be, which is not to say groups are 'anarchistic' in the sense of 'anything goes'. Society is continually in a process of construction—subject to disruption and change, but with no overall plans and nothing to announce its finish. Even Cybermind, which has an origin point, has no original social contract because it has a prehistory arising from other lists and other forms of sociality anchored in offline patterns of power[2]. It might have constitutive events, but even those are temporary. Although it is *possible* the 'spelling wars' convinced the original members that conventions of 'formal' writing were not relevant or even harmful, one year later, few members had any awareness of this, and the debate could theoretically start again. That it didn't is significant, but this implies more about the pre-existing ideas of members and their cultural embedding than anything contractual. Most online 'social contract' is impermanent and continually renegotiable, involving variable parties, and different levels of agreement. The difference between this kind of 'contract' and the agreements normally referred to by that term is too significant to ignore.

In the same way that exchange or trade is not always 'capitalism', but our terms are steeped in the conventions of capitalism (hence the benefit of terms like 'gift' and 'prestation' to try and discuss non-market exchange), so conventions cluster around terms like 'contract'.

Comparison between mailing lists and Melanesian prestations might only be possible because anthropological writers tend to abstract 'the gift' from its social background, and to treat it as an 'element' (in Mauss' words), or constituent particle, without concern for its content or context. A frequent criticism is that the focus on 'the gift' leads to a downplaying of the class and power, economic, ecological and other survival factors within which exchange operates (e.g. Harris 1968: 487-8; Weiner 1977: 218-9). Although such factors both influence who can participate on a list and their life experience, their effects on email as exchange, on Cybermind, are minimal. Another objection might be that relations on a mailing list do not exist outside the exchanges and those in Melanesia do, thus altering the nature of exchange. However, many relationships do not exist prior to exchange, and Melanesians may make exchanges to constitute relationships[3]. Weiner writes: "In the Trobriands, where exchange is the basic framework around which formal patterns of social interaction are organised, objects... can be read as objectification of desire and intent" (1977: 212). Cheal writes that "gifts are in fact used to construct a wide range of possible social worlds as stable arenas for social interaction... it is a formative social process in its own right" (1988: 136); although 'stable' is perhaps a relative term.

However, the 'truth' of the model is not as important as whether it allows us to look at the data in an interesting way. The operative words in any comparison are 'more like' not 'identical to' and, of course, there are huge variations in Melanesian societies. There is no suggestion that kinship, land tenure, or production of food (all important in Melanesia) are important to the internal organisation of online society. The point is simply that analyses based upon the existence of State-like formations, or contracts, may be even less useful.

"The Gift"

Mauss opens his essay on the gift as follows: "We intend in this book to isolate one important set of phenomena: namely, prestations which are in theory voluntary, disinterested and spontaneous, but are in fact obligatory and interested". He aims to answer the question "what is the principal whereby the gift received has to be repaid? What force is there in the thing given which compels the recipient to make a return?" (1954: 1).

One force active here is Mauss' selection process. If consideration is restricted to prestations which are obligatory and interested, then the gift which is being observed is obligatory and interested. Excluding counterexamples by definition, easily leads to the almost tautological explanation of a connection between the giver and the gift which demands return[4]. Such a solution deletes social modes of origin or closure of the gift. Beginnings and endings are not found within the item exchanged, but in the social relations constructed around and through it.

Exchanges do not always balance, nor are they obliged to do so. Focusing on a compulsion for gifts to be returned leads us to bypass situations in which gifts are ignored, or not returned (and the effects of this), and situations in which things are requested or taken. Transactions are multivalent and, as Firth argues, the degrees of balance between the obligations to give, receive and return, may vary with the situation or define the tenor of that situation. There may be "significant areas of choice and uncertainty" (1967: 10). Gifting can be fraught[5]. Cheal points out that even in WES societies there may be no attempt to obtain symmetry; imbalances are expected when a person takes responsibility for nurturing another (1988: 57). Blau suggests that 'social exchange' is caught between the polarity of pure calculation and pure generosity, neither of which exists (1964: 112). In a 'gift economy', participation may be more important than winning or losing (Cheal 1988: 139). 'Reciprocity' is not always 'accounting'[6].

Cheal further remarks that Mauss does not investigate differences in patterns of exchange arising between intergroup and intragroup exchange (1988: 173), or the possibility that exchange changes with group categorization. This distinction between intergroup and intragroup exchange proves important when discussing gender and intimacy online (see below).

Mauss makes the useful remark that in exchange "the veritable *persona* is at stake" (1954: 38). Firth comments on this passage that:

> giving is an extension of the self, and hence the obligation to give is bound up with the notion of the self, its social bounds and social roles (1967: 10-11).

Strathern extends this position, arguing that it is only the Western practice of separating subject from object which produces distinctions between gifts and persons, or gifts and social relations: "objects are created not in contradistinction to persons, but out of persons". Gifts do not have to 'stand for' or signify relations but can act as supports or constituents (1988a: 171-2). Email simply makes these features of the gift more obvious.

The ambivalence of the gift, especially the 'poisoned gift' (Mauss 1997), is taken up by Derrida, not only in his book on Mauss (1994a), but in his discussion of Plato's use of the term *'pharmakon'* with respect to writing (1983: 131-2). Pharmakon refers to both what we call a 'medicine' or a 'poison', essentially it is a powerful potion. In the story of the origin of writing told by Plato in the *Phaedrus*, writing is described by its inventor as a beneficial pharmakon, and by the God-King as a harmful one. Derrida tries to overcome the idea of writing as harmful, while keeping the ambiguity of pharmakon, which he then claims undermines other such resolutions, such as the superiority of speech to writing, or the original to derivation. It is simpler just to state that gifts can be ambivalent, and responses uncertain.

In online life we might say, "email is a text which approaches speech". The more it approaches speech, the less it is like a prestation. Email is also ambivalent in that without email there is no list, but with too much email people protest or leave. Email, like a pharmakon, the 'gift', or the cyberbody has unstable values between which it slides, being both destructive and constructive.

Derrida asks what authorises Mauss to gather events in the category 'gift', which may have no unity of meaning, and accuses anthropologists of carelessly making cross-cultural assumptions about the universality of the category of 'gift' (1994a: 26)[7]. Yet Derrida partially answers this question himself: Mauss is seeking the distinctive trait of the gift which distinguishes it from 'credit' or 'debt' in Western terms (ibid: 41). Within Mauss' schema this distinction is more important than any common trait named by 'gift' (assuming such a trait was nameable). Trying to find this ideal and what it would entail leads Derrida to claim gifts are both impossible and that we desire them (ibid: 29). Derrida seems to be expecting all categories to be concepts.

Exchange, Melanesia and Mailing Lists

I will argue that in a mailing list:

1) Prestation of text gives the space of prestation, the existence of the prestator and the existence of the group.
2) The hierarchy of prestation not only expresses and gives status but also makes the particular presence of the place manifest.
3) Time is measured by volume, each gift creates a particular instant, or passage, of experienced time.
4) Gender is perceived as having a relationship with exchange, particularly in making the offlist intimate.
5) Property tends towards distributional.

Exchange and Social Order

Malinowski argued that if we look at social control as it emerges out of people's lives, their seeking for socially valid status (in co-operation and competition), their self-constructions of identity; the interplay of obligations, performance, mutuality, negotiations and reciprocity, then we shall obtain "much more satisfactory results than if we were to discuss questions of authority, government and punishment" (1926: 13).

Within this perspective, norms become dynamic. As Malinowski writes, observance of the rules of behaviour

> is at best partial, conditional, and subject to evasions;... it is not enforced by any wholesale motive like fear of punishment, or a general submission to all tradition, but by very complex psychological and social inducements (1926: 15).

Positive ordinances for increasing sense of self-worth and accumulating recognition are much more developed and effective than prohibitions or punishments. Further, these 'ordinances' are "essentially elastic and adjustable, leaving a considerable latitude within which their fulfilment is regarded as satisfactory" (ibid: 30-1). Within parameters, conventions are situational and negotiable; they vary with the persons involved, the general mood and recent history of the group (including shifting patterns of alliance).

Malinowski emphasises the non-systematic nature of the values, the disjunction between what people say should be done, and the fact that people were continually breaking these prescriptions. Trobriand society may function 'better' because people are able to break the norms. Conflicting collections of norms allow people to choose a variety of effective behaviours, which serve their 'selves' and society far better than any set of imposed prescriptions.

For a human system to work and adapt to exigencies, some conscious 'rules' or values must be breakable, as they cannot apply to all situations. The 'work to rule' is a well-known and effective disruptive process in the WES world. People in hierarchies deceive their superiors so the system can function, which in turn allows those superiors to exist. Zizek suggests that the distancing people enact from their ideologies, helps the people guarantee to themselves that they are not merely a 'cipher' for the rules while, at the same time, reasserting their identity with the 'essentials' of the ideology. Breaking the rules becomes a form of honouring the 'greater aim' (1997: 21-2, 25). Even if it was possible to have a 'social contract', then it's enforcement could be destructive of social processes, and societies without one could survive better. Modes of ordering produce their own chaos, and may need that disorder in order to function.

Order, Status and Reciprocity

Malinowski proposes that social order depends on dynamic patterns of reciprocity and distribution which necessitate interdependence. These patterns are intimately bound up with self-identity and self-presentation[8]. "Every chain of reciprocity is made the more binding by being part and parcel of a whole system of mutualities" (1926: 23). No one can be entirely self-supporting. The help and co-operation of others, not all of whom a person will have personal connection to, is necessary at all times.

In these kinds of societies 'capital' is not accumulated, kin have demands upon accumulation, and its main function is to be ceremonially given away, whereupon the givers "feel a manifestation of power and an enhancement of personality" (ibid: 29).

As well as building self-worth, identity and puissance, and allowing participation in socially valuable activities, exchange also acts as a series of messages about others, and satisfies and expresses the feelings a person might have or gain as a result of this social activity. In other words, it acts in feedback; a satisfactory or unsatisfactory pattern of exchange gives a sense of self-worth, which can then be expressed in further exchanges and vice versa.

If texts are regarded as prestations, then mailing list sociality is governed by the gifting of messages to a group, and this gifting is connected to presenting or putting forward one's name or self-identity. High-status people are those who gift prodigiously and appropriately. However, it is not simply the volume of their giving which determines status, but the reception of the gifts by the rest of the group. To follow the list, it is necessary to read most mails and thus the more your mailbox appears to be full of posts by people you do not value or whom you dislike reading, the more likely you will leave, or protest. Thus, there can be arguments about the worth of someone's prestations[9]. So the volume of mail from people roughly corresponds to their status, or readability, within the group via feedback.

The ideal message-gift will be pertinent to the group's interests, well formed according to the requirements of the list, readable, easily digested and short. The effort involved in unwrapping the gift should be less than the nourishment provided by it. Frequent short messages might put forward a name more effectively than infrequent long messages, even if the total bulk of text is the same[10]. Forwards of other people's messages from other lists might have less value than original work, yet carry more status than no gift at all. It is unlikely people keep a detailed mental account of exchanges and derelictions of exchange, unless these are marked. The state of exchange is probably reflected in imprecise feeling states and intuitions.

Therefore, there is no easy and universal method of evaluating message-gifts. Methods will vary from list to list, time to time, and possibly from member to member, although without some coherence within these various valuations the list might split apart. Conflict can arise over these interpretations as when I was informed by two different people that at one time a list member whose prestations I considered fairly central to the list was being pressured by some other members to leave Cybermind and enrol in FOP because of the perceived irrelevance of their mails. Similarly, the split-off group 'Offlist' was partially formed as a result of different valuations of messages.

A mail is a prestation which not only expresses its contents but expresses and incarnates the feelings or strategies of the giver to an active audience. It is more intimate than a normal gift and more tied to the social life of the giver, as the messages constitute their persona and to some extent their body. We might compare 'good prose' and layout to physical beauty, and to the use of magic by people participating in *kula* exchange to establish their attractiveness and even to seduce potential exchange partners (Malinowski 1922: 335-6). We have seen how style can be taken as a maker of physical attractiveness in Chapter 7. Weiner argues that gifts establish the 'social space' of interaction, while magic "allows one to intrude upon the personal space of another" (1977: 213-4). In online life, words, gifts, magic and identity are not as separable.

Balance is precarious; if you make too many gifts you get flamed: if you make too few you are forgotten or, in effect, do not exist for others. The gift 'brings forward' the person or 'makes their name', even more so if the gift is accepted and answered. Constant putting forward is encouraged due to group turnover. Rejection of the gift is tantamount to rejecting the giver. Responding to the gift gives recognition to the original giver, and is also a measure of their status. It creates and reflects prototypicality.

Recognition equals a powerful existence. The gift requests acknowledgment, but cannot demand return from anyone. In mailing list society this relationship to response can be 'two-edged'; as the receivers are mainly non-specific and invisible, this gift can fall into emptiness. The receivers are not shamed by silence, but as the giver is specific, and because existence in list society depends on acknowledgment, unacknowledgment is a risk run by the giver. The gift can be ignored and hence vanish.

Silence is more severe in online society than offline, because in an offline snubbing you are acknowledged in the snub; you see the person turn the other way and so forth, whereas on a list such response can be absent. This gives the suspension of being, or asence, which is only temporarily (and precariously) resolved on acknowledgment. The absence of a marker, such as a physical body, means people literally move in and out of existence for themselves and for others.

Breaking the conventions of good gift giving in online society will usually either lead to the person being ignored (and hence losing, or not maintaining or increasing, prestige or existence), or being told to post differently. We might say these positive directions are such that (quoting Malinowski again) "the breach... is penalised but not punished" and "premiums [are offered] for an overdose of fulfilment" (1926: 58). Someone "who would persistently disobey the rulings of [exchange]... would soon find himself outside the social and economic order—and he is perfectly well aware of it" (ibid: 41). Despite occasional requests (e.g. MacKinnon 1997: 231ff.), punishments in online society are not graded to match the disruption. The difficulty of officially grading such sanctions through codification is another way in which the norms of such a society differ from the legal procedures of a State, and resemble those of stateless societies.

Gifts and Recognition

In many traditional Melanesian societies, status ultimately depends on the ability to give gifts and make ceremonial exchange. In the Trobriands, the heir of a chief will have certain advantages and ritual acknowledgments, but if they are 'stingy' they will not be respected. Further accomplishments can add to status among which ritual knowledge, the ability to make sorcery, fight or orate are the most important. Magic and oratory are often intimately linked to successful prestations. A good orator can literally 'make' the prestation, and magic increases the appeal, power, presence of the gifts and the awe of the receivers. Similarly the oratory within a text, at least in part, makes the text what it is, and visibly situates it within the flow of other gifts. Although Mauss self-confessedly marginalises the 'aesthetic' (1954: 77), presumably to favour the 'use value', it is the aesthetic which makes the gift and the giver. Allowing the question of what makes a well-responded-to, or appreciated, gift broadens the nature of perceived responses, recognizing the power among the receivers who evaluate the giver's work. It allows for the social response of 'gift denigration', and for the occasion in which receiving a gift can increase status.

In Melanesia sometimes people with little status may gift a local big man to help his exchange and be recognised as helping and gain some recognition and status without the big man's status being threatened. Recognition and the gift cancel each other to some extent. If a big man of equal or competing status gave such a gift then things would become problematic. Similarly in societies where the hierarchy is more stable than in Melanesia, a gift from a high-status person to a low-status person can increase the status of the receiver.

Recognition and response to a low-status person's post by a person of high status, can bring the post to the attention of people who might otherwise have skipped it or read it hurriedly. These people may then respond, or become more likely to recognise the name and read that person's posts in the future. This undoubtedly increases the self-worth of the initial giver, and may lead to their further 'socialisation' and participation within the group. Lack of acknowledgment can lead to the person's departure, as mentioned in Chapter 5.

Such formal exchange puts the person within a series of mutualities and obligations. People will, perhaps, start forming almost unconscious alliances, responding to each other's post-gifts, then exchanging email off list. Communication fails without acknowledgment and online life cannot exist without exchange.

Problems of Response

It is useful to consider the differences between responses, which are not reciprocal. On one occasion in 1997 a person kept re-posting another person's mail back to the list, with no added comments. This was perceived as aggressive or disruptive by the person whose mails were being treated this way and by several other list members—a gift was being rejected. Similarly, a one-line reply attached to a long post often implies that the length and effort is either unworthy or equalled by a trivial response.

Exchange can be, to use Bateson's terms, 'complementary' or 'symmetric' (1958: 178-9). Thus (complementary) I can give you cowrie shells and you applaud or (symmetric) we both give each other pigs. In neither case is the audience passive. Symmetric relationships might tend to become more competitive than complementary ones and the best-known example of symmetric response is an Arms Race. As the audience on a list only appears as another prestation, symmetric relationships may develop more easily than complementary ones, and thus feedback loops get out of control. This contributes to the fear of flame wars where the aim is to overwhelm the other with their inadequacy to make return. Triumph in, or reinforcement of, symmetric exchange might lead to events like the potlatch (ibid: 183, 193ff.). The debates over Iraq constitute an exemplar. Response to a disagreement and thus denial of identity tended to be another such response, further denying membership and existence.

The attitudes of 'lurkers' are hard to analyse, but my own experience would suggest they might feel mild irritation with posters, along with a tendency to delete mail unread and thus refuse to accept a gift, or they might adopt a strategy of reading the list as if it were a book or a magazine—again rejecting the gift, or seeing it as a 'windfall'. However, if too many lurk, accepting but not giving, then the mailing list will disappear.

Dispute: Sorcery and Secrecy

As in online society, so in the Trobriands, disputes become matters of public debate, which are settled by prestation, by oratory and by status. Malinowski describes what can be seen as a Melanesian flame war as follows:

> the rare quarrels which occur at times take the form of an exchange of public expostulation (*yakala*) in which the two parties assisted by friends and relatives meet, harangue one another, hurl and hurl back recriminations. Such litigation[11] allows people to give vent to their feelings and shows the trend of public opinion, and thus it may be of assistance in settling disputes. Sometimes it seems, however, only to harden the litigants. In no case is there any definite sentence pronounced by a third party, and agreement is but seldom reached then and there (1926: 60).

People allied to both sides, and thus losing on exchange and patterns of social action, often help to bring the disputants together and to solve or patch over the dispute. Similarly with a mailing list, people who are bombarded by the dispute of others, such that it becomes difficult to read all their mail, may try to intervene to lower the volume of mail arising from that dispute.

The chief, or other 'big man', can interfere in these disputes, but throughout Melanesia he has only the power gained from respect, fear, or mutual obligation. This power varies and is risked every time it is used. Perception of a too arbitrary use of power could mean that followers would move away, or use sorcery against him, a risk he may not want to take as he could lose even the ability to give. We might think of list moderators in these terms as well. Formally they have the supposed power of a Trobriand chief to impose sanctions, but in practice their ability to use these sanctions is limited by their status on the list, the agreement of the group, and any offlist power base. As Uberoi claims "rank is not to be understood as a reflection of authority" (1971: 43). If a moderator was unable to persuade others of the appropriateness of their actions and/or the value of the environment they offer, then members of that list could depart. It is reasonably easy to find other lists or to set up a new one. Most lists will have people of similar or greater status than the moderator, which can cause further fractures and problems for the moderator, if the moderator is acting without support. A person may 'surrender' power to a moderator if: they trust the moderator to make the right decision; to avoid personal blame; or to avoid continued dispute with another about their own position. However, this surrender is at best temporary, in another dispute this same person may argue fiercely with the moderator. The leader has the dubious privilege of becoming the scapegoat and focus for blame.

A Trobriand chief can let it be known he will have sorcery employed if people do not settle down and allow normal social functioning. With sorcery not only can misfortune which happens to the victim be interpreted as resulting from the sorcery, but it can nearly always be circumvented by other magic (Malinowski 1926: 80-1) and thus, if unsuccessful, be denied without risking the chief's status. However, problems arise as the person competent in sorcery is "often a dreaded competitor of the chief or headman" (ibid: 122), and so an unpopular decision invites uncertain retaliation. Sorcery may reinforce hierarchy at the same time it enables its destabilization (Kapferer 1997: xiv).

If we think of sorcery as an 'in the background and hidden' activity of uncertain magnitude, we might compare it to actions taken offlist to discomfort or remove someone. As moderators are the only persons with the power to remove people, they tend to get embroiled either willingly, through perhaps gathering 'secret' support for an otherwise unilateral decision, or unwillingly when people with a private dispute attempt either to influence the moderator against the other person or engage in a struggle to get rid of the other person. Such offlist 'sorcerous' struggles, while apparently rare on Cybermind, did occur. Obviously some lists will be more prone to this than others. On other Lists I have heard suspicions that 'troublesome' people just 'disappeared'. Hiddenness implies that this lessens chances that people will notice the removal and object which intensifies the sorcery. The only time I know this happened on Cybermind, Alan had actually been gathering support offlist for the action (see Chapter 10).

Sorcery is not just hidden hostile activity but a mode of interpretation of happenings (Barth 1975: 131). It is related to the control and disruption of intellectual or social history and status, and the explanations of disruption or incoherence which people give. For example; pondering whether malfunctions are a sign of an attack, or whether a particular unknown new and 'rude' person is being deliberately hostile on someone else's behalf. Similarly, malicious offlist gossip could be a hidden attempt to destroy the reputation a person has gained through public prestation.

In online society, 'secret knowledges' such as programming or familiarity with the workings of the internet, can give both power and status. These knowledges work 'magic', sometimes making it possible for pseudonymous people to be identified, making people disappear or 'die' and, in certain circumstances, putting words into their mouths. The uncertain possibilities of the power of programming add to this effect. Fear of hackers is fear of this kind of sorcery. On one occasion when the List was undergoing disruption, the internet supplier of one of the List members involved was being disrupted by hackers at the same time. Although list members thought it unlikely the two events were connected, they did suggest it. Moderators, like a Trobriand chief, may fear the possibility of such action being taken against them.

'Public' and 'Private' Violations

In general, violations occurring out of public view can be ignored, even if people would say that the breaking of the value was serious. One example Malinowski gives is of a young couple who had sex, which was prohibited as their mothers were sisters. Apparently people knew of the affair but ignored it. However, the young woman's ex-lover insulted her 'secret' lover in public and drew attention to the offence. The male offender donned ritual attire, climbed a tree, and addressed the community complaining about the man who had driven him to this, and leapt to his death. A fight broke out and the ex-lover was wounded. Public opinion was not outraged by the crime, it had to be mobilised by an interested party and the victim punished himself. Malinowski does not tell us what happened to the young woman (1926: 78-9). Suicides resulting from insult will be talked about for years (cf. page 95ff.), and this talk will serve to remind people of the potentially disastrous consequences of these 'flame wars'. He comments:

> The principles according to which crime is punished are very vague... the methods of carrying out retribution are fitful, governed by chance and personal passion rather than by any system of fixed institutions... These institutions and usages, far from being legal in their main function, only very partially and imperfectly subserve the end of maintaining and enforcing the biddings of tradition. We have not found any arrangement or usage which could be classed as a form of 'administration of justice', according to a code

and by fixed methods... All the legally effective institutions we found are rather means of cutting short an illegal or intolerable state of affairs, of restoring the equilibrium in social life and of giving vent to the feelings of oppression and injustice felt by individuals (ibid: 98-9).

Likewise in online society what happens offlist is of little concern to the list, unless it intrudes into the flow of list life, becoming 'public'. There may be no agreed upon code of offences among list members. Similarly there is no "arrangement or usage" resembling a State's administration of justice in online life. Sometimes people not in the dispute will try to persuade the disputants to take the argument to private mail, thus preventing it from being a problem for themselves. In most situations an apparently sincere apology and pledge not to continue the currently offensive behaviour leads to any sanctions being abandoned. Even if the person publicly 'suicides' by getting themselves thrown off the list (and thus attempts to spread blame as did the young man in the anecdote), or unsubscribes with a torrent of abuse, contacts can still be maintained (as could the 'offence'). In one such case of public suicide the person was back on the list within six months, though soon departing as they felt that response to them was not as plentiful as previously. People will likewise discuss flame wars to remind each other of the disastrous consequences of dispute.

Time and Exchange

It is the delay between messages on a mailing list which makes the gift model even vaguely persuasive[12]. The more interchange approaches real time (as on MOOs), the more the main functions of conversation approach the general use that speech has for things other than the 'mere' exchange of ideas, and the less content any given message might have. Utterances resembling "hmm" might be needed in MOO conversation, but such markers are rare in the extreme on email Lists.

Pauses also have functions in normal conversations, indicating times to switch roles, confirm comprehension and so on. Pause effects are subtle in mailing list and email. Too long a gap within a thread and people will not return to it, while too short a gap between replies can be a cause or symptom of dispute. When Glen posted 25 mails in a row with no break between them (see Chapter 9), this caused problems. Flame wars tend to have little pause, fast replies keep the memory, or mood, of the dispute/hurt alive. And as inability to make adequate response, or continue the exchange, is usually taken as defeat, quick replies can become more common.

The most important time effect is fairly difficult to prove, but from my own experience, other people's comments and the distorted time perceptions noticed when people describe past events, it appears that time is experienced as a function of numerical volume of mail. As Rose wrote (8 Dec.94): "Elapsed time seems dependent upon message volume, to some extent". Threads, which attract a large number of posts, will be felt to have lasted a longer time than threads with a small volume. In a sense the prestations create the sense of time.

Time also eradicates whatever status or history a person has developed, though perhaps less so if it is a bad history. People who are not present (not *presenting*) will be forgotten—there will generally be no monuments to them. The members of the group will change and nothing a person previously did will be visible to these new members. Status and recognition is a matter of the now, and of continual effort[13].

Place and Exchange

Electronic communication fora are usually thought of as places. It is hard to name them, or sometimes even to speak of them, in other than spatial terms, and the type of space that people describe the forum as has consequences for behaviour and persuasion (Marshall 2001). The spatial quality of a MOO is effected by the description of a 'room', but in a mailing list the quality of the place is determined by the messages. Obviously the content and style of the messages will be important and, as shown in Appendix I, with the vast majority of posts coming from a small minority of list members, the dominant group determines the sense of place and mood to a great extent.

How the reader perceives the location is affected by the way they have their mail program organised. If all the mails from Cybermind are listed as 'from Cybermind' the group might be perceived as a whole volume, but if the program reveals the author directly, then the names of prominent posters become direct markers of presence. In this second case, however briefly, the prestations from individuals are laid before the reader. They occupy screen space on opening the net link, which perhaps is analogous to the places in which 'ordinary' prestations are displayed. The items constitute the space and create emotional tone and thus influence the ways the space is interpreted. The particular physicality and quality of space for humans is made by the human use of the space. On a mailing list, this is simply more extreme; the 'space/time' would not exist without the humans and the prestations which 'open it up'.

Gender, Gift and Intimacy

Cheal argues that within the conventional Western 'gift economy' most giving occurs within the so-called 'private sphere' as a means of managing the emotional aspects of relationships, particularly the display of 'love' which is the presumed basis of enduring personal relationships. As such, gifting is performed primarily by women to women (1988: 5-6, 18, 75). Gift exchanges which involve men will usually have at least one female participant (ibid: 44, 64, 178-9)[14].

On a mailing list there are basically two forms of sociality; 'onlist' and 'offlist'. Offlist exchanges tend to be dyadic, so approximating the ideal WES world intimacy of the couple. If we take the distinction between 'private' (or 'intimate') and 'public' or ('communal') as divisions which come easily to WES people, then it is worth investigating whether the 'traditional' association of women with the intimate or offlist sphere, and men with the public or onlist sphere has any effect upon modes of prestation.

If gender is the prime way WES people establish intimacy and make intimate exchange, and if in the embedding society this almost always involves women, then relationships directed at the 'private' or offlist dyadic sphere will be influenced by, or even depend upon, gender. Establishing that at least one of the dyad is a woman, allows closeness to manifest more easily[15]. If it is common that 'maleness' is identified with aggression and flaming, and that, in contrast, women are identified with more harmonious interaction, then such identifications probably increase any difference in offlist exchange. As argued previously, among Cybermind members, gender is usually taken as clear.

Looking at gendered patterns of exchange in the discussion lists LINGUIST and Megabyte University, Susan Herring found that women participated "at a rate that is significantly lower than that corresponding to their numerical representation". She also states that "the messages contributed by women are shorter... a very long message invariably indicates that the sender is male", and that "messages posted by women consistently received fewer average responses than those posted by men... [T]opics initiated by women are less often taken up as topics of discussion by the group as a whole" (1996b: 480).

There is, as far as I can see, no concerted and deliberate attempt by males on Cybermind to monopolise onlist space. The statistical evidence presented in Appendix I shows women are among the most voluminous posters, that the response rates to males and females is similar, and that the average length of posts is also similar. This ratio may have changed after the Iraq War and the death of Rose. There were less people posting to the List and less of them were female.

As well as documenting the apparent 'actuality' of these factors, it is important to discover whether people think they are the case or not, and discover if women conduct significant levels of exchange and comment offlist. The formation of the 'breakaway' women's list 'emma' might be a way of dealing with the perception of such problems (see Chapter 10).

Although offlist questions are hard to resolve, anecdotal evidence suggests that most continuing offlist prestations involve at least one woman, and that intimate prestations will also tend to involve a woman. Thus, one male inquired about my health and condition to a mutually known woman before asking me. I had similarly assumed that a particular woman had smoothed things over between myself and another male. So the question arises as to whether women see offlist exchanges as independent from the list, or as maintaining the network of the list, in the way that Cheal argues that women are supposed to maintain the networks that maintain family connections via gifts? Is the association of the private-intimate-and-offlist, connected with an association of the offlist with the female?

Another possible effect of differences in offlist and onlist constructions might be that some women feel more comfortable in engaging in offlist exchanges than they do engaging in onlist exchanges. This might even be exaggerated by expectations of group unity being based primarily on personal bonds. In this case a person by posting to the list risks rejection of their 'love' and the discovery that, by this criteria, they do not belong to the group. This feeling of greater comfort posting offlist does appear to be the case for some women, but I do not know how general this is or whether it affects many males.

Some questions on this topic were put to the list directly in late May 1997 and, although only a few replies were gained, they are of interest. Most respondents did not think that lengthy mails tended to originate with males—the sole respondents who thought they did was an offlist female respondent ('X') who had drawn my attention to the Herring article and thus might have expectations derived from that. Neither did people think that women had more tendency to make more frequent short posts than men—even Rose who was the maestro of frequent short posts.

There was some disagreement as to whether more competitive prestations came from males and more nurturing or binding prestations came from females. Rose, for example, wrote "Yeah—I think so". Alan wrote "Yes". X thought it was probably true in general but perhaps not so much on Cybermind as elsewhere. Morrigan denied this difference of response while thinking it was more complex: "No, there is such a degree of cross over anyhow, like how does age and class and race and country of origin effect the personality of the poster". Caitlin, though expressing reservations and agreeing with the need to do a close count, wrote:

> not in my experience. I find that women posting on lists can be just as competitive and confrontational as men and men can be just as nurturant and binding as women. I do think that many people have this impression, but I'm not sure it's 'true'.

She also agreed with Morrigan about cultural complications.

It appeared hard for women to answer the question of whether "most continuing off-list prestations involve[s] at least one woman?" As the question did not have to refer solely to a person's own exchanges, but to what they knew about others, this difficulty implies lack of knowledge of the behaviour of other List members offlist. Alan responded: "most of my correspondence off-list is with women, with 'bursts' or 'cycles' of correspondence with men. With men, it seems to revolve around specific issues". This was also the case for myself, with the possible exception of correspondence with Alan himself. A few offlist correspondences with males on this subject suggest this might be the case in general.

Rose considered that "women are perhaps _more_ 'mutually supportive' off-list than on? ('They aren't listening—now we can talk!')". While she considered that most praise about her posts came from males, she thought this was probably because she was female. Morrigan also suggests an audience effect and wrote:

> I've found, personally, that women become more open off list more easily. Women seem to make themselves more vulnerable to me a lot quicker than men do, but maybe that's because I am another woman, ie it has nothing to do with the originator but with the audience. Some men consistently appear to maintain an 'arms length' kind of tone. Sometimes I wonder whether this is because of the innate sexual tension that is there between women and men when there is something of a creative nature [or because her male partner was on list as well].

Caitlin wrote:

> Men are more likely to write me to tell me they enjoyed something I wrote. I haven't noticed any huge difference in the ways that people write me based on their gender [...] Usually, when I strike a chord, the mail I get backchannel is filled w/personal revelation and I haven't noticed any difference there. I haven't noticed men being somehow more careful w/me due to issues of sexual tension, either. Certainly that sort of tension exists, but I'll note that women are as likely to flirt w/me in email (and I w/them) as men are

In response to the question:

> Do women see off-list exchanges as independent from the list?, or is there a tendency to perceive these exchanges as maintaining the network of the list?, or the networks of particular groups off list?

Rose wrote "No. No. No.", while X wrote:

> I think this is not an 'either/ or' answer rather it is an 'and'. That is to say that yes I think of off list exchanges as independent from the list in the same sense as I think of socialising with someone I work with as separate to the group mileau. However while there is a separation, there is not a divison (if you can follow) the list, or group is still there. It informs conversation and likewise the off-line, or out of group contact, can be brought back and shared with others, if appropriate.

Morrigan replied:

> I see off-list exchanges as both independent and dependent. All mutual exchange is development and that development is taken back onto the list. The other day [her partner] made a friendship band out of silk embroidery threads for me. It's not a complicated process, but it is intricate and time consuming, ordering the threads and tying the knots to produce something that is so totally different from each individual thread. For me the List and back channel is like that.

She added that:

> more men write to me than women, but (in the main) the women wish to engage in a more prolonged exchange, offer more information about themselves/feelings, etc. It's back to that thing about the tension between the sexes, maybe the men don't want to be pushy in any way, intrusive.

And Caitlin added:

> We're having this conversation because of something you or me said on the

list, but, depending upon the direction the conversation takes and the relationship that may develop from said conversation, the exchange may become completely unrelated to this list and the community. Or maybe not.

Rose also thought that women would probably be more comfortable in offlist exchanges but that "ain't me personal pat'urn, right? I'll natter wherever I ain't bin turned off!". X wrote "can only answer for me. yes. and it has exactly to do with the exchange thing. the potential for 'not being met' if/when one posts. For me posting to the list is always risky". Morrigan wrote:

> Yes, I feel very stupid most of the time, intellectually challenged. I don't think this has to do with the nature of this particular List, rather the nature of society. Women like me (no degree, no career, three kids, no job) are pretty much dispossessed and it's hard to contribute from that base. Off list is different because there's more intimacy.

Caitlin added that it wasn't the case for her:

> but then shyness in either the virtual or physical world really isn't a problem for me. I'll talk to just about anybody, just about anywhere. I do know that I am more self-confident in this way than most of the people I know.

These exchanges also show some of the variations involved in people's construction of list 'culture' and, perhaps, the facility with which this group constructs culture around various themes and categories. Despite these variations there is clearly enough commonality for people to appear to understand each other. In summary, people seem to feel that gender is important, though more important in constituting offlist life than in influencing onlist life—with the exception that at least two women felt somewhat nervous about making public prestations, feeling the risk that their gifts would be rejected or ignored[16]. However, at the same time it appears the women responding seem dubious about a hard distinction between onlist and offlist life. Perhaps this is because of an implicit suggestion that onlist life is *real* list life, when it appears that, at least on occasions, offlist life is more vital than onlist life, or cannot easily be separated out, or transforms onlist life for them. There is a "separation but not a division".

Property

When Malinowski describes the case of ownership for canoes, although he specifically states that a canoe will have an owner, "ownership" of a canoe is complex, as are the claims that people may have to use a particular canoe.

> Ownership... is defined by the manner in which the object is made, used and regarded by the group of men who produced it and enjoy its possession... in using the craft every joint owner has a right to a certain place in it and to certain duties, privileges and benefits associated with it... it is the sum of duties, privileges and mutualities which bind the joint owners to the object and to each other (1926: 19-20).

If most people who need a canoe can position themselves somewhere in a web of relationships which allows them to use a canoe when needed, or to become part of a building party for a canoe, then given that a canoe needs a group to be operated, it becomes exceedingly unlikely that anyone would or could simply remove a canoe from the orbit of its 'owners' to their own *personal* use.

On a list, list mails are public prestations: they are given freely; they are not 'for sale'; there is no fixed value which calls for immediate return; the author's stack of gifts is not diminished by someone else using them; nor is any status gained by the prestation lost if another uses it elsewhere (to some extent the reverse might happen). It is also exceedingly difficult to maintain, or accumulate, anything we might call capital. It is equally difficult to dissipate any accumulation, or to run the risk of depletion though overgenerous 'gifting'. It is also difficult to appropriate something 'belonging to' someone else within the group, to use within the group. The structure of Lists implies that rarely will any member be able to appropriate a source of gifts, or distribute them to a particular subgroup, who thereby gain gifts that they can give to others. In general, on a List, everyone receives more than they give.

However, it is still more complex than this, because not only is a mail a public gift, in the sense that it helps constitute the group, the place of the group, and gains its value because of the group, but it clearly arises from the group, usually in direct or indirect response to something that someone else has crafted.

In much of the series of exchanges under the headings of 'systems of peace', and 'systems of property' which I was having with other members of Cybermind, and which eventually became this chapter, parts of the 'property' of the others were clearly embedded within the 'property' of mine and make it what it is. There has been a form of group ownership constructed through almost every mail which made this exchange ; almost all of which included excerpts from previous mails. Further, the exchange only exists because of the group—even if most of the group was largely silent. This particular exchange emerged from a post about an African cultural performance that a list member had witnessed which, in turn, emerged from something else, and so on.

We might say that like the Trobriand canoe, this chapter is only existent because of a web of connections and contributions; yet writing it, and publishing it, changes the models.

For information to become sellable, in an 'information economy', it must be in short supply. People must be prevented from accessing it for little or nothing. Parts of information must be isolated and not ascribed to a mixed origin, like the Trobriand canoe, but to an origin that breaks from previous discourse. Capitalism replaces economies of multiplicities, or of extravagant dissemination and dispersion, with ideologies of ownership and accumulation. Perhaps the Internet restores these other economies.

Questions about what 'constitutes property' become contested. Concepts of "property" in cyberspace change with the players. As the demographics change, as the ways of charging, or gaining access change, as the kinds of things 'cyberspace' is used for change, so will the concepts of property. Laws will be made to enshrine these concepts; either to catch up or to try and import or preserve ways that property is defined in the embedding society.

The mode of dissemination and appropriation in corporate capitalism automatically affects concepts of information, when information is defined as property within a society 'dominated' by corporate capitalism. Legal theorist James Boyle writes:

> information presents special [social and conceptual] problems and the discourse of authorship *seems* to solve its problems... The author stands between the public and private realms, giving new ideas to the society at large and being granted in return a limited right of private property in the artefact he or she has created (1996: xii).

Boyle claims that the notion of the corporate author does for information what economic notions of natural markets did for the industrial revolution. It provides a method by which what is an intertwined production, or a naturally occurring phenomena can be appropriated by the corporate sector (1996: xii). If information equals property, then information cannot be free (as in the old Hacker slogan). The claim of corporate authorship suppresses both the claims of sources and of audience in order to provide the break from public discourse, which allows 'private ownership'. It puts boundaries around texts.

The border between 'public' and 'private' in the WES world is, as we have seen, a paradoxical and shifting area. In capitalist property relations, rather than acting to establish intimacy, this border is where the magics of creation and ownership are used to appropriate ideas and render them commodities. The division separates whole areas which are deeply unclear and in tension; the construction of the category of 'originary author' acts as a bridge between them, and it is a border which has been permeable or reconstructed in online society.

If, in the way they were built (through the free exchange of software and techniques), internet societies originally behaved in such a way as to function as if information was a matter of prestation, then attempts to model information as 'property for sale or to be owned' destroys these 'original' models and the society changes, as surely as tribal or prestation-based societies before any totalising 'economic' model of exchange. Intertwined mail, forwards and accounts of other writings, even references to web sites, become subject to the demands of ownership and copyright. Or as Rose wrote (2 Mar.96):

> Some one has suggested that I copyright that thing that wrote itself last night, and this reopens an old thought-box. We discussed this, here, a long time ago, and it was my opinion that if I posted something to the List, it was a 'gift' (something like that...).
>
> Well, somebody seems to be thinking $$, here, and suddenly I ain't so pure and generous any more. How does one copyright something retroactively? I mean—it would burn my butt if somebody *else* made money from my sweat without my permission... ;)

Therefore the model of the information society/economy may in itself be hostile to the traditional Internet society, in that it changes the ways people who use this model can behave, from the 'inside' as it were.

It changes messages from prestation to property[17].

Chapter 9: Control and Crisis

Introduction

Points made in earlier chapters about list structure, authenticity, framing and exchange, are applied here to analyse a dispute that arose on Cybermind. The analysis shows the interrelationship between identity categories and norms, and demonstrates the ways people make sense of events online by reference to offline history. In this dispute different framings produced a positive feedback loop as people misinterpreted one another. 'List values' were actually generated in a condition of crisis—these values were not explicit or coherent before the conflict—they intensified in opposition. The dispute ultimately has its origin in cultural, rather than personal factors[1].

These events were chosen as the person involved, Glen, was an articulate dissenter and I engaged in offlist correspondence with him. He appeared on the List on three occasions about four to five months apart. The first two times he was present for about a month before leaving; the third time passed quietly before he left. Debates over Glen took considerable amounts of space, and he was mentioned by other list members when he was not onlist and in offlist correspondence, which indicates the importance of the encounter. Although almost no one argued publicly in favour of him, some did argue in favour of his right to behave as he was doing, and the spread of ways of dealing with him was marked. My impression of uniformity at the time was inaccurate. Glenn did not join Cybermind with the intention of disrupting the list, and hence we cannot simply explain the disruption by 'hostile motivation'.

The first discussions Glen was involved in, in March 1995, largely concerned his idea that behaviour on the net could be analysed as a form of capitalism (which put him outside 'mainstream' political positions on the list), and his assertion that debate should be fierce and aggressive to be open and honest.

The second time Glen appeared on the List in June/July of that year the reaction was far more hostile. However, that 'heat' was intensified by events one month before, when Gordon had deliberately attempted to disrupt the list (see Chapter 10). These previous events shifted the interpretive tools of the group into more sensitive modalities.

On this second occasion the argument moved to the Holocaust. Glen was, in my opinion, perceived as holding a position which he did not hold; although he might have had some pleasure in pushing the argument, or in aggravating people who reacted to him. He seemed to expect people could and should establish some kind of 'distance' from the Holocaust. The group reacted strongly. Several recognized people read him as casting doubt on the reality of the Holocaust. This particular misreading, and the application of the category of antisemitism to him, was intimately connected with the norms of the list. It enabled categorisation of a problem member or outsider, thus framing group dissatisfaction, focusing tools of persuasion, and motivating action. The debate was terminated by Glen acceding to several requests from Alan to discontinue the topic and, shortly afterwards, leaving the group.

Alan's behaviour shows his reluctance to unsubscribe someone, even though he threatens it, and even though in the previous month he had unsubscribed Gordon—the first time anyone had been unsubbed for non-technical reasons. Although supposedly able to rule autocratically, the structure and values of the list made his alliances difficult and unclear. He could claim support for unsubbing but it was not obvious who these supporters were, or whether they would maintain their support. Further, some recognised list-members were not wholeheartedly in approval of unsubbing. Despite the manifest hostility of many, Glen was recognized and was therefore, even if ambiguously, a list-member.

When he first left Cybermind, four people wrote to the list farewelling him. According to Glen, at least one other person wrote to him offlist "saying she didn't agree with me on anything but would miss me nontheless". Many more popular people have departed the List to considerably less expression of regret, showing the ambiguity of recognition.

Given this degree of accommodation and complexity, the problems seem primarily 'cultural'—to do with differing interpretive framings between exchange, authenticity and strength of expression, political categorisation, ambience, cosmology and powerlessness.

Both sides read things in ways which were not intended by the sender, and both concretised the 'self of the other' with these interpretations. Successful categorization simplified and intensified arguments. During the dispute some people allocated Glen to a very narrow outsider category.

Exchange and Hierarchy

When Glen first joined the list he initially posted infrequently, but soon became one of the most voluminous posters on the list. He wrote at considerable length, replied to every post mentioning him or which interested him, and inspired voluminous posts in return. He was the third most prolific poster on his first encounter and, when he returned, he became the fifth most prolific poster. By volume of words, his place would probably be even higher.

The volume of his posts disrupted the stability of the prestation hierarchy, whereby those posting a lot should be those valued by the group or, at the least, be non-disruptive of the group. Furthermore, his posts were generally critical of positions held by List members, so this volume intensified the mood of forcible colonisation or attack, and further marked him as an outsider. During his second appearance, he began to mail all his posts simultaneously, which made him even more visible. On one occasion twenty five of his posts were delivered to the list in a space of a few minutes. It was difficult to ignore him. As Glen replied to everything and quickly, a prestation move was only ever closeable by letting him make the last prestation, which would imply acceptance of his position. The speed of his responses also meant replying was not always possible. The discourse approached the conditions of flame war, even without abuse.

Group hostility towards him increased with the volume of his mail and declined while he was too busy to make more than several posts a week. His third encounter in which he made a total of twelve posts over sixteen days, never making more than three posts a day, was uncontroversial. To reiterate: occupation of List space creates List space.

Many list members commented on what they perceived as Glen's inability to engage in *exchange*. Thus, they alleged he refused to accept comments from others, and was more interested in giving his own opinions than receiving any. He was perceived as violating reciprocity by not recognising others. His prestations were perceived as a mode of attack, which was reinforced by his violation of the prestation hierarchy. For example David wrote:

> it seems to me, you don't want to really engage with other people in discussion.... I naively thought you would be capable of listening to those on the list who take the time to engage in 'communication' with you. However it's become all too obvious that you are far too busy trying to work out what you're going to say next to bother with listening.

Another member expressed their perception that the gifts were not made in 'good faith':

> you are not listening, you are not communicating, you are not learning. You are typing to hear yourself type and to see how many buttons you can push on how many people.

Several other people also agreed that Glen did not listen, or did not display the empathy that listening to others required.

Authenticity

Authenticity and its conventions were supported by both sides, but for Glen affective involvement at a fairly high and continual level was required to maintain interest. This demand for excitement and a demand for what he called "hard-core, interactive analysis" and a more 'aggressive' debating style[2] contrasted with the general preferences of the list for an even-tempered, low-aggression style—even though recognised members were frequently quite vituperative towards each other. As he wrote to me, "I'm trying to move away from campy, inefficient 'you-scratch-my-back' smalltalk into *true communication*" (my emphasis). Other members restated the group's official preference for calm discourse with low aggression, writing that Glen's method will "more than likely engender flames which then have to be doused before productive dialogue can take place". As we might expect Glen (9 Mar.95) disagreed, claiming that high affect is a mark of true exchange and authenticity.

> Well with respect to honesty and integrity, I've found the latter method a MUCH more effective method of communication.
>
> I'm not going to straddle any fences. I'm not going to hide behind some facade of humility.
>
> And I'm certainly not going to pretend to give someone respect [...]
>
> And, anyway, flames do not have to be 'doused' as you say. There is much to learn in the way someone flames me as there is in their more civil comments.

The display of certain types of affect and engagement (which to Glen imply authenticity and openness) interacts with the interpretation of the display of these types of affect as hostility and disruption of communication. The interrelation of the group's claims about concern or recognition of others with Glen's interpretation of these displays as avoidance and dishonesty, increases his feeling of avoidance and dishonesty and thus increases his displays which are interpreted as hostility and so on.

Political Categories

Glen's favour of aggression, tended to lead to him being politically typed, and assigned into offline world political categories, mythemes and social power. This was congruent with his general political line. For example, during the arguments about the nature of capitalism, some people suggested Glen read Marx. He replied that Marx was boring and that:

> I don't like Marx's emphasis on the working man as a victim... I take full responsibility for the good and bad things that happen to me. if I spend my life on an assembly line dissatisfied with and disassociated from my end product, then it's my fault. In short I think of Marx as an elitist.

When I argued that historically capitalism was based on the dispossession of people from the land and had rendered people incapable of supporting themselves, he replied:

> the peasants let this happen to them (and please don't respond to that with, 'how should they have stopped it? I don't know how they should've or even if they could've... but they still let it happen.

Similarly, in a discussion of harassment of women in the workforce, he insisted that women should vocalise their distress and take legal action if possible but, at the same time, women should not take snide comments to heart but "brush them off". In his opinion the problem was of no necessary or continuing concern to others:

> If in the end you fail, then you fail. Period. I cannot waste my life and billions of dollars trying to help every underdog in the universe. I have things to do.

It is not clear how such a concern would stop *him* from 'doing things', but we can think of the 'conservative-right's' determination that 'well meaning people' interfere with the process of other people taking 'personal responsibility' for themselves, and thus destroy the moral sense of these other people. Empathy was a potential trap and waste of time.

List members who commented tended to perceive their identity in terms of groups (either belonging or not belonging) and in terms of relatedness to others. Glen appeared to perceive his identity in much more individualistic terms (as a category of one). His learning is motivated by relevance to him, and not dependent upon others, just as what happens to him is not dependent upon others, and he only has to relate to or help those who are important to him. These value positions take their force in relation to each other. Normally, members of Cybermind would, as is the social convention for US citizens, portray themselves as individuals, but here List members become more group centred and Glen more individualistic as they differentiate themselves from each other, or try to make sense of the already perceived difference.

The 'Holocaust Debate'

After a short series of arguments recapitulating themes from the previous encounter, Glen's writing moved from the verge of non-specific abuse (writing that "intellectuals need a huge kick in the butt once and a while"), to a direct challenge (or 'honest expression' of frustration) from him to Alan:

> If my lack of knowledge and understanding of Marx[3] gets in the way of your understanding or relating to anything I write, then use your #@!$%^&*$# delete key. Or better yet, flex your muscle as list God and take me off, never to return again.

For his part Alan introduced a link between anti-intellectualism and anti-semitism:

> Yes, Glen, the intellectuals need a huge kick in the butt once in a while, and you're just the one to give it to them! Wow! Arbeit macht frei!

and:

> quite frankly I am frightened of the anti-intellectualism I see all over this country. You can call me paranoid if you want, but for better or worse I _am_ an intellectual, and that has also been a charge against Jews in the past, and intellectuals and Jews have often been close to the first to go.

The normative position expressed here stems from Alan's self-identity as intellectual, Jewish and marginal to the power structures of his country, and particularly to the supposedly mainstream 'Republican Revolution' of the mid 90s. For him it was a matter of survival, as he makes clear elsewhere, "we're losing our freedoms, our ability to exist in this world".

Such survival anxiety is general among the group. Later posts refer to government cutbacks in expenditure on arts and education, where survival income originates for some recognised list members. Glen is made a prototypic representative of a group engaged in the destruction of a way of life (i.e. as racist, pro-capitalist, selfish, anti-culture, anti-intellectual), just as, for Glen, Alan takes a social role as "Knowledge Keeper" or "academic elitist". Both categorise the other as powerful and themselves as not, thus expressing a general sense of alienation from power. It would, however, be impossible to get list-wide support to expel someone for not being 'intellectual'. The value is being elaborated in relation to Glen. If the list became 'dominated' by ponderous essays with heavy citation and referencing, the focus of dissent would change, just as during the Iraq War some members wanted light humorous posts.

Glen was not aware of the significance of the phrase "Arbeit macht frei"[4] used by Alan, but its connection with the concentration camps was explained to him by dobie and Mitchell. Glen replies:

> Well, I don't mean to push buttons; but, on the surface, the phrase sounds exactly the same as the common American dream, i.e. work hard and you can achieve anything.
>
> Is the difference between the two simply one of where they've been in the past? Simply one of history? If so, then I would entreat you to let go of the specific relation to the phrase and shift your emotion instead to the *use* of the phrase.

Dobie expresses surprise at this request and argues for its impossibility. Within the group the possibility of empathy towards the victims of the Holocaust is a fundamental moral act. This discussion then blends with another ongoing discussion of morals as 'gut feeling', Glen writes:

> I would even go so far as to claim that it is Intellectualism or ideological abstraction that *causes* the persecution of others. The main reason the Holocaust went down was because people listened to the 'reasoning' of their leaders when they should have been going with their instincts.

Alan replies (8 July.95):

> Glen, this is the core of where you're wrong, and where your wrongness is dangerous. Read Theweleit's Male Fantasies; it was _precisely_ gut feeling that led, among the Freikorps and others, to Nazism. Gut feeling doesn't 'know' morality whatsoever [...]

Again, for Glen it is the strength of 'feeling' that propels the intellect, while active group members argue that the strength of hostile emotions disrupt discourse. Glen had also been protesting that List members 'constant' reference to academic writers[5] was a mode of avoiding having to think for themselves, as well as a low excitement interaction, so Alan's reference to Theweleit (intended to ground the discussion in a body of work), is to him another example of avoidance.

Glen goes on to claim there is an overemphasis on anti-semitism, which might lead to social barriers:

> Yes, anti-semitism is wrong. Yes, the holocaust was probably horrible and there are fanatics out there who claim it never happened. And, yes, if you feel strongly about it, study it and fix it a permanent place in your world-view. But, don't lower yourself to the same level as the racists by thinking that Judaism separates you from the rest of humanity.[...]
>
> I do intend to get past, as quickly as possible, those barriers to communication that come about because of a refusal on one or more of the parties in a discussion to say what they want to say when they want to say it.

Glen may think separation is overcome through aggressive communication, but Steven finds these posts "offensive" and "hurtful", while Alan writes that anti-semitism is on the increase and this increase is related to the rise of the far right. These are points which Steven seconds, but Robert and Tom dispute as they often identified with US Republican politics, and need to state they are not inimical to the group, and they don't support anti-semitism because of their politics. Neither Tom nor Robert are perceived as outsiders when compared to Glen, and no one disputes with them at this moment; what makes an insider varies with situation. Alan writes that he too is offended. The term 'offence' indicates discourse is becoming intense, thus contradicting the developing values of Cybermind and indicating to Glen that communication might soon start to happen. As a result, this means the process will not stop. However the intensity not only has to do with Glen's mode of presentation but with people's theories about the world.

Robert, while defending the record of the Republicans in the US Congress, refers to Glen's post when he writes that allegations that there "is a war being waged on the freedom of people [...] reminds [him] of glen saying he thinks that the holocaust never occurred because he didn't witness it". The statement that the "the holocaust was probably horrible" also draws rebuke from Caitlin, dobie, Steven, and Angela, and puzzlement that anyone is bothering with him, from Mike, Fred, Laura, Kaona, Mitchell, and KK.

Suspicions of racism provided a socially powerful focus for people's discontent with Glen, although the way this was handled varied. Rose writes about a mosquito in the room with her, which she decides to ignore to concentrate on the important things on her computer screen. Several people narrate their experiences with people who survived the Holocaust. Laurie wrote about the denial of evil and how it is present within all of us, and how denial leads to projection upon others:

> we, each and every one of us, carry within us the seeds of a holocaust in the actions and attitudes that carry indifference and hostility to the needs and rights of others.

Steven, Johnson, skip, js, Amethist and kmc joined in Laurie's discussion. So a common moral reaction was a universalism suggesting we all might be capable of immoral or persecutory acts. This is again not surprising given group valuation of empathy.

Glen then posted twenty five posts in a row, an early one of which states:

> Just to make sure it's documented... I NEVER claimed that the holocaust didn't occur because I never witnessed it.
>
> I NEVER said that. I NEVER implied that. And if you think that I did imply that, either you don't understand English or you speaking out of context.

Later, in the same stream of posts, he tried to explain what he meant by "probably horrible":

> The word 'probable' is used to indicate the existence of possibilities not under consideration. If I were to say, 'the holocaust was horrible,' I would be implying that I knew the horror myself, or, at least, knew that someone who I trust expressed to me that it was horrible.

A few people (Amethist, Laurie, Alan, Steven and later Jerry) commented on the number of posts and twenty minutes later (presumably after reading them) Alan wrote:

> I'm writing publicly because I'm extremely angry with Glen, and if the spamming keeps up, I'll be forced to uns*b him. I don't want to do this.

> At this point, I consider him a somewhat nasty anti-semite, but that's my business. But I don't want to have thirty posts from him in a row—or from anyone else—taking up bandwidth; this is not fair to a lot of the subscribers who pay for accounts, and it's not fair because it tends to dominate a list. [...]
>
> I'm also writing this to open it up for discussion; I'm not going to take unilateral action, particularly if the spamming stops.

Several members of the group also think Glen is occupying too much space and Glen agrees to consolidate his posts. Andrew, Toni, Jerry and KK write in support of Alan's management of the list, and his statements about Glen. Tom, Steven, Laurie, Steve, Caitlin and Jacques all write that they consider Glen unreachable or determined to be ignorant.

There are some counter proposals and reactions. For example, Amethist asks "Why doesn't the group try to make peace with Glen?" Johnson, Jose, Mitchell, and myself argue that although Glen is prolific he is not spamming, and banning him is not a good thing to do. Rose agrees that Glen is not spamming but that she trusts Alan's judgement; Steven, who has been clearly upset by Glen's actions, asks a question:

> Isn't 'community' a consensual thing. The paradox for me is this:
>
> A section of the seder discusses the four children (trad. sons): the smart child; the less-smart child; the child that cannot ask and the child that separates from the community. They each ask about Passover...the first two children ask about why WE celebrate passover; the fourth child asks 'What do YOU mean by Passover.' My question is, for all you riddle freaks...is this last son part of the community or apart from the community?

Of those who respond, most think the fourth child is a member of the community, even some who have been critical of Glen's presence. It is unlikely that anyone who replied was unaware of the metaphorical leaning of the question[6]. Dobie and Craig argue that Glen is not anti-semitic. Alan adds (20 July.95):

> I won't tolerate anti-semitism here in this space, because to do so would be an ad hoc support on my part. I would rather see the list collapse than be a sounding-board for anti-semitic or other racist ideas.

This is a clear threat, but the only option Alan has, if he is to *lead*, is to put the existence of the group at stake, and the justification is the authenticity of his reaction and the strength of his feelings. However, threatening the group is not an option he can follow through with—the values of the group forbid it to some extent. There are protests at this threat. Skip writes, although not defending Glen:

> on the Net, we are going to find ourselves forced to confront any number of things that make us uncomfortable (people, philosophies, ideas, images...), that previously kept more or less to themselves and were easy to avoid. We might as well learn how to do that.

Alan responds:

> Lists are not open spaces. They are communities that take work to maintain.
>
> I received a tremendous amount of mail supporting my decisions, as well as mail asking me to unsub him directly. I did neither. I will if the discussion continues.

If on Cybermind a sense of 'community' partly results from off-topic posts, then these off-topic posts can also increase the prospect of dispute and fragmentation of the list, as they too define List space and place and open the possibilities of fracture.

People expressed support for Alan, but none (however many wrote directly to Alan), wrote to the List asking for Glen to be removed, although several wrote that whatever Alan decided to do was acceptable. It is as if those of the group who wanted to take action against Glen abstained from the responsibility of asking for action, letting Alan be the focus for any dissent or blame that might arise.

Glen made several more posts on one day, and then left voluntarily without announcement.

Conclusion

The clash shows the importance of framing, of modes of exchange, and of the ways that people push each other into becoming prototypes of out-group categories and thus making it harder to read them in the way those people might have intended. These identity categories then have huge effects on persuasion and on the rhetoric of life, and the trajectory of events. The debate also shows the uncertainty of power on the List; if the positions had been pushed to a complete confrontation, it is not really clear what would have happened.

Usually the exposition of norms and values (or explicit formulations about others and the world) on Cybermind is inexplicit or implicit, and even when norms *are* explicit there are always exceptions, contestations and areas of vagueness. This inexplicit nature of values may allow a voluntary group more diverse membership, or give an appearance of greater unity, as there is no call for everyone to agree on these norms, or for them to be continually enforced[7]. However, in times of stress (some of which will be generated by external events), focal points can appear, perhaps only visible with hindsight, around which 'proto-norms' cluster. These cluster points give the eventuant norms the appearance of greater unity than they actually possess. Norms and values become perceptible in opposition. They are organised around category membership. If somebody behaves in a particular way, or has certain features, then they *are* something. Norms validate identity and are reciprocal, in that they require others for their validation, whether that validation is through acceptance or rejection. Norms arise in the grouping of things together which are different, and the excluding of things which might be similar. They thus grow out of interactions between groups, or between people within groups, and are generated within the same categorizational processes which drive the extension of both sympathy and conflict.

Glen violated the prestation hierarchy by his volume of mail. He attacked member's ideas, and disrupted processes of closure on the list by answering all mail referring to him, thus involving more and more of the list in interaction with him, in ways which generated hostility or impatience. The structure of the list made it impossible for people to participate on, or follow, the list without encountering the consequences of Glen's interactions with people. He occupied and created far more space than his status warranted.

The etiquette and values Glen brought to frame, and hence interpret, List behaviour, led him to perceive the group as distant, remote, unconcerned with honesty and 'interactive communication', and deeply involved in protecting their status as an elite. On the other hand, the framings used by many on the List (but not all) led to him being perceived as aggressive, intending to argue with no clear point to make, and unconcerned with the empathy they regarded as necessary for communication or listening. It was easy to categorise him as a hostile part of the alienated and uncertain social situation for which Cybermind was a response. He could be perceived as symptomatic of threats to existence in the offline world.

Both sides perceived the other as trivial, ignorant or arrogant. Glen's refusal to accept references to authors, or go away and read them, was seen as arrogant, and his desire for the intensity he called amusement was interpreted as frivolous or aggressive depending on the circumstance. List member's frequent reference to texts outside the immediate communication, was seen by him as trivialising and arrogant, blocking out the non-educated. The List's refusal to accept his 'aggressive' and 'honest' communication style was also seen by him as devaluing intellectual honesty and as retreat or exclusion.

These incompatible framings led to an increase in the behaviours which 'the other side' found upsetting. Glen's attempts to ensure 'honest communication' were perceived as aggressive or ignorant, and met by defence or reference to books in order to expand the terms of reference, which he then perceived as avoidance. This increased his attempts at 'honest communication'. The cycle was broken in the first encounter by pressure on Glen's time, and a decrease in his mails, which lowered List perceptions of his hostility, and the second time by Alan insisting that a subject was closed. However, breaking the cycles decreased intensity and engendered dissatisfaction in Glen and led to his departure.

The debate also crystallised values in coaction. Conflict created values, it made it easier for Glen to be categorised as prototypic of the 'Rightism' which appeared to threaten people's lives. With this framing in place, it became impossible for some to hear what he was saying and easier to make it even more prototypic of 'Rightist' positions which he did not hold, such as racism; even when this was brought up by a normally right wing member of the List trying to distinguish himself from Glen. Simultaneously, Glen became more expressive of his need for intensity and the expression of particular types of affect which could be interpreted as aggression. Conversely, Cybermind became more formally expressive of the necessity for mutual concern and empathy and of the disruptive nature of aggression or hostility. Glen's expressed value, that it was not necessary to have concern for unknown others, intensified because of demands of application of concern. To the List, this merely demonstrated his self-centredness and inability to communicate, and the futility of attempts to communicate with him. The framings led to symmetric exchange, positive feedback and hostility. Equilibrium was too difficult to attain.

These conflicts occurred despite considerable values and concerns held in common. Both sides considered Cybermind as a 'place' to expand the mind or increase understanding through discussion, but the differing framings and etiquettes made this almost impossible. Both sides valued the 'confessional' nature of the group. Glen admitted this made him uneasy, although he revealed much about his off-list life[8], but there was no agreement on the communicative styles which maintained this possibility. Both sides behaved as if emotions made something 'true' (or guaranteed discourse), and as if emotions underlay dialogue. However, the emotions which were thought to have this property were different and constructed as contradictory. As well, both sides valued open communication and perceived communication as a way of solving problems and divisions, but proved incapable of doing so, again largely because of the ways they interpreted the others. Both sides reacted to each other in terms of wider social concerns. Each perceived the other as representative of, or a manifestation of, wider and disastrous social movements. Cybermind tended towards the arguments and tropes that Lakoff (1996, 2004) claims are used in the US by 'Liberals' and Glen to those used in the US by 'Conservatives', even though questions of political faction arose only rarely. Both sides perceived communication, elitism, discrimination, exclusion and racism as problems (i.e. the construction of compulsory outgroups), but both sides perceived the other as exacerbating the situation. Both sides saw elitism and isolation as a problem, but the arguments gathered mainly around the nature of the 'other'. Glen perceived this as a problem for the group, and the list perceived it as a problem for the individual (i.e. Glen). As a result, conflict was almost inevitable.

Chapter 10: Invasions, Fragmentation and the Mobilization of Gender and Politics

Introduction

This chapter considers some examples of stress on Cybermind, including occasions when the list was apparently deliberately attacked, when the group fragmented into independent lists. In all these cases, offline world factors intruded—particularly issues involving either gender or politics. These factors provided focuses around which the interpretations and motivations of group members could cluster. In the case of the attack, the interest is not in the motives of the attackers, but in the way the List responded to a central internet mytheme about people engaging in deliberate flame. List authority and communicative structure were temporarily altered into a form more suitable for giving the moderator support, and the attack was repelled with greater ease. Although it proved easy to deal with external disruptions, internal disruptions were hard to resolve. The structure of a list implies that as it is hard for subgroups to temporarily separate or for dispute to be ignored by list members, there will be a tendency to form separate breakaway lists, or for the list to otherwise fragment. The origins of two such breakaway lists are considered to show the circumstances which engender this kind of splitting off.

Invasion Freaks?

At one time, a person, who we will call 'Gordon', appeared, writing two letters one after the other. One gave some slogans (presumably intended to be amusing) in favour of shooting people and the second stated that he was interested in the psychology of flaming. He had, he wrote, recently been in a flame war "with a group of sanctimonious profeminist men [...], what really got them going was that my flames generally had a grain of critical truth in them". Both of Gordon's mails are easily interpreted as expressing a particular 'rightist' political disposition (due to the clustering of 'guns' and 'anti-feminism') which might immediately attract support or condemnation on any list. On the net, the subject of guns is well known to cause acrimonious debates and mail flooding[1]. However, in this case, the guns post was ignored.

In response to the second post, some recognized list members stated their preference for low aggression communication. Alan proposed that flaming silenced debate, drove people away, and broke up community. Steven queried the point of flaming and suggested it stopped people revealing themselves. Nan wrote that:

> this list has for me a precious, almost miraculous feeling of community—a sense that I think springs from an unspoken commitment to civil discourse and respect for the wonderful diversity of its members.

Gordon replied that he wasn't concerned about people leaving and: "So what if feelings get hurt [...] All of this hand wringing over hurt feelings is making us into a nation of weenies". Response was initially muted as people attempted to argue with him, or suggest he wait and see how the group worked, but his subsequent replies led to many active list members deciding he was more interested in provoking flames than in discussing them; he never for instance posted "a few of the beter falmes" he'd seen.

Mail volume escalated to become among the highest ever seen on list. Eventually, correspondence took up so much space Alan decided to unsub Gordon, while immediately offering to re-invite him back if people wanted. A large debate resulted. Many argued removal of Gordon was a violation of free speech, but most writers agreed the poster did not intend real discussion, only disruption. However, even those who agreed repeatedly wrote of their ambivalence about the unsubbing.

Although not on the list, Gordon was able to post to it mail sent to him offlist from list members, together with his comments. This was explicitly seen by some list members as proof his motivations were violatory. He finally posted a summary of the affair and claimed to be a journalist writing a story about liberal intolerance, which could be seen as trying to impose his ethnographic model upon the group, as a political act. At this point, Alan removed Gordon's ability to post to the list, and a ban on his address was temporarily imposed at the listserver. Gordon's summary, together with his journalism claims, convinced most writers he had not joined in 'good faith'. Suggestions were made to use 'traditional' vengences like filling his electronic mailbox with rubbish, or notifying his Internet supplier, which, it was claimed, might lead to him losing his account. I do not know if such talk materialised into action.

In the aftermath of the affair, mail stayed at extremely high volumes, most of it either reflections upon what had happened or requests to stop discussing it. The group's identity prototype as tolerant was shaken, and volume of mail threatened identity in another way as people, unable to cope with this volume, or the recurrence of themes, left.

Similar processes were active with Gordon as in the encounter with Glen, only in an exaggerated manner; particularly issues concerning raw communication and aggression as a flag of authenticity, and 'softer' emotions as corrupting. Although it is difficult to take Gordon's words at face value, as he began his attacks immediately on joining and made little attempt to engage in anything other than hostile exchange, two particular concerns arise. Firstly, about masculinity and secondly, about the kind of public space a mailing list resembles.

Gordon appeared to be preoccupied with both attacking and conflating 'sensitivity' and 'weakness' in males. This preoccupation with establishing, or defending, 'traditional' masculine categories, was counterpositional to that of Cybermind. Thus Gordon boasted of his attack on the 'profemen' list[2], repeatedly used the term 'weenie' (usually associated in the US with small penises) as a term of abuse, wrote that a group which was disrupted by flames was weak, wrote of the S[ensitive] N[ew] A[ge] G[uy] virus which destroyed the mind and sense of humour. He recurrently used phrases implying the naturalness of competitive or aggressive communication such as "If you can't take the heat, stay out of the kitchen", "If you go to the park you have to poop with the big dogs". He occasionally referred to women with masculine pronouns, as if the audience was naturally male. The virile body was prototypically perceived as aggressive and defined by the absence of certain emotions that were considered to be weakening or 'feminine'.

Members of the group perceived this focus on masculinity in keeping with the importance of symbols of gender on the internet. Various list members wrote that:

> flames are a particularly male/aggressive way of arguing

> this "strikes me as the white, male backlash-inspired flame war".

> this is a part of being male, is it, the urge to be a nuisance to others, just to prove how big our pricks are or something???

> you seemed to assume that the group should operate according to stereotypically 'masculine' testosterone-laced communication styles. Quite a few of us on this group are women, and our presence here does affect the communication style of the list.

Perhaps because of a determination to stir things up, Gordon repeatedly accused the group of hostility to him and of starting the flames. For example, he wrote: "I started out trying to discuss flames and, well ...got flamed"; and, "since what I considered to be relatively innocent bantering has uncorked so much hostility". He alleged the first real flame occurred when a list member suggested he might not be as good a satirist as H.L. Mencken, one of his proclaimed heroes. He also accused the group of fear: "My warning lights began to flicker —who ARE these people and what are they SO afraid of?" However, it would also be possible to see this as evidence of his own fears about encroaching weakness, and as illustrating the hypothesis that male gender uncertainty leads to heightened aggression (Ross 1993: 62-3). He is perhaps overcoming his own social alienation by attempting to identify with the 'traditional' gender values espoused by the 'conservative' elite, and crush the threat of feeling socially insecure. Of course this argument is simply counterpositional to one Gordon might make to the effect that he behaved as any authentic and virile opponent of weakness and hypocrisy would do. We each make culture for the other.

Gordon claimed mailing lists were public spaces which should be open to anybody and which had to defend their right to exist; hence his stated lack of concern about people leaving. Although there were people on the list who argued similarly, the majority position seemed to be that mailing lists were not public spaces in this sense[3]. The social divisions of public and private are not automatically agreed upon, despite their importance. Examples of List member's arguments include:

> if my favourite pub is invaded by some thug starting to exercise verbal and/or physical violence, i sure do hope that someone (preferably a collective action from the guests, but if not the janitor suits me just fine) throws him out.

> Just as they wouldn't be tolerated in a casual conversation in someone's living room (well, not mine ;-) they shouldn't be tolerated here.

> This is not USEnet, which is completely public, [...] I would compare a mailing list to a club that allows anyone to join, but which retains the privilege of bouncing troublemakers.

> I think the analogy of a drunk picking fights at village pub is a good one.

Many in the group did fear that flaming would destroy the empathetic community mood-framing of the group:

> the best discussions emerge when people listen to each other.

> This list isn't a place where you get cut down for posting your thoughts, in fact its encouraged. Most people like it here for that reason.

> His comments stifled speech, thought, and ideas and Im happy to have him silenced.

> a forum for discussion may have a much greater chance of surviving a flame war/verbal violence than a community [...] [I]t's the trust between members of a community that's on stake when something like this breaks out. if i get the feeling that i can't talk from the hearth, without the fear of being nailed by some thug who just love to nail people, then that place has ceased to be a community to me. in cyberspace, as in 'real life'.

> who's the next one posing as something else than his real self, just to conduct some creepy little quasi-psychological experiment? [...] out to expose foolish lib-er-als on the Net?

People again perceived the attack in terms of a wider US political division between 'conservative and 'liberal', while some situated Gordon's activities within more general net phenomenon; both methods show the importance of embeddedness, 'history', and 'general knowledge' as precepts for interpretation.

> I felt that he might also have been deliberately trolling, trying to bring the list down, posting for the sole purpose of causing trouble. You should also know

> that there are groups on the Net that specialize in this sort of thing.

> this guy went way beyond good nature. I've seen it happen on other lists, too, and I am dubious about the ability of this group to deal with people like him.

> I've never seen a list community recover very well from a flame war.

> In my net experience, huge, icy silences grow on lists when they're subjected to 'sniper fire' flaming.

> I saw [list A] go heavy moderation because of repeated flames; now it's a dud. [List B] also lost some heavy-hitters because of a major flame war; now it's one little cat fight after another. Finally, the whole [C] system is heavily moderated because the ownership is petrified of flames; it's not only a dud but trying to get any kind of discussion going is like pulling teeth.

Counterpositionally some members argued flames had previously cemented community on the List, that he should be ignored (using the delete key, etc), gently socialised, or just observed. One member suggested Gordon's humour made him worthwhile. These were not positions that survived Gordon's journalism claims. His suggestion he was masquerading, to criticise or hurt the list through publicity, made him appear inauthentic.

Several months later, Gordon returned to the list with at least six co-workers in tow[4]. Just previously to this attack, two list members wrote that Gordon had been spotted on the 'Freaks' and 'Weird News' lists. On the attacker's arrival, another member wrote that they had been told Gordon and two of these newcomers had been running another list, which had been shut down due to complaints. Through the then fairly new functional internet search engines it was possible to confirm that several new or 'unrecognised' list members were also members of the Freaks list[5].

Initiating this second attack, Gordon pretended to be a trainee priest who had left his seminary to become engaged to a woman whom he later discovered making porn movies[6]. He asked for advice as "cybermind does seem to have a special sensitivity". Several established members responded. Gordon blew his cover by using his old address (with a pseudonym[7]) and was almost immediately publicly unsubbed by Alan. Another new subscriber (also a Freaks member) wondered about homosexuality among priests, praised the author's narrative flair, and gave mild abuse to list members such as: "shaddup you fucking bleeding heart", and "FACE IT! YOU FOLKS ARE IDIOTS". Not surprisingly some people thought this suspicious.

As it happened, several members of Cybermind had returned a few days before these events and it was easily possible to tell who were new subscribers through a *who cybermind* request. In this case, list boundaries, of a sort, could be established, which increased the possibilities of control and action. A number of these new subscribers were being pointedly vocal and being vocal about Gordon, which is unusual in many newcomers simultaneously. Discussion of the attack moved offlist and mainly concerned the best way to react to, and identify, Gordon's fellows. Making these identifications was aided, as shall become clear, by the incompetency of the attack. Most of the people identified were silently unsubbed or left of their own accord. Some members of Cybermind who began flaming the attackers back were informed by Alan of what was occurring and asked to calm down. Alan also mailed an account of the situation to many established members of the list to organise support.

Being able to identify non long-term members and thus increase boundary strength, changed the nature of the group. Similarly, Alan's raising of an offlist group communicating through him via a BCC[8] list changed the hierarchy of the group, allowing more definite actions with less chance of alienating recognised members; they were, to some extent, 'in' on the process. This suggests that the possibility of temporarily changing group organisation is part of the 'language' of social life, even if the people involved do not know exactly what they are doing. Social 'structure' renders certain behaviour more probable, but is in turn subject to temporary manipulations.

On this occasion very few people brought up issues of freedom of speech, or giving people a 'chance', with the exception of a few new subscribers; one of whom not only attempted to set up freedom issues but wrote about the fascism of the list owner. A later mail by him, presumably meant to be sent to someone else, opened:

> I just sent this to Cybemind. I am looking forward to the response. I think that the combination of indignation and crying out that I'm hurt in this post should push a lot of hot buttons over there.

Sympathy is perceived as a trap, yet again. Another Freak sent answers to mail from Gordon to Cybermind rather than to Freaks.

One Freak, widely considered to be pretending to be a woman (showing group ways of reading gender), sent several posts about diarrhoea, attempted to start a Mac vs PC argument, and fantasised about raping a male film star. Another new person CC'd their posts denouncing Alan to Freaks rather than using the hidden BCC function. Finally, another new member forwarded a threat from Gordon:

> Try not to think that your precious list is being threatened, rather imagine that the cyber-envelope is being pushed by dissonent ideas [...] You should also know that the word is out on cybermind and your insular world will never know peace until you give up any pretense of control.

During the dispute Alan asked pip to become co-moderator (again changing the hierarchy and gaining support), and they closed the list to outside email, firming the list boundaries. People now had to be registered on the list to post to it, and for a while new applicants had their addresses looked at more closely than usual.

Alan situated the events within wider political processes of the decline of civil society and the removal of public spaces within which similarly categorized people can speak, writing:

> there should be spaces on the Net where people can discuss dedicated topics, create communities and so forth, without outside interference. These spaces are disappearing everywhere.... [On Usenet], across the board... noise and the right-wing have taken over in large measure.... Something very basic is at stake here, which is the relative health and freedom of communication on the Net. It can take just a few people to bring a list down.

Free and authentic expression was perceived as being under attack.

Given the ease in which the Freaks were detected, it is difficult to determine the point of their engagement, and after all it is not exactly hard to disrupt a List. One of them wrote that groups like Cybermind:

> have begun and will continue the downfall of the Internet. I've been here, I'm staying here, and if you people insist on coming here I have every right to bug you as much as you bug me... this should be a place were people who share the common interest in, and love of machines should be.

It is tempting to see this "love of machines" also in terms of a 'masculist' retreat from emotion or human complexity[9], particularly as the Freaks list was at least as full of the 'newbies' he supposedly despised as Cybermind.

After the crisis was over, two people independently mentioned they had heard that a lot of mail had gone offlist. One wrote:

> Is there really any benefit to emulate usenet on a private mailing list? This is probably why much of the normal stuff in here has moved to private unannounced mailing distributions

The same person, in response to a question, wrote that they had been sending mail they considered more personal (i.e. private and presumably intimate), directly to others rather than openly to the list, as would be their normal custom. The crisis may have meant people needed to re-establish 'close contact', which they did privately, given the cultural association of privacy with intimacy, and the feeling the list was exposed to view and had shifted into a more public mode. Despite this momentary quietness, life soon returned to some degree of normality. However, I do not know how much mail subsequently continued off the List. It may be that offlist mail became voluminous enough to curtail the function of the List, as too many 'private' understandings were reached, and this may be a factor in the subsequent fissioning.

Perhaps the only obvious consequence was an increased level of suspicion towards newcomers who behaved unusually, as ingroup categories had temporarily hardened, and it is probable quite a few innocent people were leapt upon. In all, despite the shifting and almost unidentified background population, Alan and others learned to defend list boundaries under stress. Gordon and several of the others attempted to rejoin Cybermind about one year later and were silently removed, and when they tried again another year later Alan suggested, in offlist mail, the possibility of letting them in to see what happened. The fear had gone.

Fission

Although the list survived external disruption, it was less able to cope with a subsequent series of internal disputes, mainly based in the politics of the Left/Right division occurring in the five months afterwards[10]. Email messages tend to have one tone or express one role, making relationships 'simplex', whereas offline it is easier to create other relationships simultaneously with the person with whom you are disputing, and to give messages which reassure at the same time as they dispute (relationships become more 'multiplex'). The only sanction for either side tends to be either getting the moderator to enforce exile, or splitting off; neither of which maintains group integrity. As it is unlikely the moderator could publicly interfere in a dispute between long-standing members without disrupting the List further, the tendency is for these members to split off, or to cease participation. Such breakaway groups are possibly common. Alan wrote (pc 16 Oct.98): "Wired was a split from fop-l, Meta-Phil-Lit from Phil-Lit, and Sub from Poetics. There's a lot of this". It is easy to set up new groups, and if moderators enforce unpopular decisions they risking losing list members. Breakaway groups can also form for discussions which most of the group considers irrelevant (as with the White Powder Gold List from Alchemy, or the 'Rossin list' from Cybermind) without ill feeling and with people still remaining on the original list.

'emma'

One of these breakaway or subsidiary groups was a gender-based list called 'emma'. I first heard of emma in January 1996 when it was mentioned in an offlist response to a survey. It was exceedingly difficult to get information about this group, largely as its governing rubric was privacy, but eventually I received two different origin stories from only three people. Both stories agree it was formed in September 1995. One story specifically said it was formed by about twenty women and "one biological male who has a female soul":

> out of disgust at the dominantly male point-of-view on both fop and cm [...] It sprang forth [...] following the weird summer on cm—and worse goings-on on fop, i guess. The original intent was to have a women's place, where friends whose voices we valued could come and speak freely without the competitive, judgmental, talking-down atmosphere some of us were feeling from particular men on the lists. (Not *all* of them, mind you).

Another person also told me that she had been told the list was a spinoff from Cybermind. The other, slightly less definite story is that:

> Emma was being formed in response to events on future culture, and that some women who were on cybermind only were invited to participate by women who were on both lists. it started out as a cc list and then somebody set up a listserv for it.

The first account agrees in part with this, that not *all* members were from Cybermind or FOP, the author writing "originally there were things posted to this list from cm and fop, mostly to explain to those who weren't privy to both lists about how/why the new list was necessary".

I only know the identities of eight members of emma, all members of Cybermind, of whom three were also members of FutureCulture, but this bias in favour of Cybermind members is possibly linked to my sources.

The list was private and by invitation only: "We decided once the list was up and running well, we'd nominate people for membership and it would have to be unanimous". The list was very active on opening but "we had a major falling out in November over whether to open the list to men, and truth to tell, it has never recovered". However another person, writing at the same time (March 1996), claimed: "It seems to be picking up lately, mostly with posts from younger, grad student women—and the topics are exceedingly personal, and I treasure that".

Construction of gender on emma focused primarily on the need to produce a 'private' list in contradistinction to the relative 'public' of Cybermind, FOP or FutureCulture, and on issues of 'intimacy' and 'aggression'; a reaction to the same divide conjured by Gordon. It illustrates the clustering counterpositions of private and public, intimate and aggressive, and female and male.

'Offlist'

The origins of the Offlist list are complex and involve some of the same background to the formation of emma. As well, a new member continually criticized people for the length of their messages, for irrelevant discussion, and for making too many forwards. One short-lived member, in the weeks before the split, was a professional philosopher who several times wrote that he found discussion on mailing lists trivial and disconnected. This appeared to trigger Alan's recurrent ambition for Cybermind to be a 'serious' discussion list. On top of this, List population was declining. In the week before the formation of Offlist one member wrote to me that Cybermind "feels more mean-spirited now. It's a colder place".

To give some examples of the tension on the list in the weeks before the split, two disputes involving considerable friction and numbers of people will be described. Firstly, there was a discussion about 70s music in which a list member ('A') remarked that "disco sucked". Another list member ('B') remarked that this statement was homophobic. Many people read B as writing that A was homophobic and protested that it was possible to dislike 70s disco without being anti-gay. The speed with which dispute escalated is noteworthy. This is the only time, in the period under consideration, in which I can remember someone being perceived to be using academic status to 'prove' their argument. The second dispute concerned Multiple Chemical Intolerance Syndrome, with one member denying it occurred and was an example of technophobia, and another member arguing that they suffered from it and were fed up with people saying it was psychological alone. Both these disputes might be considered protests against an attempt to impose an interpretation of culture[11].

To some list members the associates of B (all recognised or established) formed a noticeable subgroup[12]. Thus, two list members wrote to me:

> C, D on occasion (not much), E, and others, F maybe on occasion, B, tend to create circulations among themselves that go on for a while, are filled with injokes, are on any topic only by default, etc. That might be part of the problem.

> The people who defend it are the people like yourself [ie the author of this ethnography] who find strong community here. But for myself, [this group] has erected a wall around it, just like home-owners' associations in LA that Mike Davis writes about. It's closed off, smug.

B had been berated onlist, and apparently offlist, by Alan and Laurie for the irrelevance of their posts. I was told, by a third party, that Alan was worried about:

> a lot of people leaving. B's group didn't see it as a problem, didn't seem to see any reason to attract new subscribers and didn't care if people were unsubbing. Their posts always seemed a little cryptic to me, as though they were conducting a clique in the space, some of us being in the clique and others of us not.

Alan wrote to the list "In case you're not aware of it, for a lot of new subscribers, this place comes off looking like an exclusive in-group, no matter how much you justify it theoretically". Values about equality, open access and hostility to formal exclusivity can be easily activated in some List members, as nothing has changed in the embedding world that would diminish them.

At the time, a number of befuddled newcomers wrote to the list about such features as "the high volume of chit chat", and in reply to one such post C, a member of the subgroup, wrote that the list was going through a "'phase', tendency dying", which brought objections from A and from Laurie, and the suggestion that C wanted the list to die. Laurie wrote: "I hope it is the tendency toward exclusivity that is dying. I don't want to be a part of a list that excludes people by making them feel unwelcome". To which B replied:

> That is very sweet.
>
> Except for the implication that certain people, unnamed, have made it their business, by mechanisms unnamed, to make others feel unwelcome. *Those* people, the ones who have made this place inhospitable, perhaps *they* should be made to feel unwelcome.
>
> For instance, those people who write in modes other than journalistic plainstyle, or those who believe that the cumulative development of an idiom within a community may be of utmost value, despite the inaccessibility of a matured idiom to newcomers. And, most of all, those people who have the temerity to let it be known, on the list, that their relationships to other individuals on the list have developed certain histories and intricacies.
>
> Let such people, me for instance, be made to feel unwelcome, they have brought it on themselves. Let them unsub. Let them, if they wish, find their own corner of the Net.

As in this letter relations between on-topic and off-topic were phrased in terms of an approach to theory. Thus when C was held by others to be "essentialising gender", B emphasised the complexity of C's prose:

> I feel that in not pinning him down to something so simple as an essentializing claim, I do what I can to "read" him correctly. If in fact 'correct' 'reading' is even at stake in responding to those odd, brilliant acts of his. If 'in fact' they are 'acts' in any familiar sense. Etc., you get it.

F wrote, no doubt ironically:

> (Pip, Alan, can we add this to the 'mission statement?') that subscribers may not write about philosophy or psychology or cyberspace in verse, nor may they write aphoristically, nor may they use less than two lines of text, nor may they communicate in a way that might be construed as 'inside' even though that effect might be a function of ironic tone or just plain difficult and complex language.

And later:

> In addition, I find it disturbing that you give so much attention to 'statistics' and the voices of random 'strangers' and newbies over the thinking and writing of valuable contributors to the list; and here I defer the gesture of

vagueness by specifying, as an example, the way B's writing/thinking has (not) been handled, engaged in.

There is a certain oddness to the discussion, in that some of those criticising obscurity were often relatively inaccessible writers themselves and poetry, ellipsis and suggestivity were standard fare on Cybermind. On the other side, those claiming their right to use 'difficult', multivalent, or aphoristic expression were dogmatic about their ability to clearly understand what everyone else, outside the subgroup, was writing. 'Our' own culture is flexible but the impositions we put on the cultures of others is less so, and this intensifies with conflict and category separation.

Dobie's analysis, which draws attention to 'communicative infrastructure', is as suggestive as any:

> after some thought, I believe our true problem lies, not strictly within the realm of discourse, but the invisible structure behind/around it. [...]
>
> I find two important metaphors of social space emerging from both G's and F's posts.
>
> G mentioned rooms, as in certain discursive practices/topics being suited for "other rooms" {aka other lists}.
>
> F played with the metaphor of conference.
>
> All involve aspects of spatiality that this list, as an active entity (archives don't count) doesn't have access to.
>
> In a room, people can cluster and have little conversations that go mostly unheard by the others, huddled in their own little conversational soirees. Same for a conference (once the papers have been read, or even during ;-) People can always wander over and join in, wandering away when the conversation moves on without them...
>
> Here on the list, one either mails to the list and everyone is witness to the conversation written in text, or it is sent privately, and none save the conversants are aware of its happening, nor are those words preserved in the archive.
>
> We're stuck with a single channel of information, flowing like a river into our inboxes.
>
> And when people test the waters, and find only anathema to drink (defined each to their own; too long/too short/particular style) they first delete, then as the volume rises complain, and finally grab their towels and go home.[...]
>
> people [cannot] pick and choose which streams to dip their toes into, instead of worrying about drowning in the whole flood, all at once. [...]

> In the end, we're all constantly in each other's faces, and inevitably irritated now and again by what some see as 'off-topic' or whatever... in the end the true problem isn't really in *what* we're discussing (as F points out, G's post is generalized without specific examples of violation) I think, but rather the unfortunate linearity (aside from the ocassional time-travel email) of our communal intersection, the list.

Over a period of about two weeks various members, identified with this subgroup, left the list. When B departed, he began Offlist to which he subscribed about six or so list members, mainly in this subgroup, apparently without asking them in advance. Offlist lasted for over a year and was then terminated by B, also apparently without discussion. Many of the members of Offlist did not return to Cybermind, though they remained subscribed to FOP.

After B and friends left, I was told Alan had mailed to a group of people (clearly not including me), to discuss what could be done to lower the levels of aggression. I have no idea what was discussed within that group, but outside that group this aggression was phrased by two list members in gender terms. I have distinguished the 'names' mentioned as male or female.

> look, these [aggressive posters] are males, and the women are more quiet than at any time in the past. D[f] does post, and G[f], and I'm not sure that many more. So the discussions heads towards males, C[m] calling me [...], etc. etc. and there's no way out/in. And H[f], who I liked, has left, J[f] hardly posts at all, G[f]'s distressed, I think K[f] is as well, etc.

The second person wrote:

> i think that there is this coldness a lot of it is buffymale anger [...] and many of the women who usually speak up have gone quiet i think that L[f] and M[f] (who is back now) are needed..i think that N[f] has become a bit aggressive K[f] is frightened.. D[f] always in trouble (i love her) ..F[f] seems to clash with alan
>
> now the men the men are suddenly all mixed up in this sexuality thing..gay stuff old lovers stuff new lovers stuff no lovers stuff..

The number of people publicly involved in the specific arguments leading up to the creation of Offlist were small, and it could be thought of as a dispute between two subgroups rather than a dispute involving one subgroup versus the List (which was how it was constructed by at least one side). Differing modes of perceiving the List and differing expectations of the List formed the background to the dispute. The actions of the people who made 'Offlist' framed Cybermind as 'community' for them, but simultaneously *appeared* to cut others out of understanding. These problems were magnified by the possibility of reading all mails received at that time as relative to that dispute. As dobie implied, list structure meant there was no way to isolate the argument, or way in which the more ordinary activities of the group could continue while avoiding the dispute. That such splits were not more frequent might result from the difficulties of creating subgroups. Normally such a dispute might result in one person leaving and remain almost unnoticed. However, in this case, people who formed a subgroup (almost certainly through offlist correspondence and meetings on MOOs), displayed a mutual loyalty and identity. The formation of Offlist may have simply climaxed an ongoing process.

The same could be suggested for 'emma'. The strong, if relatively small, female presence on Cybermind, together with a strong symbolic gender division, made the expression of discontent fairly focusable and so a group could develop, not only with a view of what it wanted in a list but of how it could decide its initial membership, and therefore fissioning was possible. However, this group, perhaps in accordance with its principles of membership, did not formally separate from Cybermind. Neither did it formally argue with Cybermind, or its members necessarily depart from Cybermind, although some 'faded away'. It appears even Alan was unaware of the group's existence, despite his closeness to some of the formative members, and this was not because they feared him, but because it was not necessary for those on emma to establish the splintering.

Iraq

It is not possible to detail all the arguments and splits that developed over the several years leading up and following the invasion of Iraq in the space available. Later on in conversation with me people remembered it as a difficult time, in which people left the list because they felt they, or their country, was being attacked; a time in which friendships, or mutual acceptances shattered largely along nationality lines, especially when this was reinforced by political polarity. People also felt that they were not being read properly and their words distorted, or that prior understandings where being forced upon them. This is bound to intensify asence and threaten a person's sense of existence and belonging. The moderator, and the group, were unable to control the events without closing the List.

In general, non-American List members did not understand the charges of anti-americanism which were made against them, as can be seen in Martin's letter (31 Mar.03):

> I certainly get the impression of a very different atmosphere here (I am in London) to that in the US.
>
> I have had many discussions and arguments over the war—it's almost impossible not to ... In all those arguments I have never been accused of being anti-British (remember our soldiers are over there dying too!) nor does it seem to have occurred to anyone even those that disagreed with me that I was doing anything wrong in stating my criticism....

Chris, also British, writes (11 May.03):

> at times extremely aggressive tactics have been used on and off list to try to make this list more "patriotic".
>
> Obviously that is USA-patriotic even though list members [...] may well reside in one of the 100 or so countries worldwide

Yet the effect on Americans was equally strong. Maurizio (also non-American) writes (21 Jan.03):

> We do know that [A] left because of perceived anti-americanism. Did [B] leave for the same reason? [...]. I do know of one lurker who left because of "300 anti-American posts a day." Slight exaggeration, but you know what I'm saying.

A prominent List member, who was both anti-war and anti-Bush, wrote:

> I've pretty much dropped away—the anti-Americanism is too strong for me—it reduces me to catatonia personally—I have to be able to function—and there are far too many forwards. [...]
>
> A lot of what comes in on Cybermind is repeated damnation that seems totalizing and occasionally unfair. I know there are others who feel the same way—the silence here might be the result.

This effect probably grew, not only from political disagreement, but from the persistent use by non-Americans of the term 'American' to categorise the actions of the Bush Administration. This was commented upon by Jim who wrote (13 Mar.03): "I still feel the US population is being painted with a presidential brush". Other people objected strongly to being lumped in with the administration, but at another level also identified with their country such that 'American' included them voluntarily. Again, mutual feedback in which people made their distress known, fuelled the appearance of severe conflict. It could appear that there were conflicting subgroups (American and 'non-American'), even though these subgroups where not organised. Kathryn wrote dealing with the issue of the appearance of factions and the potential obliteration of identity (1 Jun.03):

> The factions that began to form were Americans (one faction) and everyone else (another faction). And I noticed this behaviour mainly among male members of the group. [...]I remember someone responding to another's post by saying something to effect, "I can't consider you a friend anymore, if that is what you believe". I felt it myself, I felt how the discussion of the topic itself was fascinating, but it seemed to bring up a whole lot with it, stuff that could make or break friendships. It wasn't the topic itself ("The war is wrong") it was what discussion implied ("Do people think I'm wrong/bad because I live in the country that's made a bad/wrong war?")

A way that some people attempted to deal with this asence and the sense of uncontrollable conflict was to post one-line jokes, which led to further conflict. Alan worried about the material flooding people's mailboxes and driving them away; in other words, that the patterns of exchange where not working. Thus he wrote (20 Jan.03):

> I'd really like to make a case for NOT SENDING one line responses! This may be one reason we're losing members again! We're about half of what we were now.
>
> The one-line responses tend to clutter inboxes for close to no reason at all—there have been slews of them recently. Half the witticisms seem sexually double-entendre as well.
>
> Sorry about this, but it does make this list more and more inflated and less and less interesting. If there's something of substance to say, please do, but a lot of us are now getting emails in the mid-100s/daily, and a lot of one-liners don't help.

Some people engaging in the "one liner" behaviour argued that there was not much useful content on the List anyway and that it might be the politically vocal people who were driving readers away. Mari, who was one of the main participants, explained her reactions as follows (20 Jan.03):

> at the present time, i am exhausted, physically and mentally, for a number of reasons. i am looking for happy things to keep me going. I am not looking for

long articles on war, and bush and and other heavy and quite valid subjects. they surround me, crushing me along with other things. i don't ignore them, but i have had enough response to them to last a while and i have other things on my mind.

one liners, quite frequently of sexual double-entendre are fun. i enjoy puns. and apparently others in the list enjoy them as well.

perhaps we are losing members because of over serious subject matter that has caused heated personal attacks between members. let's get serious. this is a list for the study of the psychology and philosophy of cyberspace. my psyche currently demands light & air not heavy & dark. do i not count? and tell me, how many are complaining about the one-liners, as opposed to those who are joining in?

there, this was more than one line. i will now try to keep my hands quiet here, and go to another list where jokes are welcome, as well as dark thoughts.

WA agreed writing (20 Jan.03):

> I agree that the one-liners add life to the list. They are the messages I am likely to read. I have been on no-mail since October and I have thought that I could not face CM in view of the horrible political situation, the ugliness of my own country.
>
> I will skim or delete overly heavy postings, long postings that drive me into the dumps. I know that Bush is ruining our country and planning evil for the world. My heart is already broken... That's why I stayed on no-mail for so long...

Other people wrote in likewise. Some complained that the group was not giving them the right gifts either. Earlier, just after the start of the 'war on terror', a person had written:

> Is there such a thing as off topic on this list anymore? Heck, with the bulk of the posts the name 'Cyberpolitics' would probably be more of a representation of the bulk of the posts.

Others suggested that the people who were supposedly leaving because of the one-liners may not have been regular List users anyway, and that the people issuing one-liners were. Others seconded the idea of going to other Lists or setting up a back channel for the jokes, with Jim, suggesting "that's just going to gut/subvert the list further". Alan backed down and went onto nomail. Later on still, Jim told me that; "Many of us put filters in place to weed out various subgroups [and] A LOT of the oneliner traffic was taken back channel". This may have reinforced connections and made them more of a self-identified group, in relation to another group, and later on, some people did identify the "one-liner crew" as a visible subgroup, but again there was no coordination, simply a preference and personal association.

There was no easy solution to the conflicts and the List struggled on with missing members, depression and ongoing acrimony amidst periods of relative harmony. List traffic did decline, as did the number of active people. In the three months of September, October and November of 1999 approximately 90 to 100 people posted to the list, in the three months of July, August and September of 2004 after the war squabbles, only 31 people posted. It probably was not until late 2006 that the List started to recover, but even then quarrels over the Bush Administration and Iraq, while approached with little enthusiasm could still produce a sense of crisis and alienation, and there were nowhere near the number of active posters that had previously graced the List, and it tended to be even less on topic.

Gender

The question of gender arises in all of these disputes. These gender assumptions are not invented by the list, but imported from the embedding society and then perhaps intensified, as they constitute one of the few identity markers and triggers for interpretive schemas available.

Briefly to summarise points already made: gender does not necessarily influence the number of posts a person makes to Cybermind; gender marks tend to become exaggerated; gender is connected to intimacy; and it is possible, but by no means conclusive, that offlist correspondence involving women is of great importance for the list 'community'. It is also possible that the normal low levels of hostility and absence of list wide flame wars, particularly in the first six months of fieldwork, were indeed part of the reason for the obvious presence and participation of women, particularly given the kind of verbal violence and invocation of sexual assault and harassment found more generally on the internet[13]. However, such idealism has to be seen statistically and in context; there was no statistical evidence of a decline in female participation after these conflicts other than during the continuing disputes over the Iraq War and women did participate in personal disputes.

Nevertheless, the organising category association between males and 'violence' guided perception. Some males also embraced this association either critically or as a self-identifier. There also appears to be a reluctance to observe female 'violence', dispute or assertion, even when in a 'good cause'. For example Hall's (1996) account of the SAPPHO list implies people could be removed for not appearing 'feminine'. This was not unreasonable as this list was meant to be for women only, and thus possibly a target for attack with, at that time, little security in guaranteeing sex of participants. A degree of struggle went on over whether particular definitions of this appearance were legitimate or not. Similarly, women on Cybermind seemed as determined to defend their list from attack as the men, even though it might eventually lead to a splinter group. Women were involved in internal disputes as readily as men (F and G in the Offlist dispute for example), even though men formed the majority of participants in most disputes, and women seemed to primarily flame other women. This may not be uncommon; Witmer and Katzman concluded their statistical research on "newsgroups and special interest groups on the Internet and CompuServe", by writing that "The data do not support the... hypothesis that men use more challenging language and flame more often than women" (1998: 7, 9-10).

While gender might provide a conceptual split, it also provided a method of conceptual unification. The sexual one-liners were nearly all exchanged *between* men and women, rather than made within the one gender.

More in keeping with expectations, Herring (1996a) conducted a statistical breakdown of correspondence on two lists (one predominantly male, the other predominantly female) to conclude that women were generally more informative in their postings and men more critical—although exchange of information was secondary to exchange of views. Furthermore, posts of agreement or support were overwhelmingly female, regardless of topic or list[14]. Gordon seemed to have issues around gender categories and keeping them tight. His texts suggest that he considered criticality far more important than relatedness, so it is possible the slide moves from 'praise of being critical' through 'attempting to drive off those not in agreement with one's basic assumptions', to 'seeking out people to attack'. This links the valuation of authenticity to the decision that there is only one authentic, not multiple. This has nothing to do with victory: loss can also reinforce authenticity. What is 'desired' is to establish that, in particular ways, the others are not authentic or moral. In online society (particularly on Lists and newsgroups), a very few people can set the mood for the society. Therefore it does not take many people to assume that males are 'violent' or females are 'cooperative' to drive away those who disagree, and to produce societies which are essentially gendered in tone, and eventually segregated. People like Gordon and the formation of SAPPHO, are linked. Without such fear of 'weakness', so that a congerie of associations around it has forever to be attacked, it would not be *as* necessary for 'women only lists' to form and for them to be exclusionary themselves. The only way cooperation can exist is to ruthlessly expunge its attackers, which in itself leads to fragmentation.

Clustering

Despite the widely accepted argument that 'knowledge workers' have diverse and generally non-coherent political views, this is not an adequate descriptor, particularly in times of stress. In a debate or struggle, as with gender, the political categories of Left and Right, or of nationality often appear with surprising force, gathering arguments together and exaggerating the strength of people's reactions. This occurs even though these categories are not particularly coherent in the embedding society[15].

Like categories, propositions are not linked linearly by logic or similarity, but in clusters, with varying types and strengths of links, with the links often seeming to be emotional rather than considered. Strength is determined by the frequency of association or frequency of procedure (i.e. movement from one formulation to another) as used in the embedding society. The number of comments appearing simultaneously, increases the chance of the appearance of the full cluster. In the same way as flame is partially generated by the possible number of responses to any statement, so are the full range of associations of Left and Right. This full range of associations, when being presented in a context of differentiation rather than negotiation, leads to emphasis of the whole cluster and eventually incorporates those who participate, forcing them to choose one side or another.

The force of these associations seems to be such that, within a fairly short period of time, people can assign strangers to either their own category or to another and therefore decide if the group is like them or not, or whether they should attack or defend. Polarities seem to appear as people try to resolve the counterpositions which are produced by the inadequacies of categorization within the group, or allowed by the organisation of the group and its relationship to other groups. In this chapter the problems have emerged in the relationships between the categories of public and private; aggression, authenticity and freedom; American and non-american; and masculine and feminine. Attempts at resolution by exaggerating the poles intensify contradiction or category separation, and intensify the strength of application of the interpretive schemas which generate the culture of those people now linked to counterpositionary categories.

Ultimately these category separations, occur in such force because the communicative structure of the group prevents other ways of coming to a way of living together, or walling off the problems, and because these structures tend to prevent more complex multiplex relations from being common or list wide.

Chapter 11: Constructions of Online 'Community'

Introduction

The category of 'community' is not only inherently unclear and disputed but is deeply implicated in Western political and social discourse as the subject of widespread aspiration and dispute. In particular, it functions as an important social validator. As a result, this chapter is not about whether there is a 'thing' which can be called 'community', or whether Cybermind (or 'virtual community' generally) approximates or falls away from this state; this chapter discusses how a social grouping constructs itself as being 'community', and discusses how members perceive the benefits of being on Cybermind.

In contrast to those interpretations which see 'virtual community' as arising out of a decline in offline community, it is suggested that it is more useful to recall that Westerners get a sense of *'gemeinshaft'* from their leisure groups and that this forms the basis for the nostalgia and lack experienced elsewhere. People in the West also have great practice in forming new groups, which they call communities, and many features of these groupings are also features of online groups. It further seems that some of the techniques used to build community can also weaken it.

Firstly, it is necessary to outline some of the academic and popular mythemes about community, as these mythemes form the background to usage of the term on Cybermind, and are themselves involved in wider social processes and expectations.

'Community'

> Community is, at the moment, a powerful word in the United States. It is invoked in seemingly contradictory places; among conservative leaders championing 'traditional values'; among blacks trying to reclaim a ghetto neighborhood from poverty and despair; among Christians or Jews describing their congregations; among middle-class people seeking a spiritual experience or connections along the 'Information Superhighway'; among lower- and middle-class whites trying to keep a homeless shelter from being built in their neighborhood.
>
> When invoked in these economically and politically varied locations, *community* is a powerfully suggestive, yet vague term (Bounds 1997: 1).

The most obvious thing about the term 'community' is this vagueness. Whole disciplines have been formed trying to define what it means. In a well known article, George Hillery looked at ninety four different definitions of community by sociologists, and concluded that the one thing they all had in common was that they dealt with people (1955: 119). Konig claims "one could easily append to [Hilary's] bibliography at least as many important sources again" (1968: 22)[1].

Given that the term is a congerie rather than a concept, there is little point in criticising previous definitions, or in trying to construct a new definition. Avoiding the search for a definition might help us come to see how the term is deployed.

'Community' is a term used to form groups or promote particular ways of interpreting them. It represents aspirations and can be used as a way of including or excluding; hence its role in politics. The vagueness of the term is part of its power. It can unify because it is imprecise. Different people using the term may have different expectations, but they can all appear to be talking similarly. 'Community' is a term used to try to evoke and build connections or associations, to support the feeling of commonality or difference, or to delimit and support identity constructs. It always points to an ideal: "*If* we had 'community' then [something or other] would, or should, happen". In a contrary manner it is always possible to criticise some grouping as not being community, and thus represent them as inauthentic, or unworthy of political representation[2].

Through the term 'community' assumed commonality is represented to us, and evokes the feelings and responses which make a group community *to us*, when we are not 'there' as well as when we *are* there. The term also allows exclusion, as the category 'our community' takes its value in relationship to other groups and people. However, the boundary maintenance and construction aspect of community groupings (Cohen 1985: 12-3) requires new strategies online due to the asence of boundaries. List community requires 'effort' or 'motivation' to come into being. It often cannot just happen because of who is 'about us', or because of our work or daily life. It may require more support than usual.

Nostalgia

In Western mythemes, 'community' is almost always something *we* have lost and someone else has. It is constructed in relation to a perceived alienation. For example, Bounds writes:

> We live in a time and place when Community seems vital to our individual and social well being. Yet, simultaneously, we live in a time when what have been ordinary communal relations are scarce in the face of social and geographical mobility, lost traditions and the experienced pluralism of US society (1997: 2)[3].

Community becomes a polarity, and is usually contrasted with an inferior, and later, state. The appeal of such contrasting terms as *Gemeinschaft* ('community') and *Gesellschaft* ('association'); 'status' and 'contract'; 'mechanical' or 'organic' solidarity; and 'rural' and 'urban', is well known. The usual assumption is that 'small scale' societies are more simple, harmonious, integrated, satisfying and cooperative (or stultifying and conformist), than large scale societies—something not demonstrated by ethnography[4]. Current life is perceived as a diminishment or a copy of something real.

Depending on political bent, the theory of loss of community, is often tied to the development of either capitalism, 'modernism', or the extension of a state with 'alien' usually 'liberal' morals'. Enclosure of land removed the ability of much of the population to support themselves and forced a new way of life upon them in the only space available, the city. The city becomes perceived as a source of difference rather than of harmony, of juxtaposition rather than integration, despite the evidence of 'well formed' sociality in areas such as London's Bethnal Green (Frankenberg 1969: 174ff.).

Public longing for 'community' is linked with a perception of breakdown of a relatively uniform hegemony, the attack upon civil society, or the decline in the use of terms of connectedness arising through constancy of place, localised kinship or life-long familiarity. This longing is more connected to a nostalgic imagining, than to any consensus which may have actually existed (although it is possible that civil society or kinship was at one time a buffer against the exigencies of capitalism and fate).

'Community' can, therefore, be considered to be under attack. As Glugg writes to Cybermind (7 July.95): "The following [...] makes me think [...] about the survival of community at a time when the very concept of such a thing is under fierce assault". Online community becomes perceived as a compensation: "The propensity for trying to make virtual communities is comment enough on the debility of real ones, but also on the need for them" (Julian Stallanbrass, quoted by Alan (3 June.96)). "I suspect that one of the reasons for this phenomenon [i.e. virtual communities] is the hunger for community that grows in the breasts of people around the world as more and more informal spaces disappear from our real lives" (Rheingold 1994: 6. See also Barlow (1995a), Ronell (1996), Stoll (1995: 221)) Although I am suggesting that civil society, or access to it, has declined, I am not suggesting that online activities are simply compensatory. Online groupings are embedded within the practices of 'daily life' and, as such, involve efforts to adapt to or overcome those situations.

'Virtual community' is not a 'village community' and need not be. Despite a tendency to use 'community' with this nostalgic reference, most people currently online have never lived in a village. No remembering of 'real community' needs to lie behind the desire for virtual community, only a nostalgia for imagined community. Indeed, if displacement in time is the important feature, then virtual community might be coloured by a 'nostalgia' for the future.

Contrary to this usual analysis of 'community' as absence, Elias and Dunning suggest, that in modern societies people seek an existing "leisure *Gemeinschaft*" to contrast with their "non-leisure *Gesellschaft*". They suggest non-leisure activities tend to be routinized with high levels of emotional constraints, self-imposed personal control and lack of 'freedom'[5]. They argue there is consequently enjoyment in "pleasurable arousal through being in the company of others without commitment, without any obligations to them apart from those one takes on voluntarily" (1993: 121). This implies that the contrast between representations of 'community' and its opposite is so powerful to city-based Westerners because it is rooted in their lives (as 'good times' vs 'work' or routine life), rather than absent. This dual experience gives the basis for the imagining of another kind of life, and provides yet another basis for voluntary and temporary association beyond the practical.

This distinction between leisure gemeinschaft and routine gesellschaft can be related to Victor Turner's dialectic between *structure* ("norm governed relationships between social personae" or the world of roles and statuses [Turner 1969: 128]) and *communitas* (which suspends structure to involve the whole 'spontaneous' human and "free relationships between individuals" [ibid: 132]). Myerhoff argues that although the two depend on each other and ideally oscillate, US Americans usually attempt to 'freeze' one pole or the other and as a result continually feel defeated (1975: 33-8. See also Veling 1996: 12-3).

Online community may act as a transformation, concentration and enlivening of more restrained non-leisure relationships with a perception of greater freedom and less than normal *immediate* risk[6]. The routine might tend to be perceived as inauthentic, while the online, without those particular restraints, might seem more real. Online nostalgia may not only be coloured by people's offline nostalgia for 'belonging', but arise because of people's expectations of 'continual leisure gemeinshcaft' or 'communitas', and their reluctance to allow structure or routine to be recognized as valid. 'Burnout' (See Chapter 5) might also result from attempts to prevent the supposedly role free, authentic and helpful communitas of online life, from shifting into the daily routine of structure which is necessary for its maintenance.

In 1998 I emailed twenty-one people who had been highly active on the list to ask them about what they had enjoyed about the list, why they had remained a member or left, what they had found useful about the list, and how these benefits compared with similar activities in their offline lives. I received replies from nine males and four females, most of whom replied to further questions. I shall call this the Community Survey and indicate it by the code (CS) where necessary. As most respondents did not give permission to use their names, everyone is quoted anonymously, with some spelling and typographic idiosyncrasies regularised.

Respondents all considered their connection with the list was worthwhile. However, it is significant that 'community' was often expressed in the past tense. Remarks such as the following were made:

> Unfortunately I don't currently have time to do much except skim the list for things I find interesting enough to read more carefully [...].

> there are times I'm bored to death with things because they've been said over and over again.

> I really used to enjoy CM, but nowadays I don't seem to have the time or as much interest.

> I've been less involved in CM for the last few months...[...] I was getting less interested in the interpersonal stuff going on there on the list [...] also the subject matter of the stuff on the list was of less interest to me...

> I feel that I am far less emotionally involved [with Cybermind] as my physical life is so full.

I am uncertain whether this 'nostalgia' is connected with the same factors which make 'community' generally a subject for nostalgia or if, in this case, it results from expectations that things could be better; from burnout; or from reluctance to allow the alternation of routine and leisure, or structure and communitas.

Expectations

'Real community' is nearly always associated with living together in a place[7]. However 'community', not tied to place, has been anticipated for some considerable time. In the mid-19th century, de Tocqueville remarked on the tendency of Americans to "instantly form associations" for any purpose (1994 II: 106) and commented that a newspaper "always represents an association that is composed of its habitual readers" (ibid: 113), perhaps anticipating Benedict Anderson's (1991) view of imagined communities formed via print media. In 1893 Durkheim suggested that place would lose its "present predominance" and that our activity and interest would be extended "quite beyond these [local] groups" (1960: 28-9). More recently, but still before the Internet, Melvin Webber claimed that in 'modern society', as:

> the individual's interests develop, he is better able to find others who share these interests and with whom he can associate. The communities with which he associates and to which he 'belongs' are no longer only the communities of place to which his ancestors were restricted; Americans are becoming more closely tied to various interest communities than to place communities (1963: 29)[8].

A few years later Richmond, in a discussion of 'post-industrial' migration, argued that many educated people were involved in world-wide communication networks with similar people, and defined the term *Verbingdungsnetzschaft* (a third ideal type to go with *Gemeinschaft* and *Gesellschaft*), as a social system:

> in which the characteristic forms of social inter-action take place through networks of communication maintained by means of telephone, teleprinter, television and high speed aircraft and space-craft etc... Such relationships are not dependent upon a territorial base or face-to-face contact, nor do they involve participation in formal organizations (1969: 278).

In the late 1960s, concerns about decline in community of place, continual movement, and the formation of interest groups, became part of 'popular' discourse. Alvin Toffler's best selling *Future Shock* (1970) contains chapters highlighting these issues. "Place: The New Nomads" describes the supposedly tenuous and declining connections people have with place, and the resultant lack of commitment. "A Surfeit of Subcults" describes people's involvement with groups based on an idea or interest as part of a search for identity, or as arising from leisure or work based specialization; "techno-societies far from being drab and homogenized, are honeycombed with just such colorful groupings" (1970: 252). Selecting a 'subcult' is supposed to reduce the overwhelming number of choices available to a person and give guidelines for behaviour. Constant social change prevents any identity from providing meaningful stability for long and so people soon embrace another one. Repetition of this process leads to 'serial selves' and becoming 'burnt out' (ibid: 277-81).

Sociologists still maintain similar ideas. Alan Wolfe writes "[i]n the absence of traditional understandings of community, Americans are creating new experiments with subcommunities" (1991a: 7). Although Fischer doubts that Americans have recently become more mobile, he thinks a decreased dependence upon locality for sociability is probable (1991: 86). Gergen (1991: ch 3) argues communities are no longer geographically circumscribed but are based upon symbolic relations[9], and suggests that through the 'mass media' we have a perception of greater intimacy or involvement with celebrities than we have with our neighbours[10]. He also suggests this leads people to locate their identity in symbolically significant others such as with supporters of a football team[11], or 'membership' of a TV congregation (ibid: 214-6). This may, he claims, further isolate them from their neighbours and plunge them deeper into the 'symbolic community'. Fear that online community will further separate people from their neighbours has previously been mentioned, and shows the prevalence of expectations of separation, the apparent need to combat them, and the analysis of the present in terms of a falling away from an imagined past[12].

Making 'New Communities' in Suburbia

In WES societies, many people have experience of moving into 'new communities', and having to make social connections from scratch. Herbert Gans' account of the establishment of 'Levittown' in the late 1950s makes it possible to show that some features of suburban associations appear online. This implies that these features are indicative of wider social processes, and not any specific 'deficiency' of online society.

Residents of Levittown had no pre-existent connection with other residents and initially they were more likely to be concerned with house or family than making 'community' (Gans 1967: 40). However, after a relatively short time, people attempted to contact neighbours and form informal small groups. Women belonging to categories which were in a minority in a particular area, were the main founders of groups in those areas. Other minority groups, such as college-educated women, found it harder to make friends nearby and had to establish 'community wide' associations (ibid: 50-1). People sought out association, and the most likely to seek it were those who felt different from those around them. Gans writes that:

> [These] organizations were primarily sorting groups which divided and segregated people by their interests and ultimately, of course, by socio-economic, educational, and religious differences. On the block, people who shared a common space could not really express their diversity; the community sorting groups came into being for this purpose (ibid: 61).

The group expressed the 'similarity' of its members and their 'difference' from those around them.

Internet users are also likely to seek out others who are similar (using interest, social role or even politics, as a marker of similarity), and anecdotal evidence suggests that many feel different from those around them offline. Online groups allow people to express this difference which is then often perceived to be 'therapeutic'. People who stay, frequently discover the potential of the list after arrival and often give the impression this discovery surprised them (as with Gans 1967: 141). Disputes likewise tend to be seen as matters of personality (ibid: 57), but there is also a tendency on Cybermind to fit disputes into wider political and social processes. This might occur because list members, as a 'class', tend to be more politicised or more familiar with sociological discourse than Levittowners. Only a relatively small number of list members are active in the group, as in Levittown associations (ibid: 63). This implies that a tendency to 'passive involvement' is not just a factor of online society. Finally, examples of 'community spirit' on the list tend to be restricted to a few people, or to appear in moments of crisis, just as in Levittown (ibid: 145).

Origin of the Cybermind 'Community'

Given these experiences, and the mythemes of community as declining (as previously dependent upon place, as subject to search, as now being made by interest etc.), it is not surprising that online groupings have been considered as either compensatory, as continuations of decline, or as bold innovations. Equally, given the use of the term 'community' to form groupings, it was easily applied to early Internet users and designers. Part of the standard mytheme of the internet is its subversion by programmers for unauthorized 'community use'[13]. Similar eagerness is revealed in the opening weeks of Cybermind. The first mention of community arises within the 'spelling wars' when Livia writes (3 July.94), "So far, *I've* found cybermind an interesting community. Worth coming out in as a flamer". This message presumably attempts to identify the writer as someone who belongs with the majority of the list, implying that she values the group and is defending them, and their 'place of communication', from Ann.

Other discussion of the nature of 'community' arose during the flaming. Possibly this attempted to re-establish harmony, and possibly it expressed an externally based eagerness for 'community'. People discussed the relationship of community to ethics, the difference between text and face-to-face community, and the relationship between intentional communities and 'living together' communities. Almost at the beginning of the dispute (3 July.94), Cynthia introduces:

> what might be a more interesting question for cybernevermind:
>
> what is a virtual community? if part of the sensibilities being articulated so far have to do with intellectual and emotional response (typos and obscenities are rather different triggers, though not so neatly divisible along an intellectual/emotional axis), how do these sensibilities figure into the construction of such a community? or put another way, how is a virtual community different in concept or in practice than another kind of community?

Which suggests she considered Cybermind a potential community, and points out an expected connection between norms, sensibilities, response and what people call community. Michael while mentioning twice that he did not want to discuss community in a flame war context (and thus indicating awareness of how inclusion moves into exclusion), introduced his interest in discovering more about "intentional community" asking (3 July.94):

how do intentional communities deal with disrupters? I know that, for a lot of them, the answer is simply 'not very well,' and that intentional communities are very volative and prone to collapse, but there must be some stratagies that have developed that would be interesting to look at.

Malgosia wondered if "true community" could only occur where people were prepared to help each other in material terms. Jerry wrote in response to a question as to whether a community could exist without face-to-face interaction (8 July.94):

> yes, we are a community, not merely virtually, but actually—the fact that the interactions within the community are mediated through technology does not make the community less actual [...] And in some respects the sense of community can be stronger because everyone who is part of the community interacts by choice.

The latter part of the quotation clusters choice, freedom and authenticity again. Joe stated (11 July.94) "i DO feel that the nets provide me with a community that would otherwise be lacking". Others, like Michael, while doubtful the list *was* a community, could hope it would become one (3 July.94). Alan, however, wondered (10 July.94):

> why there is a tendency on this list to define ourselves _as_ community... Certainly in the looser sense of community, a group of people defined as a particular demographics, we _are_ such; certainly in terms of empathetic knowledge of one another and deep identifications, we aren't.

In another letter, less than two weeks after the list began, he wrote (10 July.94): "On Cybermind, we have spent centikilos of space discussing 'our' self-formation as communal".

Death and Community

Within a month of the list's beginning, the question of 'community' arose again with the death of Michael Current. Despite the ongoing discourse of community recorded in the previous section, some people have regarded this death as an origin point for Cybermind's 'community'.

Only a few of the messages made to the list at that time focused on the effects of the death on the group, or made explicit attempts to build group solidarity in the face of death; although this must have been of some concern to Alan who now faced the task of running the list alone. Jane asked "What does it mean that we're here, to and for each other; doesn't the presence of even the least of us make some difference to the rest of us. Or not!" Fido wrote: "The living/dying feels ghastly but also strangely beautiful, luminous, as we sort out our own investment in this stuff, the current that passes from me to you, this net, what makes us kin"—although the nature of this 'kinship' is clearly perceived as a problem. Jerry wrote that Michael "enriched the community of this list. Can anyone still doubt that we are a community?"

These remarks about the unity and community of the group as a whole, contrast with the apparent subgroup formation that was manifesting offlist through private exchanges. Most mourning of the dead, in WES societies, is supposed to occur in private, by those 'close' to the deceased, and in accordance with this practice, the mourning moved offlist. This contrast between unities was not something which could be brought up at this time without positing the exclusion of others from the community ideal, with no conventions to decide who this should be. Six months later Fido recalled (1 Feb.95):

> Over the next few days we gathered reports, someone got a picture and mailed it around, phone numbers circulated, and stories, people called his house, Alan talked to his mother; we all talked to each other, whispered, mailed [...]

The, 'we' in this case probably referred to those who were not only already close, but who knew each other from several lists.

From just after the death, Jerry (among others) has forcefully maintained that Michael's death constituted an origin of community. Similarly KarenW wrote (23 Dec.94):

> part of what makes Cybermind precious to me *is* Michael's absence, so in a strange way, his presence suffuses Cybermind for me, as the community clearly felt *grief*, clearly *mourned* (and is still mourning, I'm sure. I feel echoes of the same feelings any time someone mentions Michael, or I drop by Marius's pages and look again at the traces of Michael throughout them, and I'm sure that my mentioning him here will raise the same feelings for others.) I really feel that it was Michael's death that brought together the community, constituted the community. So in a way, Michael's absence is the presence of Cybermind.

However as shown, people on Cybermind (including Jerry) were constantly using terms like 'community' *before* Michael's death. There is, to me, no marked difference in the type of mails before and two weeks after the death. People's perception of the death as an origin point needs some explanation.

Firstly, the association may occur because of the reiteration of mood, in a situation which was not hostile, and was a unique but shared experience (see Chapter 7). Secondly, the association may be affected by memory, and the preservation of only selected texts by participants. For example, another list member who has argued that Michael's death made the list a community, had not joined the list long before this death, did not know much about Michael, and in the weeks following the death complained the list was incomprehensible and elitist, and that they would have to leave. Later, the person seemed to remember making these complaints *before* Michael's death and being remedied after. If community presupposes a polarity state of non-community then there has to be a point at which they switch from one to the other. Michael's death becomes such a memory point, and its significance is emphasised by the lack of any coherent group history. If Hertz's formulation that societies need to re-establish their permanence in the face of death is correct (1960: 77-8), then some people may have needed to transmute memory of the death into a birth. However, without some events happening of the kind that people apply the term community to, the death may not have become significant to so many people, and then the reactions to the death by so many members together, displayed that 'commonality' to all who shared it[14].

Lest it be thought I'm imposing my interpretations over people's actual experience, I quote the following 'testimonies'. Firstly, from Shawn writing to FutureCulture about Michael, just after the death (23 July.94):

> The first days of the cybermind list [...] were some of the most exciting days of internetworking and virtual-community-building that i have experienced since i started living so darn much of my life 'out here.'

Secondly, from Mitchell (pc 7 Nov.96):

> In practice, I am unsure how much the CM community had evolved at the time of Michael's death, which as I recall was pretty early in the list's history. But while he was widely mourned at the time, The degree of community development was pretty much the same in the immediate aftermath of his death as shortly before. Michael's death, per se, was not a significant stimulus to things that would not otherwise have occurred.

Thirdly, Mike briefly outlines what it was like for those not already members of the 'community' (pc 7 Apr.98):

> I first signed onto CM the day before Michael Current died. I saw one or two of his last messages and then the incredible response to his passing which rather overwhelmed me as I had no context into which to fit what was going on. I had a very small participation in the activities.

Finally, Alan in response to a direct question wrote:

> I'd say—first, that ANY mailing list generates community; second, that part of the FutureCulture community came on to Cybermind and continued as such; third—I really think all the bonding, etc. would have occurred even if Michael had not died.

Cybermind and Community

This section approaches the question of what features enable the labelling of a group as community, by considering both what might be taken as community posts and the group's own reflections upon community in a roughly two month period between the end of June and the beginning of September 1995. This period overlaps with the second encounter with Glen, and was chosen to investigate how community would be discussed in such a situation (especially if it is hypothesised that community is defined against non members, other groups, or feared social states), and to portray that period in slightly greater depth. Occasional reference is made to the Community Survey to show that these remarks do not only apply to this time.

Extracting the group's own comments on community was done by a word search through copies of the list-digest archives, then expanding outward into other relevant mails. Deciding what constitutes a 'community post' could be fairly complex. However, as shall be seen, list members often distinguish 'community posts' by their irrelevance to the main topic (their excess) and/or by their personal nature (witness Alan (19 Jul.95): "This list has developed a sense of community, which is great, and a lot of good discussion, which is great"), and this is the model I have used. For convenience these posts are discussed under various headings.

Autobiography

As already implied, the list tended to emphasize the 'personal' and 'private'. Descriptions of offline events are often relayed to the list, and often feature reminiscence of people's lives. For example,

Caitlin and Janet, both describe their experiences in hospital and the support they received from online friends. Alan described and theorized about a meeting with a schoolfriend, possibly someone he once loved, which starts a small thread not only of sympathy but of people writing about their ex-schoolfriends and experiences at school. Rose sketched her experiences in a street parade in her hometown. Alan announced the death of Jerry Garcia of the Grateful Dead which initiated a whole series of posts, some of which describe various member's experience of youth in the 60s and early 70s. Meetings of group members were organized and reported on in London and Boston. People often wrote in to convey the commonality (and sometimes difference), of their experience.

Recreation

Another form of developing commonality is to elaborate each others jokes or 'nonsense', as in a discussion of aliens and nutrasweet (which perhaps expressed boundary anxiety after the battle with Glen), or a discussion about a group mascot (perhaps a symbol of community), which diverged into a discussion about various birds, particularly ducks, and later gave rise to a discussion of personal totems. More unusually, in this period, Amethist gave the group a series of logic puzzles which people discussed onlist. Later, one member would post a daily witticism or musing, and this would frequently be elaborated and turned into further jokes and reflections by others. This is also the basis of the one-liner joke phenomenon, in which strands of single-line witticisms bounce off each other, and branch out, often for a considerable number of emails and often with considerable skill. It is a method of declaring presence, without arguing, or simply saying 'me to', or as Skip suggested (2 Feb.07):

> I think of the one-liners and pun chains as what the neurons of the cybermind do to make sure the connection is still alive while they're waiting to receive/send actual content ;*)

Discussion of Community, Online and Offline

Community, itself, was often discussed. Community, in general, was perceived to be under threat from capitalism, racism and resurgent fascism. A new member initiated a discussion by asking whether the need for community was instinctive and asking what it was that made Cybermind (to him) so obviously a community. Caitlin started another discussion by comparing electronic community, or virtual intimacy, to the intimacy arising between regular smokers outside a building, and asked whether we make too much of the uniqueness of electronic community, while proposing that intimacy occurs much faster in cyberspace. There was a brief discussion on the effect of commercial spamming of mailing lists and its effect on list community, with one member suggesting the list tackle such problems by boycotting, or otherwise incommoding, people who spam.

Community and Redundancy

In response to continuing remarks about the excessive volumes of mail on Cybermind, dobie suggested (29 June.95), that the list should be split into two groups, one for on-topic posts and the other for off-topic posts, so that people who didn't like the off-topic material need not feel overwhelmed by volume. This discussion illustrates something of the problems involved in what members considered important to 'community'. He wrote:

> I do think we want to maintain some focus on the issues of the group, even as we wish to retain the multitude of voices and ideas that come across it each day.
>
> So here's a nutty idea...
>
> create a second list: kybermund (cybermouth in german, maybe someone else can think of a better name, maybe spell it cybermund ;-)
>
> subscribe everyone presently on cybermind to it, and then direct people to send mail that's more off-topic to the second list.
>
> *smile* I think that way, if the people are already subscribed to it, people who aren't interested in hearing all the "chatter" that I happen to like (ok,most of it) can unsub from the second less topical list.
>
> Any takers?

Jim wrote that he had a 'free list' with which this could be done, though later the same day he would write (7 July.95):

> I'm actually against it as well but I'll help implement it if it's desired. I'd probably read the 'noise' before the intelligence anyway 8^)

Only two people replied in support of the idea, while objections were fairly uniform, and demonstrate the importance of the supposedly irrelevant. Thus Mitchell wrote (30 June.95):

> Somehow it wouldn't be the same. Where is the bright line between on and off topic? I'm not even sure there is a bright line. And even if we tried to make one, I'm not at all sure how long it would last.

Jerry rephrases the idea in terms of First Tier (issues) and Second Tier (off-topic) and writes (1 July.95):

> sometimes my best headspins arise from collisions of off-topic stuf with on-topic stuff. 'sides I need a breather now and then and I don't want to have to concentrate too hard on which cybernd my post best fits in—we're a community fer ...sake so we talk about little things as well as the big—the *margins* as well as a notional centre (and that's a big reason not to segregate) [...]
>
> anyhow—from what Ive writted so far you can see the problem—is this a second tier (tear) post or a first tier one?

Kevin, in another thread, gave what seems to be a response to the proposal (30 June.95):

> Cybermind is a playpark for the mind. It is a place for games, chit chat as well as serious cerebral workout. Its like a social club, except that the patrons are so diverse that you couldn't find such a thing in RL. Thats what I love about it. Without a personal angle on things it would become very dry.

To give some further examples of people's protest; Trond writes (7 July.95):

> i'm afraid that would destroy a lot of what makes this list such an intelligent and warm virtual place. i just don't like the idea of separating the intellectual from all the other aspects of human interaction. 'information' without any 'noice' just can't make a community. imho

Tom (7 July.95):

> Cybermind would no longer be Cybermind, and I for one feel that the sense of community would be lost. While I greatly enjoy the intellectual conversations here, is the personal snippets and "off topic" stuff that makes this list *human*

Vijay, in his only post for that month, concurs (7 July.95):

> I agree with Tom—the personal, intimate nature of this list is stunning. Please dont tamper with it.

Nan (7 July.95) writes:

> split if you will, but not with my blessing. I believe spontaneous community (this Beautiful, Spammy Place) beats planned community (as proposed) hands down.

These posts imply that the 'community' of the list is seen as an addendum, or excess, to the topical posts. For most people, removing the off-topic posts would destroy the intimacy and personal nature of the list—perhaps indicating structure and not communitas[15]. This is significant, as dobie's proposal did not involve removing the 'excess' posts, but merely asked people to send the 'off-topic' posts to another list, which presumably would have similar subscribers. It is also notable that people considered the theoretical side of the list would suffer diminishment by insisting on 'on-topic' posts[16]. Fred expresses this more elaborately than most (7 July.95):

> I've learned a lot from pondering the unsplit list. As it is, and especially as one might idealize it to be. The idealized version: there's a community of readers/writers, many or most of whom want to reflect on the philosophy and psychology of subjectivity in cyberspace, who also communicate offtopic, partly as a way of providing material for reflection; and, because of the continuous undercurrent of theoretical reflection (which, one hopes, often surfaces in explicitly theoretical posts), *everything* written in that space takes on a different quality, unique to this space. That is, it should be effortless, even inevitable, to read the most uncalculated autobiographical fragment in light of whatever general speculations have recently or pertinently occupied this space. And to whatever extent writers make themselves available at 'personal' or 'anecdotal' levels, that would inflect whatever more 'intellectual' posts they offer.
>
> For Cybermind that's an idealization, mostly because there aren't as many ontopic posts/threads as there might be. But the idealized version is incredibly appealing to me. [...] I'd hate to lose this possibility.

A year or two later Alan set up the Cyberculture list for serious discussion alone. It was never as successful as Cybermind. On-topic discussions tended to be brief and most posts tended to be announcements. It was eventually disbanded due to lack of interest.

Using 'Community'

Group members use the term 'community' to indicate the importance of the group to them, to give value to the group and to suggest or show personal contact, and 'caring'. Personal contact and caring may also be thought of as excesses to the list requirements, like non-topic digressions or references to behaviour offlist.

Jerry, for example (7 July.95), distinguishes "straightforward lists" from Cybermind by reference to the personal. The "straightforward lists" are

> adversarial [...with] no real discussion, just one-up-person-ship games [...] What I get on CM is very much the sense that there are people behind the posts, rather than proto-journal articles.

kmc (12 July.95) writes:

> I have never seen people so completely caring about each other than here. Perhaps I have never really belonged anywhere before. But i've never seen anything like this in what some people refer to as 'real' life. I'm really glad to be here.

Toni generalises (20 July.95):

> interacting over the net is a form of knowing, and it does involve some requirements for mutual concern.

And on a more personal level, this care and union is implied by Tom writing (25 Aug.95):

> Feeling rather alone tonight, so I come to seek solace in Cybermind.

Although such claims are not made frequently, they are not uncommon and they occur throughout the period of fieldwork. Emphasis on care is not only proclamation, the period opens with a new member relating his disillusionment with life, which, apart from Glen, attracted concern from others, both on and off list. One member describes how his ex-lover with Crohn's disease was injured on an excursion to a public concert. This latter gives rise to expressions of sympathy and interest from others. Later on another member asks the group for help regarding her son who is seriously ill with the same disease, and is met with, largely offlist, support and help.

Cybermind's emphasis on these issues does not imply the only way 'community' can be constructed is through emphasising 'care' or 'the personal', although perhaps the tendency to use 'community', in the WES world, this way reinforces this. Any fairly consistent excess has similar effect. An excess of messages becomes a way of driving away those who do not construct their community in that manner.

Frankenberg, who uses the term 'redundancy' in his discussion of community, points out that in communication theory redundancy is a way of avoiding undetectable errors, by giving more information than is actually needed (1969: 280-1; see Chapter 1). So in online society, given there is little connection other than the messages, then redundancy, or excess, frames the messages, making an indirect series of commentaries, which reduce the chance of reading argument as hostility, and hence reduces the threat of continual splitting. Redundancy also reduces uncertainty by implying the kind of messages which will be acceptable. When Cybermind is in stress through dispute, one way of indicating presence and non-hostility is to make jokes or start off-topic discussions, as on-topic discussions may call for more disagreement which may not be wished for in the circumstances. This is an example of knowing when to keep silent but still demonstrate presence.

In the community survey I asked about how people recognized community, and though the answers add complications, the personal and 'redundant' aspects still feature. Two respondents spontaneously mentioned the concept of a "home list":

> CM was my 'home' list for a long time in that, it was the list where I felt most "at home" on the net, even if I didn't participate directly all that much or present myself personally very much. I'm not sure why it was my 'net home', maybe because the demographics of the list were closest to my own interests... other lists like FutureCulture and similar seemed to be for much younger folks and I felt comfortable with CM...

> the idea of a 'home list' makes more and more sense to me, although personally I've always felt nomadic, homeless, in real and virtual life; my feelings are ambivalent about Cybermind, which can appear druglike to me at times[17].

> In our collective explorations of grief and other emotions, there was a tremendous sense of sharing, and perhaps for the first time, the list participants began seeing each other as individual people [...] There are a zillion instances of welcoming and being welcomed by other list members online.

> [Something is 'community'] if a lot of the communication between subscribers goes beyond simply formal responses to each other's posts, be that communication on the list or off; also if a lot of what people discuss with each other on the list goes beyond a strict construction of the list's topic.

> I'd say the feeling of community is linked with the feeling that one can simply *be* and not worry about *seeming*...i.e., that one is simply accepted as one is; here we are, getting on with each other as best we can...

> I think we know community because we can recognize 'strangers', when we can't recognize who is a stranger there is no community...[...] I can recognize when other people are part of a community but I have a lot more trouble knowing when I'm part of a community...

> a community for me is a group that meet with a similar interest in the same place frequently...and are fairly passionate about being there... & we were that!!

As well as the excess to the topic as an identifier, it seems clear that patterns of ease, perceived similarity, care, and acceptance were important to people, suggesting a somewhat fraught daily life. Other answers, which will be discussed later, imply that the extension of a network of friends and contacts was perceived as valuable, and that offline life was often considered lacking in social stimulation or acceptance.

Community With or Without Glen

The dispute between Glen and the list also indicates some of the aspirations of the list to community, and some of the problems with those aspirations. Alan, for example, (19 July.95) saw off-topic excess as contributing to the dispute, as:

> The other spoon lists don't run into this problem for the most part, because their subject matter is more tightly defined[18]

Laurie (21 July.95) saw the problem as one of social control and responsibility in communities generally:

> If we categorize this as a community, and communities by definition must somehow enforce standards of good behavior to remain a productive community [...], then what are the limits of good and bad behavior in an electronic community

In a later letter on the same day she clarified her remarks, emphasising that 'community' should not be exclusionary in principle:

> If a list is centered around a given topic, but then the discussion ranges into other topics which may or may not promote communal feeling among the members, then what measures, if any are taken to return discussion to the stated topic of the list? [...] I think it would be naive to say that issues of proper and improper behavior simply don't apply to this medium, that all one needs to do is delete or killfile. To my mind that is equivalent to building walled cities or neighborhoods to keep out undesirables in that it doesn't solve the real issues of the communal space.

As shown earlier, some list members thought this kind of 'structural' question was inappropriate or had dictatorial tendencies which were incompatible with the 'communitas' of 'community', and there was little engagement with what seems to be a reasonable question, other than from Glen himself. She was not attempting to exclude Glen, rather asking how 'communities' deal with disruption. However, as presence is linked so much with what people write, her respondents perceived stopping a person's comments as removing the person. Similarly, rules could imply the destruction of free authenticity, and thus the end of the moral basis of community[19].

Steven (21 July.95) told the story of the four sons from the Seder (Chapter 9) and asked: "is this last son part of the community or apart from the community?" As previously stated, the response was generally that the son was part of the community. The model of community people wanted to embrace, even if they couldn't manage it in practice, was inclusive. Caitlin wrote (21 July.95):

> The last child is a part of the community—an important part. Community is about defining the WE, but it is also about defining our individual places in it. [...The dispute] generated some interesting discussion about who and what we are and how we think and label ourselves and each other. These things are important to community and I, for one, would be sad to see conflict and nastiness removed completely from the equation.

Skip (22 July.95):

> There are communities within communities—some of them are consensual, some of them are not—the top-level one for people (the 'community' of all humans) is not consensual; here we all are, and we're stuck with each other. [...]. So the one who asks, 'What do you mean by that?' may not be part of the immediate community (the ones that know the answer to the question), but is part of the next-level-wider community (those who can talk about the question with some sort of common language).

Jerry comments (24 July.95):

> the fourth child is both part of and apart from the community—there is no discrepency here as we are all members of multiple communities (family, student, consumer, etc) and at times these intersect in sometimes contradictory ways.

Despite community being a loaded term and, on Cybermind, conveying the ideas of care, and personal being, it seems to be difficult to use the term in any practical sense, or to agree on the limits to, or regulation of, community; an excess is perhaps automatically beyond regulation, or it is not excess. So although the term allows bonding because of its vagueness, the same vagueness might hinder coordinated group action. It also makes it more difficult to deal with a person who is perceived as disruptive, particularly if they were seen as, at least, partially of that 'community'.

Problems and Pleasures of Online Life

Community and Dispute

Disruption can arise out of nostalgia, or longing, for community, and from the use of the term as a concept, not a congerie with many referents. If people assume both that community can exist and that it implies acceptance and understanding (or that it should contrast with the restraint, or inauthenticity, of their work life), they may not consider how their posts can be read by someone of the same group who does not share their interpretive conventions. A post which is intended to be witty, or pointed, or bantering, by breaking the implicit conventions of community held by other people, can easily be perceived as an attack. A person may arrive upon a list which does not share their mode of communalising, and in distress begin to try to impose their vision of community upon it as they perceive this vision as the only one.

Increased communication does not necessarily prevent wars (as has been occasionally argued on the list). Long before the invasion of Iraq, when faced with a person writing that they occasionally found the US bent of the list difficult, another person asked "why do you hate America?" As this question contained an implicit requirement that people either not answer it, give reassurance, or deny the 'dislike', it appeared communication was not occurring when communication (e.g. writing about what one did find difficult about the US emphasis of the List) was making things worse. A previously nonexistent hostility was *created* through communication. Even people sympathetic to the original difficulty saw the responses as anti-American, and did not perceive the anti-non-American bent of some of the US responses. In this case it was lack of communication, (i.e. becoming quiet), that restored a sense of 'community'. With over a year spent in the lead up to the Iraq War, it proved impossible for people to maintain silence. People were continually provoked by external factors, by defences of America, by accusations of anti-Americanism and by use of hostile statements about Americans, rather than just about the US government, and quietness proved impossible. Attempts to overcome the disunity by the posting of jokes and one-liners may have driven some people away. Posts tended to be aggressive or irrelevant, or both.

Therefore it seems that national identity, and difference, may be reinforced by encountering others, rather than diminished as is often argued. The offline identity category of the 'we' as American was stronger than the 'we' of Cybermind. The 'other' side was grouped as non-American, rather than as German, British, Canadian or Australian. Pre-existing political factionalism or tensions were also aggravated, so that the right/left division, which tended to be pro-war and anti-war became more disruptive than previously, and debate moved quickly into abuse and misunderstanding.

Fragility and Asence
Online communities are often seen as fragile. As zoogirl writes, they are:

> unstable because they can be obliterated at the stroke of a key, which (it is arguable) real-life communities cannot (except perhaps in case of war or in certain political situations).

This is perhaps an expectation driven by the concept of 'community' rather than by behaviour in the world. There are many cultures where fissioning of groups is the norm, and even societies which are stable geographically may not be stable residentially or interactively (cf Lawrence 1984).

Email community is, however, influenced by asence. People on a list cannot be silent together, they cannot sit and share presencing. Without volume of mail there is no presence; but with increasing volume people tend to skim mail, so that appreciation of everything happening to other list members can be limited. A long recognized list member once wrote to me:

> I feel as though I was driven away from cybermind and my memory of it is nothing but pain. It ended up being one of the worst experiences of my life.

I was not even aware, until receiving this message that anything was amiss for this person, which indicates the failure of 'ideal community'. There is no doubt the events the member described to me happened. As my attention was directed towards looking for this kind of event, I presume such unawareness was not uncommon. Trauma to another can occur when a person is offlist, or set to no-mail, for example. A list member's absence is not indicated. To the person suffering the trauma, it could appear that people who might be expected to support them are not doing so, when, in fact, those people don't even know anything is happening. This adds to the feelings of asence and alienation. Texts, which are marked in terms of the intensity of the emotions involved, are not distinguished from other texts in the mailbox. Thus, in offline life, a raised voice, or tears, or some other gesture may emphasise that a person is in distress, and allow others to focus their attentions upon them; whereas in a mailbox nothing marks a call for attention. A cry of distress can be sped over, deleted unread, or submerged in comments upon a part of the letter.

A marked example of this occurred during a discussion of virtual rape when a female list member mentioned having once been raped offline. It might be supposed that in a 'liberal caring community' this would be greeted with a degree of sympathy, but one list member disagreed with a particular point of her mail, and discussion focused immediately upon that disagreement, bypassing the issue of the offline rape completely. Such events, which can be devastating for the person ignored, are an extreme form of asence; even suffering does not prove you exist. A list member, while commenting to me after reading the above, referred to the ambiguities of online public and private framings, writing that email:

> is very different from ftf or telephone—not necessarily because of lack of facial gesture, timbre of voice (as is often said) but because it […] has the capability to be both intimate and public. In the example you cite the public face of email and its position in 'argument' has eclipsed the intimate. I've seen the reverse of this happen too, where an intimate reading is preferred over a more objective one.

As well, traditions and styles of reply in online life have to be continually re-presented to exist, so it is easy for them to be laid aside. A list is made by the people who post and the way that they post; thus the nature of the group is less separable from the prominent list members than it is in the embedding society, which makes the 'generations' effect (discussed in Chapter 5) more marked. Lack of public reminiscence may also contribute to this sense of fragility. People are only able to remember publicly or discuss things which they think everyone remembers, or which are traumas, such as the 'Freaks' escapades. So not only are others shifting in and out of existence, but so are the group conventions and history. The bond is continually broken or, at least, tremulous and tending to silence.

We might expect a list to become less viable the less it could act, rather than the more certain acts were open to it. However, the less 'virtual' the community becomes, the more it goes offlist or into offline life, the less it might flourish. When people talk to each other and not to the group, then group life and presence is diminished. Pairing behaviour might redirect content from the list to the pair. The more some communal acts became possible the more a list might fall apart. As Turner et al, claim that factors which personalize intragroup membership relations decrease intragroup cooperation (1988: 65-6). "[I]nterpersonal attraction and group cohesion tend to be inversely related" (ibid: 62).

Athough asence may describe the limits of communities of a certain type, it does not mean that useful and pleasurable activities are absent.

Pleasures of the Online Life

Sometimes we can see a lyrical edge to reports about what people enjoy; although these are not overly informative, and I suspect become slightly less common the longer people are online. Just to give one example, Tom writes (23 July.95):

> Sitting here once again on a Sunday morning. I muse through the morning coffee steam about why I can't break away. The electronic attraction of cyberspace drawing me in, drawing me out, drawing no conclusions. The mind paints the cyberscape for me as I swim through the information currents (cybermind is a deep ocean green). [...]
>
> Why do I like Cyberspace? I sit here this Sunday wondering where I crossed the line. I do not think that, even if I wanted to, I could easily pull myself from the depths that I have found. It is home now, I use the tools as if they were my own limbs, action following intent. While I still love the touch of the

> sun on my face, and the caress of the warm wind on a summer night, I have now found new joys and thrills in the touch of a data stream, the caress of warm cyberspace all around.

Just over a month later, about a week after the 'Holocaust debate', Tom asked (1 Aug.95):

> I find myself wondering what the biggest appeal of the Net in general is to the online population at large...what is it that you like most about this space? I am not sure that CM is the best cross section of average net users but I would love to hear your input.

Laurie answered (1 Aug.95):

> I like being able to express myself, communicate my personality, through writing.

Nan adds that for her (1 Aug.95) Cybermind is:

> about much more than writing. I like the interactive part, the feedback from others whose opinions I value, the intrigue of new ideas and images seducing my mind to playfulness as well as serious debate. And yes, the community: much more than mere *audience*—something all writers require—this group has heart.

Rose writes (2 Aug.95) that she likes the helpfulness of people, and gives some examples. She adds:

> Perhaps altruism is a basic human trait, after all? [...] Surely by now the 'we're pioneers out here together' mentality is no more, so why are we still helping one another... if not because we *want* to, and enjoy it?!

Steven (2 Aug.95) phrases his liking of the net in terms of information and sex ("occasional steeping of the hormonal brew"), and of Cybermind in terms of intellectual stimulation and community:

> My left and right hemispheres both soak up the nutrients that are posted here. Too, as society's center is loosed in the widening gyre, there is a sense for me of groping to a new kind (or level) of connectivity; the glimmer of hope that as this rough beast slouches towards bethlehem there will be recombinant forms of resistance, love, and info-sharing.

Skip (2 Aug.95) saw it in terms of a potential change of "the Rules", a cutting across borders and boundaries and a new chance. Shawn agreed: "there is so much more virtuality out t/here than we could ever hope to actualize". John (3 Aug.95) saw it in terms of the increase of his possibilities; that he did not have to worry about appearance, or having enough money.

Although it is hardly an overwhelming theme of these replies, it appears some people regard online society as a possible new move towards a more acceptable form of human association coming through a change in what it means to be human, and as a kind of rebellion against the parts of the embedding society which they feel oppressive, or which do not bring out the best in people. Certainly it is perceived as a contrast. Whether it will remain so, once it becomes routinised is a different matter.

This section of the chapter indicates that rather than being engaged in retreat, at least some people online are exploring their sense of belonging, or not belonging, to wider social categories, and perhaps in changing those categories themselves. The list partially releases people from expectations which are no longer valid, the perhaps universal gap between desires, ideals and circumstances (Barth 1981: 7), yet others on the list recognise those expectations as worthwhile, and worth striving for. List usage comes out of people's offline lives in many ways, and goes back into their lives in equally many ways.

Chapter 12: Intersection of the List with the Offlist and the Offline

Introduction

Problems around the application of the term community are now discussed in relation to people's lives offlist. The group often attempted to organise offline meetings and these were important to list life. However, it is difficult to organise the List as a whole to do anything—even for them to specify a MOO on which they can interact. Leadership and facilitation in organising offlist events is extremely important. List structure also makes it so that most offlist contact will be as pairs, and the dynamics of this semi-secret list 'aura' is described and explained along with the relationships and love affairs which grew around the List. People recognised many benefits to being on Cybermind, and it is shown how this relates to the social pressures of their lives offlist.

Organizing as a Group

As argued in Chapter 4, the structure of lists, and their vague relationships to other groups imply that it is hard to organize as a group. I give some examples of these difficulties, which manifested between June and September 1995.

The destruction of PMC-MOO and its recreation by the Wizards, with the aim of making it more relevant to the discussion of post-modernism, was discussed with some vitriol both on and offlist. Member's main concerns focused on whether the change would destroy the 'community' and spontaneity which made the MOO worthwhile. Agreement was not uniform, but no subgroup of Cybermind protested to the Wizards, even though it was generally agreed that the MOO was no longer suitable for member's social activities. Subsequently, an attempt to establish a new MOO 'space' for Cybermind failed, even though Jim transported the Cybermind lounge from PMC-MOO to the almost empty Cows-go-MOO.

Failure of the group to establish an agreed upon MOO-space shows members had little ability to organize in terms of *group* action with respect to the wider world[1]. The help and support given to one another on an individual level only emphasises this.

Likewise, during this period there were many exceedingly long forwards about the passage of the Communications Decency Act through the US Congress, asking the 'Internet community' to protest.

It was often asserted that the proposers of the Act were not internet users and were ignorant. This Act attempted to impose what were called 'community standards' on the internet, showing the use of the term 'community' in a wider political context. Supporters of the Act (who were not obvious on Cybermind[2]) seem to have assumed 'community standards' were uniform throughout the US and could be defined. This obliterated the idea that different groups of people might establish different standards in their groups. There was no consideration, by supporters of the Act, that freedom from commercialization or advertising (a relatively common value of net users) constituted a community standard. Opponents of the bill suggested that standards should be established at the individual or, at the largest, the nuclear family level, rather than by a national 'community'. So both sides ignored the group basis of such decisions in some way.

Although it was often pointed out, that the application of these nationwide 'community standards' might result in the suppression of the list itself, there were no explicit attempts to present, say, a group petition to Congress, or to recognize those members of the group who wrote to their representatives in protest. However, it may not be the group itself which is the problem. It may well be the 'class' of people joining this particular list are not good at organising themselves into groups which act on the world, in any circumstance. So that is another illustration of the thesis that 'Knowledge Workers', or Gans' new suburbanites, find it hard to organise.

Offlist Meetings

Another important indicator of list community seems to be the interaction of people offlist. Although the group may not demonstrate much ability to coordinate its activities as a whole, it is well able to act mutually at a small group level or between individuals, both onlist and offlist. However, these activities to some extent threaten the sense of community, by removing presence from the list and making references less clear to others, or by indicating that those not involved are outsiders.

In this section of the chapter, offlist activities, both on and off line, shall be considered, so as to show how people use such small group or individual/pair types of meeting.

People organized frequent offline formal meetings of groups in the US, Australia and the UK, which were reported onlist. Organising such meetings often took months as people struggled to find mutually convenient times and locations. The posted descriptions and effort involved in organising meetings indicates they were considered important to the List[3].

To give an example, the following (abridged) mail from Rose (10 Aug.95), describes the Boston meeting during the two months just discussed[4]. The report, characteristically, is a report describing people rather than describing what the people did or said to each other:

> Eric (CM's first baby) fit so comfortably in arms that had not held a Significant Infant in a very long time... Aunt Rose felt _complete_ with his warm downy head 'neath her kisses.
>
> There is an image of Steven on the street corner by the Boathouse—a beacon sending out psychic messages to nearing Cyberminds: 'We are here. We will wait for you. Come, join us.' (Or, perhaps: 'Where the f*ck *are* you??')
>
> Speaking of 'psychic', the psychic energy (must be a correct term out there somewhere, no time to hunt for it) at the free-form banquet table at Chili's was so vibrant, so intense, that it prevented Rose from becoming-the-table-without-even-looking-at-it! [...]
>
> Nan—ah, Nan! Nan was so 'Nan', she couldn't possibly have been anyone else. I think if she'd walked by at the Boathouse without paying us the least bit of attention, one or more of us would have dashed after her and retrieved her......
>
> The families were reassuring, somehow—they exhibited Universal Family Dynamics (well, 'universal' in my experience, anyway—being 'nuclear', 'n all......) Jim (Rose), Dave (Ellen), offspring—thank you!!
>
> Sasha—ageless, a mobile quest after the unknowable
>
> Glen[nR]—sunburned and still, far deeper than the river that had scorched... ... his arms
>
> Dobie—who was so gracious in his reaction to 'you're so YOUNG!'
>
> Lurkers, Maggie and Laura—true Cyberminds, f2f (far more 'mind' than I!)
>
> Annie (Nan's friend)—*truly* 'delicious'!!
>
> —Rose, looking around her world eagerly and saying, 'OK—What's next'[5]

Online meetings between two or more groups in different parts of the world also occurred, usually via PMC-MOO and, after the 'reform' of that MOO, on LambdaMOO or Dhalgren-MOO, despite world time differences[6]. It was easier for people to meet as pairs. Possibly there was some psycho-sociological problem in organizing routine behaviours amongst group members, as one-off events always seemed to be more successful than repeated events[7]. Sometimes this was because of the absence of a person to take responsibility for organising. Thus, it was possible to organize sequential birthday celebrations on PMC-MOO for Bernadette, Laurie and Mitch largely because of the activities of one or two people. But, subsequently, no one continued the 'tradition'.

One of the most remembered joint MOO and 'flesh' meetings occurred in December 1995. Jerry recalled it two years later as one of the "two real highlights for me". It:

> led directly to the next great moment—the cybermind96 conference. After the Great MOO party someone suggested a BIG get together, and that's where the idea for a conference came from^8.

This 'MOO' party occurred on Sunday 17 December 1995 and was reported to the list by five people. Six members met in New York at the '@Café' and five in the London 'Internet Cafe'. PMC-MOO was used to communicate between the two meetings, and other people from the list also used the MOO. Various list members brought along their children or spouses, as is common at these group meetings, which demonstrates either that online community is not separate from daily life, or a need for 'safety in numbers'.

The excitement is best described by kmc who had "had a terrible cold/fever which alternated with headaches" and almost did not come. He wrote:

> The meet was wonderful, even as I stalked my overmedicated body through the streets toward the @Cafe, I already felt better, even euphoric in a way. That feeling was to intensify.

> We talked about everything under the sun and more, it felt so very reassuring in a way to meet these people one had only come into contact with through this medium of email. Conversations burst into being and grew spontaneously, like threads, but unlike threads, without the deliberateness that sometimes goes into email, without the time to search for the "right" word... Compared to email, conversations begin to feel like improvisation... on the spur of the moment, euphoric.

> It felt so reassuring because... because for the first time, stepping across the threshold of the virtual into the physical as well, full incorporation without the required projection of the physical, without the simulation of the physical in a field where it finds no place, without the accustomed virtual signifiers of ;-), but rather, to see Jim and Alan laughing as they mounted a mock-battle replay of the old os/platform-wars, and to feel again the human warmth that emanates from the physical. Reassuring, comfortable.

> At once, it reinscribes the virtual, extends it, reinforces the idea of virtual community. And yet, it also acts to undermine it in some ways, perhaps to undermine the impotency, the *lack* which the screen invokes for me. Hard to describe, though hopefully. i've communicated some of it here.

So though kmc expresses a delight in the expansion of his knowledge of others, this does not have a simple relationship with 'improving' the viability of the list for him.

Frequently people wrote, as Rose did above, that people were in some way physically as they were expected to be—there was a sense of recognition[9]. Thus for the New York meeting LAM wrote:

> At 2pm Jim walked thru the door and I just knew that it was him. (Must have been that 6th sense...because I did not receive the off list mail that he sent me with his description until I returned home this evening.)

However, other list members were in the Cafe and had not been noticed. This aptness of appearance gains contrast from cases where the person was not as expected (i.e. dobie's "youth" for Rose, although this had not been hidden by him). However, this 'unexpectedness' is far more rarely mentioned, and when mentioned (offlist) often arises on those very few occasions when people have portrayed themselves with out-of-date photographs, or when pairing interest is involved. When people are emotionally involved, disjunction between appearance as imagined and perceived becomes important. People who confidently deny the importance of the body can find that appearance *does* count, and that relationships can fail because of it.

My own experience was less dramatic. I had little idea of what people would look like, but found it easy to adapt and to assume I had always known what they looked like. Another way of relating to appearance comes from Janet (22 Jan.96):

> When I've met folks in the flesh after knowing them online, my "online" mental picture of them sometimes overshadows the physical presence to such an extent that, even knowing what someone looks like, I continue to conjur up my earlier rendering of her. I'm not sure what to do with that.

In a similar vein GlennR writes of meeting a person met through the Internet after fourteen months of correspondence (24 Apr.96):

> The strange part is, almost as soon as her tail lights disappeared over the hill... I started to lose memory of her actual appearance. A week later I had to think hard just to form her image in my mind... What's left now is no mental

image at all... [She] is now, in my mind, a construct of ideas and words—no images. In the face of contradiction between fantasy and reality, I choose neither. The words were the reality all along.

Cybermind Conference

The most difficult organizational feat was the Cybermind Conference held in November 1996. Although this conference was the work of many people, it would almost certainly not have occurred without the efforts of list member Karen Melzack, who took responsibility for everything. Karen made the suggestion to the list on 9 December 1995 while the MOO meet, mentioned above, was being organised because:

> I so much wanted to join the Meet in NY or London in the coming weeks but I can't and then I had a cyber?thought... how about a real/unreal Cybermind Conference?...in say late 1996.

Jerry (9 Dec.95) suggested persuading an institution to host it and raising corporate sponsorship. Carsten (10 Dec.95) asked if Karen would volunteer to organize it and Karen agreed. Some members expressed doubt that it would be possible to organize or to gain the money. However, by the 16th of December, Karen had made appointments to see people in three Perth universities. She discussed the conference manifesto and some papers with Alan, Jerry, Richard and myself and issued it by 22 Januart 1996. By 16 February 1996 she had raised Alan's airfare. Most of the organising of list members was done offlist in either private email, a special email list, or on the Conference-MOO. Three recognized members from the US, and nine members from Australia attended[10], while various people in Perth joined the list in the period preceding the conference. Some of the conference was broadcast over the Web via C-U-See-Me and Real Audio, and descriptions of the papers were typed over the Conference-MOO as the papers were presented, which enabled speakers to interact with list members in other parts of the world[11]. At least nine people were regulars on the Conference MOO. Photographs from the conference, comments, and stories were also sent to the list.

The conference did not have any particular effect upon the group. It did not seem to make bonds firmer between conference goers or between the group as a whole. It did not make conference goers an elite. The relationships I had with people which were already reasonably close were reinforced; but distant, or awkward, relationships remained distant. However, one of my closest list friendships probably would not have emerged without meeting at the Conference. Few people who joined the list for the conference, remained on list afterwards. I suspect few lasting contacts were made between list attendees and non-list attendees, despite some people's attempts to make contacts with non-list member attendees to help find work or get published and so on. List usage by some conference attendees may have even declined. Nevertheless, the conference was often given, in remarks to me, as an example of the strength of Cybermind's community[12].

Leadership and Facilitation

Group meetings seem to have gone into abeyance in the aftermath of the quarrels over Iraq, although individuals still met each other. This may result from the decline in population or the relative unwillingness of people to co-ordinate events. These meetings require organisation by people who take on the task of facilitation, as does the functioning of the list itself. For example, the December MOO meet was largely organised by one person; LAM[13]. At a basic level, whatever community exists on Cybermind only exists because of the gift of time from the moderators. This 'gift' is, in some ways, not an overt gift as it is doubtful most members are aware of the amount of time and effort involved. There may be conflict between needing an organizer or a person to take responsibility for group actions, and the general ideology of independent individualism, or the resistance to being organized, or engaging with 'structure'.

The same need for someone to take responsibility for organisation was also shown in one of the few successful attempts by the group to co-operate in an online project, namely the Cybermind Novel which was written as part of the NaNoWriMo competition in November 2003. Rowena drew people's attention to the competition in October of that year. Skip suggested that the List collaborate, which was received with enthusiasm. Elizabeth suggested the initial organization, subject germs (about cyberspace) and the first character; and I provided the website. About 9 members of the List collaborated over the month by writing alternate chapters and posting them onto the List. In this case the presence of discussion and the chapters on the List overcame issues of asence, which probably would have disrupted the order of writing if it had simply been put directly on the website, I took responsibility for putting all the chapters onto a website, and effectively harassed people during the occasional failure of someone to write at the time they were supposed to. I also edited the final version of the novel now on that website. Subsequent suggestions by List members that the group should write another novel given the success of the first have not resulted in group action, perhaps because of the absence of anyone volunteering to co-ordinate.

The Aura of the Offlist[14]

Alan writes (3 June.96):

> If online there are no witnesses to secret discourse, how does one then study online behavior? Concrete example—if Pip and I unsub X from the list (to take a sore point), that is invariably after discussions between us, and between us and numerous others off-list, and among others that we don't know about off-list, including of course the party unsubbed. This can get voluminous—yet what you would be studying would be only the public onlist statements—as if the Congressional Digest here in the US were the only clue to what goes on in Congress?

In offline society, to some extent, people know what is happening "backstage", or they know something is happening, even if they are not sure what. They might observe the people involved whispering to each other or going off into the bush together and guess. Whereas in online life people are not likely to know that *anything* is happening. The markedness of this dislocation may vary from person to person, but clearly affects the knowledge any one person could have of the list and how it worked.

Initially, it seemed to me that there was relatively little offlist life (apart from administration, the odd meeting or affair), but on other occasions it seemed more was happening offlist than on. This may have resulted either from increased familiarity, or a change in list behaviour, or both. Sometimes it could be postulated by a newcomer. For example Dragon wrote (16 June.96):

> as a newbie I have to admit that I have found it hard to find a place to join a discussion here. I feel very outside the lot of you. Perhaps some of that can be attributed to all the offlist chatter (of which I am not a part at all).

Thus, implying that, sometimes, interpretation may be made more difficult for those not involved in the aura[15].

Closer Individual Email Contact and 'Real Life' Contact

Activity on the list engenders a network of largely dyadic offlist contacts between list members. These contacts are far harder to describe than group contacts, as they tend not to be portrayed onlist.

Alan is the centre of a vast web of offlist correspondence[16]. He is the person people complain to, or make queries to, and it is often he who will try to make peace between disputing members. Although this reinforces his leadership role and his position as the most recognized person on list, it is also somewhat unusual. However, most active people attract some offlist correspondence eventually[17]. In the two months discussed above, I had offlist correspondence with at least ten list members. Though this might connect with my role as list anthropologist, only two of these correspondents (not surprisingly Alan and Glen) were specifically queried about list events, and most correspondence with them was personal. During 1995-96, I corresponded more than once, generally in fairly intense bursts, with at least thirty nine list members for purely social, and non research based, reasons—mainly with comments on list mail, or replies to mail directed to me.

Attempting to describe offlist contact between list members is difficult, not only because it is invisible, but because people resisted describing their offlist (private) life in email. I only received three replies to a large number of public requests for such data, which I reproduce here[18]. Firstly (pc 12 Mar.96):

> Close friends: [8 names] (of these, I've flesh-met [four]) As you can see, this is a wonderfully diverse group—I know of no other space where I could talk to [3 of the previous names] because political and social differences would probably prevent it from occurring.
>
> [A] is some kind of soul-mate; we recognized it in each other instantly. This was so in the flesh, too. Likewise, [B] and [C] and I have a heart-connection. I can talk about anything with them and we often speak in poetry and metaphors. [D] I also see on a MOO almost daily...

And an example of a less involved approach to the group (pc 15 Mar.96):

> Hmmm—I've had off-list convsersations with maybe half a dozen folks here, either reinforcing what I or someone else had said ("Hey! Good post!"), commiserating with someone's condition, following up on a thread, or asking for more info. Most discussions are onlist—that's mostly a function of not really having the time to pursue net.relationships a lot;

Bernadette made the only response to the list (15 Mar.96):

> So you want us to say how many friends we have on list? I would say roughly have 4 or 5 net.friends on the list, that I would regularly

communicate with, and what we discuss is our business, I am afraid. But conversations have ranged from computer related to politics. CM is meantioned in passing,

Such remarks can be elaborated by information given to me through private contact with seven or so list members.

The list which follows, demonstrates the involvement of members with each other and the frequency of attempts at sexual or romantic relationships, without the reader simply having to take my word. When reading this account, the following factors should be borne in mind. Much is based on gossip; often people were more inclined to talk about other people's List-based love affairs than their own. There were multiple and occasionally conflicting narratives; thus this listing is a simplification and distortion of the patterns of gossip and autobiography. However, there did not seem to be enough conflict between accounts for it to be analytically interesting. This gossip also covers a reasonably long time period (about five years), so its compression exaggerates the apparent drama. I have included only pair meetings, not group 'fleshmeets'. The background to, and consequences of, the Cybermind Conference has also been ignored. I have assumed that taking the trouble to meet in person implies a degree of closeness between people. To hide identities I have split some people into two, and combined others. I have left out contacts which made identification too obvious, or where revelation might have had repercussions in offlist life. This list is certainly not definitive; the recurrence of a few names may reflect my particular sources. Gender has not been specified; however, almost all of these offlist contacts involve at least one woman.

- 'A' journeyed to meet 'C', 'D', and 'E'.
- 'F' met 'E' on list and travelled to meet them, but the relationship failed.
- I was told that 'G' left their spouse to live with 'D' but it did not work.
- 'D' had close phone contact with 'H' and an affair.
- I was told that 'D' had netsex with 'I'.
- It was frequently rumoured that 'B' and 'D' had a passionate net affair ended by 'B'. This was denied by both 'B' and 'D'.

'I' had a relationship with 'E', which on meeting was disillusioning for 'I'.

'I' had an affair with 'J' and went to stay with them, but closeness faded away.

'I' had a short email affair with 'K' which broke up acrimoniously.

'L' had a long relationship with 'M', in which 'M' wished to marry 'L'.

'M' was reputedly being chased by 'N', who was also writing to 'L'.

It was rumoured, but in my opinion dubious, that 'M' was having an affair with 'O', but it is probable they wrote to each other frequently.

'O' had a relationship with 'P' in which they met several times.

'O' later had a relationship with 'Q' and 'Q' moved to join them.

'F' apparently had an intense MOO relationship with 'S' which failed on a visit.

Previously it appeared that 'F' was interested in a relationship with 'D' and that they had met, but it didn't work out.

It was said to me that 'A' wanted to have children with 'S'. It appeared they had an intense, probably non-sexual, relationship off list.

'L' had netsex with 'J' on numerous occasions.

'L' also had netsex with 'K'.

I was told that a love triangle existed between 'T', 'C' and 'U'.

'D' and 'C' met and were quite close friends but seem to have fallen out.

'F' and 'C' were friendly and met.

'O' travelled to meet 'F', 'A' and 'B'.

'F' paid for 'V' to address a conference.

'V' and 'O' visited each other on several occasions.

'W' met 'A' several times when they travelled to the relevant part of the country.

'L' and 'W' talked regularly on the phone, and met on several occasions.

'X' travelled to another country to stay with 'O'.

'R' travelled to another country and sought out 'Y' and several other list members.

'Z' and 'AA' met on list and lived with each other for several months.

'D' met 'BB', had an affair which hovered on marriage and 'D' travelled to meet 'BB'.

'CC' stayed with 'Z'.

'Z' went to work for 'V'.

'W' met 'F' and had occasional phone contact.

'W' lamented to me that 'DD' was married otherwise s/he would have tried to start a relationship, but had to settle for a relatively close friendship.

'DD' and 'R' met occasionally.

'L' and 'EE' had netsex and an offlist friendship for some time.

'V' met with 'FF' on at least one occasion.

'GG', who didn't have much involvement with other members, tried to help 'M' during a 'rough stretch'.

These thirty or so people are easily less than one tenth of the people who have been on the list in the time period under consideration, yet they make up a significant proportion of recognised members at the time of their activity[19]. Many parts of this network would have remained unknown to me without a particular contact at a particular time, and thus is even more likely to be abridged[20]. That I had few sources also implies this sketch of a web of contacts only represents a small proportion of offlist contacts. It is also difficult to describe when people *don't* meet. Thus, one of my contacts was in the same city as a frequent correspondent, but made no effort to meet. Other list members seem, on some occasions, to have gone out of their way to avoid offline contact with list contacts.

The degree to which list members engaged in sexual or 'romantic' contact, is obvious. There is no evidence this is a universal feature of mailing lists. It appears that most, though not all, of these contacts aimed at some kind of lasting pairing relationship, emphasizing the importance of the private pair relationship in WES construction of intimacy. It also seems that the success rate of these attempted romantic contacts was not high[21], although friendship contacts were often said to be successful. Without some idea of the 'success rate' of people's attempts to initiate lasting pairing relationships in the embedding societies, it is not possible to decide whether these failures are significant. Neither is it possible to decide whether the degree of attempted sexual activity is higher than in the embedding society for a similar 'class' of people.

Despite this, the anecdotal evidence is clear. People tell me they have had more love affairs via the Internet than in any similar time period in their offline lives, but with less translation into lasting relationships[22]. People, who were not members of the list, but who have written on netsex, frequently imply that there is less at stake in netsex (it is safer for example) and therefore that it can be engaged in more frequently and casually than offline sex. I am not certain of this kind of position for Cybermind. People seemed to find netsex as fraught or complicated as offline sex, in fact complexity might increase because of the absence of immediate feedback[23]. Online relationships and netsex *could* be as emotionally distressing as any more conventional relationship. There seemed to be no obvious gender distinction in people's emotional reactions to netsex and relationships.

The limited amount of information transmitted may allow the quicker appearance of intimacy mentioned in Chapters 7 and 11. It certainly allows others to appear more prototypic of the kind of person they might be, and hence more appealing or aggravating. Also the change from simplex to multiplex communication might be enabled to occur more rapidly, thus giving a sense of quick intimacy.

It seems probable the quest for a close relationship is more important, or more common, among list members than the quest for 'simple' sexual pleasure. Sexual pleasure may well be considered an attempt to generate intimacy (Giddens 1992: 50). A search for intimacy may be evidence of loneliness, or of alienation from one's everyday life. At the least it is an expression of dissatisfaction, and of the idea that such problems can be fixed at a personal level (perhaps forever) through intimacy. Yet at the same time it appears the intimacy can only be verified by 'everyday life' and thus the large number of visits, phone contacts, or transfer of photographs. It is possible that some people avoid offline contact as they do not want to risk the relationship in another field.

Alford argues that in WES therapy groups, pairing occurs because people are frightened of being left out, of being the only one alone, or it occurs to remove threats of symbolic death. These are conditions emphasised in list life by asence. Alford also suggests sex and pairing is a compensation for being unable to get the group to cooperate or work together (1994: 35-6), which, as we have seen, is also a problem in online groups. It can, therefore, be suggested that pairing may produce a concrete cooperation which is otherwise rare, and is used to lower asence. These factors may be emphasised by the theories of individualism widespread in WES societies. The pair could be the only social unit people are able to emotionally recognise, or not feel overwhelmed by and risk losing their individualistic self-construction.

Another feature of these relationships is the amount of travel involved. At least nine of these contacts required overseas travel, or projected travel, and at least another six involved traversing significant distances. The money and effort of such journeys also suggests the importance people place upon these relationships and face-to-face contact, especially given the apparently low incomes of some of the people involved[24].

Offline Benefits

In the Community Survey, several people wrote that they joined the list because of the topic but remained because of their perceptions of community, as for example:

> I first joined the list because of my interest in the analysis of online social systems. Not everything on the list proved of interest (e.g., most discussions of philosophy), but enough did that I stayed with it. Eventually I found myself responding to more and more things, and adding more ideas of my own _sui generis_, and developing a feeling of community with the various people on the list.

and:

> I came for the ideas and stayed for the people. Staying on list only for ideas would be frustrating to say the least.

Some people mentioned that they used the list to try out their writings, and that in some cases this eventually led to publication. This is important for people on the fringes of academia and the art world, and also because of the group/class valuation of 'creativity' as is shown in these three posts:

> for me, there have been several uses—including self-publishing and distributing my own work... It's led for me to other publications, conferences, meetings as well.

> Did it help me get a job, or a paper published? Well, I got a couple of online publications out of it, and it certainly provided some experience in electronic communities that I was able to draw on for my book (and my second PhD book) So, yes I have had direct help from the list.

> I try out most of my writings on the list sometimes getting a good idea where they can be improved from people's comments.

This function of the group can directly improve people's survival chances, as these people write:

> the general discussion and the 'leads' offered in posts certainly help contribute to my areas of work.

> [Cybermind] definitely was part of the cornerstone to my career now.

One writer commented that "professionally I haven't found CM all that useful", yet detailed a number of professional contacts made through the list, and elsewhere wrote "I got my current job largely through my participation on an e-list". Laurie (23 Mar.98) conducted a survey which asked whether people "ever collaborated on a project with someone as a result of meeting in an online forum". Of the eleven respondents known to me, nine unambiguously replied in the affirmative, one other member changed their mind to 'yes', and the other remarked that it had been discussed.

Almost everyone specified friendships or meeting people as a benefit of the list. The implication of most responses seems to be that wanting to increase one's contacts is 'natural', and thus presumably common in their society. Another series of quotations:

> I met a number of people who I wouldn't have otherwise met, some of whom have become quite good friends, people I can discuss things with.

> It has been a pleasure meeting CM members IRL from time to time (there have not been many, and I wish there could be more).

> I think almost everyone, on the net or not, likes new experiences, and getting to know new people with whom they have things in common.

> meeting a number of people some of whom I feel very close to.

> I have formed a number of genuine friendships with people I would never have met under rl (non-cyberspace) conditions.

> I have certainly formed some long term friendships—ones that I value as highly as my face-to-face friendships.

> The net extends one's RL by bringing one into contact with people one would never have gotten to know otherwise.

Finally one person mentioned the help that they had received from the group in a moment of distress:

> The response to my request was fantastic and I will always appreciate cm answering me and helping me in my hour of need... it was a surprise:)

In an unsolicited remark, giving an example from another List, someone wrote (22 Jan.96):

> For reasons too complex to go into in this forum, I found myself without most of my real-life "friends" over the past year. I've developed a cybercommunity in which to dwell [...] and have been fortunate enough to have a "flesh-meet" with some of the individuals.

Comparisons

The Community Survey also asked how people compared Cybermind with other lists and to their offline life. Was the Internet an extension of life, or a substitute, or a compensation for an unsatisfactory life? I approached these questions a little more indirectly than the others, only bringing up specific issues in requests for further elaboration. Perhaps because of this responses tended to be varied. These variations show the different ways the list fits into people's lives.

There is nothing in my offlist life to compare. And the list has always been supportive. [...] I have been more 'myself' here than ever in physical life, and my 'self' has been generously accepted.

I have a somewhat different persona in c-space than IRL and thus I can do things with/through that personae which are more difficult IRL. I write to a group better than I talk to a group for example and I think I'm easier and nicer on the net than IRL.

It feels like more of a separate compartment; I don't find myself talking about my everyday life much on CM, and I don't talk about cybemind much in everyday life...[...] Its easier to carefully formulate one's responses, [...] or make requests to powerful people...

the physical separation from others, and the anonymity of some parts of cyberspace, facilitates indulging one's baser instincts with the accountability reduced. Then again some benign things are easier too,

Is CM like physical life? No, it's not. In some ways, it's only a pale imitation of physicality. I can't truly look someone in the eye and tell them what I think, or see their face when they say something. I can't, on the 'net, pull out my guitar and play. I can't, on the 'net, hold onto a friend for a reassuring hug. All that I have to go on are words, but the words are so much more intense.

it's more like a neighbourhood bar, perhaps, for me..., or cafe/coffee shop...

To ask if it is different from my real-life interactions, is kind of an odd question—at least it feels odd, because the interactions are between people first and foremost. I mean there are obvious differences—like time lag, and like you are seeing someone through the texts they produce, but in important ways I've found little real difference between online interactions and off-line ones.

The variations within these responses are obvious, and suggest that people have many ways of integrating, or relating, their online and offline lives—the group does not have to have only one beneficial function for people to find it useful or helpful.

Conclusion

Finding a degree of 'community' seems to have been expected by many people who posted to Cybermind.

Construction of a group as a 'community' in the WES world is not isolated from sociological theories, or from political struggles which focus on 'recovering community', 'forging a new community', or gaining representation for a community. These competing mythemes often present community in terms of a current absence. They imply community has occurred in the past or will occur in the future, but rarely that it occurs now among 'us'. Ideas that community has been destroyed by urbanisation, capitalism, modernism, ease of movement, decline in kinship responsibility, or even by television, are part of the discourse of community. Community is treated as if it was an essence rather than a term used to give aspirations, or create unities and differences among and between groups. Being recognised as community gives a group social validity and justification.

Constructions of 'community' in the embedding society are not only political and nostalgic, but are inherently vague and involve considerable differences in interpretation. The vagueness of the term allows it to be applied to the same group with relatively different references and yet give the impression of unity. We are all members of the community even though we value different aspects, and occasionally conflict on vital issues because the term is vague enough to include certain categories of people in a way that is satisfactory to all, if different. Yet different usages elsewhere are important in arguments over recognition.

Consequently, many definitions of community would exclude Cybermind because:

a) It consists of people separated in time and space.
b) It is part-time or 'leisure' based rather than full-time and survival oriented.
c) It is voluntary, rather than compulsory or a matter of birth.
d) The boundaries are permeable and unclear.
e) The people involved change continually.
f) It is conflictual as much as consensual.
g) Cooperation as a group is tenuous—things do not get done without 'pushing'; and
h) It is largely incapable of functioning as an entity in relation to the outside world.

Despite this a large proportion of long-term or recognized members declare it to be, or to have been, a 'community', and have gained benefit from it. It may not succeed in everything, but it succeeds well enough at some things.

In Victor Tuner's terms we can see members of Cybermind as seeking communitas rather than structure. Outside of crises, they will try to avoid structure. Elias and Dunning have suggested that 'leisure' activities, like living on Cybermind, take some of their meaning from their contrast with more restrained, or routine, activities. They act as outlets for altered and, by contrast, more enjoyable states of mind, and function as idealised examples of *Gemeinschaft*, which explains both the attraction of, and nostalgia for, 'community' in the WES world; it is something we have glimpses of, and which represents an 'escape' from the workplace. This contrast may also explain people's reluctance to engage with 'structure' when that is so strongly associated with work.

Three factors constitute the group being categorised as community within the dominant construction on the List. These factors can all be characterised as forms of 'excess', as functional lists could easily exist without them. Firstly community arises in the excess of messages not on topic. Secondly these excess messages have to be of a set of particular types or styles. Thirdly friendship, and contacts between people which occur offlist, also help categorizing a group as community by people involved in these contacts, and this can also be thought of as an excess to the formal requirements of a list. Excess can also threaten constructions of community.

Thus, if 'community' is characterized by an excess or redundancy of messages over an imagined basic set of messages, which could be characterized as 'on-topic', then the feeling of online community is partially a matter of volume, but this is 'two-edged'. With no volume the list has little presence, but with large volume people will leave or begin skipping messages and skim-reading, which leaves them unable to follow what is happening, weakens their sense of belonging, and lowers their chance of responding to friends when needed. This excess then weakens the feelings, which are important to their labelling of community.

Secondly, community is characterized by the excess being of a certain type. Excess, which is contrary to the general norms of the group, does not make community, although it might engender common cause in reaction to it. Excess especially contributes to feelings of community on Cybermind, if it appears to be personal in reference, or the expression of concern or support, and does not if it can be construed as an expression of anger or hostility.

Thirdly, communication offlist, meetings and friendships with others (whether offline or online but offlist) are also conducive to people construing the list as community. This third excess is also dangerous to list content and coherence, as people involved offlist become less involved onlist and take their mutual conversation offlist thus diminishing the presence of the list in other people's mailboxes and possibly setting up references which are meaningless to those not involved, as was alleged by some members in the case of the Offlist group.

Therefore, it appears that two of the contributing factors to constructions of community also generate strains within the group, which lead to feedback limits on that construction.

Excess provides messages of security and friendship in an environment in which the primarily simplex relationships have little inherent redundancy which can maintain the connection when the relationship is stressed. The excess also serves to reduce uncertainty and makes more explicit what is acceptable behaviour. As messages give a sense of place, the excess demonstrates the framing locale.

Clearly, the kind of redundancy favoured on Cybermind is not the only kind possible. An excess of 'flames' (or almost anything else) could serve a similar set of functions. Different kinds of excess would select for different kinds of memberships. Excess drives away those who are not prepared to put effort into the group and who do not wish their 'community' to be constructed in these kinds of ways.

The strength of these selection processes seems demonstrated by the remarkable coherence of Cybermind's population across professional groupings. Most members are 'middle class intellectuals', primarily with an Arts background (see Appendix I). There have been members with scientific, usually computing, backgrounds but almost no members of the 'business managerial class'. Few members, if any, could be classified primarily as 'manual workers'. Likewise the political leanings of the group are noticeably similar. Therefore the offline world provides a background set of common knowledges and conventions.

Although virtual 'communities' are important to their users, they are also perceived as fragile due to asence and the ease of disconnecting from others. As the atmosphere of the community depends upon its being continually re-presented, it is vulnerable to change at any moment—whether because of the activities of newcomers or because of the lack of activities by the established and recognised.

Online, the majority of active participants define, or present, the procedures and framings which make community. In that sense, the silent or the inactive are disempowered. There is little to have internal power struggles over, except the nature of the community itself, but such power struggles are never really resolved. Community is maintained by people not pressing an issue past the point which causes people to leave; particularly people recognised by the group.

On Cybermind plurality is the ideal, but in a group perceived as fragile, plurality cannot survive past a certain level or people have nothing to say, and no common framings to interpret the saying of others. Plurality is only present up to a point, often depending on events elsewhere and externally based categories. Gans argues that Americans cannot handle conflict because they cannot accept pluralism (1967: 414). However, it might simply be that in a society without multiple modes of connection between people, conflicts tend to be threatening to relationships as there is little else holding them together. Simplex relationships can also encourage the speedy application of prototypes, which then tend to become exaggerated and subject to 'mythical expectations'[25]. Thus, counterpoised to the fury of flame and the imposition of outsider categories, we see people engaged in a search for romantic coupling.

Experience of community is also shaped by asence. Asence can lead to flame war because of lack of reaction and indistinct boundaries on the self (or in some cases on the group), or because of over-expectations of harmony and understanding being violated. Paradoxically such 'exaggeration' can lead to a greater sense of involvement at the same time as the bonds are perhaps being destroyed. Such 'war' does not require that people are naturally aggressive, merely that the situation magnifies the possibility of such a response. Asence is also increased by generational succession, which can lead to radically different views of community and its composition throughout the group, and between 'generations'. This generational problem may add to the difficulties of organizing as a group and of re-telling, or sharing, anything like a uniform history of the group, which might increase feelings of fragmentation.

Online boundaries are vague, amorphous and permeable at best, although this may be emphasised by firm boundary patterns in parts of WES societies. With large portions of the list invisible and changing, borders cannot be drawn with precision. The group may try to exclude those who attack values held by the majority of the active members, with values often becoming more explicit, or even forming, in the defence. However, this active exclusion, or boundary enforcement, does not occur on many occasions, and it tends to focus on either unrecognised outsiders or those recognised as disruptive from previous encounters, and is not something active members can agree upon with ease. Glen left of his own accord and, although people were not happy with his mode of argument, the majority of people put responsibility for excluding him onto Alan. This might be part of a general WES pattern of avoiding responsibility, or avoidance of conflict, rather than anything specific in list behaviour.

Such factors may induce some people to decide that online societies must fail, and contradict the aspirations of some of their members. However, it is more useful to discuss what kind of action and experience is possible, or probable, with these 'asent' boundaries.

Construction of 'virtual communities' is part of a more complex social process, which has been anticipated and recognised for some while and described by the mythemes of sociology and media commentary. According to these stories, people in WES societies are more isolated than used to be the case. They are held to move frequently, and have contacts with people who are distant from them in space, via various technological apparatuses such as cars and telephones. They have continual experience of dealing with strangers. They form associations at a personal level, often using an 'interest', or symbolic focus as a method of bonding. In such group associations only relatively few people will be active, and even fewer of those will take on organizing or propelling the group.

In such a society with perceptions of 'shallow' kinship ties, few place-based ties, and now with diminishing 'professional ties' (particularly for people outside the corporate managerial world), it may seem a useful strategy to extend one's social connections to make a 'survival net', particularly when the future is uncertain. One way of making such a net is by using the Internet as a tool of association. This then feeds into the seeking of private offlist sexual relationships, as the sex/pair bond is, for WES people, the most obvious mode of establishing intimacy, connection and support—ideally resulting in two people becoming one.

Written support and sympathy at an individual or small group level is also easily possible and obviously rewarding to those who receive it, as is the ability to express personal anger or disappointment with the world. Indirect support for career or activities in a member's offlist life (such as providing references, pointing to work, or helping publication) is also possible and significant in some cases. Extended friendship, in the sense of compatibility and excitement, is also possible. However, it appears far more difficult for the group to organize itself as a group in a coherent manner, perhaps because it does not act against or toward other online groups. Actions of any complexity involving more than three or four people tend to require someone to take responsibility for coordination and, in general, this does not occur. The suspicion must arise that this lack is a behaviour learnt outside the list, although perhaps exaggerated by the list[26].

It also appears that some personal changes are possible because of the nature of the group. People who are nervous of others can be less threatened; people who are flustered and inarticulate can use the delay to become articulate; people who are self-conscious can hide and leave with no regrets if things do not work out. Such factors are often reported by people, both to the list and to myself, as important and life changing for them.

So people seek out a new community which allows safe self-expression; that is friendly, passionate and exciting, warm and welcoming, in whatever ways we wish these things to be. Yet any actual group of people may fail this ideal, which eventually leads to disillusionment, burnout, and turnover in population. However, there is no need to assume that permanent bonding is always what is needed, or even that the revitalization produced by online 'communitas', cannot be taken back into the routines of offline life.

Thus it seems that there are several interrelated processes occurring in the construction of online 'communities'. There are processes generated in the embedding societies and brought online; there are processes generated by the organization of communication online; and there are processes generated by the way that people interact with the demands and expectations of others after their arrival in those 'communities'. Thus, although the behaviours may be predictable by looking at how the embedding society functions, the actual history may depend upon the particular interactions of the people involved. Without Alan's persistence, his own writings and his tolerance of off-topic posts, the particular group history of Cybermind would be different, and so on.

People bring their prior experience and expectations to these new communities, but at the same time (given the widespread lack of long term experience using Mailing Lists or MOOs), people have to develop something which is slightly different from the offline world

—if only because conventional institutions do not seem to work—and yet similar because of the anchors necessary to their survival offline. At least part of the attraction of online society is this very sense of creativity and possibility, and the hope of founding a new world.

Conclusions

'Culture'

At the beginning of this book, it was suggested that 'culture' might usefully be considered as gained knowledges (tacit or explicit), which are not uniform throughout society and which vary in significant ways. These variations are affected by the techniques and cumulative pathways of learning which are available to people. It was suggested that culture, as knowledge, draws people's attention to the world in particular ways, and thus influences their perceptions of the world. Disjunctions between knowledges may have important social consequences. Furthermore, we must be careful in deciding what, if anything, of the events we observe are misperformance or noise. Such apparent misperformances or noises, might actually be vital parts of both the organisation of society and the experience of members. Society is a mode of producing chaos as much as producing order.

Categorisation

Having made these propositions, it was necessary to explore categorization as a component of human knowledge. I argued that categories, although affected by the nature of the real, were also affected by the learning situation, the relations of power, or emotional states, and so on. The different things/events grouped in a category were often not members in quite the same way and some members were better examples than others. These 'better examples' were called prototypes. Prototypes had the property of being more easily recognizable, memorable and activated than non-prototypic members. Category members, if identified as belonging to a category, could then appear to take on the properties of the prototype. This proved to be important, not only in explaining the course of online disputes, but also in the ways that these disputes were conceived by the participants.

Given that categories have the potential to diverge in use, communication cannot be a transfer of contents, but a complex feedback process in which interpretation is as important as intention. A major factor in communication was the framings brought to the situation by the participants. Although these framings might allow divergent interpretations, they made 'conceivable' coaction possible. Interactions between people could often be driven by the different framings brought to them, even if the 'concerns' were superficially similar. Framings, which were discovered to be important in the online world, included: locale, mood, exchange, redundancy, etiquette, conflict, and the public/private division. Categories also tend to 'cluster', so that the activation of part of a cluster activates the other parts of the cluster. This also provides some conceptual stability between people—although, again, clusters need not be uniform throughout 'society'.

A distinction was then drawn between concept and congerie, by specifying that categories in which the members could be linked by similar properties, or by definition, could be called concepts. Everything else was called a congerie and would have varying links between members. Concepts were more likely to form where their members were manipulable and there was some kind of pressure towards system. Vague congeries often filled in the gaps of signification or terminated explanation, becoming almost magical in their references. 'Community', 'information', and 'authenticity' are congeries which are important online. These terms gain their puzzling and occasionally overwhelming complexity because of their function in discourse, and because they gather disparate things or events together.

Where the objects and events of the category are difficult to manipulate, then social control, or the attempt to influence or regulate the behaviour of others, may be a major factor in producing category matching or coherence. As survival frequently depends upon co-operation, and co-operation in turn depends upon the relative mutual coherence of categories, which renders actions compatible and predictable, then we can expect large proportions of dialogue to be concerned with making these categories mutually coherent. When people attempt to coact through the exchange of text alone, then the intensity of social control may increase, to make communication appear coherent. Online social control occurs between people maintaining, or imposing, categories upon others; and people exploring and developing the adequacies of their self-categorization, often by attempting to become prototypic.

Categories affect groups. A group, or category, need only to be named to affect the behaviour of people towards that group and those named by that category. The precise nature of this effect is produced by the kind of interactions between the groups so categorised. Prototypical category members are more persuasive, or influential, to other category members than are non-prototypic members.

Prototypicality varies with outgroup comparison, and becomes more extreme when the framing of relations between the groups is overtly conflictual.

In online life the connection between category, social control and communication becomes clearer, as it is more emphasized. The online world is largely a world in which people do not reinforce, shape, or share their categories within the constant contact of 'everyday life' and the resistances of the world. By virtue of this isolation, and its textual nature, communication is shifting; restrained only by offline convention and thus subject to category slide and misinterpretation. Therefore, a fairly constant power struggle over category coherence may arise. This struggle is perhaps the primary mode of co-operation currently possible in online life. In this constant negotiation, category-norms are constantly put forward, recreated, validated or found to be wanting. Category-norms are produced in the discovery of difference. 'Net culture' is created *for* those who become 'others', or who become 'us', and *in response* to those who become 'others'. Every person is their own ethnographer creating the model of the society within which they operate, and of the groups with which they interact.

Control and Communication

Based on these theories, the Mailing List Cybermind was investigated from several different perspectives in order to get as full a picture as possible. The main perspectives employed were: the Embedding; Structures of Communication; Boundaries; the Control/Power System; Exchange; and Returns. All of these connect together in their effects, either to reinforce each other or to disrupt each other.

Given that online society emerges from offline society, it was necessary to briefly outline processes in Western English speaking (WES) worlds which affect the people who make up the main population of Cybermind.

The Embedding

List members were categorized as loosely belonging to the category of 'middle class intellectuals', although this category itself has significant internal divisions which were reflected in the list, as most members were involved with the arts and humanities rather than with business or administration. It was argued, largely through the words of List members, that changes in the balance of power which were enabled by information and communication technology, have rendered the corporate sector dominant. The corporate sector has been able to sever its connection with place, and to integrate at an international rather than national level to a far greater extent than other sectors. This was seen as allowing corporations to evade regulation and taxation, thus limiting their interdependencies with other participants in the State.

Diminished dependence of the wealthy upon a productive labour, or middle class, has led to a perceived decline in working conditions, income and stability of work for those classes, and a perceived decline in State support for them. Workers have become contingent, flexible or disposable, unable to resist the pressures towards 'Just-in-Time' production and distribution, which has been enabled by increased speed in processing and transport. Relative value of incomes is widely seen to have declined, with more of the wealth being distributed to the upper echelons of society and most people engaged in a 'race to the bottom'. The 'market' has become a rationale for attempts to preserve the status quo while increasing its inequalities. This worship of the market seems to have reduced the opportunities for people to make their living in devalued artistic or intellectual pursuits. Universities are now expected to behave like corporations and to do research for corporations.

The middle-class intellectuals of Cybermind feel distanced from the power opportunities of their societies and unable to do much to change or influence the actions of those they perceive as powerful. This was reinforced by the apparent electoral success of the Right in the United States of America. A sense of depression was increased by continuing mythemes of ecological doom, which processes seem largely ignored by their leaders in favour of continuing the wealth of a few or not risking 'the economy'. Whatever the truth, it appears that, online at least, the polarity categories of 'left' and 'right' function as terminating and framing congeries, which exaggerate each other and fragment discourse.

It is doubtful that the common explanations for these social processes, by the mythemes of the 'Information Society' and the 'knowledge worker', are of much use in helping people deal with the situation.

There is also a continuing mytheme of decline in kin contacts, availability and support, at the same time as potential support from the State is diminishing. Forming 'voluntary associations', or networks of friends, has been one way people have attempted to gain support and contacts, which may be useful in helping their survival. These groups can be abandoned when necessary to pursue the flexibility demanded by capitalism, or can also be used to attempt to find new and effective ways of 'authentic' being in the world. Internet groups are an extension of this process, giving a wider, if more tenuous, range of people to choose from. These groups are usually based upon 'shared interests', which give some feelings of commonality and a common vocabulary and real world reference with which to engage.

The embedding world provides widespread linguistic conventions. In particular the most easily used 'modes of framing', which as explained earlier are contested ways of interpretation which are both found within the message and imposed upon it. These modes of framing can then produce lines of fracture or co-operation, as they already define who the other is and what your relationship to them is.

The main framings used on Cybermind seemed to be:

1) *Authenticity*, the search for the truth of the other, and the attempt to express the truth of the self. Online life was often held to remove social markers which stopped people from perceiving the truth about others, yet conventions around authenticity and awareness of the potential of deceit implied that authenticity could only be validated offline. As such, authenticity was often connected to 'the body' and hence to gender.

2) The *public/private divide* or the public/intimate divide, which is often painted as binary opposition but is more a shifting and contested continuum. This division implicitly corresponds to the divisions possible on a Mailing List with the offlist or offline becoming private or intimate and authenticity becoming even more important. Intimate relations tended to be marked by the presence of a woman. People would also argue about what kind of public the onlist was. Was it open to dispute and impersonation, or should it be taken as a more harmonious authentic community, which respects a level of secrecy?

3) *Political divisions*. As already suggested above political divisions were major framings and major lines of fracture, as were the divisions of nationality. There is no particular sign that the Internet will cause such divisions to be replaced or to diminish.

4) Sustained *mood*, reference to emotions or to the body, constituted a framing, when contrasted with the normal disjointed set of moods produced by the dispersal of subjects on the List. Thus, flames or mourning could seem to overpower other messages and produce a coherent and memorable occasion. Sustained mood was

also present in more intimate netsex events in which people endeavour to maintain contact.

5) *Patterns of exchange* also constitute a framing, but will be discussed later.

6) *Etiquette*, by which is meant the way communication is carried out, constitutes the final framing. On the whole, people on Cybermind seemed to prefer the display of non-aggressive or non-intense patterns of behaviour, with marked empathy, especially from newcomers.

The distinction between categories and framings is hard to make. In some ways categories are often framings, especially when the interaction is primarily in text. However, as remarked above, categories are not stable—they are rarely sharply defined, they are more congeries and can be disputed. Successfully putting someone in a category defines them, defines how people should act towards them, and renders them more or less persuasive depending on whether the category is in-group or out-group, and how prototypic the person is seen to be. Putting a person in a category, especially if it is framed by conflict, may make them seem more 'prototypic'.

The framing of authenticity was investigated in more depth. It was suggested that authenticity may have grown out of a 'democratic' reaction to previous aristocratic courtesy markers, which arose during the change to more equitable power balances and recognized interdependencies, during the late 19th century and the first three quarters of the 20th century. Authenticity also correlates with the WES division between public and private, which regulates both interpretation of behaviour and exchange. Personal authenticity contrasts with mythemes about public deceit, and displays some of the problems arising with the maintenance of trust in a society celebrating public competitiveness. Authenticity also correlates with a general lack of ritual elaboration, lack of formal etiquettes, and a supposed lack of ascribed roles, and takes its value in opposition to these formalities. However, a problem arises immediately because authenticity needs to be framed to be indicated and known, and thus inevitably involves a set of etiquettes. People on Cybermind commonly used conventions about authenticity being indicated by strength of response (which could lead to flaming being perceived as genuine); breaking 'rules' (even such things as spelling errors, or 'obscenities'); references to underlying emotional or body states; or references to offlist events. The more private a communication, the more likely it was to be perceived as authentic. Because of the connection between authenticity and body states and between authenticity and the private or intimate sphere, gender became particularly important in framing communication. 'Female' gender was a prime marker for safety in intimacy. Hence, people generally worried about the gender of people they were engaged with, particularly in offlist, or other private, communications. People on Cybermind were usually considered to present 'true' gender onlist.

People's use of the conventions of authenticity gives rise to problems. The contrast between being who you are online and increased capacity for deceit has already been mentioned. Likewise complications arise through the relationship between authenticity and aggression, within which it was possible to consider aggression as a primary indicator of authenticity whilst, simultaneously, considering aggression as inhibiting authenticity.

Incompatible etiquettes of authenticity sometimes lead to disputes, in which the techniques employed by one group of people to ensure authenticity could be perceived by another as ensuring lack of authenticity. In one such case, a member demanded intense high-affect communication to gain authenticity, while many of the group responded by demanding the considerate, low-affect communication, which to them indicated 'community'. This was perceived by the first person as avoidance and trivialisation and so he intensified his presentation, while the group perceived his behaviour as disruptive and so intensified their presentations. As a result of this mutual construction of culture, both sides intensified their differences, leading to category separation, which was also enabled by the activation of a cluster of categories around the supposed political polarities of 'left' and 'right'.

Structures of Communication

It was proposed that the organization of communication was vitally important for the kinds of behaviour which were enabled or restricted online.

Mailing lists, by virtue of their communicative organization, had the potential to be autocratic, as the moderator controls access to the list and can therefore remove anyone they do not like. However because of WES cultural factors, this autocracy may be difficult without offline rewards or an offline power base. Moderators may find it impossible to gain a long-term supporting group who are dependent upon them for resources or status and who could, in turn, distribute such resources and status to others. Similarly the moderator usually depends on others to make the list interesting to others and to maintain viability. Therefore, the moderator has a tendency to be questioned, and to risk losing recognized members of the list when taking an unpopular decision. This uncertainty of power could be reinforced by the importation of values of 'freedom' or 'free speech' from the embedding societies. These particular values gain strength from their association with the authenticity which is held to guarantee the truth of communication. Cybermind was founded in an argument over issues of 'free speech', and although it may have proved impossible to maintain these values (as complete freedom of speech leads to noise and the lack of ability to verify truth), they still prove effective as rhetorical tools when used by established members. It is much easier for a moderator to be autocratic towards people defined as 'outsiders' either by their lack of familiarity to the group or by their socially defined position, or by ongoing conflicts.

Complex hierarchy is much more common in MOOs, where Wizards can gain supporters by having resources or favours to distribute, and programming powers over the environment. Status can also be gained through programming skills as well as through communicative skills. These factors lead to a tendency to form committees and to have semi-codified forms of procedure; the application of which can depend on contacts and patronage. Similarly as people have more invested in their characters, rooms and props, there is less tendency to object to decisions by leaving.

The communicative structure of Lists and MOOs enables different modes of group formation. On Lists it is relatively hard for subgroups to form onlist, unless political or national categories are used. When they do form it is usually because of offlist association, and they tend to either be invisible or to produce tensions leading to either conflict on the list, or to the subgroup breaking away. On MOOs the presence of 'rooms' allows more complicated subgrouping and relationships, or lack of relationships, between subgroups. As a result, struggles between subgroups appear less likely to lead to the splintering of the group.

Although people on Cybermind belonged to many online groupings, these groupings rarely interacted as groupings, unless they expressed some offline category division. Online groups, in general, have no other necessary interactive or category relations between each other. Therefore, online groupings can only rarely become primary categories for self-identification, and are usually overwhelmed by offline self-identifications, such as gender, politics or nationality.

These online structures of communication also gave rise to experiential factors. Important among these was the suspension of being between presence and absence which I called *asence*. Online it is difficult to be sure of the quality of one's presence because of lack of acknowledgment from others, or lack of a sense of closure to a communicative exchange. Exchange and presence stops with agreement, but may continue with argument. Likewise it is not always possible to be certain of the presence of your audience, or to continually adjust communication according to their response. This can be disorienting and can lead people to attempt asence reduction by provoking response (as in flame, although flame also results from communicative structures), or by using an easily referenced body response, as with netsex or, in a less dramatic manner, through the use of emoticons or the exchange of jokes.

Furthermore, as presence, either personal or involving the demonstration of the framings and conventions of the group, requires continual prestation, these presences are always on the verge of fading away. This can lead to generational problems in which a group of newcomers change the functioning of the group completely, by their own presentations, especially if supported by someone already recognised. Given that the populace of a list may be continually changing, there is a tendency for people to lose recognition or status, and for the style or 'community' of the list to be continually on the verge of disappearance and in need of re-presentation. Asence can feel exhausting, as it can never be resolved for long. Again, this may increase the importance of social control to those who wish to maintain their sense of continuity. Yet, although social control through argument may create presence, it can also drive people away if they are adverse to flame.

The structures of a Mailing List also tend to create 'lurking', as not everyone can write without List volume becoming unmanageable and this further increases uncertainty about audience response. The boundaries of a List are not clear.

Boundaries

Lack of boundary or clarity to the group reinforces asence and uncertainty. Online boundary problems can be contrasted to attempts in the offline word to draw boundaries around groups, or to worry about those lack of boundaries. In particular, this orbits around the body. Online the body is ambiguous. It feels open, with little resistances—even extended. Given that materiality seems to be defined by marked boundaries, and given the mytheme of the separation of mind and body (or even of 'information' as active force), the online body can be seen as ghostlike, or 'energetic', even a matter of pure spirit. It can sometimes be portrayed as cyborg, but this body is also riddled with ambiguities, potentially broken boundaries and lack of control. The online body is in some ways powerful, it can access information and travel with speed, yet at the same time it is generally unable to influence the offline world very much. It is subject to injuries which render online presence difficult by constantly intruding on awareness, and the person can feel constrained by the categories of others. Bodies are caught in an oscillation between being 'virile' and powerless. Attempts to make boundaries online, by saying that a person cannot be hurt online and so forth, are not only dubious but just do not work for Cybermind.

Exchange

Hierarchy within a List roughly corresponds to visibility. In general those who are more influential, recognized, liked, or listened to are also those who post the most. These posters demonstrate List 'community', as well as construct or manifest its space and its sense of time intensity. As only a relatively few members of any list participate onlist, those particular members exert considerable influence over the interpretations made, the List locale or mood, the kind of messages recognized, or responded to, and the kinds of reinforcement given. Without presentation, the person and the place of presentation disappears. Therefore, existence becomes a constant round of prestation, perhaps comparable to Melanesian exchange, while remembering that the audience is active, and people are capable of ignoring or rejecting prestation. If people post outside their status range then others tend to protest, or people leave, especially if the audience is forced to take notice of this breakage by violation of self-category norms. Power is manifest in exchange, although this may be without strict rules and is always open to being contested.

Gender is implicated exchange, in that it is possible that many women tend to cultivate private/offlist exchanges, which can be vital for the health of a list and are part of the way that List members build 'community'.

Power/Control System

The control system and power ratios have been implied in almost everything written above. Moderators can find it difficult to control a List without an offlist power base. Attempting to control the list is a way people avoid asence and collaborate in an environment in which collaboration seems difficult. Rhetoric is the main basis for the power exercised by general list members, although 'secret activities' can occur offlist, which in some ways resemble secret sorcery, and whose extent can be uncertain. The most obvious rhetoric involves the categorisation of others. Effective categories are based on categories marked in the offline world, and seem to gain their effect from difficulties in maintaining complex relations, or from fear of the outsider. These categories tend to be more effective against unrecognised people than against recognised people; unless the categorisation is already established. Thus, it is easier to remove newcomers, or those who have not developed a pattern of exchange. It is possible to slightly change List structures to deal with situations, sealing the List off from newcomers, or setting up CC lists to gain support, but these strategies have tended to be temporary on Cybermind. Power and control are ongoing issues, never determined forever.

Returns

As implied above, the group can function in several ways: it helps people to make contacts in a hostile and uncertain environment, which is perhaps why, when it becomes hostile itself, people leave. These contacts can be either professional or personal. Intimate, primarily offlist, pairing contacts were important and frequent, while professional contacts have helped people to gain publications, work and so on, thus helping their survival.

Community

The question of returns leads into issues of 'community'. Investigation was carried out into how an online grouping might constitute itself as 'community'. As the term community seems to be a terminating congerie, it is fruitless to search for the essence of community, but it is useful to see what enables a particular group to be so classified by its members. Community correlates with the discourse of authenticity because community is continually contrasted, in sociological and political mythemes, with inauthentic groupings; and though sought for, it is usually posited as being elsewhere in time and space. Yet, at the same time, being identified as community can lead to political legitimacy and recognition.

Elias's conceptualisation of a leisure *gemeinschaft*, and Turner's conception of *communitas*, led to the suggestion that some WES people's nostalgia for community was based on an idealized, or exaggerated, version of the experience of non-work, non-routine, leisure activities. Efforts to maintain such freedoms (*communitas*), then labelled community, can prove to be failures, because people refuse the oscillation into the 'routine' process (structure) necessary to maintain their functionality.

The categorizing of Cybermind as community by List members was shown to depend on three factors, which were indicated by their supposed excess to the formal requirements of the list. Firstly, community was indicated by an excess of off-topic messages, which acted to provide framing redundancies, and create mood and locale. This excess indicated the kind of messages which would be acceptable, and indicated how these messages should be interpreted. Secondly, on Cybermind, this type of excess should indicate 'caring', and 'the personal'; perhaps shifting the list into the private side of the public/private contrast. Thirdly, community was indicated by the presence of offlist contacts between members.

While Cybermind seemed largely unable to organize itself as a group, with the exception of the conference and the novel (which may have arisen from factors in the offline world, such as WES middle-class problems with accepting leadership in supposedly egalitarian groups, or their fears of being overwhelmed by groups), evidence was presented to suggest that people were able to organize shifting and temporary patterns of either small subgroup or pairing association. Online life does enable the successful seeking of friendship, contacts and support, of a nature which was found, by people, to be valuable. It renders the gathering of temporary support and association considerably easier than in offline life. At the least, people simply found people with compatible interests, experience and politics with whom they can engage in non-routine 'play', when the embedding society is perceived as hostile to such aspirations.

Discussion of world, political and existential problems (in a relatively safe zone in which thought experiments can be ventured) may help people to accommodate to, or constructively act (at an individual level) in their engagement with traditions that seem inadequate to deal with contemporary life and alienation. Online life could, however poorly it functions at present, act as a bridge between the shifting forms of public and private action. Experience in dealing with online disputes, however, would not seem to prepare people for offline disputes in a 'pluralistic society', as it seems too easy to dissociate from either the group, or from the people one is disputing with.

Paradox

One factor arising in this analysis is the complexity of feedback processes. Normally feedback is considered to be either positive (increasing the effect) or negative (decreasing the effect). However, many online feedbacks seem to change from positive to negative after a certain point. Ordering processes can become disordering processes. Thus, volume is necessary to give the group presence but, past a certain point, dealing with volume causes people to leave the group, skip mail and so on, thus apparently weakening the group. As a result, off-topic mail, as well as indicating community, can also strain it. For similar reasons, a popular List, will always tend to have mostly invisible members or lurkers, as the strain of everyone posting volubly diminishes the appeal of the list, yet without everyone posting most will be unknown. Similarly, the offlist pairings and groupings, while also indicating community, tend to take explanatory posts and framings away from the List, either diminishing volume or making the List harder to follow, thus weakening group category identity.

Some common procedures, particularly those around authenticity, also seem to produce 'contradictions'. Thus the authenticity which bonds, is indicated by strong expression which can also indicate, or produce, the conflict which separates. Although it is often held that the public should match the private, it is the difference between them that generates intimacy. Authenticity in intimacy requires the discarding of the tools, or rituals, or etiquettes, of communication, thus rendering it harder to understand one another, or resolve ambiguity, and increasing the possibility of divergence and separation. People claim they can only be their authentic selves online, but their online relationships can only 'truly' be validated offline—again leading to a conflict between a process and its method of validation. We can even note that 'intellectual discussion', when used as a vehicle for negotiating personal ties, risks generating conflict as people risk having parts of the category structure which forms their self-identity, as well as their position in the group, challenged. Thus the way of making contacts and status continually risks those contacts and status. These particular dynamics might accelerate the appearance of intimacy, closeness and understanding between people, but then help the appearances to disintegrate in quite marked ways.

Also notable is the tendency for supposed polarities to oscillate, or undermine each other. Thus, although in WES society public and private are dealt with as if they are absolute oppositions, they are always opposites in relation to the situation. What is public or private constantly shifts with the situation, even in the same location. Lists can sometimes be considered to be public and sometimes to be private, and it is easily possible to apply the 'opposite' framing to that intended. Authenticity, while supposedly contrasted with etiquette, requires etiquette. The cyberbody oscillates between impotence, as it can't act on 'the real world', and omnipotence as it can do anything online. Gender, while supposedly unimportant, or potentially a suppressor of real self, is vital to establishing the real self in intimacy. We may note that groups (or things in general) are often considered to be either restrictive or enabling, but are usually both; the enablement cannot occur without the restriction and vice versa. As an example, there are only a limited range of sounds, and combination of sounds, a person can use if they wish to be considered to be speaking a particular language. Similarly, leadership, while needed to enable action online, may be perceived as disempowering others. The machineries, which allow middle-class intellectuals to make new and potentially satisfying contacts, are the very machineries which have been forcing such contact by enabling the changes which have rendered their lives less secure and less satisfying.

In some way, it appears that the processes of gaining conceptual order, particularly when done through oppositions, generate problems and chaos. In attempts to solve these problems, WES people frequently emphasize one side of the polarity so as to overwhelm the other. As shown, authenticity may apparently blank out the awareness of ritual and etiquette, rendering communication more problematic than necessary. Another common response is to make these suppressed aspects appear outside the group, and exaggerate it there. Thus outsiders can become interpreted in ways different to the ways they intend, which generates the conflict which reinforces these interpretations.

If, as has been the case in the WES world, categories tend to be conceived as hard bounded, with contents linked by the same similarity, and in polarity (as something is inevitably either a member of its category or else a member of its opposite, rather than, say, a member of both at different times), then a group must be considered as categorized by either one pole or another. Yet most processes are not logical opposites or polarities. A man is not the opposite of a woman or vice versa, and there exist processes that are not men or women. Likewise if categories are treated as referring to things which are always similar, then apparent contradictions are set up by process. For example, a group differs from itself at another time. The referents of categories can always be changing rather than stable.

In a now lost work, Protagoras reputedly argued that every argument has an equally valid opposite argument, and that contradiction is impossible (Freeman 1949: 349; Sprague 1972: 12-13, 21). If such a position can be entertained, then we cannot even assume that axioms lead to particular conclusions. Therefore, the logics of social conceptions cannot be assumed beforehand, but the kinds of connections have to be investigated; any 'logic' can only be seen 'post hoc'. In this book, I have tried to investigate what happens if we focus on a logic of categorisation and action, as categorization cannot be abstracted entirely from the things categorized or from the actions possible or probable. I have tried to follow the assumption that culture is not necessarily uniform, but variant; that culture is learnt and individual, but learnt from and with others and is thus social. I have tried to show how the patterns which appear to arise are generated by people bringing to a particular organisation of communication, patterns of behaviour which have arisen in the embedding society. All these patterns are such that without the individuals interacting there would be nothing we could label as social, and without the social there would be nothing we could label individual. As Barth writes: "Somehow, people's various limited horizons link up and overlap, producing a world much greater, which the aggregate of their praxes create, but which no one can see. It remains the anthropologist's task to show how this comes about, and to chart that larger world which ensues" (1989: 140).

To perform this task fully, it may be necessary to risk some form of apparently 'psychological' postulates. Psychology grows with society, in interaction, coaction and interdependency with others. Yet the formation of categories is only one part of psychology, it does not pretend to be the whole. A full sociology, or anthropology, calls for us to investigate other social aspects of the mind, and only with this investigation can these further psychological factors be elucidated.

Appendix: Demographics and Statistics

Introduction

One of the advantages of online fieldwork is the possibility of counting and making comparisons which are not entirely subjective, and this Appendix gathers some attempts to elucidate this ethnography through enumeration. The primary subjects covered are the composition of the population, behaviour by gender, and some consideration of abstract patterns of communication. Most of the data comes from:

a) Two general surveys spaced about one and a half years apart with a much smaller survey from 2007.
b) Personal counting of threads and posts made in four equally spaced months over the year of 1994.
c) A counting of posts made in July, August and September of 2004.
d) Surveys conducted by other lists members.

General Population

The population of Cybermind varies almost from week to week, or even day to day, as people try the list to see whether it suits them and drop off if it doesn't. People also leave temporarily, because of pressure from work, or overload of mail, or absence from their computer. Consequently, no figures given here can be considered absolute for any period of time; it is more than probable the population changed while the surveys were being conducted.

During the period of study, the total population has varied between about 100 to almost 400 people. The majority of these people, as perhaps might be expected, seem to have had their computers situated within the United States, but there has always been an active contingent from outside that country.

On the 18th May 1995, during the first survey, there were 268 people on the list, of which roughly 5% came from Australia, 5% from Canada, and 14% from the UK. The remaining people were almost all situated in the US, although there was a small group from Europe (mainly Germany and Norway). Another count made during the second Survey on the 4th of November 1996 gave a total of 314 non hidden subscribers[1]. The proportion from the UK had dropped to 4.5% with the proportion from Australia and Canada remaining almost the same. Distribution throughout the world had increased from 26 countries to 37, although the next largest inputs remained Germany and Norway. There has been no obvious prolonged presence of African (other than non-black South African), Chinese or Southeast Asian nationals connecting from their country of origin during the time I have been present[2]. Thus, as was remarked by one of my correspondents from Iceland, there is an obvious domination of proceedings by native-born speakers of English. The extreme density of some of the text regularly presented to the group demands an exceedingly high proficiency in English to decode, and may well act as a further barrier to 'internationalisation'.

Surveys

The first survey was taken during May 1995; the second survey was taken just before the Cybermind Conference in November 1996; the third survey was taken in January 2007. In the first survey, 44 people out of a population of 268 replied; a response rate of 16%. For the second survey, 51 out a possible total of 329 people responded, making a similar response rate of 15.5%. In the third survey only 15 people responded. There was some overlap between the samples, as I encouraged people to respond to all surveys, and 86 different people responded to the first two surveys. The response sample differed slightly from the list population in several ways. In the first two surveys the rate response from the non-US world was higher than might be expected. For example in the second survey it was probable that 59% of the list population hailed from the US[3] while only 45% of the respondents did. Australians made up 16% of the respondents while making up only 4.5% of the population. This could possibly reflect pronounced activity by those Australians on list (something often mentioned to me by those Australians), or be an artefact of the conference which was being organised in Australia, or a side result of the ethnographer's nationality. People from the UK made 10% of the respondents as opposed to 4.5% of the population.

Gender, and Age

Whereas it was possible to give gender identities to almost all of those who replied to the survey, it was not possible to do so for the list as a whole on either occasion[4]. For the first listing over 50% of the list was unassignable by me and for the second listing just over 30% was similarly unassignable—assigning was done by name or familiarity with the person. With the 2004 figures the number of participants was small and genderable without survey. Comparing the results for all surveys of the population to which gender could be assigned:

Table 1: Gender

	Responses to Survey 1	Genderable Population of List at Survey 1	Responses to Survey 2	Genderable Population of List at Survey 2	Responses 2004
Female	26%	27%	36%	26%	31%
Male	74%	73%	64%	74%	69%

Although the gender ratios of response to the survey changed by what appears to be a significant amount, the ratio of identifiable males to females on list was fairly constant[5].

Of the 44 people who responded to the first survey, the ages ranged between 20 and 56 years. In the second survey, the ages ranged between 19 and 60 years. Four people did not give their age. Using fairly arbitrary age grades this gives the following results.

Table 2: Age.

	Average[6]	Median	≤25	26-35	36-45	46+
Survey 1	33	31	13	14	13	4
Survey 2	36	34	6	21	14	6
Survey 3	51.5	50	1	1	1	12

The general population had aged slightly between the first two surveys and significantly between the second and third surveys. This might be unexpected given that we could have presumed younger people would have a greater degree of access to computers and the Internet, and for this number to have increased with time.

The average age of the women in the first survey was 38 and all but one were over 30, while in the second survey 5 women were under 30 and the age distribution of women was similar to that of the general list population—returning the same median and average. This change could represent a sample variant, but it could also suggest that a bias (whether of obstacle or inclination) against younger women using computers and the net had declined in the period between surveys. The third survey did not have a significant female response.

In the first survey, 32 of the respondents were male, 10 female and 2 unknown[7]. The increase in the sample size of the second survey (from 44 to 51) was entirely due to an increase in the number of responses by women from 10 to 18.

The significantly greater proportion of apparently male to female members on List is to be expected from anecdote that the main users of the net are male, and the history that has produced this state of affairs. It is the more striking, because Cybermind would not consider itself a 'sexist' community, and many of the more prominent posters in its history have been female. (See below).

Education and Survival

Education standards among the respondents of all surveys was uniformly high. In the first survey a maximum of 5 of the respondents did not have some university education. Five had PhDs, and at least 2 were working towards their PhDs. Where it was possible to identify the kinds of education, 21 had taken Arts at university and 7 taken Science. All of the people educated in the sciences were working with computers. In the second survey the trend was even more marked. Of 51 respondents 7 people either had Ph.Ds or were working towards them, 14 had or were working towards Masters Degrees, and a further 3 had non-specified postgraduate qualifications. Of the 86 total respondents to both surveys, at least 73 people (85%) had, or were obtaining, a university education, which is a significantly higher than the proportion in the general population[8]. In the third survey all but one person had some form of higher education.

Category of profession is more difficult to specify, as a wide variety of jobs were described ranging from 'pest-control' to 'attorney', but by far the largest number of people in the first survey (12 or 27%) described themselves as 'students', the next highest categories were 'computer related' and 'arts related'—these categories being imposed after the survey. In the second survey the number of students remained relatively high at 9 (18%), but the largest category was those who described their profession as 'teacher', being a total of 13 people or 25%. Some of these people specifically mentioned they taught at universities. Only 4 people in the first survey gave this as their occupation. In both surveys few respondents implied that their profession was permanently academic at a grade higher than tutor; however, personal contact suggests this figure might be higher than the replies suggest. It is clear that there is little formal academic involvement on the List. Those people who are academic staff did not tend use this fact as a status or authority tool onlist, even though 'academic knowledge' might serve that function on occasions. Another, possibly significant fact was that a relatively large proportion of the list (19 in the second survey) seemed to make their livings from work which might be described as uncertain; such things as 'art', 'research', 'writing', or contract work; or described multiple 'professions' and so on. Given the somewhat varied fate of the teaching profession, relatively few people described what might be called dependable professions such as law, medicine, or computer programming. No people described themselves as filling business management or executive positions.

Information about jobs is increased by a series of questions posted to the list by Mike Murphy and Amanda White (30 Nov.95) for their "cultural anthropology class". This will be called the "Murphy/White survey". Eighteen list members answered the questions on the List. Fifteen of the 18 respondents were employed, although 3 of the jobs would not normally be called 'professional'—i.e. Xeroxing, 'various', and liquor manufacturing. Five of the jobs specifically involved computers, and 6 involved education.

All in all, members of Cybermind appear to be solidly 'middle class intellectuals', members, of a class whose social position and security is perhaps becoming increasingly precarious, and who might be seeking out new ways of dealing with their situation and forming new ties.

Time on the List

Length of time that respondents had been on Cybermind and whether that was continuous was queried. Thirty nine people responded to this question in the first survey and, as expected, the results ranged from since or close to inception (8 people, 3 of them women) to one week. Obviously such estimations are bound to be fairly inaccurate, but the average of the estimates was just over 4 months. It is interesting that the majority of the respondents had not been with the list very long; 10 claimed to have been on for 1 month or less, and more than 50% estimated that they had been on for 4 months or less. Of the 10 people who had been on the list less than a month, only 4 were still active 3 months later. Six months later only about a half of those who had responded appeared to still be present on the list. In the second survey, 19 people claimed to have been with the list for over 1 year and the average time people estimated they had been onlist was 9 months. Given the list had existed for a further one and a half years between surveys, and that the was less than one year old at the time of the first survey, this kind of result might have been expected. However, of the 44 people in the first survey, 30 or 68% had left the list by the time of the second survey showing the volatility of the population. Another list of members taken in March, four months after the second survey, showed that 15 or 29% of the 51 people who had responded to this survey had left the list.

Of those who had in the past temporarily unsubscribed, the majority of them said they had done so out of necessity and for the minimum period of time possible—again suggesting a desire for cohesion among those who make it to becoming long-term users.

Reading and Mailing

The reading habits of participants was also queried. The vast majority also read lists other than Cybermind. Only 6 people in the first survey read no other lists. The number of lists participated in by other respondents varied from 1 to 15 in the first survey with someone claiming to read 60 lists in the second. Those people with the highest number of lists tended to state that they did not participate heavily in most of these lists, and they were constantly trying out new lists and dropping ones that no longer interested them, which suggests a countervailing tendency to demand quick gratification from lists. The average number of lists read (including Cybermind) was 4 to 5 in the first survey and 8 in the second. Such figures have to be regarded as approximate only, due to people giving answers such as '4-5' or 'a few'. Some people wrote that they subscribed to lists but deleted all mail on them unread[9].

People were also asked to describe their mailing habits to Cybermind in terms of frequency. A surprising number, 9, of the respondents in the first survey described themselves as rare or infrequent posters and 3 said they never posted. In the second survey 8 people wrote that they posted rarely and 9 wrote that their response was either their first post or among their first posts. This suggests again that the survey was quite useful in accessing normally silent list members, although at the same time it perhaps gives a bias away from the characteristics of long-time members. Interestingly, of the 13 people in the first survey who had been on the list for longer than 6 months, 5 described themselves as infrequent, or rare posters (a significant proportion of the 9 all told who described themselves in that way). A compilation of 20 respondents who had been recurrent on the list for at least one and a half years was examined in August 1997, and of those 20 people I would describe the posting patterns of 12 as 'rare', 4 as making a couple of posts a week, and only 4 as making more than 1 per day. This suggests that any consideration of Cybermind's 'community' has to consider voluntary but interested non-involvement. Offhand it appears it may be the case that these people were more interested in the issues discussed than in 'community', and thus only posted when they felt they had something relevant to contribute. Perhaps older members, with their presence on the list established in their own minds, needed to engage in less 'display' or 'creation of presence' behaviour, or are affected by having responded to similar arguments before. It is also possible some of these people have most of their contact with other list members offlist.

The question of how people read Cybermind was perhaps the most delicate, given that most people chose to respond to the questions publicly. It was probably not to be expected, given the emphasis on 'community', that people would openly write that they ignored most postings—which, given the list volume, might actually be an expected result. In some ways this question might be the most difficult to answer as well, as people probably do not observe their reading patterns, and may well maintain different patterns depending on mail volume or on external factors.

Granted these difficulties, the majority of respondents (27 or 63%) in the first survey claimed to read by order of arrival and several emphasised they read everything. However, it was clear at least 4 of the people who read by order were, as one said, "free with scan and delete". The next largest category (but much smaller with only 8 people or 20%) was that of the explicit skimmer—those who employed "blanket delete", who deleted "uninteresting threads", or employed "slash and burn". This kind of technique must occasionally lead to some dislocation as threads widen into other topics, and prior argument vanishes. It may also lead to the tendency of readers to focus on a particular 'cast' of regular writers to help speed selection of material read, and thus narrow the perceived membership of the list. In the second survey, replies were far less elaborate with people simply reporting an ideal. Here 21 people wrote that they read by order of arrival, with an extra 6 reading the list in digest format; which effectively produces the same result. Seven people reported they read personal mail first. In the third survey everyone who responded read by order of arrival, but 2 went into reading by threads on occasions.

One of the few explicit accounts of how a list might be read which includes Cybermind, comes from Hoberman who writes:

> The more mail one gets, the less attention each individual message is likely able to grab: one prioritizes the mail by sender or topic using the delete key to act as an initial filter for the information. Each deletion or save represents a summery judgement on the part of the individual as to the value of the information (1996: np)

Another list member writes (10 Mar.96):

> after reading a couple three posts on a thread I delete the rest on that matter if I'm not grabbed. Also, if a post is lengthy and I don't have the time, or interest after a screen or two, away it goes.

Personally, I read all posts in order of arrival. I would sometimes abandon more lengthy theoretical posts if they did not seem useful, or produce a strong reaction. For the first nine months of my time on list I either printed out, or stored on disk, all list mails[10]. After this period, I only kept 'interesting mails' stored on disk.

The final question in terms of list use was "why do people subscribe to Cybermind and what do they like about it". In the first survey 19 people (or 43%) specifically mentioned they liked the 'community' or the 'people', only 11 people (25%) said they read it because of their interest in the ideas discussed (several of these were the 'rare' posters). In the second survey the number of respondents who mentioned 'people' or 'community' declined to 16 or 31%. Several people commented that they found the list challenging, and a learning experience, and three people specifically mentioned Alan as a major attraction. In the third survey, almost everyone described the list as interesting, with a few people adding that it was open and diverse.

Offlist Interests and Connections

Other questions were asked to find out general background interests (tastes in books, films, music and politics). Taste in books, films and music, as reported in all three surveys, was eclectic in the extreme; the only unifying factor, being the 'non-mainstream' character of most examples given. This could be taken to imply a fairly high level of interest in these subjects—almost everyone answered these questions volubly—and perhaps a self-identification of most members with 'intellectual' or 'fringe' art movements, and implying a possible self-perceived marginal status to the wider society and its forms. In the second survey there might be slightly more uniformity with more people nominating particular science fiction films and novels. Five people mentioned William Gibson and five people the movie *Bladerunner*, for example.

The only significant uniformity was in politics, where most people in all surveys described themselves as 'left' or 'liberal' in inclination (this includes statements about being 'centre left'): 24 in the first survey and 32 in the second survey for a total of 46 out of 77 different people who replied to this question in both surveys. This is still only 60% of the answering population, but there was no other block of similar magnitude. Only 5 people described themselves as being 'right', 'elitist' or 'neo-conservative', which is less than those who described their politics as 'centrist' or 'mixed'. A number of people described themselves as anarchist but this was usually qualified with the word 'left'. Only one person described themselves as 'libertarian', which is the term usually given to pro-capitalist anarchists. In the third survey, the result was even more uniform. No one specifically described themselves as right, conservative or right of centre. It is as if the group attracted people who described themselves as of 'left' orientation. The hypothesis that people who self-define as 'right' enter and then drop out due to uncongeniality of the environment is significantly weakened by the newness to the list of a significant portion of the respondents who described themselves as 'left' and who could not be expected to know this model was dominant. Of course such a response is bound to express largely US ideas of what might be 'left', and several respondents seem from other postings to be significantly located towards what would have once been called the 'right'.

I am not trying to argue the political position was uniform, merely that people labelled themselves in a particular way, which implies certain biases. Although political arguments have arisen frequently, the majority of people on the group wish to be known as 'left' or 'liberal', which is a significant factor in group identity, and has caused problems for some members with different views. There may be some significance that in the second survey several people further described their politics with such epithets as 'disillusioned', 'angry', 'sullen', 'confused', 'skeptical' or cynical' which suggests the socially expected alienation from mainstream politics.

Strangely, given the keenness with which fleshmeets are organised, or people met offlist, or the term was 'community' deployed, few people who responded to the first survey said they had regular correspondence with other people from Cybermind off list. Of those who had been on the list for over four months, the rough average number of off list correspondents from Cybermind was just over 2. This figure is undoubtedly exaggerated as several of those replying stated that these correspondences were irregular or vague, and 2 respondents claimed about 9 such correspondents. In the second survey, despite the longer time that people had had to build relationships, the results were similar. For those who had been onlist four months or longer the rough average number of correspondents was again claimed to be 2. This was also unexpected given the work involved in organising the conference which was occurring at that time.

The second survey raised some issues not mentioned in the first. From the results of these questions it seems that people on the list have a fairly intensive involvement with the Internet. 38 out of 51 people claimed to use the Internet once per day or more—which might be a basic requirement if one is to follow the amount of mail that Cybermind can receive. Twenty one people stated they used it for periods of 2 hours at a time or more, whereas 13 wrote they used it for 2 hours or less. 10 people wrote they used it for varying amounts of time, and 7 did not respond. In the Murphy/White survey 16 of 18 respondents claimed they used the Internet daily, and 13 estimated they used a computer for more than 4 hours each day. All respondents wrote they used or had used the net for research for a range of topics from pharmacy to astrology, although most nominated research topics related to their profession or academic interests.

When asked if computers and/or the Internet had added to their quality of life 36 replied 'yes', 9 were ambiguous or made remarks to the effect that it had certainly changed their lives, and only 4 responded 'no'—which is perhaps to be expected, as we might think that few people would join a group supposedly devoted to the psychology and philosophy of the Internet otherwise.

Active Population

Out of the 200 to 350 people on the list, only about 20 to 40 people are regular contributors at any one time. In the three months from July 2004 to the end of September 2004 only 31 people posted in total, showing the decline after the Iraq War. In general, some of these people have posted at a high volume for their entire time on the list, while other people's postings come in cycles. Thus, people may engage in high volume periods, when they have time (lack of time is a regular complaint) and the subjects being discussed interest them, and fade out almost completely at other times. Many, or perhaps most, of the people on the list never contribute to discussion, or contribute to such a small extent they remain unknown to the vast majority of readers. This apparent absence may be emphasised by the marked presence of other people and the volume.

What follows is an attempt to get some idea of the pattern of flow of messages in Cybermind in four months of one year. The months chosen were March, June, September and December of 1995, largely because of ease of access in the archives and for reasons of even spacing through the year. I did not want any two months to be more likely to be influenced by extraneous factors than the other months.

Looking at the activity during these months, we appear to have the following posting patterns.

The 5% most prolific posters during a month account for an extraordinary proportion of the list mail. Around a third of all posts will come from 5 or 6 people. The 20% most prolific posters in each month made between 64% to 70% of all posts. In other words, the next highest 15% of posters added roughly another third of all posts to the third made by the 5% most prolific posters. The obvious conclusion, is that the final third of all posts is contributed by the remaining 80% of posters.

At the other extreme, not accounting for the even larger number of people who do not post at all, at least one quarter of those people who post will only post once[11].

The question of the number of times people post can be looked at in at least two ways. Firstly, what we might call 'Absolute' in the sense of asking "how many people post more than 10 posts a month, 20 posts a month?" and so on. Secondly what we might call 'Relative', in the sense of recognising that activity varies from month to month, and so we ask "how many people post more than 0.5%, or 1%, or 2% of the total posts in a month?"

With the absolute figures, the minimum number of people to make 10 or more posts is 32 and the maximum 42. In all cases, over 27% of the active population made 10 or more posts in a month. The minimum number of people to make 20 or more posts was 16 and the maximum 27. In all cases at least 15% of the population made 20 or more posts, and for June and September the proportion was over 20% The minimum number of people to make 30 or more posts was 9 and the maximum was 17. The variation in proportion was 8% to 18% of the posters.

This suggests that although the list is volume dominated by a relatively small number of posters, there is a body of people who are almost continually active at a much lesser level.

This is reinforced by the 'relative' figures to some extent. In general between 35% and 45% of the active population make more than 0.5% of the total numbers of posts each, between 23% and 30% of this same population each make 1% or more of the total posts each.

Looking across time the following 17 people made posts in each of the months sampled: Alan, Caitlin, Carsten, GlenR, Gerald, jon, Laurie, MikeG, Mitchell, Nan, Pip, Paula, Robert, Rose, skip, StevenS and T-Bone. This does not, of course, mean that they were on the list continuously—a reasonable amount of list-hopping could be expected. Similarly other people might have been on the list for each month but not posted in one or more months.

The following 28 people were active in 3 months with the following key to their activity (a) March, June, September; (b) June, September, December; (c) some other combination of months. I more than suspect that at least two of these people were present in all four months.

Bernadette (b), BruceL (a), DanielP (c), DavidH (b), DaveW (b), fanny (b), frank (b), Fred (b), Gauti (a), GlennY (b), hirch ra (a), Jacques (b), Jakob (c), JaneH (b), JanetH (b), Jerry (b), Jim (a), Juan (a), kmc (b), Kim (a), KK (a), laura (a), Matt (c), MichaelB (a), Phil (a), Sasha (c), TomE (b), Vijay (a).

Arranging this data in columns to look at those posters who each made 1% or more of the total posts, ranked by number of posts.

Table 3: Most Frequent Posters

People who are listed below the ** in the columns are those who made less than 1.5% of the total posts.

March		June		Sept.		Dec.	
Name	No.	Name	No.	Name	No.	Name	No.
Alan	137	Alan	166	Alan	187	Alan	152
dobie	91	Rose	126	kmc	169	Rose	94
glen	63	kmc	106	Andrew	117	TomE	72
Rose	62	StevenS	95	Rose	88	Andrew	69
StevenS.	56	dobie	91	Laurie	68	Jacques	43
Laurie	43	Mitchell	79	Richard	56	Skip	43
jon	39	Laurie	72	Caitlin	55	MikeG	37
Sean	36	TomE.	73	Wisdom	50	Karen	31
Amethist	36	DaveW.	68	Jacques	44	MPGS:	30
Jim	36	Nan	48	T-Bone	44	Jerry	29
SusanN	33	Jerry	45	Fred	38	jon	28
Robert	27	Robert	43	TomE	38	Laurie	25
Koop	27	Skip	43	Mitchell	35	Lotus	25
Ian	27	Dick	41	Paula	33	DaveW	23
Kevin	26	T-Bone	38	DaveW	33	Carsten	22
hirch ra	23	fanny	33	Jerry	31	Fred	20
StevenB	22	jon	32	DavidH	29	Jeffrey	19
MikeG	22	Carsten	29	Hartwin	28	**	
T-Bone	22	**		Kayo	26	Christina	16
pip	21	MikeG.	28	fanny	25	kmc	15
Nan	20	Zav	25	JohnS	25	Pip	14
**		Pip	24	**		Robert	14
Calum	15	Trond	24	Karen	24	Wisdom	14
Carsten	15	Glugg	23	Jim	22	Sue Ellen	13
Fran	15	Dwayne	22	Kim	21	Bernadette	12
Caitlin	14	Caitlin	22	Pip	20	matt	12
DanielP	14	Carole	21	jon	20	Radhika	12
DavidS	14	DanielP	21	Jodi	17	MikeW.	12
Glynn	14			Nan	17		
				Robert	17		

(Errors are bound to have crept in due to use of varied pseudonyms and the transfer to America Oniline, which made the general name 'Cybermind Participant' one of the big posters of December).

It has often been said to me that the active population of Cybermind is about 20. Given that, in this period it appears there are usually about 100 posters per month, this figure of twenty may well stem from a vague consciousness of the number of those people who make more than 1% to 1.5 % of the total number of posts.

Of the 64 people who appear in the preceding table, 35 appear only once (though in 5 cases, not appearing more frequently was a matter of only 1 or 2 posts), and a total of 17 only posted in one of the months sampled (5 of these in December).

As might be expected, the majority of those people who appeared on Cybermind in 3 or 4 of the sampled months have also appeared amongst the posters who post between 1% and 1.5% of the total posts for at least one of these months. Five of these people appear in all 4 columns, 9 appear in 3 columns, 8 appear in 2 columns, and 7 in 1 column. Nine people didn't appear—although for several the non appearance was effectively a statistical artefact.

At the other end of frequency, of those who posted only 1 or 2 posts in a month, 147 people did not appear in the other months sampled while 30 did. If we remove those who first appear in December, then 112 people only posted once or twice. In other words, it appears that of those posting once or twice, 80% were not posting three months later.

It should also be emphasised that of the 17 posters who posted in each of the four months, 5 posted only once or twice in one of those months. Of the 28 people active in three of the four months 18 made only 1 or 2 posts in at least one month. So it cannot be assumed that low posting is a necessary correlate of disinterest. As I have suggested earlier, it appears that for some people active participation in 'community' is not necessary—nor what their involvement with Cybermind, for them, is about.

The main conclusions which can be drawn from this is that far more people were active onlist during the course of a month than I had thought from reading the List (the smallest number of people posting being 94) and the List is, by volume, clearly dominated by a fairly small number of the total number of people who post. However there seems to be a significant body of posters who are long term and who post regularly, but who would not show up amongst a count of the continually most prolific posters. This was so even in the 2004 figures, where several long-term posters seemed to only appear once or twice in the three months selected.

As well as clearly displaying the dominance of the list by the 20% of its most prolific posters, the following table also clearly shows that a large number of list members make few, if any, posts. Never less than one quarter of people who posted made only one post. When we consider that it appears that at least 50% of list members in a month will not post at all, this means that the greater majority of the list is effectively silent.

Table 4: Comparative Volume

Month	Posts	Posters	A	B	C	D	E	F	G	H
Mar	1229	120	452	37%	914	74%	32	75	39	33%
June	1983	122	663	34%	1396	70%	42	64	37	30%
Sep	1673	94	611	37%	1151	69%	42	49	25	27%
Dec	1241	112	473	38%	835	67%	35	68	29	26%
2004	1561	31	513	33%	1065	68%	17	11	6	19%

Key:
- A = number of posts made by the 5% most prolific posters.
- B = percentage of the total number of posts made by the 5% most prolific posters.
- C = number of posts made by the 20% most prolific posters.
- D = percentage of the total number of posts made by the 20% most prolific posters.
- E = number of people making 10 or more posts.
- F = number of people making 5 or less posts.
- G = number of people who made only 1 post.
- H = percentage of the total number of people who posted, who only made 1 post.

Activity by Gender

Given the overwhelming proportion of males to females on the list, it is perhaps inevitable that the majority of posts will originate from males. However, the following table, while not implying the list is not predominantly controlled by men, shows that women on this list are not silenced. The proportion of posts made by women is pretty much in line with the proportion of women in the list population, including the most prolific sections of that population. There is however, clearly a change in these ratios after the arguments around the invasion of Iraq.

Table 5: Presence of Women

Month	A	B	C	D	E	F	G	H	I
Mar	28	23%	269	21%	25%	194	21%	17	23%
June	25	20%	463	23%	20%	303	22%	11	17%
Sep	25	7%	507	30%	27%	294	26%	8	16%
Dec	29	26%	342	28%	27%	205	26%	16	26%
2004	9	31%	342	22%	17%	207	24%	4	40%

Key
- A = Number of Women posting.
- B = percentage of active population that is female.
- C = Number of posts made by women.
- D = Percentage of total posts made by women.
- E = Percentage of women in the 20% most prolific posters.
- F = Number of posts made by such women.
- G = Percentage of the posts made by the 20% most prolific posters made by women.
- H = Number of women making 5 or less posts.
- I = percentage of those making 5 or less posts who are women.

In order to investigate a possible correlation between gender and response rates (such questions as whether males responded primarily to other males, whether female posters were ignored and so on), I considered 900 consecutive posts from March 1994. Of these 900 posts it was possible to classify 798 of them as ether male responses to males, male responses to females, female responses to males, female responses to females, males starting a thread, or females starting a thread. The remaining posts were either by people of unclear gender; posts in which it was not obvious to whom the poster was replying; and posts addressed generally to the list but not initiating a new thread.

In this final sample of 798 posts, 598 (or 75%) were made by males and 200 (or 25%) were made by females. Distribution of responses were as follows:

Table 6: Response Rates and Gender

	M to M	M to F	F to M	F to F	M start	F start
number	386	126	123	48	86	29
Percent	48%	16%	15%	6%	11%	4%

Clearly 63% of these posts were responses to males, and 22% were responses to females.

If we take the percentage of these responses as a fraction of all posts by that gender—for example, the percentage of all female posts to males as a fraction of all female posts and tabulate them, then:

Table 7: responce and gender

M to M	M to F	F to M	F to F	M start	F start
65%	21%	61%	24%	14%	15%

There appears to be little significant difference between the response rates of males and females to each other, although males responded slightly less to females than females did, and females responded slightly less to males than males did. Both genders tried to initiate threads equally.

Comparing the number of posts by a gender and the number of responses to people of that gender, then 85% of male posts were responded to and 87% of female posts were responded to.

In order to investigate whether the posts sent in by males were longer than those sent in by females, I looked at one week between the 11th and 18th of April 1995. After allocating posts by gender, I counted the original lines of text, ignoring text which had been quoted. I also ignored a few posts which were primarily lists of Internet sites, or computer programs. Altogether the count involved 264 posts, and some 3,549 lines of text. There were 200 posts from identified males, and 64 posts from identified females. Obviously just over 24% of posts came from women, which is slightly less than normal. The males wrote 2,686 lines of text, for an average of 13.43 lines of text per post, and the females wrote 863 lines of text for an average of 13.48 lines of text per post. Although further counting throughout the year and looking at different circumstances might turn up a different result, this does suggest that average length of posts is reasonably similar between genders on this list.

These rough figures suggest that on Cybermind there was little statistical difference in people's responses to others by gender. The question of type of response (i.e. whether responses to females are more hostile or dismissive than responses to males) has not been investigated due to the difficulty of making such evaluations.

Summary

Most of the population of Cybermind comes from the US, with Australia, Canada and the UK the next most significant origin points. Thus the list involves primarily the English speaking world.

There is a fairly wide spread of ages represented ranging from the late teens to the late 60s, with the average and median ages falling in the 30s. There seems to be a slight aging of the general population between the two surveys, though a youthening of the female population towards the age distribution of the general population.

At least 70% of the population is probably male and, as a result, the list predominantly consists of posts by males—though the distribution of posts between males and females is similar to that of the distribution in population. People seem to respond in equal percentages to people of both genders, and each gender appears equal in its attempts to initiate threads, and in the average length of posts.

Education is high amongst members, most of whom seem to have been to or are attending university. The importance of education is further emphasized by this being the single most important site for member's occupation or income. However, it appears there was a significant increase in the number of those who taught for a living between surveys.

There is a fairly high turnover and dropout rate, although there is a relatively small core of long-time or recurrent members—many of whom do not post very frequently or display much in the way of active involvement. The fairly low spread of reported off List interaction between people suggests that long-term members do not substitute private mail contact for public action.

Tastes among members are fairly eclectic, although could possibly be described as somewhat self-consciously 'non-mainstream'. The only marked unity was the quite large proportion of people who described themselves as being 'left oriented' in politics. This seemed to be the case even for those people who had just joined.

Members also seemed to engage in fairly heavy Internet usage in terms of time and in terms of other lists followed. As might be expected among people who used the net frequently, the Internet was almost uniformly considered to be beneficial to their lives.

The list is dominated in volume by a relatively small number of posters. About 5% of active posters make about one third of all posts; the next 15% of active posters make a further third of all posts; and it appears that more than half the people subscribed at any one time will not make any posts in that month. Somewhere between 20 to 40 posters are likely to be 'clearly visible' at any one time, although about 100 different people are likely to post in a one month period. It seems probable that many people post only a few times and then leave. However, it must be remembered that many long time posters do not post frequently and would not be visible to the newer members.

The average length of threads is short in both time and volume, with the majority of posts occurring within three days or less. However, there will at most times be a thread occurring which will last for two weeks or more. The actual flow of subjects is both longer and shorter than this, as threads change subjects, and new threads spin off into separate conversations and cross into other threads via the people involved.

Glossary

Terms in italics in the definitions are defined elsewhere in the glossary.

aka	'Also known as'.
alt	Prefix for a *newsgroup*, indicating that the newsgroup is 'alternerative'.
asence	The suspension of certainty between presence and absence which is experienced online. Asence is often resolved by acknowledgment. See Chapter 5.
ASCII	'American Standard Code for Information Interchange': usually used to refer to alphanumberic text; i.e. standard typed text.
ARPA	The 'Advanced Research Projects Agency'. An office of the US Department of Defense, which funded the construction of the *ARPANet*.
ARPANet	The experimental computer network, which is usually considered to have formed the basis for the Internet. Work began on it in 1968.
aura	The 'total communication' which occurs in the background or off the particular Internet social formation it surrounds. For example offlist mail, *MOO* use, phone calls etc. between members of a mailing list.
backchannel	A specific example of *aura*. Communication which is invisible to most group members.
BCC	'Blank Carbon Copy''. Like a *CC*, only the person the mail is addressed to is not aware of the other people the mail is being sent to.
btw	'By the way'.
burnout	Exhaustion or boredom resulting from 'too much' Internet usage.
CC	'Carbon Copy'. Most email programs allow people to CC posts to other people, as well as the main persons addressed.
CDA	The 'Communications Decency Act', which intended to restrict the possible nature of communication on the Internet. It was appended to an act to deregulate

	ownership of communication. It was passed by the Republican Congress, signed into law by President Clinton, and found unconstitutional by the US courts.
cluster	A group of categories which, while not inherently connected, appear to reinforce each other, and be evoked simultaneously.
coaction	Mutually interdependent actions, they can be cooperative, conflicting, interactive or simply necessary for each other.
concept	A category in which members are linked by similar properties and can be defined.
congerie	A category in which members may be linked by differing properties.
crosspost	Posting an item to several different internet groups at the same time. Usually by using the CC function.
darknet	Alan's term for the less visible parts of the internet.
emoticon	An attempt to indicate expression, through *ASCII* characters. Sometimes called a 'smiley', after the most common version, which represents a smiling face. :) or :-) emoticon; indicating a smile. :(or :-(emoticon; indicating a frown or, more usually, sadness.
FAQ	'Frequently Asked Questions'. Usually a file, which gives an outline of the way an internet group works, and responses to the frequently asked questions made by newcomers.
Flame	Vituperative, or critical post. There is no precise definition. It is argued at the time. The definition of something as a flame is often a rhetorical/political act.
flame war	When a group of people engage in *flaming* with each other.
fleshmeet	An offline face-to-face meeting of people who have primarily known each other online.
framing	Rituals, things, events, or symbols which surround communication. A frame can be considered to be those parts of the environment of the message, which though in some ways independent of the message, help resolve the meaning of the message, by indicating appropriate methods of interpretation. There is usually no obvious, primary frame, so groups or

Glossary

	people may frame the communication differently.
ftf	'Face-to-face'.
<g>	'Grin'.
generation	Term implying the arrival of a whole group of new people onto a list, in a very short space of time.
IMO	'In my opinion'
IMHO	'In my humble opinion'.
IPL	'In Physical Life', or 'In Personal Life'; i.e. offline.
IRL	'In Real Life', i.e offline.
killfile	A list of those addresses from which postings will not be perceived.
List	Short for *Mailing List*.
listserv	A software program used to run *Mailing Lists*; or the computer the list is run from.
lurker	A Person who reads a *List* or *newsgroup*, but rarely contributes. See Chapter 6.
mailing list	A group of people linked by all receiving the same mail. See Chapter 4.
moderator	The person who administers a List, or occasionally a newsgroup.
MOO	In this book MOO includes MUDs (Multiple User Dungeon, or Multiple User Domain), and MUSHs. MOO stands for MUD Object Oriented. Places like Second Life, can be seen as graphic MOOs. See Chapter 4.

MOO commands:

connect <name> <password> allows you to enter the MOO.

After having connected, Interaction requires knowledge of several basic kinds of command. The basic '*say*' command ["<text>] operates as follows:

you type: "hello
you read: you say "hello"
others read: [Name] says "hello"

There is also an *emote* command [:<text>] which allows the person to describe the actions of their persona:

you type: :hugs corvi
everyone reads: [Name] hugs corvi

It is also possible to choose to activate larger formulaic expressions called '*verbs*'. If you have

programming rights then you can activate unique self prepared verbs. In this case you might type:
>hugs1 corvi
>everyone reads: [Name] hugs corvi while whooping loudly
@dig allows you to describe your room.
@go <destination> 'teleports' you to that destination
@join <name> takes you to the person called [name]
look <object> gives you the description of the object, if it has one.
@quit quits the MOO
@page <name> <text> allows you to type to [name] without the text being visible to anyone else. The person does not have to be in the same room.
@sethome <location number> means that your character is visible at that location, even when you are not using it. The character will often be described as 'sleeping'

mytheme	Theory, myth, story etc. Directs attention to aspects of the world. Implies the "theory dependence of observation".
netsex	When people describe activities they find sexual to another person over the Internet. At the time of writing this most commonly seemed to happen on *MOO*s or IRC, but could happen in private email, or in talk.
newsgroup	An Internet bulletin board, that is distributed throughout the net. Unlike *Mailing Lists* and *MOO*s it does not require a computer to act as its home. See Chapter 4.
pc	Personal communication
PL	Personal Life, or Physical Life; i.e. offline.
post	To send an item of text, usually an email, to a *Mailing List*
prestation	A 'gift', something formally given.
prototype	A good example of a category.
RL	'Real Life' i.e. the offline world
sigfile	A piece of text attached to the end of a letter, often giving the person's email address, workplace etc. but often including *ASCII* decorations and nowadays graphics.

soc.	*Newsgroup* prefix, indicating 'social'.
spam	Unwanted multiple postings. Usually advertisements sent to unconsenting internet users, or to many newsgroups.
terminator	A term, name, phrase etc., which ends explanation. In some ways it is like an axiom.
thread	A series of *posts* linked by a common heading.
troll	A person, or message, which is perceived as trying to initiate *flame war*, by saying something which will obviously upset many in the group it is posted to. Defining something as trolling is usually a political act.
WES	'Western English Speaking', used to include those social formations which are known as Western, but where the people usually speak English. Includes Australia, the UK, the US, Canada, and New Zealand.
Wizard	A person who has power on a MOO.

Notes

Introduction

1. In 1999 Schaap wrote that the "ongoing research has not yielded a full-length monograph about a particular online community" (1999: np). If we exempt unpublished theses, and informal accounts, such as Horn (1998) and Hafner (2001), then this statement is still nearly correct. The collections edited by Jones (1995a, 1997a & 1998a) and Smith & Kollock (1999) contain formal ethnographic accounts of online societies but, as chapters, they are brief. Baym (2000) is a good account of a soap opera fan newsgroup. Kendal (2002) has written an excellent study of life on a MOO. Hine (2000) has many valuable reflections on doing ethnography online, but is narrowly focused on a set of discussions about a trial in the US, and makes almost no attempt to socially situate the people involved in this discussion.
2. A Mailing List is a group of people who all receive the email directed to the group. For a more detailed description see Chapter 4.
3. There is a vast, and well-known, literature on fieldwork and ethnography commenting on 'reflexivity', and the socially positioned role of the anthropologist themselves, in gathering 'data' and turning it into narrative and theory. For some samples see Bateson (1946 {1991: 44ff.}), Rabinow (1977), Hammersley & Atkinson (1983), Clifford & Marcus (1986), Rose (1990), Marcus (1999).
4. Of interest here is Bourdieu's (1991b) analysis of how the requirements of philosophy modified 1930's German political discourse in the writings of Heidegger.
5. *Coactivity* can be defined as actions taken by people who may never interact in person, which may be necessary for either to function socially. 'Coaction' includes, not only 'interaction', but 'mutual action', which is not interactive; cooperation, as well as conflict.
6. See in particular Barth's study of the way that the interpretation of Baktaman symbolism and ritual changes with initiation grade (1975).
7. Barth, at one time, suggested anthropologists made "a number of loosely connected, partial models of society" (1981: 24). We probably should not assume that other people make, or are directed by, coherent, complete or logically consistent models.
8. A local newspaper told the story of how in the Singapore Stock Exchange the position formerly occupied by the man, who bankrupted Barings Bank through bad trading, was afterwards empty 'because of bad Feng shui'. Here the journalist creates a Chinese culture to explain this event. I know nothing about the customs of the Singapore Stock Exchange, but probably people there are engaged in a highly competitive and hazardous activity—largely depending on contacts, reputation and luck. No one need believe this desk has bad feng shui, but if they assume others believe then, no matter how well placed the desk, occupying it might lose them some of their reputation—other people may expect them to make bad deals and so on and eventually their career could crash as a result. If the story is correct, then it is noteworthy that traders of European origin have not set up in that position either. Of course something else could be happening; this paragraph just gives another model.

9   Later in the book it is suggested that WES demands for authenticity imply that uncovered 'unpleasantness' is a guarantor of truth. We tend to take conflict, rather than cooperation, as the mark of social transformation (e.g. Moore 1987: 730).
10 Obviously not always, or else this point would be harder to make. I am not arguing that all human groups necessarily have a concern with boundaries at all times.
11 Labouring the point, 'power' is not a uniform thing. In the terms used in Chapter 1, the category is not a concept but a congerie.
12 In many ways Elias' view of power, first formulated in the 1930s, resembles that of the later Foucault. Foucault also emphasizes that power is not simply a blocking, a rule, a mode of subjugation or something which can be acquired. There is not a simple division between power and those subject to it (1979: 83-5, 92-3). Power is productive, resistance is not exterior to power, and power is relational (ibid: 95; 1997: 291-2). Foucault also proposes that power relations have different forms, and different rationalities. Unfortunately Foucault also ties power to the myth of authenticity, 'how can the subject tell the truth about itself?' (1998: 451-2), a point which is here subject to investigation and not taken as a premise.

Both Elias and Foucault, link power with the 'self-cultivation', whereby a person disciplines themselves, or is disciplined, using prescribed tools to become a good example of their ascribed, or desired, social category. Here Foucault is much more subtle, as Elias tends to reduce the myriad ways of self cultivation to a supposedly unproblematic, and probably uniform, 'self control'.
13 It is difficult to think of a WES discourse about society which is not sociological in some sense. Even 'fundamentalist' religious politicians like Pat Robertson make claims such as new technology will change access to distribution of messages and hence change society (1994: 190ff.).
14 Bourdieu writes that the anthropological task is to "uncover the most profoundly buried structures of the various social worlds" (Bourdieu & Wacquant 1992: 7, emphasis added). In his discussion of Western Art, Bourdieu unmasks 'taste' and the 'poverty of artists' as 'symbolic capital', which "is to be understood as economic or political capital that is disavowed, misrecognized and thereby recognized, hence legitimate, a 'credit' which, under certain conditions, and always in the long run, guarantees 'economic' profits" (Bourdieu 1993: 75, cf.169). Those artists on Cybermind who rarely gain any economic profit might disagree, but their rejection by, and of, the 'bourgeoisie' certainly indicates their personal authenticity and reinforces their self-categories. Bourdieu claims that magic is also misrecognised and unveiled by the anthropologist as well (ibid: 81). Economic reason, when visible, presumably does not need to be unveiled.

In this book I treat sociological and anthropological documents, not only as analyses, but as ethnographic documents - items of culture.
15 One of the most telling stories is of Franz Boas' impatience that the Kwakiutl were too busy engaging in potlatch to tell him anything interesting (Rohner 1969: 38).
16 It might seem unnecessary to labour propositions such as an informant's statement is not necessarily: a) what they always hold to be true; or b) an actual reason for, or description of, how they act; or c) uninfluenced by the ethnographer as audience. However, it is easy to forget this and assume, for example, like Runciman that it might be possible to settle Sahlins and

Obeyesekere's dispute over Hawaiian interpretations of Captain Cook "for sure" if we could travel back in time to ask and observe Hawaiians (1998: 24). Possibly so, possibly not. There might be no unity on this issue among Hawaiians either, or it might not be a meaningful question to them.

17 Often the 'best' information gathering occurred face to face or over the phone, which shifts social life into a modality not characteristic of the group in general, but certainly part of its member's operation.

18 Only one person ever insisted that use of their words should be cleared with them first. Some names have been changed where permission cannot be assumed.

As well, the book was kept on the web as it was being written and list members were asked to check any use of their names or words, and notify me if they objected.

19 Population data are described in Appendix I.

Chapter 1

1 'The Real' has properties (independent of the human mind, but capable of generating it), but these properties can be apprehended in many different ways. The Real resists theory - hence falsification is possible. The lack of 'fit' between available discourse and the Real, and the resistance of the Real to 'signification' can be an important generative, as argued by Bachelard (in McAllester Jones 1991: 24). In slightly different terms Barth brings this to anthropology, writing: "Events are the outcome of interplays between material causality and social interaction, and thus always at variance with the intentions of individual actors... We need to incorporate both a dynamic view of experience, as the outcome of individuals construing events, and a dynamic view of creativity, as the outcome of the struggle of actors to overcome this resistance on part of the world into our model of how culture is generated" (1989: 134).

2 Anthropologists have long had an interest in categories, but have generally ignored both category theory and questions of how people learn categories. Durkheim and Mauss proposed that animal categories corresponded to social categories (1963). Durkheim claimed that classifications "have taken the forms of society as their framework" (1915: 145) and develop historically: "the idea of genus was in the first instance merely another aspect of the idea of the human group" (1975: 171). However, if humans can form categories of human groups, then they are already forming categories and we cannot assume priority. Durkheim also assumes some categories are 'things' actually given in nature, and then arranged in classes (1915: 145), and then later has the problem that 'primitive peoples' are always "confusing things that seem obviously distinct" to him (ibid: 235-6). This arises as he does not investigate the ways people learn categories and go about gathering together things he considers distinct. As Worsley further points out, category 'systems' learnt in different situations (e.g. 'religious', 'technical', 'linguistic' etc.) can be radically different, even for the same people (1997: 119ff.).

Levi-Strauss proposed that animals provided good tools with which to think about social categories, and then shifted his interest from categories to the terms themselves, "which never have any intrinsic significance. Their meaning is one of position" (1972: 55). His analysis thus separates experience and categorization, or

form from content, and does not explain how the units of bricolage are learned (ibid: 17ff.).
3. It is taken for granted that emotions and thought are not separate types of thing, cf. Ratner (1999).
4. 'Similarity' refers here to a heuristic rather than to a given, it is not a concept itself, but a congerie. Some similarity grows in what Ellis calls 'functional equivalence', in the experience of what people do with things, or do about things (Ellis 1993: 31). Functional equivalence may arise from properties in the world as these properties are used or uncovered. It is hard to use what we call mercury in the same way as we use what we call gold, and neither behave exactly like a rat. However this does not mean there is a universal placing of exactly the same things in the categories of 'gold', or 'rats', or the same reactions to them. Functional equivalences can differ so radically that some categories appear 'irrational' or 'magical' to non-society members.
5. See, for example, Bloor's account of research into syphilis (1983: 34-6). I argue this point at length in Marshall (1992), to try and explain the nature of alchemical language. It should not be assumed that a 'clear' concept is always 'better' than a 'confused' congerie (cf Wittgenstein 1968: #71). Ahsen similarly argues that 'unvivid', or 'unclear' images are often sources of creativity, (1986a, 1987a, 1987b).
6. He writes of mana: "these types of notions, somewhat like algebraic symbols occur to represent an indeterminate value of signification, in itself devoid of meaning and thus susceptible of receiving any meaning at all" (1987: 55). "I see in mana... the conscious expression of a semantic function, whose role is to enable symbolic thinking to operate despite the contradiction inherent in it. That explains the apparently insoluble antinomies attaching to the term... force and action; quality and state; ... omnipresent and localised. And indeed mana is all those things together; but is that not precisely because it is non of those things, but... liable to take on any symbolic content whatever?" (ibid: 63-4). The term takes its value in allowing the termination of explanation.
7. Elias suggests that this fallacy is particularly prevalent in the social sciences when theoretical models, such as 'family' or 'structure', are taken as real (1978: 13-5), or when processes are reduced to static objects (ibid: 112ff.). It might be suggested that his 'civilising process' is an example of such - a trend which becomes taken as a reality in itself.
8. *Arete*, or "excellence or goodness of any kind... is an abstract noun connected with aristos, excellent ... the irregular superlative of agathos" or good. *Aristokratia* equals "rule by what are called aristocrats in ordinary English" (Urmson 1990: 30-1, 10-11). Aristotle noted, what I'm calling, the congerie nature of agathon (op. cit).
9. The possible divergences may be infinite, but not every divergence is equally probable. Each interpretation of Shakespeare's Hamlet may be different, but I have yet to find someone arguing that it is about the mating habits of elephants.
10. Derrida, in his argument with Searle, implies that 'transfer of meaning' is a problem, because if meaning depends on context, then "a context is never absolutely determinable" (1988: 3). Therefore the "hypothesis [that] 'the author says what he means'... cannot even be formulated". Once the "inadequation between meaning and saying, as well as the alleged 'corruption' of the text...

[has] been acknowledged to be 'always possible'", this cannot be left out of analysis. "A corruption that is 'always possible' cannot be a mere extrinsic accident... This possibility constitutes part of the necessary traits of the purportedly ideal structure" (ibid: 77). However Derrida's interests do not focus on the sociological consequences of this 'fact', and the problems it poses. Furthermore, he seems to expect that it is easily possible for people to read him accurately (ibid: 146-7).

For Searle, category matching between people is not a problem. He first argues that some things have functions because an individual ascribes them that function (like using a stone as a paperweight) and some things have functions because of collective intentionality. On occasions "I am doing something only as part of our doing something" (1995: 23). He answers the question of the relation between 'I' and 'We' intentionality, by begging the question and arguing that it is the "sense of doing (wanting, believing etc) something together" (ibid: 24-5). "The form that my collective intentionality can take is simply 'we intend,' 'we are doing so and so' and the like" (ibid: 26). And that is it. He ignores: pre-existent processes involved in making a 'we'; the possibility of different 'we's; the relationship of this 'we' to the 'I' or the 'they' (i.e. to different categories of groups); how it is that people come to know they are coacting together; and how they ensure that they agree upon what they are doing and how to do it. In Searle's world there seems no room for conflict over, or misunderstanding about, what 'we' are doing—despite his display of incomprehension in his argument with Derrida.

11 The term 'frame' is borrowed from Agar (1994: 130), although it is not unique to him (cf. Bateson 1972: 184ff.; MacLachlan & Reid 1994). I have turned the term into a verb, to imply that framing is not 'set', but active. The idea goes back, at least, to Malinowski's 'context of the situation' (1947: 306ff.).

12 *Performative* is the term proposed by Austin for when language is concerned with 'making something so', as with statements such as "I thee wed" or "I name this ship". Performative utterances are often surrounded by ritual, ceremony, audiences and institutions—it is so only when the audience interprets it as so and people may dispute the adequacy of these conditions.

13 The concept of locale comes from Giddens, who also argues that locales give the experience of "the 'fixity' underlying institutions" (1984: 118). In his later work he abandons the notion because non-local influences can nowadays determine these locales (cf. 1990: 19). However, this is because the reach of the groups with dominant power ratios in certain locales has extended and changed not because the idea of locale has lost its use.

14 Barth, although not making use of this theory in his study of Sohar, points out that some identity categories are mutually exclusive (e.g. Shiah/Sunni) while some are associated (e.g. Baluchi and Sunni) (1983: 36). He further points out that some socially effective categories do not act together as social units (e.g. ex-slaves) even though the members are all affected by the categorization process of others (ibid: 44, 48).

15 Unless, that is, they were economists, when the view of humans as innately competitive seemed to override cooperation (Ridley 1996: 146).

16 This usage descends from Cancian, who proposes distinguishing between three kinds of norms: ranking norms, which evaluate individuals on the basis of how

well they conform to a standard; reality assumptions about what constitutes good and bad actions; and membership norms which are the standards for including or accepting a person within a group (1975: 2-3). These are only distinct if one holds a 'standard view' of categories. Within the view presented here, people 'suffer' group membership based on assumptions about reality, which are graded so that they can better or worse approximate the category prototype. Group membership implies expectations about actions and evaluation already. As Cancian suggests later: "individuals conform to norms in order to validate an identity" (ibid: 137).

17 It is frequently alleged that 'reality norms' are less important online, and some people do claim this is so for them. However, these allegations may occur as WES mythemes of individualism and authenticity already imply that such weakening is beneficial. I will argue later that reality norms such as gender norms become very important online.

18 Biernat et al (1996) found that US college students would embrace positive stereotypes associated with their fraternity or sorority, as highly self-descriptive. They did not deny negative stereotypes as valid, but claimed they were general. In that case it seemed that everyone is really 'bad' in the way that we are supposed to be.

19 From a different perspective, Bailey argues consensus will not eventuate if there are more than about fifteen active people involved and, that if relations are multiplex, then arguments cannot be isolated and tend to cause total paralysis (1965: 2, 5).

20 Moore argues that people both attempt to fix and to manipulate the situation. We can investigate the limits of manipulability and the various influences of different peoples and positions (ibid: 220-1). We can also look at the way in which indeterminacy is done away with and generated (ibid: 232-3). Or whether people attempt to fix determinacy on others or on themselves.

Chapter 2

1 In accordance with the tendency for corporate agglomeration, AOL took over Compuserve, allied with Netscape, and became powerful enough to merge with one of the world's largest media companies in Time Warner, although this was not greatly successful (Klein 2003, Munk 2004).

2 The earliest remaining list mail is from Marius Watz and dated 1 Jul.94. It opens "I now step into this new space, created by two net.persons I have come to admire and respect [...] I have hopes for this space as I always have when I enter a new room". (Note the casual use of metaphors of space, and the expectations produced by this framing). Mitchell Pravatiner recalls seeing the announcement of Cybermind on some other list on Friday 1st of July and joining that day. A letter posted on Wednesday the 6th by Alan talks of Cybermind's first week, implying the list began about that time. Because of the date of this letter I refer to the period from the beginning of the list to, and including, the 6th July as the "first week".

3 Eventually issued as the May/June 1995 issue (Vol.19, No.3). Alan is unsure whether he had an Internet account before he took on the editing or not (pc 11 Nov.96).

4 Thinknet was originally a newsletter concerning philosophy on the Internet started by Kent Palmer. Later it became an "experiment... to have multiple email

lists each dedicated to a specific philosophy". This was established on World.std.com by September 1993. Eventually Kent Palmer allied with the Freelance Academy run by Lance Fletcher to form DialogNet. Kent writes that although Michael was the moderator of the Deleuze list he was not "not handling any of the administrative load of the list" which was being done by Kent himself (pc 5 May.99). A division of labour that I think was perhaps bound to result in conflict, although Kent does not agree.

5   On the 27th of September 1999, Alan forwarded some mail to Cybermind from Michael's mail archives, which suggests that Alan 'introduced' himself to Michael in early May of 1994, and that they had begun to discuss founding a new list by the end of that month.

6   The glyph :) is an 'emoticon', defined by Raymond as an "ASCII glyph used to indicate an emotional state in email or news... invented by one Scott Fahlman... around 1980" (1994: 162-3). They represent facial expressions, and hence act as framings to help interpretation. People also indicate emphasis by enclosing words within asterisks, i.e.. *help*, and sometimes expressions will be written within angle brackets or within asterisks such as: *smile*, or <grin>. See Chapter 7.

7   "Walkers-in-darkness", a list for those suffering from depression.

8   In a now undated mail to Cybermind (either 6 or 7 July 94) Michael writes "One of the reasons that the Spoon Collective [...] was formed was because the previous owner of one of the other Spoon lists found the language and manner in which a particular debate was being conducted to be objectionable and tried to put a stop to it". In another mail Alan wrote (10 Jul.94) of a case where: "An administrator of a number of lists sends a post complaining about a particular email thread. He speaks of governance; the list members feel by and large they are under the aegis of free discussion. and that the post implies control. Eventually, the list changes administrators as a result of misunderstandings".

9   Kent Palmer informs me (pc 5 May.99) he has one higher degree in Sociology, and that he had read *Anti Oedipus* and *A Thousand Plateaus* before starting the deleuze list. However he "did not care very much for the kinds of people that he found were using Deleuzian philosophy as a rationale for hedonism and nihilistic behavior".

10 In response to the question "Roughly when did Michael and Malgosia form spoon?" Alan wrote (pc 13 Mar.96): "Not sure but I imagine it to be around 2-3/94. I came in almost immediately and Steve Meinking was part of it as well".

    A world.std.com official, Elizabeth Lear, informed me that "Records show that Spoon was a customer of World starting June 9, 1994" (pc 15 Nov.96). It is certainly possible that Malgosia and Michael were discussing forming a break-away List several months before they took the action, but time distortion is common online.

11 Kent wrote to me (pc 5 May.99) that the administrative burden of Thinknet was proving too great for him alone - "The whole issue was administrative load which [I] could not handle and which eventually caused [me] to become very ill. [... I] was happy to off load the lists to other administrators but had hoped that this could be done under a single umbrella organization.[...] The reason that the lists were on the verge of being shut down was because [I] could not alone manage to do all the administration that was needed".

12 Kent Palmer writes (pc 5 May.99) that this was true of him as well.

13 It appears that this has involved little money. He wrote to the list of receiving about $6,000 in grants, over his lifetime.
14 According to a letter on Cybermind, posted sometime after his death, he had been sacked from his previous job as a political lobbyist for a gay organisation as that group suspected he had AIDS.
15 The metaphors used in this opening sentence are heavily reminiscent of the genre writings of cyberpunk (from which they are trying to separate themselves), and of the type of techno-adventurism associated with the FutureCulture list and its founder Andy Hawks. 'Cyberspace', as mythic entity, was meant to transform the human.
16 The current version of the manifesto (2007) deletes the remarks about discussions of MOOs, IRC, VR and Cyberpunk, further opening the List; not that anyone was ever berated for such discussions.
17 There is no attempt to spell out what this hegemonic bias might be, it is unspecified - perhaps to be inclusive - but possibly the term is meant to suggest an academic and artistic elite, and to suggest that Cybermind remains 'outside' it. A later version changes the word to "totalizing".
18 Alan stated (30 May.95) this paragraph was written by himself and Michael, and adopted by the other Spoon lists "at the time". On questioning, Alan was not able to remember any incident which might have precipitated the addition of this paragraph (pc 10 Nov.96). The paragraph appears in an announcement of 10 Jul.94, and it was possibly introduced as a result of discussions on the list between 5-7 July 94.
19 Obviously people are reluctant to talk about these differences to an anthropologist who is making them public. However, it would seem that Alan's sense of friction arose from the kind of organizational problems described by Malgosia above. Those who were programmers with access to the majordomo program often appeared, to him, to make decisions on behalf of the collective without consultation.

One of Alan's few direct remarks on the split was "Cyb and Fop didn't belong there; they're academic, tight-assed - we've been wild. We had to protect our lists; the others didn't" (pc 15 Mar.96). This statement emphases Alan's construction of Cybermind as anti-academy, more radical than the other Spoon lists, and as more vulnerable. The split with Spoons occurred during the attack on the list by the 'Freaks', which is discussed in Chapter 10.
20 His copy is undated, but preserved between posts dated 22 June and 5 July.
21 The impact of FutureCulture on early Cybermind is something I discovered through reading, in March 96, Greg Ritter's moving essay on the death of Michael Current and its effect on that list (Ritter 1995). Almost all the people described in Ritter's essay as belonging to FutureCulture I recognised from Cybermind, although many had left by the time I read the essay, and few seem to appear in the first month's records. However those that did post, frequently mentioned FutureCulture as their Net Home or used it as an example of online community.

Chapter 3

1 This account sees the State as a site of conflict and collaboration, as argued by Elias and his followers, rather than as a monolithic body of power (Elias' briefest explanation is Elias (1970); see also Mennell 1995). McGrew, for example, writes

"the State is a highly fragmented and in some respects de-centred apparatus of rule" (1992: 76).

2   In the Communist Manifesto, the no longer fashionable Marx and Engels, claimed capitalism:
> cannot exist without constantly revolutionising the instruments of production and thereby the relations of production and with them the whole relations of society... [E]verlasting uncertainty and agitation distinguish the bourgeois epoch from all earlier ones (1968: 38).

They held that capitalism inevitably spreads over the globe giving a "cosmopolitan character to production and consumption in every country". It destroys national industries, compels every nation to adopt the capitalist mode of production, creates enormous cities making the country dependent upon the city, and "creates a world after its own image" (ibid: 39).

This 'image' involves six features: firstly, massive inequality; secondly, the concentration of wealth, property and power in progressively fewer hands; thirdly, working people becoming an "appendage of the machine"; fourthly, deskilling of labour; fifthly the decline in the size of middle class; and finally the increasing precariousness of survival for most people (ibid: 41-4). Capitalism converts "every occupation hitherto honoured... into its paid wage labourers" and reduces all connections between humans, including family ties, to monetary ones (ibid: 38). The State finally becomes a committee for managing the common affairs of the capitalist class (ibid: 37).

3   'Class' is both a category and a framing. It can be imposed, or it can come out of a socially based theory of class, even from formal sociology. Ascription of class membership allows interpretation of behaviours and prescribes norms and expectations for that member.

However, such categorizations are congeries, there is considerable difference within the middle classes. We can further distinguish between those members associated with business, with government, with the humanities, with the sciences, with the arts, and with the professions. Cybermind members are primarily associated with the humanities and the arts. However, the opportunities of most people assigned to 'the intellectual middle class' have come to differ from the opportunities historically predicted by membership of that class.

4   There is an extensive literature on gangs, but these are usually locality or directly survival based and are frequently not voluntary. The essays in Redhead et al, *The Clubcultures Reader* (1997), give no indication of how people in dance clubs go about organizing themselves or making contact with others. Despite the book's claims about ethnography, most of the essays could have been written without the inconvenience of attending any such clubs. D.W. Brown's (1995) study of the use of convention by strangers is useful, but the examples are disjointed and philosophic rather than ethnographic. Jenkins' (1992) study of 'fan' cultures shows active audiences in action: transforming separation into connection, passivity into participation and orthodoxy into critique; but no specific groups are considered in detail. Fine's (1983) account of role-playing gamers is an interesting attempt to investigate the creation of leisure fantasy worlds, but only vaguely situates the activity in its social environment.

Chapter 4

1. As all my experience has been on MOOs, and to avoid writing 'MOO, MUD or MUSH' continually, I have subsumed them all under the category of MOO.
2. Connection via the web (blog or youtube), by newsgroup or IRC channel, etc. did not seem that favoured by members of the list, although many list members had websites. Consequently I have ignored those organizations of communication.
3. Mailing Lists seem to have been the first form of group communication developed on the Internet. On the history of Mailing Lists, see Hauben & Hauben (1995: Ch10), Thomas (1995), I.Hardy (1996), Hafner & Lyon (1996: 200ff), and Hauben (1997),

    In November 1995 Treese (1993+) put the number of internet Mailing Lists known to the Indiana University Support Center at 12,850, while in April 97 he claimed the number of mailing lists in the liszt.com directory was 71,618. With the popularity and ease of things like yahoo-groups the number of Mailing Lists is now truly huge.
4. Lists can change of course. The Alchemy list only became fully moderated after the moderator received complaints about irrelevance and rudeness (and was threatened with legal action for censoring posts—which he had not done). Cybermind became a closed list (i.e. only people on the list could post to it) after an 'attack' from outside. The process leading to this latter change is discussed in Chapter 10.
5. List members sometimes discuss what effect the various styles of moderation have upon the vitality of lists but, as yet, there is little evidence for any direct effect, and it probably changes with the list subject and the demographic it attracts.
6. Divergence from thread subject is encouraged by the reply function in most mailers. A single press of a key will set up a new letter with the old subject header and, sometimes, the previous letter quoted within for comment—changing the subject heading takes extra work.
7. Usually quotations from the previous letter are set off by '>'s, though some mailers may use other markers. Thus if Rose writes (3 June.95):

    Do inanimates have emotions? No, of course not!

    Zav's reply (4 June.95) to this line looks like:

    3/June/1995 03:22pm Rose:
    >Do inanimates have emotions? No, of course not!
    Maybe not emotions but don't some North American Indian tribes
    believe every object has a soul, or a manitou as its referred to.
    Be careful what you say.....you might hurt your floors feelings.
    Zav :)
8. Literature on the history of MOOs is sparse but literature on the sociology of MOOs is immense. Curtis (1996), Bruckman (1996), and Dibble (1998), are much reprinted and cited. Kendall (2002) was mentioned earlier. There is a growing literature on graphically based worlds which have a lot in common with MOOs such as Taylor (2006). These worlds are being impinged by corporate activity, brand names, and a real cash economy, trading places and buildings in the MOO and special artefacts and characters (Castronova 2005). This reinforces my remarks about the personal investment which occurs in these types of internet forums.

9 A short explanation of the most common MOO commands is given in the Glossary, under MOO Commands.
10 Bernadette writes (pc 5 May.99): "it is common to allow players to create their own rooms without needing a prog bit. Some moos won't let you have a prog bit until you have built your own room- a demonstration of basic moo competence".
11 For more on MOO 'space' and List 'space' see Marshall (2001).
12 Which sometimes reached more than 10 minutes from Australia. My opinion was that the lag was not that significant a barrier (as people did not complain about connect time charges), suggesting that formal group communality is more fragile than people would like to think. The lag on PMC-MOO seemed to diminish soon after.
13 Kendall notes that in the MOO she studied, anonymity was not really accepted either (1999: 69-70).
14 MOO users will often enter the MOO as anonymous 'guests' in order to spy on other users, or make comments they don't want to be sourced back to their character. This implies characters are expected to be consistent, and linked to all their actions.
15 Bernadette writes (pc 5 May.99) "most MOOs are based on what is called the lambda core software (lambda core was written by the people who bring us lambda moo), although some programmers modify the core. The core is public domain software and freely available".
16 I'm influenced by, but do not explicitly use the terminology of, Mary Douglas's ideas of 'grid' and 'group'. particularly as developed by Atkins' (1991) in his study of the social context of the letters of St. Paul (which could be considered as constituting an early text-based society).

Douglas has proposed many different definitions of 'grid' and 'group', which she considers as two independent variable dimensions of social life. Her simplest statement about them occurs in her Foreword to Atkins' book: "One dimension [group] measures the extent to which the social unit has borders closed to the outside world.... The other dimension is structure, ('grid' in the jargon). The more a community is structured, the less it can be counted egalitarian" (1991: xi-xii). All Internet groups seem to be low/grid low group, with newsgroups the lowest and MOOs the highest. However this does not prove a particularly useful discovery as WES society appears to be low grid low group and so these groups manifest social behaviours similar to their embedding society.
17 Lambda MOO, one of the earliest and most popular of MOOs, has a large file labelled 'Manners' which it is suggested all new participants read, and which acts as an informal code of law.
18 Bernadette disagrees (pc 5 May.99): "I seem to remember a history, on lambda, of people fighting with the wizards - the wizards job at lambda is full of unpopular decisions". For examples of deference to Wizards see Reid (1999: 119).
19 See also Douglas on problems of leadership in groups where leaving is easy and boundaries vague and unenforced (1987: 38ff.).
20 Category definition for the moderator of a Mailing List is not particularly complex. They are simply the person running the list—there is little else to distinguish them from other list members, unlike normal hierarchical categories which may include numinous or magical intangibles like 'birth', 'gender', 'talent', 'charisma', 'blood' etc.

21 There were occasional discussions which could be called religious. On the whole these discussions tended to favour less institutionalised forms of religion, and resembled the general vague mystical thought usually considered 'New Age', with considerably less emphasis on 'positive thinking' than is characteristic of such thought. One 'born-again' Christian member, sometimes expressed concern about what her fellow congregation members would think of her long-term membership of Cybermind.
22 I can only think of one rather unusual instance when Alan was having severe problems moderating FOP and asked Cybermind whether he should resign from moderating altogether.
23 This might be an example of the estranged relationship that WES people have to power. Something similar to what Elias & Scotson (1994) call 'blame gossip' is more likely to be directed towards these vague and, largely unencountered others, rather than at specific outgroup members. But this is more like the blame gossip they describe of the relatively powerless people in Zone 3 of Winston Parva, who criticised the snobbishness of those in Zone 2, but whose gossip had little effect on those it criticised.
24 This lack of cooperation might be a feature of non-hierarchically linked WES groups in general, rather than a specific feature of Internet groupings.
25 It has been suggested to me several times, that this filter was so effective 'Comms-MOO' got almost no new members and thus slowly declined until it was almost always empty. Whether true or not, this story shows the problematic around boundaries.

Chapter 5

1 When I joined the list I did not notice many long-standing relationships and people. Some, people who were, at that time, 'important people' soon unsubbed forever. A number of people who were to become important to the list arrived at about the same time, and it seemed common for new people to arrive in 'bunches'. Much later, after an absence of five months it seemed that the majority of posters to the list were unknown to me. I estimate the 'generation' period on Cybermind varies between six months and two years, even if some people have managed to remain active almost for the whole period of the List's life.
2 My own experience of lurking on several lists was that I tended to speed-read posts, to treat them as content specific, and had little idea of who the different participants were—nothing separated out the 'voices'. Despite this, list members were usually still generous in their response when I did ask questions, and this then helped my recognition of people.
3 It is generally assumed this silent membership is fairly stable. Looking at chronologically arranged 'who lists' of the people on the list, and the statistical evidences in Appendix I, my impression is that many people did remain lurkers for considerable time periods. However, there is a continual stream of silent people staying for only a short time.
4 In this case, Alan had not been informed, as according to one of the women involved they had not wanted to worry him and had solved the problem themselves, feeling the lurker was (16 Mar.95) "more immature than malicious".

5   An obvious example is alt.flame, but there were more localized and subject-specific groups such as aus.flame.gareth.powell devoted to a once well-known Australian computer journalist.
    It is important to recognise that terms like 'flame' and 'troll' (a name usually given to a person who appears to want to start a flame war) are not objective terms but, as I hope to show here and in later chapters, they are largely terms of abuse and policing usually applied to people who are outsiders to the group. The terms are interpretations, applied to largely uncertain things such as deciding the intention of another person. The success of using the labels depend upon rhetoric, the importation of assumptions about hostility from the external social world, possible use of external group ties, and the application of social control. If we ignore these factors, then we ignore an important part of the constant struggle of online life and people's attempts to manufacture group tradition and identity.
6   During the dispute (4 July.94) he forwarded what was alleged to be the alt.syntax.tactical FAQ. There is an article on this group by Hill (1995). See Chapter 10 for an account of another group's attack on Cybermind.
7   'Flames', 'psychopaths' and 'below' could signify a virtual hell. Legislative control from above is perhaps analogous to the God from whom there is no appeal, while the human tries to steer the middle way between extremes.
8   The ignoring only affected Ann, no one else was prevented from reading Livia, and Livia herself was not affected other than symbolically. Symbolism becomes taken as concrete.
9   The usual suggestion is that when online, people can avoid argument, but in fact all they can avoid is participating. Any involvement with the list as a whole will lead to awareness of the argument.
10 For example Dery (1993: 559), Reid (1999: 115), Donath (nd #2.1.1.1).
11 In another mail in the same thread Alan remarks that flaming is generally less prevalent on MOOs, particularly those MOOS which "demand a ritual entrance [...] the worst flames I've seen, say, on PMC-MOO, have been by long-time users who deliberately go in as Guest so they can flame/post anonymously...". It is possible that people on MOOs tend more to harassment of individuals, rather than to group-wide flame wars.
12 It perhaps needs to be suggested that despite this tendency of communicative structure to multiply 'hostility', the tendency of people to respond to flames with flames, may still result from WES social conventions as well.
13 Baym mentions the idea of flaming as play, or ritualized insult (1998: 59). This did occasionally occur on Cybermind but not often. When I once wrote a parody flame in the middle of a discussion, I was vaguely troubled that members who did not recognize me, might not read the parody as intended, and thus a real dispute might develop.
14 Cohen points out the importance of this procedure in the modern construction of ethnic resistance (1985: 109).
15 Ian wrote in early 1995: "I just noticed that I've saved almost 1,100 Cybermind/FOP posts! I still re-read some of them from time to time". A thread on 'hoarding cybermind posts' also ran for a short while.

Chapter 6

1. The issue of 'race' did not seem important upon Cybermind (although see Marshall 2007a), but Shirky's comments on the hiding of characteristics are apposite: "The net far from being a socially neutral space, is largely white and male. When most people on the net don't know what race you are, they don't ordinarily assume you could be any race at all; they assume you are white" (1995: 42). Cf Burkhalter (1999).
2. Barth implies that in the city of Sohar in Oman, 'politeness' is actually a key factor in the generation of social life (1983: 98ff., 249).
3. Mary Douglas's discussion in Natural Symbols (1973), and Trilling (1974) form the basis for this section. Modern WES distrust of ritualism is also mentioned by Elias (1985: 23-7). Not all members of WES societies may hold these views. Explicit discussions about the artificiality, deceitfulness and status-enforcing nature of 'formal etiquette' or politeness arose on several occasions on Cybermind, (see in particular, the threads 'the nature of the beast' and 'Reserve ! =untrustworthy' in March 95).
4. We can think of the early anthropological puzzlement when people explained that they did things because they had always done them that way. We demand that to do something, people must have an explanation, and preferably one that can be phrased in utilitarian terms such as 'placating the dead', or 'expressing social unity' or 'keeping order'. See also Elias' comments on our inability to understand the central importance of etiquette in European Court Society (1983: 36ff., and passim).
5. Trilling writes: "At the behest of the criterion of authenticity, much that was once thought to make up the very fabric of culture has come to seem of little account, mere fantasy or ritual or downright falsification. Conversely, much that culture traditionally condemned and sought to exclude is accorded a considerable moral authority by reason of the authenticity claimed for it, for example, disorder, violence, unreason" (1974: 11). Authenticity "is implicitly a polemical concept, fulfilling its nature by dealing aggressively with received and habitual opinion" (ibid: 94). See also Taylor (1991: 63-5).
6. Taylor (1991), for example, criticises "debased authenticity" in the name of true authenticity. Almost all the criticisms, by others, that he reports, are criticisms of "narcissistic" or "self-indulgent" forms of authenticity. A rare critical voice is Oscar Wilde: "What is interesting about good society... is the mask that each of them wears, not the reality that lies behind the mask" (1966: 975). "A mask tells us more than a face" (ibid: 995). "The first duty of life is to be as artificial as possible. What the second duty is no one has yet discovered" (ibid: 1205). The absence of counterposition is more marked as authenticity is not demanded in all non-WES cultures; see Doi (1988) on Omote and Ura in Japan.
7. See, for example, in a therapeutic context, Dreher (1995: ch8), where the possibility of multiple authentic selves is portrayed as a great discovery and as appropriate to contemporary life.
8. Bensman and Lilienfeld write: "friends use their friendship to unburden themselves of secrets that they hold within themselves, a burden that ordinarily causes a sense of isolation from the public and official culture, which rejects the kinds of thoughts, actions, or information contained in the secret. Revealing the secret, then, is a release from the pressure of public opinion. But the demand for

intimacy is based on the necessity and the opportunity to reveal such situations with the understanding that the other will not reveal such information to still others". Gossip "creates a culture for a friendship circle for network; it sustains the entire circle. It is a kind of quasi-public information in a relatively intimate network or group". "[T]he culture so created contains secrets; violation of public norms... the informal culture so presented is always at odds with the public, 'official' culture". "[I]ntimate behaviour involves the willingness of individuals to express aspects of themselves to intimate others who are willing to tolerate and accept behaviour that is not accepted, not tolerated, or frowned upon in public or official circles" (1979: 148-9, 156).

9 An executive probably does not want the kind of relationship they have with their underlings to be the same as the one they have with their spouse. My address, or my license number has to be available to some people, or it serves no function, but it does not have to be available to all.

10 In a well-known incident, the network provider Prodigy defended itself against charges it censored criticism of itself but refused to police racism by arguing that their 'bulletin boards' were electronic publications and could be edited as they, the private owners, chose. Others conceived these 'boards' as public places like parks; still others like shopping malls and subject to those restrictions; others like public carriers such as telephone companies or the US mail (Boyle 1996: 112). 'Freedom of (public) speech' under US law is limited by 'private' ownership of places or communication channels i.e. the methods people have of communicating (Shapiro 1996).

11 This is not unique to Cybermind. Bromberg quotes a MOO interviewee as suggesting the Internet brings out "what you're like deep down inside" (1996: 146). Barlow writes that "between the word that I type into my computer and e-mail to you and the word that comes out on your end there's nothing but the digital transformation taking place. It's not mediated" (1995: 36, 40).

12 In further list correspondence she elaborates:
> Only a minimum of my personality seems expressible offline because it is hidden by the surrounding shell of my body and my social role. Online, however, I can communicate, not from the surface of the shell, but out from within the shell. I feel that online I can write from out of who I really am, not from who other people around me think I am.

Online life might sometimes be seen as a 'spiritual purification', involving a shedding of the 'material' obstructions to truth and freedom. See Chapter 7.

13 Note also the etherealisation of the underlying authentic mind (as described in Chapter 7) and the supposed freedom from embedding culture. Although I disagree with Reid, it needs to be stated: a) this might happen on IRC but not elsewhere online; b) it might be a historical phenomena which is now over; c) it might be a position now rare but becoming more common; and d) it is an improvement over previous positions that the "medium is not conducive to emotional exchanges...[it is] more serious, business-like and task oriented" (q. op.cit), which probably resulted from studies of work oriented, rather than sociable, networks. Multiplicity may also be a form of self-cultivation associated with a younger generation than those on Cybermind. See for example Clark 1998: 179.

14 F.W.H. Myers quotes Ribot, *Les Maladies de la Personnalitie* (1885), to the effect that the part of personality which "emerges into consciousness is little compared with what remains buried but operative nevertheless... the Self is a coordination. It oscillates between two extremes at each of which it ceases to exist; —absolute unity and absolute incoherence".

Myers adds that this view is [c.1900] "the view prevalent among experimental psychologists [they] have frankly given up any notion of an underlying unity" (Myers 1927: 12).

15 Slater in his account of an IRC channel quotes 'Rock Dr.' as writing: "If I'm trying to develop a real friendship, then I like to know the truth" (1998: 106). How to find out this 'truth' is then a problem to be solved (ibid: 92). It usually involves gaining more offline data, quizzing others privately, making phone contact, meeting offline, and so on.

16 To give a further example of the supposed therapeutic effect of online authenticity in terms of revealing hidden and therefore genuine parts of the self, I quote a member writing (25 Feb.96):

> I am not afraid in cyber... [...] I have poured out my most negative and self depreciating thoughts to a particular email friend to an extent and with a regularity which would have been impossible in PL... in some ways the *deferred presence* of the recipient has parallels with psychotherapy.

Counterpositions do exist. Another member writes (19 Feb.96): "The 'isolation of depression'/ if you'll allow 'depression of isolation' is symptomatic of the Net as well, the Net constraints add to my general feelings of helplessness in the face of it".

17 The one-line reply in itself is part of an email convention. Large amounts of the original letter may be quoted, and the one line appended usually appears to be intended as an amusing and/or dismissive comment. It is an obvious form of one-upmanship. However, if a one liner appended to a large letter is not made by a recognized person, it may be construed as indicating incompetence and be taken as a 'waste of bandwidth'.

18 Ann did not teach composition, she was quite clear about her profession.

19 Later, but within this first week, he writes (3 Jul.94):

> I know for a fact there are a _lot_ of poor people (economically) on the Net; this is _not_ an arena where elitism should be tolerated.

Cynthia writes:

> authority, i'd argue, is highly overrated. granted that the net tends to be available to and used by elite folks but 'elite' doesn't always translate the same way. moreover, woldn't it be more interesting to be talking to varieties of people, not just those who talk like you do?

Michael also talks of net democracy, the blurring of boundaries and the mixing of people (3 Jul.94):

> One of the best things about the deleuze list I mentioned in a previous post, I think, is the mixture of the so-called 'experts' (and we have nearly all of them in the English-speaking world on board) with folks who are not, and even never have been, part of academia. This isn't easy to negotiate, but I think it is _more_ possible in cyberspace right now than it is outside it.

20 Clash being a well-known late 70s politically motivated punk rock band, with anarchistic left leanings—making them a suitable metaphor.
21 In another context Laurie writes (4 Feb.95): "funny how the language of writing seems to be transcended here; I constantly find myself 'saying', 'conversation', 'talking', 'hearing', 'voices'".
22 For many people reading on a computer, particularly reading mail, often seems to be hurried. See Chapter 6, Appendix I.
23 Usually to not read mail one needs to read it briefly to check it is not worth reading. In this context it must be wondered how much the problems with the mail server mentioned by Mitchell in Chapter 2 increased this problem.
24 As examples of the assumption in academia, Donath writes: "The body, which anchors identity in the real world, is absent" (nd: #1). Giddens argues that, in the offline world, the body is the visible carrier of self-identity (1992: 31).
25 One of my correspondents considered themselves plagued by their net lover's 'x's, '*'s or other glyphs.
26 For example, with 18th century French aristocracy, it would be plausible to assume that if they were going to use such signs they would use signs which represented those gestures which normally expressed degrees of deference and status: bowing, curtsying, kissing the hand and so on. Their code may even demand specific formulaic responses.
27 For example, Don, a linguist, draws attention to the frequent use of ellipses (...) which is rarely remarked. She writes that these are "one of the most significant features of texts of this kind" (Don: unpublished).
28 Another example of text as body is that writing in capital letters is often considered to be shouting. In December 1994, three new members arrived on Cybermind, for whom the convention was to indicate the reply to mails, not by setting off in >s (as described in Chapter 4), but by the use of capitals. They were told by nine list members to stop this, that it was shouting, and that the lack of letter distinction made it hard to read. Members never protested at the lack of distinction in people's frequent use of no capitals, as it did not clash with the group preference for low aggression communication, as 'shouting' did.
29 Mark Poster is more extreme writing: "one may experience directly the opposite gender by assuming it and enacting it in conversations" (1977: 223). Cf Marshall (2004a).
30 See also Clark writing of online teenage dating (1998: 166-9). Springer makes a similar point when talking of cyberpunk novels and films; "despite the fact that people alter their sexual identities... the texts do not radically restructure relations between the sexes" (1996: 66).
31 The pronouns e, em, eir, eirs, eirself are known as spivak. When people set their gender to 'spivak' in general they play with their anatomy rather than their gender (i.e. it is usually possible to classify them as a male or female spivak, or it is assumed that they are concealing gender rather than that they don't have one). For the origins of spivak on LambdaMOO see Danet (1998: 141).
32 O'Brien remarks that in her experience a person who maintains vagueness about 'real gender' is "generally 'dropped' from the interaction" (1999: 90).
33 To save space it should always be assumed the words 'female' and 'male', or 'man' and 'woman' are shorthand for "person presenting themselves as having that sex".

34 The dynamics will obviously be different on male gay lists.
35 Sudweeks et al. claim that it could be expected that as WES female discourse is supposed to be more emotional than male, women online would make more use of graphic indicators of emotion. They found this to be the case (1998: 6, 9).

Chapter 7

1   This chapter builds on themes elaborated in Marshall (2003c, 2004a, and 2006a: 935-61).
2   E. Martin describes these phenomena in detail. However, her argument that, over the last 40 years, there has been a shift from the maintenance of external barriers to the maintenance of personal immune systems may arise from trying to make a range of conflicting theories fit into a single mytheme. She gives plenty of contemporary examples of boundary anxiety towards foreign substances (1994: 37-9, 53-4, 67, 230ff.). Recent Australian advertising campaigns have promoted a 'war' on bacteria in the household, focusing on children ingesting germs if those bacteria are not 'wiped out'. This indicates that the appeal of barrier models of defence are still strong, even when it is widely thought that anti-bacterial agents may induce the evolution of resistant bacteria, and diminish the development of the immune system.
3   The terms of sickness, and thus boundary issues, are used in describing society and its boundary problems; we are often said to live in a 'sick society' suffering 'epidemics', or 'plagues' of social problems (Helman 1992: 53-4, 67, 230ff.).
4   Evan McKenzie, writing in 1993, claimed that over 30 million Americans (one eighth of the population) live in these enclaves (q. Boyer 1996: 151). This points to separation from the rest of the populace, as well as to defence.
5   Two replies were forwarded to me from FOP by Bernadette and are referred to as FOP 1 and FOP 2 making a total of fourteen replies—this includes a reply from Alan. Two different replies came from the same person using different pseudonyms. These two replies are similar enough to be treated as one.
6   We might expect that societies which would not 'carry across' the body sexually would have strong systems of classification of roles or behaviour generally, and/or strong group boundaries, in contrast to the relatively unstructured society of the WES middle class, with its fairly loose classifications of roles and order (Douglas 1973: 101).
7   People may use photographs which are not accurate depictions of themselves as they are now, which is perhaps 'rational' if they want 'casual' sex, but which sets themselves up for probable rejection when they find, as they do, the person "of their dreams". Use of inaccurate photographs of list members was not reported to me as common—although people commonly exchanged photographs through email. When it is discovered, it is taken as evidence of inauthenticity, and often ends the relationship.
8   As some members expressed some embarrassment at their contributions to these discussions, I have in many cases neither dated the remarks or attributed them. I have indicated male or female writers, often by [m] or [f]. See Parker (1997) for an autobiographical account, by a non-Cybermind member, which makes many of the same points made by members.

9 For an overview of academic research, which portrays netsex as almost entirely pathological see Griffin-Shelley (2003).

10 Plato *Republic* 435e-444e, 580d-581a; *Phaedrus* 246, 253c-255b; *Timaeus* 69d-72d. Aristotle *De anima* 414-15; Peters (1967: 166-76). Descartes arguments about animal spirits are in the *Passions of the Soul* (2007) and his letters to Elizabeth of Bohemia (Atherton 1994: 9-21). See Broadbent (1975), on the play with such complex mind body divisions in 17th century literature and Marshall (2006d) on the use of ghosts in philosophy and politics.

11 The analytical arguments over this history are intense, as might be expected. As well as Marshall (1992), which gathers the social, political, linguistic and epistemological arguments, good, if also slightly dated, introductions to the debate are Easlea (1980), Hunter (1981), Merchant (1990), and Shapin (1994).

12 For the change in ghosts between the medieval and contemporary periods see Finucane (1982). It might be worth drawing attention to the contrast between the apparent increase in preoccupation with both body and State boundaries over this period, (as described by Elias), and the growing etherealization, and detachment, of the ghost.

13 See the reports of research in Frude (1982: 62, 75, 77, 83), Weizenbaum (1993: 6-7), and Reeves and Nass (1996).

14 It is possible to allege that otherwise unempowered people could produce political change or, at least, reach the numbers of readers previously reserved for mass-media, through writing on the net. However, such power does not seem currently common, and may never be a common experience. The volume of writing on the net is such that any single opinion may get lost, unless already marked by social position.

Chapter 8

1 Initial versions of parts of this chapter were posted to Cybermind as the threads "systems of peace" beginning 9 Oct.96, and "systems of property" beginning 29 Oct.96. I am particularly indebted to comments made on various portions and versions of this chapter to the following members of Cybermind (in alphabetical order): Toby Cockcroft, Jerry Everard, Lynne Harding, Richard MacKinnon, Kerry Miller and Alan Sondheim.

2 Hume argues (1987: 465ff.) that 'social contracts' can only occur because of pre-existing social events and conventions. Deleuze suggests that for social contract theorists society is a negativity or set of prohibitions whilst, for Hume, society provides an extension of ability and satisfaction (1991: 38-47). I assume both. Society enables and restricts.

3 Gasche objects to the idea of an inaugural gift, as a "prestation is always already a counter-prestation". The concept of the inaugural gift "effaces its obligatory character, its inscription in a game that has always already begun" (1997: 111-12). However, people do often originate relationships with gifts. In WES societies these may be small such as a cigarette, or drink etc. The network of exchange may 'always already' exist, but this particular part of it may not.

4 Sahlins (1974: ch 4) describes Mauss' errors with respect to the Maori concept of hau (which is supposed to demonstrate this connection), in more than sufficient detail for this part of Mauss' argument to be abandoned. Hyde comments on

Sahlins' remarks that the increase of the gift occurs not after its first giving but after it is given away again: "in gift exchange it, the increase, stays in motion and follows the object, while in commodity exchange it stays behind as profit" (1983: 37). Similarly the previous addresses often left attached to email forwards gives the item a history and truth value.

5   Mauss, himself, quotes examples of fraught exchange (1954: 26, 52, 92n3) but closes his work with the remark: "In these primitive and archaic societies there is no middle path. There is either complete trust or mistrust. One lays down one's arms, renounces magic and gives everything away" (ibid: 79). This is clearly not the case, even from the data he presents, and seems to be used primarily to demonstrate the Western struggle between 'reason' and 'emotion', and to explain the absence of continual warfare (ibid: 80).

6   Bourdieu seems to argue that all exchange is commodity exchange, accounting does take place and people deceive themselves about this to enable the society to function. Therefore our Western economic categories are 'real' and universal. He extends this 'economic imperialism' to the 'cultural' via the category of 'symbolic capital'—which allows all social activities to be commodified. Symbolic capital serves to save the theory of accounting precisely where it is not visible. People's "systematic emphasis on the symbolic acts... prevent the economy being grasped as an economy, that is as a system governed by the laws of interested calculation" (Bourdieu 1997: 205-6, see also 212-13, 232-3). It is simpler to assume difference is possible. See also Hyde's brief discussion of WES kidney donation, and the donor's initial non-concern with accounting, and subsequent avoidance of it (1983: 65, 69).

7   Although there has not been the debate in anthropology over the term 'gift' that there has been over terms like 'money' and 'currency' (or over the terms 'magic' and 'religion'), this allegation of carelessness seems slightly unjustified. Malinowski goes to great lengths to distinguish the particular Trobriand vocabulary of 'gifts', and this is replicated in Mauss. Mauss might use the term 'prestation' to remove some of the expectations around the term 'don'. Strathern writes: "a culture dominated by ideas about property ownership can only imagine the absence of such ideas in specific ways.... To talk about the gift constantly evokes the possibility that the description would look very different if one were talking instead about commodities" (1988a: 18-19). Cheal writes "in truth there is no such thing as 'the gift'" (1988: 172). Derrida's criticism here sits uncertainly with the implicit universalism of his own 'perfect gift'.

8   Following the pun, we could suggest that the self-presentation is a giving of the self—that the present (gift) presents (reveals) itself in the present (moment of time) as presence. The meanings can be almost randomly distributed with equal effect. However, perhaps this is more of a warning about where our language wants to go than illumination.

9   A notable instance arose on Cybermind when some people strongly argued that a recognised member should stop primarily forwarding messages from other lists, while other people argued that these prestations were worthwhile. In this case forwards were perceived as less valuable, or even as illegitimate, as they are not presentations of the person making them and have no transparent authenticity.

10 Cheal makes a similar point about the Western gift economy and adds that sociologists tend to notice and focus upon the obvious, but rare, large exchanges rather than the small-scale and constant background exchanges (1988: 113, 200n7).
11 Malinowski doesn't really need this word with its legal connotations, but it does show the difficulty of avoiding standard formats.
12 Mauss (1954: 34), Bourdieu (1997: 198-9, 231) and Derrida (1994a: 38, 40-1) all emphasise the importance of the time factor in prestation. Godbout & Caille further suggest that in mercantile relationships people seek to eliminate time from the exchange (1998: 95).
13 A non-presenting moderator, or list owner, may keep status and presence by tending and continually updating a web site which all list members are aware.
14 Because of difficulties with the division between 'public' and 'private', Cheal suggests a new polarity of 'intimacy' and 'community'. 'Intimacy' concerns the reproduction of the life and personal relationships of those whose relations supposedly depend on the emotional attachment between members; and 'community' concerns the collective reproduction of actors and social statuses (1988: 107).

This new distinction simply creates more problems and Cheal may need to posit a further pole which lies outside the 'gift economy' — the 'society', say of a town where people have identity and roles, coact and share some common allegiances, but do not gift. It could also be argued that intimate social forms do involve reproduction of roles and statuses, such as those between parents and children, or husband and wife. For the same reason his research does not demonstrate, as he claims, that gift transactions are autonomous from 'structural' determinations such as class or role (1988: 14, 168).
15 Van Gelder describes a male who was once mistaken for a woman by another woman who was "open in a way that stunned him". He then deliberately embraced a female persona and became intimate with many women. When this was discovered some of these women considered it violatory. Van Gelder asks "why a man has to put on electronic drag to experience intimacy, trust and sharing[?]" (1996: 546).
16 People with a particular lack of confidence in exchange might not reply to such questions at all. Therefore the replies select for some degree of confidence. 'X' was someone with whom I had frequent offlist correspondence.
17 The arguments of this chapter are applied to the open-source movement and considered in relation to society in general in Marshall (2003b, 2006c).

Chapter 9

1 In allowing me to write this chapter I would like to thank Alan and Glen for their generosity and their permission for me to write whatever I pleased despite the risk that they ran in doing so.
2 Glen's homepage, which was not existent at this time, listed among his interests "confrontational rhetoric".
3 Despite the looming of Marx in debates with Glen, Marx was of little importance in discussions on the list, and was rarely mentioned. Marx has a symbolic value by which each side can further distinguish itself, and thus appears in this kind of situation.

4   "Work makes free". The slogan over the gates of Auschwitz.
5   Partly this recognises limitations of list volume and of member's time to describe theories with any accuracy, and partly this represents the group's version of US conventions of 'self-help' or the virtues of, as one member put it, having people do the "work of learning".
6   Responses to this metaphor are further discussed in Chapter 11
7   This itself is a value statement more likely to appeal to certain types of groups than others—perhaps those with a low concern about boundary maintenance. On occasions people would even refuse to tell puzzled newcomers what the list 'was about', preferring to keep the topic undefined and unrestricted.
8   His very first post was largely autobiographical and was received positively by the high-status dobie, which could have been a 'good introduction' to the list.

Chapter 10

1   Marius blamed the subject of guns for a major flame war on FutureCulture, when discussing the 'Spelling War' on Cybermind.
2   According to one list member who asked around: "The substance of his posts generally centered on varying aspects of how profemen was populated by sensitive new age wimps. Their style was not very different from the ones he posted here".
3   Hardly anyone argued that few public spaces in this sense exist in WES societies. This extension of 'toughness' could be alleged to be part of the way the right engages in destroying public space and the rights of the 'weak'; i.e. those with less power resources (cf. Schiller 1989: 89ff.).
4   Two other new members behaved 'suspiciously', but they were never confirmed as participants and were not unsubbed.
5   Much later I was informed that these particular people had a reputation for attacking lists. Another list owner wrote to me that they were known for CCing, [derived from 'Carbon Copy'], or copying, their disruptions to Freaks. Even though in this attack some posts were CC'd to Freaks, it is possible the Freaks list was not involved in attacks on other lists, on any continual or coherent basis, as some members of Cybermind were at one time on Freaks and apparently witnessed no activity of this kind.
6   Although it is possibly coincidence, or because of the group he is attempting to disrupt, this message likewise implies a fear of 'intimacy' and betrayal, together with a distrust of women.
7   As he also had an address unknown to people on Cybermind, it cannot be assumed this was not deliberate—perhaps an attempt to see how long it would take for him to be recognized.
8   'BCC' from "Blank Carbon Copy' - a standard feature in mailing programs which allows a user to copy a mail to one person to another without the first person being able to see the second address.
9   Perhaps reminiscent of those who enforce the split between the body and the online spirit-self which is invulnerable, see Chapter 7.
10 Fieldwork may have indirectly contributed to the problems. My posting of the results of the first survey in which I mentioned the 'left-liberal' orthodoxy of the

list and the absence of political dispute may have triggered a series of pronounced political arguments, largely initiated by one 'right identified' member.
11 As I was not a neutral party in these debates, it is fair to mention my position. I supported A rather than B in the disco debate. In the chemical intolerance debate I was concerned whether representatives of chemical corporations should be the only people who approved the release of new chemicals into the environment. In the dispute on the question of the behaviour of the subgroup associated with B, I argued that their posts were not disruptive and were occasionally interesting — basically that they were not doing anything which was new to the list.
12 Several people made allegations to me, of intermittent love affairs occurring between these members. This may simply have been an interpretive 'causality' link to explain the apparent closeness and separation from others.
13 See Spender (1995: 193-212), Brail (1996), Gilbert (1996), Hall (1996), C.B. Smith et.al. (1998: 112).
14 In attempting to replicate the experiment, I found it exceedingly difficult to separate 'information' from 'critique' or 'support' from 'non-support'.
15 For example, we could divide the left into: a) those who consider capitalism beneficial but needing mild regulation to ensure maximum social benefit; and b) those who consider that unless democracy and a degree of equality are established first, then capitalism is largely detrimental. We could similarly divide the right into those: a) who consider that capitalism is fundamentally beneficial and that all obstacles to its unregulated functioning should be removed; and b) those who consider that 'traditional' moral virtues and discipline are the fundamental basis of a good society. The divisions within the left and right are as conceptually significant as those between left and right, yet these inadequate polarities appear to capture people.

Chapter 11

1 Bounds merely gives six different definitions (1997: 2). Veling, a theologian, makes an interesting attempt at a definition by specifying eight continua which distinguish a group from a community. This implies that few groups are going to be ideal type 'groups' or 'communities', but his attempt at definition is weakened by his prior commitment to seeing certain types of Christian groupings as superior to others (1996: 4ff.).
2 This accusation of inauthenticity surprisingly common in sympathetic accounts of online groups. For example, Nunes writes "Cyberspace... like a Disneyland for Enlightenment conceptions of community,... [is] a simulacrum of community, deferring the moment of realisation that community no longer exists" (1997: 173; see also Lockard 1997: 224-6). The nostalgia for 'community' (discussed in the next section of this chapter) gives Nune's critique whatever force it has.
3 Nostalgia may not be intended; but the phrase "what have been", the use of the term "lost" and the suggestion that communal relationships were once not scarce, all imply the existence of a preferred state in another time or place.
4 For example, Jackson writes of the Walpiri of Central Australia: "There are so many competing interests in a desert community, so many competing points of view, that contentious issues simply cannot be settled to the satisfaction of everyone" (1995: 38). "Networks of ties developed which were different for each

person" (ibid: 64). He also writes of the Walpiri as having "an extraordinary degree of independence and individuality" (ibid: 57). However assumptions about the integrated nature of "small communities" have passed into ordinary and much academic discourse. Frankenberg, for instance, describes the expectations of his university colleagues that the 'community' he was studying would be 'simple' (1969: 238-9).

5 In order to maintain normal 'middle class' relationships in WES societies, manifestation of self-control is important. Visible excitement, or exaggerated body movement, indicate a person could be dangerous (Elias & Dunning 1993: 41). Work tends to be the place where a person is most under the control of others, and is at their most subservient. Even CEOs bow before the market.

6 This might extend to perceiving the online as 'a game', in Elias's terms a "mimetic leisure pursuit", which "is meant to elicit excitement of some kind imitating that produced by real life situations, yet without its dangers and risks.... Imaginary danger, mimetic fear and pleasure, sadness and joy are produced and perhaps resolved" (Elias & Dunning 1993: 42). However, it may not be that easy to decide if something is an imitation, or 'imaginary', as opposed to 'valid' in its own right.

   Collins points out that games "and entertainments, after all, are manufactured fantasy worlds for the display of specially cultivated skills" (Collins 1975: 83). He suggests that as skills are class distributed, participatory games are not class free, and serve to make distinctions within classes (ibid: 84). Games feed back into life: mimetic battles and real battles can be related, not separate.

7 See Hillery (1955: 118), Elias (1974: xix), Frankenberg (1966: 15).

8 De Tocqueville associated ease of association with equalising democracy. Individuals alone were powerless and isolated, frightened of the majority and jealous of power. Voluntary associations were necessary to generate action and coherent feeling. Without these associations America could easily become tyrannous (1994 I: 191-5, 263ff., II: 107-8).

9 Gergen (1991: 277 n18) attributes this idea to Cohen (1985), but Cohen argues that all communities are based on symbolic relations. However Cohen thinks 'modern' symbolic communities tend to be based on symbols of threatened ethnicity etc, which arise from challenges to pre-existing geo-social borders and structural bases (1985: 50, 76).

10 Gergen states that such celebrities provide stability among the chaos of social interaction, locations for issues that concern us socially, and serve as talking points with others. He quotes Cynthia Heimel, who argues that "celebrities are our common frames of reference.... Celebrities are not our community elders, they are our community" (1991: 56).

11 A view shared by Elias and Dunning who write: "sport has come to function as one of the principal media of collective patterns of identification" (1993: 221) and, as we could add, of collective separation.

12 See also Healy, who in writing of 'cyber-community', instances Robert Bellah's 1985 description of lifestyle enclaves tied to leisure and consumption which "celebrate... the narcissism of similarity" (1997: 61-2).

13 As an example of this story, Bruce Sterling writes:

By the second year of operation, however, an odd fact became clear. ARPANET's users had warped the computer-sharing network into a dedicated, high-speed, federally subsidized electronic post-office. The main traffic on ARPANET was not long-distance computing. Instead, it was news and personal messages. Researchers were using ARPANET to collaborate on projects, to trade notes on work, and eventually, to downright gossip and schmooze.... Not only were they using ARPANET for person-to-person communication, but they were very enthusiastic about this particular service -- far more enthusiastic than they were about long-distance computation (1993: np).

There is also plenty of evidence that management and the military were equally excited by email and Mailing Lists and encouraged their development.

14 This posited relationship between 'community' and death is not uncommon. For example, Blanchot argues that the possibility of community opens in the presence of someone else's death (1988: 9-11), and the group psychoanalyst Rosenfeld writes: "An interesting aspect was the theme of the dead member, which usually emerges as a consequence of the moment of fusion. What has died are the external roles with which each of the participants is invested at the beginning of the group. It is a process both of self-assertion and of relinquishment, which reinforce each other, so that each may attain the status of group member" (1988: 57). Perhaps 'community' makes death 'meaningful', or group bonding allows someone to be missed.

15 The debate also suggests that different lists are easily reacted to as different and unrelated groups, even if they have the same participants.

16 Almost a year later (showing the recurrence of the 'on topic debate'), Mitch writes (22 Jul.96): "I cannot help comparing our experience to that of [another list dealing with virtual culture] which adheres to the ideal of serious academic material, and on which traffic dropped to almost zero within a year after it got started. Viewed in that light, we may well be better off having taken the course we did".

17 Just to give one other quote, not from the Survey, WA wrote (23 Jan.96):
> This is a dwelling, a home. If work was shitty, if worries pile up, I can kick off my shoes here, trust (I hope) someone somewhere to glimpse what I would like to be, what I would like the world to be. It strikes me over the months how much we agree, not in our ideas but in our loves and aspirations.

18 There is evidence other members of the Spoon Collective thought Alan had brought these problems on himself by refusing to prevent off-topic communications.

19 Clearly, a value of 'freedom' need not be necessary for construction of community in the WES world. A moral or fundamentalist community can also take its value by contrast with the (disordered) mundane world. In this latter case, 'structure' is perceived as more needful than 'communitas'.

Chapter 12

1 Wilbur implies FutureCulture had far more success in organising a dedicated MOO 'space' on MediaMOO, but even this eventually petered out (1997: 18-19).

2   For example, all 18 respondents to a survey conducted by Mark Murphy and Amanda White (30 Nov.95), which asked about Internet censorship, opposed censorship of pornographic or 'hate' web sites and the application of anything other than personally based controls. Discussions in 2001 about selling Nazi Memorabilia via Yahoo's shopping site were not so clear-cut.
3   An extended description by Alan, of the first 'fleshmeet' in New York, was one of the first non-archival materials to make the original Cybermind web page, which shows its importance.
4   There were two other accounts of this particular meeting posted to the list by dobie, and Jim. Two other members posted accounts of why they missed the meeting.
5   It might be possible to see this letter as expressing a joy in being able to 'flesh out' people, known only by email. It helped to add extra dimensions to the author's knowledge, and help the resolution of messages.
6   It was, in practical terms, impossible to choose a time in which many people in the US, the UK and Australia could all be online together. Formal MOO meets tended to be between US and Australian members, or US and UK members.
7   For example, an attempt to do another 'worldwide' 'flesh' and MOO meet a couple of weeks after the December MOO meet described below passed unremarked.
8   The sequence of events in Jerry's recollection is not entirely correct. The conference was suggested before the MOO party occurred. My own recollection of events was even more inadequate—thankfully archives can be correctives.
9   Quoting Rose again (16 Feb.96): "Even if a mental image of the physical Other has been formed (and I don't do this—don't know why not), there is a recognition factor.... a sort of '*YES*!—it's you!!' Amazing.....". To the contrary, Lotus Blossom wrote at a different time (12 Dec.95) "I have often found that who a person is in her or his mind (coupled with whatever my imagination adds to fill in the blanks) is quite different from who that person is f2f [face to face]".
10 This is far fewer than originally expressed either interest in coming, or determination to come. Several of those keenest dropped off the list during the time it took to organise. The cost of airfares was probably a consideration in some other cases.
11 The MOO was distinctly less formal than the conference and the discussions on MOO tended to be 'subversive' of attempts by presenters to be 'serious'.
12 At times, people suggested that this might be the first such conference organised around a Mailing List or the first to use internet video. This is almost certainly not the case, but it does illustrate how the conference reinforced ideas of the list as special.
13 It seems to me that a disproportionate number of group events were organized by women. If so, the decline in numbers of women after the Iraq War might explain the loss of group meetings offline.
14 Alan's definition (11 June.96):
    By list 'aura' I mean the private email, telephone calls, panty exchanges, snail mail letters, packages and private or public/private photographs, fleshmeets, everything and anything that doesn't appear _directly_ on the list, or isn't a part of software give-and-take.

15 There are always counterpositions. One new list member wrote to me (16 Mar.96) that "in the six weeks or so that I've been on CM, I have probably posted more often to people I know only through CM *off-list*, than I have posted to the list itself".
16 Alan wrote [to FOP] (11 June.96):
   I have heard of such incredibly baroque interrelationships among list members that soap opera pales in comparison. I have heard of opportunities and missed opportunities and honest and dishonest consummations, failures and conquests and meetings gone by the wayside. I have not heard of larceny, rape, murder, armed robbery, kidnapping, or parking violations, but nothing would surprise me at this point..
17 Obviously the longer a person is onlist the more likely this is to occur. There is some suggestion that offlist correspondence is again more likely if the person is female.
18 In February 1998 Morning Glory polled members about their offlist interactions with each other. She received close to seventy responses offlist. At the time of writing, her report on this data was not completed and the original data was not available as she promised privacy to those who responded offlist. However the fact that about 90%+ of people replied offlist, rather than onlist as usual for surveys, demonstrates the care with which people hide their offlist interactions with each other.
19 As the listing describes people's reports of their own and other's memorable interactions, it automatically tends to include 'memorable' list members. Thus, it is easily conceivable this list omits interactions with those who did not post often.
20 For example, as a result of a discussion initiated by someone else and my expression of interest, three people wrote to me to claim they had netsex with another member of the list, in each case without saying who. Without those spontaneous comments I would have had no idea these three people had had any such interactions. Their remarks have not been included in the above list.
21 I only know of two love affairs that lead to the participants living together, for a period of several years, in the list's history and one of them broke up relatively acrimoniously with one of the people leaving the List forever. The other resulted in marriage.
22 Just one example (CS): "I've had sexual and love relationships and sometimes both [...], coming from the list... more than and more intense than would have happened in real life.."
23 Caitlin responded to a person claiming netsex was not 'serious' (16 Aug.95):
   But if you privilege the flesh so much that you ignore the potential consequences and implications of behaviors in this space then you are, indeed, playing a game. Unfortunately, it's a dangerous one [...] and the potential for all kinds of damage hovers in the air like a murder of crows waiting to strike.
24 Such effort to make contact is long established. Hiltz and Turoff write about a online conference held in 1976-7: "During and following [this conference] a very significant portion of the participants altered their business and vacation travel plans so as to include a face-to-face meeting with one another" (1993: 114).

25 The idea of projection grew within therapy, and the therapist/client relationship must be among the most simplex of all relationships, particularly if, as in orthodox psychoanalysis, the therapist does not speak.
26 A possible explanation from the consideration of 'therapeutic groups' might be that people (of this 'class') fear the overpowering of their individuality or independence by the group (Bion 1961: 168; Kreeger 1975: 24; Rosenfeld 1988: 128; Alford 1994: 2, 4), and that this fear is exaggerated by the vagueness and asence common in cybersocieties.

Appendix I

1 The listserve used by AOL allowed people to hide their names and addresses; therefore, such people have generally not been included in the counting. Only 15 out of 329 people concealed themselves in this manner.
2 This is a statement from memory, but it is a memory born by other list members as well. The statement specifically excludes people of Indian, African or other origin posting from outside those countries of origin.
3 It has been assumed that addresses without a country termination originate from the US. This is not entirely the case, but the number of addresses for which it was not true were, hopefully, small enough for any resultant error to be insignificant — particularly when compared to other sources of error. At this time yahoo and google addresses were not common or available.
4 Gender was not requested in the surveys as I felt that this might actually add to the confusion, if people demonstrated their much proclaimed freedom to vary or choose gender.
5 For comparison, Burstein & Kline, quote a Georgia Institute of Technology report from July 1995, which claimed that only 15% of Internet users were female (1995: 102). The situation nowadays is significantly different in terms of general population, but the percentage of active women posters on Cybermind has declined significantly.
6 According to Riche the median age in the US in 1994 was 34.5 (1996: 377).
7 Indeterminacy here is more a matter of my ignorance than deliberate vagueness.
8 Riche states that in 1995, 23% of the US population over 25 had a bachelor's degree or higher (1996: 377).
9 Ian Murray asked Cybermind what lists members read on 20th March 1995, receiving 13 replies of equal diversity. The minimum number of lists read by a respondent was 2 and the maximum was 36. The average number was 13.
10 To add to these descriptions of reading I quote Pound:
> I usually get around two hundred mail messages a day, so it is necessary for me to have it presorted [into folders]... I read my mail, reply to a few messages, delete a few messages, save a few others to files in my directory, and occasionally forward a message or two to someone else; I repeat this process for a few other folders, but usually not for all of the ones with new mail - just the ones that I expect to be most interesting (1996: 103).
11 Unfortunately I can no longer find the 'who' lists taken during two of these months so the proportion of people who post to those who don't, cannot really be considered, though the evidence from other months suggests that it is less than half.

Bibliography

Adamse, M., & Motta, S. (1996) *Online Friendship, Chat-room Romance and Cybersex*, Health Communications, Deerfield Beach.
Agar, Michael (1994) *Language Shock: Understanding the Culture of Conversation*, William Morrow, New York.
Ahsen, Aktar (1986) "Prologue to Unvividness Paradox", *Journal of Mental Imagery*, Vol. 10, No.1, pp 1-8.
────1987a) "Epilogue to Unvividness Paradox", *Journal of Mental Imagery*, Vol. 11, No.1, pp 13-60.
──── (1987b) "Principles of Unvivid Experience: The Girdle of Aphrodite", *Journal of Mental Imagery*, Vol. 11, No.2, pp 1-52.
Alford, C. Fred (1994) *Group Psychotherapy & Political Theory*, Yale UP, New Haven.
Allen, J., Abraham, P., & Lewis, P. ed. (1992) *Political and Economic Forms of Modernity*, Polity Press, Cambridge.
Anderson, Benedict (1991) *Imagined Communities*, Verso, London.
──── (1992) *Long Distance Nationalism: World Capitalism and the Rise of Identity Politics*, CASA, Amsterdam.
──── (1994) "Exodus", *Critical Inquiry*, Vol. 20, Winter, pp 314-27.
Angell, Ian (2000) *The New Barbarian Manifesto: How to Survive the Information Age*, Kogan Page, London.
Argyle, Katie (1996) "Life After Death", in Shields 1996.
Argyle, K., & Shields, R. (1996) "Is there a body in the Net?", In Shields 1996.
Aronson, E., & Mills, J. (1960) "The Effect of Severity of Initiation on Liking for a Group", in Cartwright & Zander 1960.
Atherton, Margaret (1994) *Women Philosophers of the Early Modern Period*, Hackett, Indianapolis.
Atkins, Robert (1991) *Egalitarian Community: Ethnography and Exegesis*, University of Alabama Press.
Austin, J.L. (1962) *How to do things with Words*, Oxford University Press.
Bagdikian, Ben (1997) *The Media Monopoly*, Beacon Press, New York.
Bailey, F.G. (1965) "Decisions by Consensus in Councils and Committees" in Michael Banton (ed.) *Political Systems and the Distribution of Power*, Tavistock, London.
Barlow, John Perry (1994) "Jack In, Young Pioneer!", Keynote Essay for the 1994 Computerworld College Edition.
http://www.eff.org/pub/Publications/John_Perry_Barlow/virtual_frontier_barlow_eff.article
──── (1995) "Is there a There in Cyberspace", *Utne Reader*, No.68, March-April 1995, pp 53-6.
──── (1996) "A Cyberspace Independence Declaration"
http://www.eff.org/pub/Publications/John_Perry_Barlow/barlow_0296.declaration
Barlow et al (1995b) "What We Are Doing Online", *Harpers*, August pp. 35-46.

Barth, Fredrik (1975) *Ritual and Knowledge among the Baktaman of New Guinea*, Yale Univerity Press, New Haven.
—— (1981) *Process and Form in Social Life*, RKP, London.
—— (1983) *Sohar: Culture and Society in an Omani Town*, Johns Hopkins University Press, Baltimore.
—— (1987) *Cosmologies in the Making: a Generative Approach to Cultural Variation in Inner New Guinea*, Cambridge University Press.
—— (1989) "The Analysis of Culture in Complex Societies", *Ethnos*, Vol. 54, pp. 120-42.
—— (1993a) *Balinese Worlds*, Chicago UP.
—— (1993b) "Are Values Real? The Enigma of Naturalism in the Anthropological Imputation of Values", in Michael Hechter et al. ed. *The Origin of Values*, Aldine de Gruyter, New York.
—— (1995) "Other Knowledge and Other Ways of Knowing", *Journal of Anthropological Research*, Vol. 51, No. 1, pp. 65-8.
Bateson, Gregory (1958) *Naven*, Stanford University Press, Stanford.
—— (1972) *Steps to an Ecology of Mind*, Chandler Publishing, San Francisco.
—— (1991) *A Sacred Unity: Further Steps to an Ecology of Mind*, HarperCollins, San Francisco.
Bauman, Zygmunt (1992) "Life-world and Expertise: Social Production of Dependency" in Stehr & Ericson 1992.
Baym, Nancy (1995) "The Emergence of Community in Computer-Mediated Communication", in Jones 1995.
—— (1998) "Emergence of Online Community", in Jones 1998.
—— (2000) *Tune in, Log on: Soaps, Fandom and Online Community*, Sage, Thousand Oaks.
Bell, Daniel (1976) *The Coming of Post-Industrial Society: A Venture in Social Forecasting*, Penguin, Harmondsworth.
Bensman, J., & Lilienfeld, R. (1979) *Between Public and Private: The Lost Boundaries of the Self*, Free Press, New York.
Benthal, J., & Polhemus, T. eds. (1975) *The Body as a Medium of Expression*, Allen Lane, London.
Berreman, Gerald D. (1972) *Hindus of the Himalayas: Ethnography & Change*, University of California Press.
Biernat, M., Vescio, T.K., & Green, M. L. (1996) "Selective Self-Stereotyping", *Journal of Personality and Social Psychology*, Vol. 71, No. 6, pp. 1194-1209.
Bion, Wilfred (1961) *Experiences in Groups*, Tavistock, London.
Blanchot, Maurice (1988) *The Unavowable Community*, Station Hill, New York.
Blau, Peter (1964) *Exchange and Power in Social Life*, John Wiley, New York.
Bloor, David (1983) *Wittgenstein: a Social Theory of Knowledge*, Macmillan, London.
Bounds, Elizabeth (1997) *Coming Together/Coming Apart*, Routledge, London.
Bourdieu, Pierre (1991) *The Political Ontology of Martin Heidegger*, Polity Press, Cambridge.
—— (1993) *The Field of Cultural Production*, Columbia University Press, Oxford.
—— (1997) "Selections from the Logic of Practice" and "Marginalia - Some Additional Notes on the Gift", in Schrift 1997.

Bourdieu, P. & Wacquant, L.J.D., *An Invitation to Reflexive Sociology*, Polity Press, Cambridge.

Boxall, F. (2003) *The new age of corporate management weird scenes inside the goldmine*. PhD thesis. Department of Anthropology, Macquarie University.

Boyer, M. Christine (1996) *Cybercities: Visual Perception in the Age of Electronic Communication*, Princeton Architectural Press, New York.

Boyle, James (1996). *Shamans, Software and Spleens*, Harvard UP, Cambridge Mass.

Brail, Stephanie (1996) "The Price of Admission: Harrasment and Free Speech in the Wild, Wild West", in Chernny & Weise 1996.

Breslow, Harris (1997) "Civil Society, Political Economy and the Internet", in Jones 1997.

Brinkgreve, Christien (1982) "On Modern Relationships: the Commandments of the New Freedom", *Netherlands Journal of Sociology*, Vol. 18, pp. 47-56.

Broadbent, John (1975) "The Image of God, or Two Yards of Skin", in Benthal and Polhemus 1975.

Bromberg, Heather (1996) "Are MUDs Communities? Identity, Belonging and Consciousness in Virtual Worlds", in Shields 1996.

Brook, James & Boal Ian (1995) *Resisting the Virtual Life: the Culture and Politics of Information*, City Lights, San Francisco.

Brown, David W. (1995) *When Strangers Cooperate: Using Social Conventions to Govern Ourselves*, Free Press, New York, 1995.

Bruckman, Amy (1996) "Gender Swapping Online", in Ludlow 1996.

Bukatman, Scott (1993) *Terminal Identity: The Virtual Subject in Post-Modern Science Fiction*, Duke University Press.

Bulan, H.F., Erikson, R.J. & Wharton, A.S. (1997) "Doing for Others on the Job: the Objective Requirements of Service Work, Gender and Emotional Well Being", *Social Problems*, Vol. 44, pp. 235ff.

Burkhalter, Byron (1999) "Reading Race Online", in Smith & Kollock 1999.

Burstein, D. & Kline, D. (1995) *Road Warriors: Dreams and Nightmares Along the Information Highway*, Dutton, New York.

Butler, Judith (1993) *Bodies That Matter: on the Discursive Limits of 'Sex'*, Routledge, New York.

Cancian, Francesca (1975) *What are Norms?: a Study of Beliefs and Action in a Maya Community*, Cambridge University Press.

Cano, Diane (1997) "Oneness and Me-Ness in the baG", *Paper Presented at the Bion 97 Conference*. http://www.loris.net/cano.html

Cartwright, D., & Zander, A., eds (1960) *Group Dynamics: Research and Theory*. 2nd Edition, Harper & Row, New York.

Castells, Manuel (1996) *The Information Age, Economy, Society and Culture. Volume 1: The Rise of the Network Society*, Blackwell, Oxford.

―――― (1997) *The Information Age: Economy, Society and Culture Volume 2: the Power of Identity*, Blackwell.

―――― (2000) *Rise of the Network Society, Second Edition*, Blackwell, Oxford.

Castronova, E. (2005) *Synthetic Worlds: The Business and Culture of Online Games*, University of Chicago Press.

Cerf, Vinton & Aboba, Bernard (1993). "How the Internet Came to be" originally in Aboba, *Online User's Encyclopedia*, Addison Wesley.
http://www.zilker.net/users/internaut/internt.html
Chambers, Iain (1994) *Migrance, Culture, Identity*, Routledge, London.
Cheal, David (1988) *The Gift Economy*, Routledge, London.
Chernny, L. and Weise, E.R. eds. (1996) *Wired Women*, Seal Press, Seattle.
Clark, Lynn Schofield (1998) "Dating on the Net: Teens and the Rise of 'Pure' Relationships", in Jones 1998.
Clifford, J., & Marcus, G. (1986) *Writing Culture: the Poetics and Politics of Ethnography*, University of California Press.
Cobb, Jennifer (1998) *Cybergrace: the Search for God in the Digital World*, Crown, New York.
Cohen, Anthony (1985) *The Symbolic Construction of Community*, Horwood & Tavistock, London.
Collins, Randall (1975) *Conflict Sociology: Toward an Explanatory Science*, Academic Press, New York.
Constant, D., Sproull, L. & Kiesler, S. (1997) "The Kindness of Strangers: on the Usefulness of Electronic Weak Ties for Technical Advice", in Kiesler ed. 1997.
Critical Art Ensemble (1994) *The Electronic Disturbance*, Autonomedia, New York.
────── (1996) *Electronic Civil Disobedience and Other Unpopular Ideas*, Autonomedia, New York.
Curtis, Pavel (1996) "MUDding: Social Phenomena in Text-based Virtual Realities", in Ludlow 1996.
Danet, Brenda (1998) "Text As Mask: Gender, Play and Performance", in Jones 1998.
Derrida, Jacques (1983) *Dissemination*, Chicago UP.
────── (1988) *Limited Inc.*, Northwest University Press, Evanston.
────── (1994a) *Given time:1. Counterfeit Money*, Chicago UP.
────── (1994b) *Specters of Marx*, Routledge, New York.
────── (1996) *Archive Fever: A Freudian Impression*, Chicago UP.
Dery, Mark (1993) "Flame Wars", *South Atlantic Quarterly*, Vol.92, No.4, pp559-68.
────── (1996) *Escape Velocity: Cyberculture at the End of the Century*, Grove, New York.
Descartes, Rene (2007) *Passions of the Soul* (1650 translation).
http://net.cgu.edu/philosophy/descartes/Passions_Letters.html
De Tocqueville, Alexis (1994) *Democracy in America*, Everyman's Library No. 179, London.
Deuel, Nancy (1996) "Our Passionate Response to Virtual Reality", in Herring 1996.
Dibble, J. (1998) "A Rape in Cyberspace"
http://www.juliandibbell.com/texts/bungle.html
Doi, Takeo (1988) *The Anatomy of Self: the Individual Versus Society*, Kodansha International, Tokyo.
Don, Alexanne (forthcoming) "Analysing Computer Mediated Conversation: approaching the Text"
Donath, Judith S. (nd) *Inhabiting the Virtual City*,
http://persona.www.media.mit.edu/Thesis/ThesisContents.html

―――― (1999) "Identity and Deception in the Virtual Community", in Smith & Kollock, 1999.
Douglas, Mary (1969) *Purity and Danger: an Analysis of the Concepts of Pollution and Taboo*, RKP, London.
―――― (1973) *Natural Symbols: Explorations in Cosmology*, Barrie & Jenkins.
―――― (1987) *How Institutions Think*, Routledge, London.
―――― (1991) "Foreword", to Atkins 1991.
Dreher, Henry (1995) *The Immune Power Personality*, Dutton, New York.
Drucker, Peter (1993) *Post-Capitalist Society*, HarperBusiness, New York.
Durkheim, Emile (1915) *Elementary Forms of the Religious Life*, George Allen & Unwin, London.
―――― (1960) *Division of Labor in Society*, Free Press, Glencoe.
―――― (1975) *Durkheim on Religion: A Selection of Readings with Bibliographies and Introductory Remarks*, ed W.S.F. Pickering, RKP, London.
Durkheim, Emile & Mauss, Marcel (1963) *On Primitive Classification*, Cohen & West, London.
Easlea, Brian (1980) Witch-hunting Magic and the New Philosophy, Harvester, Brighton.
Elias, Norbert (1970) "Process of State Formation and Nation Building".
http://www.usyd.edu.au/su/social/elias/state.htm
―――― (1974) "Towards a Theory of Communities", in C. Bell & H. Newby ed. *The Sociology of Community: a Selection of Readings*, Frank Cass, London.
―――― (1978) *What is Sociology?*, Columbia University Press, New York.
―――― (1983) *The Court Society*, Blackwell, Oxford.
―――― (1985) *The Loneliness of the Dying*, Blackwell, Oxford.
―――― (1996) *The Germans*, Columbia UP, New York.
Elias, N., & Dunning, E. (1993) *Quest for Excitement: Sport and Leisure in the Civilising Process*, Blackwell, Oxford.
Elias, N., & Scotson, J. (1994) *The Established and the Outsiders*, Sage, Thousand Oaks.
Ellis, John (1993) *Language, Thought and Logic*, Northwestern UP, Illinois.
Everard, Jerry (1999) "Crossing Cultures in Cyberspaces: Navigating Realities Between the 'Real' and the 'Virtual'", *New Observations*, No. 120, Winter, pp. 8-9.
―――― (2000) *Virtual States: The Internet and the Boundaries of the Nation State*, Routledge, London.
Fernback, Jan (1997) "The Individual within the Collective: Virtual Ideology and the Realization of Collective Principles", in Jones 1997.
―――― (1999) "There Is a There There: Notes Towards a Definition of Cybercommunity", in Jones 1999.
Ferree, Marnie, C. "Women and the Web: Cybersex, Activity and Implications", *Sexual and Relationship Therapy*, Vol. 18, No. 3, pp.385-93.
Festinger, Leon (1960) "Informal Social Communication", in Cartwright and Zander 1960.
Festinger, L. & Aronson, E. (1960) "The Arousal and Reduction of Dissonance in Social Contexts", in Cartwright & Zander 1960.

Fine, Gary A. (1983) *Shared Fantasy: Role-Playing Games as Social Worlds*, Chicago UP.

Finucane, R.C. (1982) *Appearances of the Dead: A Cultural History of Ghosts*, Junction Books, London.

Firth, Raymond (1967) "Themes in Economic Anthropology: A General Comment", in R. Firth ed. *Themes in Economic Anthropology*, ASA monograph No. 6, Tavistock, London.

Fischer, Claude (1991) "Ambivalent Communities: How Americans Understand Their Localities", in Wolfe 1991.

Foucault, Michel (1979) *The History of Sexuality Vol. 1: an Introduction*, Allen Lane, London.

——— (1997) *The Essential Works 1: Ethics*, Allen Lane, London.

——— (1998) *The Essential Works 2: Aesthetics, Method and Epistemology*, Allen Lane, London.

Fox, N., & Roberts, C. (1999) "GPs in Cyberspace: the Sociology of a Virtual Community", *Sociological Reveiw*, Vol. 47, No .4, pp 643ff.

Frankenberg, Ronald (1969) *Communities in Britain: Social Life in Town and Country*, Pelican.

Frederick, Howard (1993) "Computer Networks and the Emergence of Global Civil Society: The Case of the Association for Progressive Communications (APC), *GASSHO*, Vol.1, No.3. http://www.dharmanet.org/News/gass0103.nws

Freeman, Kathleen (1949) *Companion to the Pre-Socratic Philosophers*, Basil Blackwell, Oxford.

Frude, Niel (1983) *The Intimate Machine: Close Encounters with the New Computers*, Century, London.

Gans, Herbert (1967) *The Levittowners: Ways of Life and Politics in a New Suburban Community*, Allen Lane, London.

Gasche, Randolphe (1997) "Heliocentric Exchange", in Schrift ed. 1997.

Gergen, Kenneth (1991) *The Saturated Self: Dilemmas of Identity in Contemporary Life*, Basic Books, New York.

Giddens, Anthony (1984) *The Constitution of Society*, Polity Press, Cambridge.

——— (1990) *The Consequences Of Modernity*, Stanford University Press, Stanford.

——— (1991) *Modernity and Self-Identity: Self And Society in the Late Modern Age*, Stanford UP, Stanford.

——— (1992) *The Transformation of Intimacy: Sexuality, Love & Eroticism in Modern Societies*, Polity Press, Cambridge.

Gilbert, Pamela (1996) "On Space, Sex and Being Stalked", *Women & Performance*, Vol. 9, No. 1, pp. 125-49.

Glover, T.D., Shinew, K.J, & Parry, D.C. (2005a) "Association, Sociability, and Civic Culture: The Democratic Effect of Community Gardening", *Leisure Sciences*, Vol 27, pp. 75—9.

——— (2005b) "Building Relationships, Accessing Resources: Mobilizing Social Capital in Community Garden Contexts", *Journal of Leisure Research*, Vol. 37, No. 4, pp. 450-74.

Gluckman, Max (1955) *Custom and Conflict in Africa*, Blackwell, Oxford.

——— ed. (1962) *Essays on the Rituals of Social Relations*, Manchester UP,

—— (1962a) "Les Rites de passage" in Gluckman 1962.
Godbout, J.T. & Caille, A. (1998) *The World of the Gift*, McGill Queens UP, Montreal.
Gouldner, Alvin (1979) *The Future of Intellectuals and the Rise of the New Class*, Seabury Press, New York.
Greenberg, Stanley (1996) "Private Heroism and Public Purpose" *The American Prospect,* No. 28 (September-October 1996) pp. 34-40.
http://epn.org/prospect/28/28gree.html
Grusin, Richard (1996) "What Is an Electronic Author? Theory and the Technological Fallacy", in Markley 1996.
Hafner, Katie (2001) *The Well: A Story of Love, Death & Real Life in the Seminal Online Community*, Carol & Graf, New York.
Hafner, K., & Lyon, M. (1996) *Where Wizards Stay Up Late: The Origins of the Internet*, Simon & Schuster, New York.
Hall, Kira (1996) "Cyberfeminism" in Herring, 1996.
Hamman, Robin (1996-8) *Cyberorgasms: Cybersex Among Multiple-Selves and Cyborgs in the Narrow-Bandwidth Space of America Online Chat Rooms*, MA thesis, Department of Sociology, University of Essex.
http://www.socio.demon.co.uk/Cyborgasms.html
Hammersley, M. & Atkinson, P. (1983) *Ethnography: Principles in Practice*, Tavistock, London.
Hardt, M., and Negri, A. (2000), *Empire*, Harvard University Press, Cambridge.
—— (2004), *Multitude: War and Democracy in the Age of Empire*, Penguin Putnam, New York.
Hardy Ian R. (1996) *email_history*, History Thesis Paper, University of California at Berkeley, 13 May 1996.
http://server.berkeley.edu/virtual-berkeley/email_history
Harraway, Donna (1989) *Simians, Cyborgs and Women*, Routledge, New York.
Harris, Marvin. (1968) *The Rise of Anthropological Theory*, Thomas Crowel, New York.
—— (1975) *Cows, Pigs, Wars and Witches: The Riddles of Culture*, Hutchinson, London.
Harrison, T.M., & Stephen, T. (1999) "Researching and Creating Community Networks", in Jones 1999.
Haslam, S.A., McGarty, C. & Turner, J.C. (1996) "Salient Group Memberships and Persuasion: the Role of Social Identity in the Validation of Beliefs", in J.L. Nye & A.M. Brower eds. *What's Social about Social Cognition? Research on Socially Shared Cognition in Small Groups*, Sage, Thousand Oaks.
Hauben, Michael & Ronda (1995) *Netizens: On the History and Impact of Usenet and the Internet*, October 1995.
http://www.columbia.edu/~hauben/project_book.html
Hauben, Ronda (1997) "ARPANET Mailing Lists and Usenet Newsgroups Creating an Open and Scientific Process for Technology Development and Diffusion", Draft Paper, June 1997. http://www.umcc.umich.edu/~ronda/msg.hist/
Hayes, R. Dennis (1995) "Digital Palsy: RSI and Restructuring Capital", in Brook & Boal 1995.

Hayles, N. Katharine (1996) "Boundary Disputes: Homeostasis, Reflexivity and the Foundations of Cybernetics", in Markley 1996.
Healy, Dave (1997) "Cyberspace and Place: The Internet as Middle Landscape on the Electronic Frontier", in Porter 1997.
Hefner, Philip (2003) *Technology and Human Becoming*. Fortress, Minneapolis.
Helman, Cecil (1992) *The Body of Frankenstein's Monster: Essays in Myth and Medicine*, Norton, New York.
Henwood, Doug (1995) "Info Fetishism", in Brook & Boal 1995.
Herring, Susan (ed.) (1996) *Computer Mediated Communication: Linguistic, Social and Cross-Cultural Perspectives*, John Benjamin, Amsterdam.
―――― (1996a) "Two Variants of an Electronic Message Schema", in Herring 1996.
―――― (1996b) "Gender and Democracy in Computer-Mediated Communication", in R.Kling 1996.
Hertz, Robert (1960) *Death and the Right Hand*, Free Press, New York.
Hill, Hall (1995) "Bigfoot", *Infobahn*, Vol. 1, No. 1, pp. 40-5, 84.
Hillery, George (1955) "Definitions of Community: Areas of Agreement", *Rural Sociology*, Vol. 20, pp. 111-23.
Hiltz, S.R., & Turoff, M. (1993) *The Networked Nation: Human Communication via Computer, (2nd Edition)*, MIT.
Hine, Christine M. (2000) *Virtual Ethnography*, Sage, Thousand Oaks.
Hoberman, David (1996) *Body, Text and Presence on the Internet*, unpublished Honours Thesis, Department of Anthropology, Tufts University.
Holmes, David ed. (1997) *Virtual Politics: Identity & Community in Cyberspace*, Sage Publications, London.
Hopkins, Nick & Reicher, Steve (1997) "Social Movement Rhetoric and the Social Psychology of Collective Action: A Case Study of an Anti-Abortion Mobilization", *Human Relations*, Vol. 50, No. 3, pp. 261-86.
Horn, Stacy (1998) *Cyberville: Clicks, Culture and the Creation of an Online Town*, Warner Books, New York.
Hume, David (1888) *A Treatise of Human Nature*, Oxford Univeristy Press.
―――― (1987) *Essays: Moral, Political and Literary*, Liberty Classics, Indianapolis.
Hunter, Michael (1981) *Science and Society in Restoration England*, Cambridge University Press, Cambridge.
Hyde, Lewis (1983) *The Gift: Imagination and the Erotic Life of Property*, Vintage, New York.
Ito, Mizuko (1997) "Virtually Embodied: the Reality of Fantasy in a Multi-User Dungeon", in Porter 1997
Jackson, Michael (1995) *At Home in the World*, Duke University Press.
James, P. & Carkeek, F. (1997) "This Abstract Body: from Embodied Symbolism to Techno-Disembodiment", in Holmes 1997.
Jenkins, Henry (1992) *Textual Poachers: Television Fans & Participatory Culture*, Routledge, New York.
Jensen, Carl (1996) *Censored: the News That Didn't Make the News and Why, the 1996 Project Censored Yearbook*, Seven Stories Press, New York.
Jones, Steven G. ed (1995) *Cybersociety: Computer-Mediated Communication and Community*, Sage, Thousand Oaks.

───── (1995a) "Understanding Community in the Information Age", in Jones 1995
───── (1997) *Virtual Culture: Identity and Community in Cybersociety*, Sage 1997
───── (1997a) "The Internet and Its Social Landscape", in Jones 1997
───── (1998) *Cybersociety 2.0*, Sage, Thousand Oaks.
Kapferer, Bruce (1997) *The Feast of the Sorcerer: Practices of Consciousness and Power*, Chicago UP.
Katz, James & Aspden, Philip (1997) "A Nation of Strangers? Patterns of Friendship and Involvement in Internet Users", *Communications of the ACM*, Vol. 40, No. 12, pp. 81ff.
Kendall, Lori (1996) "MUDder? I Hardly Know 'Er! Adventures of a feminist MUDder" in Cherny & Weise, 1996.
───── (1998) "Meaning and Identity in Cyberspace: The Performance of Gender, Class, and Race Online", *Symbolic Interaction*, Vol. 21, No. 2, pp. 129-53.
───── (1999) "Recontextualizing Cyberspace: Methodological Considerations for On-Line Research", in Jones 1999.
───── (2002) *Hanging out in the Virtual Pub: Masculinities and Relationships Online*, University of California Press.
Kiesler, Sara (1997) *Culture of the Internet*, Lawrence Erlbaum, New Jersey.
King, Storm (1995) "Effects of Mood States on Social Judgments in Cyberspace" http://www.concentric.net/~astorm/mood.html
Klein, Alec (2003) *Stealing Time: Steve Case, Jerry Levin and the Collapse of AOL-Time Warner*, Simon & Schuster, New York.
Kling, Rob (1996) *Computerization and Controversy: Value Conflicts and Social Choices, (2nd Edition)*, Academic Press, New York.
Kolko, Beth, & Reid Elizabeth (1998) "Dissolution and Fragmentation: Problems in On-Line Communities", in Jones 1998.
Konig, Rene (1968) *The Community*, RKP, London.
Kosko, Bart (1994) *Fuzzy Thinking: the New Science of Fuzzy Logic*, HarperCollins, London.
Kreeger, Lionel (1975) *The Large Group*, London, Karnac, London.
Kurzweil, Ray (1999) *The Age of Spiritual Machines*, Orion Business Books, London.
Lakoff, George (1987) *Women, Fire and Dangerous Things*, Chicago UP.
───── (1995) Interview with Ian A. Boal "Body, Brain and Communication", in Brook & Boal, 1995.
───── (1996) *Moral Politics: What Conservatives Know That Liberals Don't*, Chicago UP.
───── (2004) *Don't Think of an Elephant: Know Your Values and Frame the Debate*, Scribe Publications, Melbourne.
Latour, Bruno (1993) *We Have Never Been Modern*, Harvard UP, Massachusetts.
Lawrence, Peter (1984) *The Garia: An Ethnography of a Traditional Cosmic System in Papua New Guinea*, Melbourne University Press.
Levi-Strauss, Claude (1972) *The Savage Mind*, Wiedenfeld & Nicolson, London.
───── (1973) *Totemism*, Penguin University Books, Harmondsworth.
───── (1987) *Introduction to the Work of Marcel Mauss*, RKP, London.
Lipner, Mia (1997) "Requium Digitatem", A Special Audio Installment (Cassette Tape) for *Women & Performance*, Vol. 9, No. 1, 1996.

Lockard, Joseph (1997) "Progressive Politics, Electronic Individualism and the Myth of Virtual Community", in Porter 1997.
Ludlow, P. (ed) (1996) *High Noon on the Electronic Frontier: Conceptual Issues in Cyberspace*, MIT Press.
Mackie-Mason, J.K. & Varian, H.R. (1994) "Some Economics of the Internet", paper presented to the Tenth Michigan Public Utility Conference at Western Michigan University March 25—27, 1993
http://www-personal.umich.edu/~jmm/papers/Economics_of_Internet.pdf
MacKinnon, Richard (1995) "Searching for Leviathan in Usenet", in Jones 1995.
——— (1997) "Punishing the Persona: Corectional Strategies for the Virtual Offender" in Jones 1997.
——— (1998) "Social Construction of Rape in Virtual Reality", in Sudweeks et al.. 1998.
Malinowski, Bronislaw (1922) *Argonauts of the Western Pacific*, RKP, London.
——— (1926) *Crime and Custom in Savage Society*, Routledge, Kegan Paul, London.
——— (1947) "The Problem of Meaning in Primitive Languages", in C.K. Ogden & I.A. Richards *The Meaning of Meaning: A Study of the Influence of Language upon Thought and of the Science of Symbolism*, RKP, London, 1947.
Manning, Frank E. (1973) *Black Clubs in Bermuda: Ethnography of a Play World*, Cornell University Press, Ithaca.
Marcus, George (1996) *Late Editions 3: Connected, Engagements with Media*, Chicago UP.
——— (1999) *Ethnography through Thick and Thin*, Princeton University Press.
Markley, Robert (ed.) (1996) *Virtual Realities and Their Discontents*, Johns Hopkins University Press, Baltimore.
Marshall, Jonathan (1992) *Alchemy in England: the Social Transformation of a Discourse*, MA (hons) Thesis, Department of Anthropology, University of Sydney.
——— (2001) "Cyber-space, or Cyber-topos: The Creation of Online Space", *Social Analysis*, Vol. 45, No. 1 pp. 81-102.
——— (2003a) "Resistances of Gender", *M/C: A Journal of Media and Culture*, 6, http://journal.media-culture.org.au/0308/06-resistances.php
——— (2003b) "Internet Politics in an Information Economy", *Fibreculture Journal* issue 1
http://journal.fibreculture.org/issue1/issue1_marshall.html
——— (2003c) "The Sexual Life of Cyber-Savants", *The Australian Journal of Anthropology* vol. 14, No. 2, pp. 229-248.
——— (2004a) "The Online Body Breaks Out? Asence, Ghosts, Cyborgs, Gender, Polarity and Politics", *Fibreculture Journal*, Issue 3.
http://journal.fibreculture.org/issue3/issue3_marshall.htm
——— (2004b) "Governance, Structure and Existence: Authenticity, Rhetoric, Race and Gender on an Internet Mailing List". *Proceedings of The Australian Electronic Governance Conference* 2004, Centre for Public Policy, University of Melbourne.
http://www.public-policy.unimelb.edu.au/egovernance/papers/21_Marshall.pdf

—— (2006a) Four articles for Elieen M Trauth (ed) *Encyclopedia of Gender and Information Technology*, Idea Group, 2006
—— "Online Life and Gender Dynamics", pp 926-31.
—— "Online Life and Gender Vagueness and Impersonation", pp932-38.
—— "Online Life and Netsex or Cybersex", pp.939-45.
—— "Online Life and Online Bodies", pp.946-51.
—— (2006b) "Categories, Gender and Online Community", *E-Learning*, 3(2) http://www.wwwords.co.uk/elea/content/pdfs/3/issue3_2.asp#10
—— (2006c) "Negri, Hardt, Distributed Governance and Open Source Software", *Portal: Journal of Multidisciplinary International Studies* 3(1). http://epress.lib.uts.edu.au/ojs/index.php/portal/article/view/122
—— (2006d) "Apparitions, Ghosts, Fairies, Demons and Wild Events: Virtuality in Early Modern Britain", *Journal for the Academic Study of Magic*. Issue 3.
—— (2007a) "Mobilisation of gender and race in an online world", in *Transforming Cultures* E-Journal.
—— (2007b) "Cybermind: Paradoxes of Gender and Relationships in an Online Group" in Samantha Holland (ed.) *Remote Relationships in a Small World*, Peter Lang.
Martin, Caitlin (1999) "Why MOO?", *New Observations*, No.120, Winter, p11.
Martin, Emily (1994) *Flexible Bodies :The Role of Immunity in American Culture*, Beacon, Boston.
Marx, K. & Engels, F. (1968) *Selected Works in One Volume*, Progress Publishers, Moscow.
Mauss, Marcel (1954) *The Gift: Forms and Functions of Exchange in Archaic Societies*, RKP, London.
—— (1997) "Gift,Gift", Schrift ed. 1997.
McAllester Jones, M. (1991) *Gaston Bachelard: Subversive Humanist, Texts and Readings*, University of Wisconsin.
McGrew, Anthony (1992) "The State in Advanced Capitalist Societies", in Allen et al. 1992.
McLaughlin, M.L., Osborne, K.K., & Smith, C.B. (1995) "Standards of Conduct in Usenet", in Jones 1995.
McRae, Shannon (1996) "Coming Apart at the Seams: Sex, Text and the Virtual Body" in Cherny & Weise 1996.
Mennell, Stephen (1992) *Norbert Elias: an Introduction*, Balckwell, Oxford, 1992.
—— (1995) "Civilisation and Decivilisation, Civil Society and Violence", *Inaugural Lecture at the University of Dublin* http://www.ucd.ie/~sociolog/inaugurl.htm
Merchant, Carolyn (1990) *The Death of Nature: Women, Ecology and the Scientific Revolution*, Harper & Row, San Francisco.
Meyrowitz, Joshua (1985) *No Sense of Place*, Oxford University Press, New York.
Miller, D. & Slater, D. (2000) *The Internet: an Ethnographic Approach*, Berg, Oxford.
Mitra, Ananda (1997) "Virtual Commonality: Looking for India on the Internet", in Jones 1997.
Moore, S.F., & Meyerhoff, B., (eds.) (1975) *Symbol and Politics in Communal Ideology*, Cornell UP, Ithaca.

Moore, Sally Falk (1975) "Epilogue: Uncertainties in Situations, Inderterminancies in Culture", in Moore & Myerhoff 1975.
—— (1987) "Explaining the Present: Theoretical Dilemmas in Processual Ethnography", *American Ethnologist* Vol.14, No.4 pp. 727-73.
Moravec, Hans (1988) *Mind Children: the Future of Robot and Human Intelligence*, Harvard University Press.
Munk, Nina (2004) *Fools Rush In: Steve Case, Jerry Levin and the Unmaking of AOL Time Warner*, HarperBusiness, New York.
Myerhoff, Barbara (1975) "Organization and Ecstacy: Deliberate and Accidental Communitas among Huichol Indians and American Youth", in Moore and Myerhoff 1975.
Myers, Frederic W. H. (1927) *Human Personality and it's Survival after Bodily Death*, Edited and abridged by S. B. & L. H. M., Longmans, London.
Nunes, Mark (1997) "What Space Is Cyberspace? The Internet and Virtuality", in Holmes 1997.
O'Brien, Jodi (1999) "Gender (Re)production in Online Interaction", in Smith & Kollock 1999.
Odzer, Cleo (1997) *Virtual Spaces: Sex and the Cyber Citizen*, Berkely Books, New York.
Parker, Carol (1997) *The Joy of Cybersex: Confessions of an Internet Addict*, Mandarin, Kew.
Peters, F.E. (1967) *Greek Philosophical Terms: A Historical Lexicon*, New York UP.
Pickard, Meg (1998) *Under Construction: (Re)Defining Culture and Community in Cyberspace*, MA (Econ) Social Anthropology Dissertation, University of Manchester. http://members.aol.com/megpic/net/
Pliskin, Nava & Romm, Celia (1997) "The Impact of E-mail on the Evolution of a Virtual Community during a Strike", *Information & Management*, Vol. 32, No. 5, pp. 245-54.
Poole, Roger (1975) "Objective Sign and Subjective Meaning" in Benthal and Polhemus 1975.
Porter, David (ed.) (1997) *Internet Culture*, Routledge, New York.
Poster, Mark (1997) "Cyberdemocracy", in Holmes 1997.
Pound, Christopher (1996) "Framed, or How the Internet Set Me up", in Marcus 1996.
Rabinow, Paul (1977) *Reflections on Fieldwork in Morocco*, University of California Press.
Randall, Neil (1997) *The Soul of the Internet: Net Gods, Netizens, and The Wiring of the World*, International Thomson Computer Press, London.
Ratner, Carl (1999) "A Cultural-Psychological Analysis of Emotions", http://www.humbolt1.com/~cr2/emotion.htm
also in *Culture and Psychology* Vol. 6, No. 1, 2000, pp. 5-39.
Raymond, Eric S. (1994) *The New Hacker's Dictionary (2nd Edition)*, MIT.
Redhead, S., O'Connor, J. & Wynne, D. (1977) *The Clubcultures Reader*, Blackwell, Oxford.
Reeves, B., & Nass, C. (1996) *The Media Equation: How People Treat Computers, Television and New Media Like Real People and Places*, Cambridge University Press 1996.

Reid, Elizabeth (1991) *Electropolis: Communication and Community on Internet Relay Chat* Honours thesis University of Melbourne, 1991.
http://www.irchelp.org/irchelp/misc/electropolis.html
―――― (1999) "Hierarchy and Power: Social Control in Cyberspace", in Smith & Kollock 1999.
Rheingold, Howard (1994) *The Virtual Community: Finding Connection in a Computer World*, Secker and Warburg, London.
Riche, Martha Farnsworth (1996) "United States Population: a Profile of America's Diversity - the View from the Census Bureau", in *World Almanac and Book of Facts 1997*, K-III Reference.
Richmond, Anthony H. (1969) "The Sociology of Migration in Industrial and Post-Industrial Societies" in J. A. Jackson ed. *Migration*, Cambridge UP.
Ridley, Matt (1996) *The Origins of Virtue*, Viking Press, London.
Riley, Denise (1992) "Citizenship and the Welfare State", in Allen et al. 1992.
Ritter, Greg (1995) "The Word and The Body"
http://www.gallaudet.edu/~ghritter/Writing/wordbody.html
Robertson, Pat (1994) *Collected Works*, Inspirational Press, New York.
Robins, Kevin & Levidow, Les (1995) "Soldier, Cyborg, Citizen", in Brook & Boal 1995.
Rohner, R. (1969) *The Ethnography of Franz Boas*, Chicago UP.
Ronell, Avita (1996) "A Disappearance of Community", in M.A. Moser & D. McLeod ed. *Immersion Technology: Art & Virtual Environments*, MIT.
Rosch, Eleanor (1973) "On the Internal Structure of Perceptual and Semantic Categories", in T. Moore ed. *Cognitive Development and the Acquisition of Language*, Academic Press, New York.
―――― (1975) "Cognitive Representations of Semantic Categories", *Journal of Experimental Psychology: General*, Vol.104, pp.142-233.
Rose, Dan (1990) *Living the Ethnographic Life*, Sage Publications, Newbury Park.
Rosenfeld, David (1988) *Psychoanalysis and Groups: History and Dialectics*, Karnac Books, London.
Ross, Marc Howard (1993) *The Culture of Conflict: Interpretations and Interests in Comparative Perspective*, Yale University Press, New Haven.
Ross-Smith, A. & Kornberger, M (2004) "Gendered Rationality? A Genealogical Exploration of the Philosophical and Sociological Conceptions of Rationality, Masculinity and Organization", *Gender, Work and Organization*, Vol. 11, No. 3, pp. 280-305.
Ruesch, J. & Bateson, G. (1987) *Communication: The Social Matrix of Psychiatry*, Norton, New York.
Runciman, W.G. (1998) *The Social Animal*, HarperCollins, London.
Sahlins, Marshall (1974) *Stone Age Economics*, Tavistock Publications, London.
Salus, Peter H. (1995) *Casting the Net: From ARPANET to INTERNET and Beyond....*, Addison-Wesley, Reading.
Schaap, Frank (1999) "Males Say 'Blue', Females Say 'Aqua', 'Sapphire' and 'Dark Navy'. The Importance of Gender in CMC", Paper Presented at the *15th Twente Workshop on Language Technology*: University of Twente.
http://www.people.a2000.nl/fschaap/articles/males_say_blue.html

Schiller, Dan. (1999) *Digital Capitalism: Networking the Global System*, MIT.
Schiller, Herbert (1989) *Culture Inc.: the Corporate Takeover of Public Expression*, OUP.
────── (1996) *Information Inequality: The Deepening Social Crisis in America*.
Schrift, Alan D. (1997a) "Introduction: Why Gift?", in Schrift 1997.
Searle, John (1995) *The Construction of Social Reality*, Allen Lane, London.
Sennett, Richard (1994).(1998) *The Corrosion of Character*, W.W. Norton & Company, New York.
Shapin, Steven (1994) *A Social History of Truth: Civility and Science in Seventeenth-Century England*, University of Chicago Press.
Shapiro, Andrew L. (1996) "The Privatization of the Internet: Keeping Online Speech Free—Street Corners in Cyberspace", in Jensen 1996, pp. 304-9.
Shields, Rob (1996) *Cultures of the Internet*, Sage, London, 1996.
────── (1996a) "Introduction: Virtual Spaces, Real Histories and Living Bodies", in Shields 1996.
Shirky, Clay (1995) *Voices from the Net*, Ziff-Davis Press, Emeryville.
Slater, Don "Trading Sexpics on IRC: Embodiment and Authenticity on the Internet", *Body & Society*, Vol.4, No.4, pp. 91-117.
Smith, C. B., McLaughlin, M. L., & Osborne, K. K. (1998) "From Terminal Ineptitude to Virtual Sociopathy", in Sudweeks Et al. 1998.
Smith, K., & Berg, D (1987) *Paradoxes of Group Life*, Jossey Bass, New York.
Smith, M. A., & Kollock, P. eds. (1999) *Communities in Cyberspace*, Routledge, London.
Sondheim, Alan (1988) *Disorders of the Real*, Station Hill Press, New York.
────── (1991) *Textbook of Thinking*, Open Lock@ Press, New York.
────── (1994) *Cut Desert: The Confused Suplement*, Privately Published, New York.
────── (1996) "Throws of Addiction", *Women & Performance*, Vol. 9, No. 1, pp. 105-9.
────── (ed.) (1997) *Being on Line: Net Subjectivity*, (Lusitania Vol. 8).
────── (1998) *For Jennifer and Julu*, nominative press, Salt Lake City.
Spender, Dale (1995) *Nattering on the Net: Women, Power and Cyberspace*, Spinifex, Melbourne.
Sperber, Dan (1975) *Rethinking Symbolism*, Cambridge University Press, Cambridge.
Sprague, R.K. (1972) *The Older Sophists*, University of South Carolina Press, Columbia.
Springer, Claudia (1996) *Electronic Eros: Bodies and Desire in the Postindustrial Age*, University of Texas Press.
Stehr, N. & Ericson, R.V. (1992) *Culture and Power of Knowledge; Inquiries into Contemporary Societies*, Walter de Gruyter, Berlin.
Stehr, N & Ericson, R (1992a) "Culture and Power of Knowledge in Modern Society" in Stehr & Ericson 1992.
Sterling, Bruce (1993) "Short History of the Internet". Originally "Science column #5" in *Magazine of Fantasy and Science Fiction*, feb 1993.
http://info.isoc.org/guest/zakon/Internet/History/Short_History_of_the_Internet

Stoll, Clifford (1995) *Silicon Snake Oil: Second Thoughts on the Information Highway*, Doubleday, New York.
Strathern, Marilyn (1988a) *The Gender of the Gift*, California UP, 1988
——— (1988b) "Self Regulation: an Interpretation of Peter Lawrence's Writings on Social Control", *Oceania*, Vol. 59, pp. 3-6.
Sudweeks, F., McLaughlin, M., Rafaeli, S. eds. (1998) *Network & Netplay: Virtual Groups on the Internet*, AAAI Press, Menlo Park.
Sullivan, Michael (1987) *Sociology and Social Welfare*, Allen & Unwin, London.
Taylor, Charles (1991) *The Ethics of Authenticity*, Harvard UP.
Taylor, John (1989) *Linguistic Categorization: Prototypes in Linguistic Theory*, OUP.
Taylor, M.C., & Saarinen, E. (1994) *Imagologies: Media Philosophy*, Routledge, London.
Taylor, T.L. (2006) *Play Between Worlds: Exploring Online Game Culture*, MIT, Massachusetts.
Thomas, Eric (1996) "The history of LISTSERV", 1996 version.
  http://www.lsoft.com/listserv-hist.stm
Toffler, Alvin (1970) *Future Shock*, Random House, New York.
——— (1980) *The Third Wave*, William Collins, London.
——— (1984) *Previews and Premises: an Interview*, Pan, London.
——— (1990) *Power Shift: Knowledge, Wealth and Violence at the Edge of the 21st Century*, Bantam, New York.
Treese, Win (1993+) *Internet Index*
  http://new-website.openmarket.com/intindex/index.cfm
Trilling, Lionel (1974) *Sincerity and Authenticity*, Oxford University Press.
Turkle, Sherry (1984) *The Second Self: Computers and the Human Spirit*, Simon and Schuster, New York.
——— (1995) *Life on the Screen: Identity in the Age of the Internet*, Simon and Schuster, New York.
——— (1996) "The Cyberanalysist", in Brockman 1996.
Turner, John., Hogg, M., Oaks, P., Reicher, S. & Wetherall, M. (1988) *Rediscovering the Social Group: A Self Categorization Theory*, Blackwell, Oxford.
Turner, Victor (1969) *The Ritual Process: Structure and Anti-Structure*, Cornell University Press.
Uberoi, J. P. Singh (1971) *Politics of the Kula Ring*, Manchester UP.
Urmson, J.O. (1990) *The Greek Philosophical Vocabulary*, Duckworth, London.
Van Gelder, Lyndsy (1996) "The Strange Case of the Electronic Lover", in Kling 1996.
van Knippenberg, D., Lossie, N. & Wilke, H. (1994) "In-Group Prototypicality and Persuasion: Determinants of Heuristic and Systematic Message Processing", *British Journal of Social Psychology*, Vol. 33, No .3, pp. 289-300.
van Krieken, Robert (1998a) *Norbert Elias*, Routledge, London.
Veling, Terry (1996) *Living in the Margins: Intentional Communities and the Art of Interpretation*, Crossroad Publishing, New York.
Vygotsky, Lev (1986) *Thought and Language*, MIT, Massachusetts.

Webber, Melvin M. (1963) "Order in Diversity: Community Without Propinquity" in L. Wingo ed. *Cities and Space: the Future Use of Urban Land*, Resources for the Future.
Weber, Max (1948) *From Max Weber: Essays in Sociology*, Translated and Edited by H. H. Gerth & C. Wright Mills, RKP, London.
Weiner, Annette (1977) *Women of Value, Men of Renown*, University of Queensland Press.
Weizenbaum, Joseph (1993) *Computer Power and Human Reason*, Penguin, Harmondsworth.
Wertheim, Margaret (1999) *The Pearly Gates of Cyberspace: A History of Space from Dante to the Internet*, Doubleday, Sydney.
Whigham, Frank (1984) *Ambition and Privilege: The Social Tropes of Elizabethan Courtesy Theory*, California UP.
Whittaker, Steve, & Sidner, Candace (1997) "Email Overload: Exploring Personal Information Management of Email", in Kiesler 1997.
Wilbur, Shawn (1997) "An Archaeology of Cyberspaces: Virtuality, Community, Identity", in Porter 1997.
Wilde, Oscar (1966) *Complete Works*, Collins, London.
Witmer, Diane F., (1998) "Practicing Safe Computing: Why People Engage in Risky Computer Mediated Communication", in Sudweeks et al. 1998.
Witmer, D. & Katzman (1998) "Smile When You Say That: Graphic Accents As Gender Markers in Computer Mediated Communication", in Sudweeks et al., 1998.
Wittgenstein, Ludwig (1968) *Philsosphical Investigations*, Basil Blackwell.
Wolfe, Alan (1991) ed. *America at Centuries End*, University of California, 1991.
―――― (1991a) "Introduction: Change from the Bottom up", in Wolfe 1991.
Wolfe, Mark (1994) *A Phenomenological Critique of Human Presence in Simulated Worlds: a Communications Basis for Virtual Reality*, unpublished MA Thesis University of Calgary.
Worsley, Peter (1997) *Knowledges: What Different Peoples Make of the World*, Profile Books, London.
Wouters, Cas (1989) "Sociology of Emotions and Flight Attendants: Hochschild's Managed Heart", *Theory Culture and Society*, Vol.6, pp. 95-123.
―――― (1995a) "The Integration of Social Classes (Etiquette Books and Emotion Management in the 20th Century Part 1)", *Journal of Social History*, Vol.29, pp107ff.
―――― (1995b) "The Integration of the Sexes (Etiquette Books and Emotion Management in the 20th Century Part 2)", *Journal of Social History*, Vol.29, pp325ff.
―――― (1997) "On the Sociogenesis of a Third Nature in the Civilizing of Emotions: Developments in Dealing with Strangers and Strangeness and with Feelings of Superiority and Inferiority"
http://www.usyd.edu.au/su/social/elias/confpap/wouters1.html
Wuthnow, Robert (1994) *Sharing the Journey: Support Groups and America's New Quest for Community*, Free Press, New York.
Zizek, Slavoj (1997) *The Plague of Fantasies*, Verso, London.

Index

Agar, Michael, 3, 21, 311
Age of members, 283-4
Alchemy Mailing List, 74, 75, 84, 198, 316
Allen, Bruce, 56
America Online, 31, 39-40, 102, 312, 334
Anderson, Benedict, 218
Angell, Ian, 57-8
'Anti-Americanism', 46, 205-6, 234-35
AOL (see *America Online*)
Archives, 40, 54, 102-3, 202, 225, 291, 313, 332
Argyle, Katie, 4, 130
Aristotle, 141, 310, 325
ARPANET, 31, 331
Art Papers, 32
Asence, 11, 20, 76, 89-92, 94, 101, 102, 114, 118, 121, 125, 126, 130, 132-3, 145-9, 158, 204, 214, 216, 235-7, 254, 260, 261, 273, 301, 334
Askanas, Malgosia, 33ff.
Association, Temporary, 49-51, 208, 210, 218, 220, 224, 262, 268, 276, 330
Aura, 241, 248-54, 301, 332
Authenticity, 11, 35, 78, 96, Chapter 6 *passim*, 130, 132-3, 135, 137-8, 148, 178-9, 184, 191, 192, 194, 209, 214, 217, 233, 269, 270, 271, 272, 275, 277, 278, 308, 312, 320, 321, 322, 324, 329

Bachelard, Gaston, 309
Backstage, 248
Barings Bank, 307
Barth, Fredrik, 3, 4, 29, 162, 239, 279, 307, 309, 311, 320
Bateson, Gregory, 73, 90, 160, 307, 311
Baudriallard, Jean, 55
Bell, Daniel, 62

Blair, Tony, 55
Boas, Franz, 308
Bodies, 6, 11, 106, 107, 114, 118ff., 121, 123, Chapter 7 *passim*, 323, 324, 325, 330
Bodies — virile, 145-7, 191, 192, 274
Boston meeting, 243-4
Boundary, 3, 6, 11, 14, 16-17, 25, 44, 74, 86-87, 99, 102, 119, 125-9, 132, 142, 144, 147, 173, 195-7, 214, 226, 261-2, 273-4, 308, 317, 318, 324, 325, 328
Bounds, Elizabeth, 213-14, 329
Bourdieu, Pierre, 61, 307, 308, 326, 327
Boyle, James, 109, 172, 321
Buchanan, Pat, 65
Burnout, 11, 95, 101-102, 147, 217, 218, 263
Burns, George, 103
Bush, George (II), 45, 46, 48, 55, 56, 58, 60, 64, 65, 66ff., 205-6, 207, 208
Butler, Judith, 144

Cancian, Francesca, 24, 26, 28, 311-12
Capital Letters, 323
Capitalism (see also *Information economy*), 10-11, 16, 47, 48, 53, 63, 72, 108-09, 151, 152, 172, 179, 258, 315, 329
Castells, Manuel, 49
Category, 4, 5, Chapter 1 *passim*, 29-30, 90, 176, 265, 309, 317
Category bias, 25
Category norms, 10, 24, 26, 30, 267
Chaos/order, 3, 53, 156, 265, 267, 330
Cheal, David, 121, 152, 153-4, 166, 167, 327
Cheney, Dick, 63, 64, 67
China, 56, 57, 63
Clash, the 323

Class, 11, 12, 80, 108-9, 116, 126, 141, 142, 145, 152, 168, 213, 220, 242, 253, 255, 260, 268, 315
Cluster, 28-29, 30, 142, 152, 210-11, 266, 271, 302
Coaction, 17, 18, 19, 265, 302, 307
Communications Decency Act, 43, 86, 241-2, 301-2
Communitas, (see *Structure/Communitas*)
Community, 7, 11-12, 74, 77, 184, 213-17, 225ff., 242, 258, 263, 275-77
Conflict, 22, 270
Congerie, 15, 29, 83, 105, 117, 121, 145, 148, 210, 214, 234, 266, 302
Concept, 15, 29, 155, 234, 266, 302, 320
Control system, 6, 48, 267, 275
Counterpositions, 4, 8, 23
Culture, 1-5, 9, 13, 119, 170, 192, 200, 202, 235, 265, 271, 279, 307, 308, 309
Current, Michael, 7, 32ff. 43, 103, 129, 222
Cyberculture Mailing List, 82, 229
Cybermind Conference, 45, 129, 246-7
Cybermind Lounge, 43, 76-7, 241
Cybermind Manifesto, 35-7, 83, 103, 314
Cybermind — members/population, 7, 10, 40, 282ff.
Cybermind Novel, 247-8
Cybermind — origins, 7 ff., Chapter 2 passim, 222ff.
Cyborgs, 35, 125, 141, 274

Dasgupta, Partha, 64
De Tocqueville, Alexis, 218, 330
Death, 104, 129-32, 222-5, 331
Descartes, Rene, 141, 325
Derrida, Jacques, 111, 154-5, 310-11, 327
Dibble, Julian, 134
Douglas, Mary, 17, 103-4, 118, 125, 317, 320, 324
Durkheim, Emile, 218, 309

Education of members, 284-5

Elias, Norbert, 6, 22, 25, 51, 73, 81, 106, 109, 216, 259, 276, 308, 310, 318, 330
Ellis, John, 16, 310
Email and speech, 116, 154
Embedding, 1, 4, 5, 18, 47, 84, 86, 116, 121, 146, 148, 166, 172, 193, 200, 208, 210, 216, 239, 256-69, 272, 276, 317, 321
Emoticons, 119, 122, 302, 314, 324
'emma', Mailing List, 45, 167, 198-9, 204
Established/outsider relations, 25, 81, 104-5, 200, 261, 272
Etherealisation, 127, 142, 145, 321, 325
Etiquette, 21-2, 106, 107, 110, 112, 114, 123, 270, 323
Ethnography/fieldwork, 1-3, 5, 7-10, 38, 190, 267, 281, 307, 308, 315, 328-29
Excess, (see *Redundancy*)
Exchange, 7, 11, 20, Chapter 8 passim, 177-8, 270, 274

Fiction of Philosophy (FOP), 38, 82, 85, 198, 318
Fieldwork, (see *Ethnography*)
Flames, 96-101, 112, 121, 123, 129, 163, 189ff., 260, 319
Fleshmeets, (see also *Boston Meeting*), 43, 242-50, 256, 290, 332
FOP, (see *Fiction of Philosophy*)
Forwards, 51, 199, 205, 241, 313, 319, 326, 334
Foucault, Michel, 112, 132, 308
Framing, 5, 18ff. 28, 30, 106, 265-66, 270, 302-3
Frankenberg, Ronald, 215, 231, 330
Friedman, Thomas 55
FutureCulture Mailing List, 31, 32, 36, 41, 45, 69, 81, 82, 85, 96, 198-9, 224, 225, 231, 314, 328, 331

Gans, Herbert, 219ff., 242, 261
Gender, 11, 120-2, 123, 135, 136, 145, 151, 166-70, 191, 198ff., 208-10, 274, 278, 282-3, 295-97
Gender–changing, 121-2

Gergen, Kenneth, 218,330
Ghosts, 11, 125, 141-4, 145, 146, 148, 149, 274, 325
Giddens, Anthony, 49, 253, 311, 323
Glen, 26, 43-4, 146, 163, Chapter 9 *passim*, 225, 232-34, 249, 262
Gluckman, Max, 4, 27
Gordon, 43-4, 176, 189-97, 209
Gossip, 318, 320-21
Gouldner, Alvin, 71
Grid/group, 317
Group structure, 79ff.

Haliburton, 67
Harris, Marvin, 22, 73, 152
Haunted computer, 141-3
Herring, Susan, 166, 167, 209
Hierarchy, 11, 38, 79ff., 104, 106, 156, 177
Hillery, George, 214, 330
History, 11, 24, 48, 61, 87, 89, 102-04, 128, 156, 162, 165, 175, 193, 224, 237, 258, 261, 263, 284, 316, 321, 326
Holocaust debate, 176, 180-85, 233, 238
Hopkins, Nick, 25
Hume, David, 23, 325

IATH, (see *Institute of Advanced Technology in the Humanities*)
Ideal type, 3, 218, 329
Identity, (see also *Self category*) 22, 23-5, 29, 113-14, 116
Images of others, 245-6, 324, 332
Immersion, 127-28
Information, 2, 9, 16, 20, 58, 66, 78, 136, 140, 144, 145-6, 172, 202, 209, 228, 231, 238, 253, 274
Information Economy/Society, (Chapter 3 *passim*) 47ff. 52, 53, 102, 145-46, 148, 172-3, 266, 268, 320-21 329
Information Economy as alchemy, 146
Infrastructure, 6, 202
Institute of Advanced Technology in the Humanities, 38ff.

Iraq War (second), 7, 46, 48, 55, 60, 66, 67, 68, 86, 160, 167, 181, 204-208, 235, 247, 291, 332

Jokes/Joking behaviour, 46, 119, 200, 206-208, 226, 231, 235, 273

Kendall, Lori, 118, 120, 133, 307, 316, 317
Kolko, Beth, 120
Kosko, Bart, 16
Krugman, Paul, 59,
Kurzweil, Ray, 142

Lakoff, George, 14, 17, 188
Lamda MOO, 78, 243, 317, 323
Leadership, 162, 184-5, 247-8, 249, 276, 278, 317
Leisure *gemeinschaft*, 216-17, 218, 259, 276, 315, 330,
Levi-Strauss, Claude, 16, 309-10
Levittown, 219ff.
Liminal, liminality, 17, 149
Locale (see also *Place/space*), 20, 76, 98-9, 110, 260, 266, 274, 276, 311
lurkers/lurking, 11, 90, 92-5, 118, 160-1, 243, 273, 277, 318

MacKinnon, Richard, 129, 151, 159
Mailing Lists, (*passim*) 31, 73ff., 84, 316
Malinowski, Bronislaw, 155ff. 326
Mana, 16, 117, 310
Martin, Caitlin, 76
Martin, Elizabeth, 108, 324
Marx, Karl, 73, 179, 180, 315, 327
Matter, 144
Mauss, Marcel, 16, 152, 153-5, 159, 309, 325, 326, 327
McRae, Shannon, 120
Meaning, 3-5, 17, 19, 214, 233, 259, 260, 309, 310
Memory, (see *Images of others* and *History*)
Men, (see also *Gender*) 121, 141, 145, 191
Meyrowitz, Joshua, 110-11

Moderation/moderator, 33, 43, 44, 73-4, 80-81, 84, 85, 87, 88, 130, 161-3, 194, 196, 198, 247, 271-2, 275, 316, 317
MOOs, 73, 76, 132, 272, 303-4, 319, 332
Mood, 11, 20, 99, 108, 129ff., 148, 164, 193, 209, 269-70, 276
Moore, Sally, 28, 50, 312
Moravec, Hans, 142
Moyers, Bill, 58-9
Multiplex, (see *Simplex/multiplex*)
Murdoch, Rupert, 66
Myerhoff, Barbara, 50, 216
Myers, F.H.W., 322
Mytheme, 10, 22-3, 49, 52, 71, 108-9, 122, 125, 145, 148, 213, 221, 258, 268, 312, 324

Netsex, 11, 20, 94-95, 118, 125, 132-41, 148, 236, 253, 260, 325, 333
Norton, Richard, 53
Nostalgia, 214-218, 234, 276, 329
NSFNET, 31

'Offlist' Mailing List, 45, 189-204
Off-topic (see *Topics/off-topic*)
Offlist meetings, 242ff.
Online society, Standard descriptions of, 2
One line replies, (see also *Jokes/joking behaviour*), 115, 160, 206, 322

Pain, effects of, 127
Palmer, Kent, 32ff. 312-13
Paradox, 134, 173, 260-61, 277-9
Performative statements, 19, 129, 311
Persuasion, 9, 14, 23-4, 25, 29-30, 176, 185, 266, 270
Place/space, (see also *Locale*), 20, 103, 165, 171, 185, 192, 196, 218-19, 260, 274, 277, 316, 321
Plato, 16, 141, 154, 325
PMC-MOO, 43, 44, 45, 77, 78, 80, 85, 241, 243, 244, 317, 319
Political divisions, 48, 51, 64ff, 83, 152, 156, 158, 161, 163, 179-80, 182, 187, 188, 189, 193, 196, 210, 268, 269, 289

Posting habits of members, 291-95
Potter, Harry, 65
Power, 1, 6-7, 10, 18, 74, 79-81, 85, 86, 146, 147, 149, 179, 180, 181, 185, 214, 261, 267, 268, 271-2, 274, 275, 278, 308, 311, 314, 315, 318, 325, 330, 334
Private, (see *Public/private*)
Prodigy, 321
Property, 54, 57, 109, 151, 170-73, 315, 326
Protagoras, 279
Prototype, 10, 14-16, 21, 24, 25, 26, 27, 29, 83, 95, 130, 136, 158, 185, 187, 191, 253, 265, 266-7, 270, 312
Public/private, 11, 22, 88, 106, 109-11, 123, 163-4, 192-3, 197, 225-6, 269, 278, 327, 328

Race, 24, 36, 320
Reading habits of members, 286-88
Recognised members/Recognition, (see also *Established/outsider relations*), 44, 81, 86, 88, 94, 95, 104, 160, 176, 178, 181, 194, 195, 200, 252, 262, 263, 275,
Redundancy/excess, 12, 21, 30, 133, 225, 227-29, 230-31, 232, 234, 259-60, 276, 261
Reich, Robert, 56-7
Reicher, Steve, 25
Reid, Elizabeth, 112, 120, 321
Religion, 9, 71, 83, 142, 309, 318, 326
'Religious Right', 64ff, 110, 308
Repetitive Strain Injuries, 127, 145
Response, 17, 18, 21, 26, 75, 89, 90-91, 97-98, 102, 112, 126, 154, 157-61, 164, 166, 168, 231, 270, 296-97
Returns, 7, 237-9, Chapter 12 *passim*, 275
Richmond, Anthony, 218
Rifkin, Jeremy, 57
Ritual, 4, 27, 28, 80, 86, 91, 107, 108, 110, 118, 130, 132-3, 148, 159, 277, 307, 311, 319, 320
Rosch, Eleanor, 15

Sahlins, Marshall, 308-9, 325-6

INDEX

Schaap, Frank, 307
Searle, John, 311
Self category, 4, 14, 23, 25, 27, 35, 62, 84, 86, 185, 208, 274, 277, 308
September 11 2001, 45, 56
Shirky, Clay, 101, 320
Simplex/muliplex, 12, 27, 30, 44, 95, 99, 100, 136, 197, 253, 260, 261, 334
Slater, Don, 11, 322
Social contract, 151-
Social control, 5, 74, 79-81, 99, Chapter 9, Chapter 10, 267
Social Security, 60
Sondheim, Alan, *passim* 7, 8, 32ff. 52-3, 69, 73, 113, 248
Sorcery, 23, 29, 159, 161-3, 275
Spelling Wars, 96ff., 114-17, 152, 221-2, 328
Spivak, 121, 323
Spoon Collective, 34ff. 331
State, the, 47, 109, 152-3, 268
Status, 10, 18, 21, 29, 76, 87, 91, 92, 102, 103, 104, 106, 107, 108, 109, 121, 151, 155ff., 200, 271-3, 274, 277-78, 285, 320, 323, 327,
Strathern, Marylin, 3, 154, 326
Structure/Communitas, 216-18, 229, 233, 247, 259, 263, 276, 331
Structures of communication, 6, 39, 40, Chapter 4 *passim*, 100, 171, 186, 202, 204, 211, 241, 271-3
Symbols, 4, 21, 133, 148, 312

Taylor, Charles, 105, 320
Taylor, John, 14, 15, 16
Temporary association, (see *Association, temporary*, and *Voluntary group*),
Terminators, 16, 18, 22, 27, 28, 29, 145, 266, 268, 275, 310
Therapeutics of being online, 113, 220, 322
Therapy groups, 51, 254, 320, 334
Theweleit, Klaus, 181, 182
Thinknet, 32-34, 312-3.
Threads, 74-5, 164, 165, 287, 288, 296-7, 298-9, 316
Thurow, Lester, 57

Time, 128, 163-4
Toffler, Alvin, 62, 219
Topics/off-topic, 7, 19, 20, 46, 49, 74-5, 82, 84, 94, 104, 147, 166, 185, 201, 208, 209, 225, 227-29, 231, 232, 254, 259, 263, 276, 277, 287, 328, 331
Travel, 135, 252, 254, 333
Trilling, Lionel, 105, 108, 320
Trobriand Islands, 11, Chapter 8 *passim*
Turkle, Sherry, 112
Turner, John, 23ff., 237
Turner, Victor, 17, 216, 259, 276

Uberoi, JP Singh, 161
Unmasking truth 108

Values, 11, 28-9, 32, 40, 48, 50, 74, 156, 163, 176, 180, 181, 185-88, 331
Verbingdungsnetzschaft 218
Voluntary group 18, 49-51, 71, 216, 268, 315, 330
Vygotsky, Lev 14

Walpiri, 329-30
Webber, Melvin, 218
Weiner, Annette, 152, 158
WES (Western English Speaking) Societies, 1, 4, 47ff.,104, 105, 108, 119, 125, 166, 262, 330
Wilde, Oscar , 320
Wittgenstein, Ludwig, 15, 310
Wizard (MOO) 44, 76ff., 241, 272, 317
Wolfe, Alan, 219
Women (see also *Gender*), 41, 100, 179, 198ff. 236, 296
Wouters, Cas, 107,
World.std.com, 37-9
Wuthnow, Robert, 49-50

Zizek, Slavoj, 156

Colin Lankshear, Michele Knobel,
Chris Bigum, & Michael Peters
*General Editor*s

New literacies and new knowledges are being invented "in the streets" as people from all walks of life wrestle with new technologies, shifting values, changing institutions, and new structures of personality and temperament emerging in a global informational age. These new literacies and ways of knowing remain absent from classrooms. Many education administrators, teachers, teacher educators, and academics seem largely unaware of them. Others actively oppose them. Yet, they increasingly shape the engagements and worlds of young people in societies like our own. The *New Literacies and Digital Epistemologies* series will explore this terrain with a view to informing educational theory and practice in constructively critical ways.

For further information about the series and submitting manuscripts, please contact:

> Michele Knobel & Colin Lankshear
> Montclair State University
> Dept. of Education and Human Services
> 3173 University Hall
> Montclair, NJ 07043
> michele@coatepec.net

To order other books in this series, please contact our Customer Service Department at:

> (800) 770-LANG (within the U.S.)
> (212) 647-7706 (outside the U.S.)
> (212) 647-7707 FAX

Or browse online by series at:

> www.peterlang.com